Restoration through Redemption:
John Calvin Revisited

Studies in Reformed Theology

VOLUME 23

The titles published in this series are listed at brill.com/srt

Restoration through Redemption: John Calvin Revisited

Edited by

Henk van den Belt

BRILL

LEIDEN • BOSTON
2013

Library of Congress Cataloging-in-Publication Data

Restoration through redemption : John Calvin revisited / edited by Henk van den Belt.
    pages cm. — (Studies in Reformed theology, ISSN 1571-4799 ; v. 23)
    Includes index.
    ISBN 978-90-04-24466-5 (hardback : alk. paper) — ISBN 978-90-04-24467-2 (e-book)
1. Calvin, Jean, 1509-1564. I. Belt, H. van den, 1971–

    BX9418.R38 2013
    230'.42092—dc23

                                                                    2012041304

This publication has been typeset in the multilingual "Brill" typeface. With over 5,100 characters covering Latin, IPA, Greek, and Cyrillic, this typeface is especially suitable for use in the humanities. For more information, please see www.brill.com/brill-typeface.

ISSN 1571-4799
ISBN 978-90-04-24466-5 (hardback)
ISBN 978-90-04-24467-2 (e-book)

This book is printed on acid-free paper.

Printed by Printforce, the Netherlands

CONTENTS

LIST OF ABBREVIATIONS

CO   John Calvin, *Joannis Calvini Opera quae Supersunt Omnia*, ed.
        Wilhelm Baum, Edward Cunitz and Edward Reuss (Brunswick:
        Schwetschke and Sons, 1863–1900).

CCSL   *Corpus Christianorum: Series Latina.* (Turnhout: Brepols, 1954–).

NPNF   Philip Schaff and Henry Wace (eds), *A select library of Nicene and
        post-Nicene fathers of the Christian Church* (Oxford: Parker, 1890–
        1900).

PL   J.-P. Migne (ed.), *Patrologiae cursus completus accurante* (Paris:
        Migne, 1844–64).

LIST OF CONTRIBUTORS

J. Todd Billings, Associate Professor of Reformed Theology at Western Theological Seminary

Johan Buitendag, Professor of Systematic Theology and Christian Ethics, University of Pretoria

Jaeseung Cha, Associate Professor of Foundational and Constructive Theology New Brunswick Theological Seminary

Ernst M. Conradie, Professor in the Department of Religion and Theology and teaches especially Systematic Theology and Ethics

Roger Haight, S. J., Scholar in Residence at Union Theological Seminary

I. John Hesselink, Former President and Former Albertus C. van Raalte Professor of Systematic Theology at Western Theological Seminary

Rinse H. Reeling Brouwer, Extraordinary Professor at the Protestant Theological University, The Netherlands

Phillipe Theron (1942–2010) was Professor in Systematic Theology at the University of Stellenbosch

Henk van den Belt, Extraordinary Professor of Reformed Theology, University of Groningen

Gijsbert van den Brink, Extraordinary Professor of the Theology of Reformed Protestantism at the Protestant Theological University and Associate Professor of Christian Doctrine at VU-University Amsterdam

Cornelis van der Kooi, Professor of Western Systematic Theology at VU-University Amsterdam

Amie van Wyk, Emeritus Professor of Potchefstroom University (now Northwest University), South Africa

Nico Vorster, Research Professor in Systematic Theology at the Faculty of Theology, Northwest University, South Africa

Robert Vosloo, Professor of Systematic Theology and Ecclesiology at Stellenbosch University, South Africa

Paul Wells, Adjunct Dean of the Faculté Jean Calvin, Aix-en-Provence, France and Affiliate Professor at Northwest University, South Africa

INTRODUCTION:
REVISITING CALVIN: ANALYSIS, ASSESSMENT, AND RECEPTION

Henk van den Belt

John Calvin has exercised a tremendous influence and his theology has played an important part in the development of the Christian tradition. The commemoration of the 500th Calvin anniversary in 2009 offered an opportunity to revisit his theological heritage during the 8th conference of the International Reformed Theological Institute (IRTI). The conference was held in France, and hosted by the Free Faculty of Reformed Theology, now called 'Faculté Jean Calvin,' in Aix-en-Provence. The aim of the conference was to look back at Calvin's theology from the perspectives of current Christianity and the Reformed tradition in particular and trace his influence in the different contexts of the approximately hundred participants, scholars and students from all over the world.

Paul Wells, from Aix-en-Provence, opened the conference with an analysis of Calvin's paradoxical legacy. A remark by this lecturer—that Calvin was a "scarecrow" because of his character and his polemics—found its way to a headline in the Dutch *Reformed Daily*.[1] This volume shows that much more can be said about his influence and legacy in and outside of France.

There are at least three ways to revisit Calvin. In the first place one can turn to the sources and analyze Calvin's theology, either by closely reading the Reformer or by studying his sources. A different approach pays more attention to the present context and returns to Calvin's theology from that perspective; revisiting Calvin then means assessing his theological heritage in order to apply that to contemporary theological issues. Finally, one can also carefully listen to how others have understood the Reformer. We are not the first readers of his theology and the way others have understood and interpreted him can offer new insights into our own understanding and to the application of his heritage for our own context. The contributions to this volume all fit into one of these categories, although in some of them more than one perspective is chosen.

---

[1] "In Frankrijk werd Calvijn een 'vogelverschrikker'" [In France, Calvin became a 'scarecrow'], *Reformatorisch dagblad* 7 July 2009.

The Visitation of Christ

The early Lutheran and Reformed churches replaced the hierarchical structure of the regional church by a system of church visitation, the first one
initiated by Luther and Melanchthon in the electorate of Saxony in 1527.
Also, from Geneva regular church visitations were conducted in the surrounding villages as a way of monitoring the evangelical character of the
region, for which Geneva functioned as a model.[2] This practice expressed
the mutual responsibility of the evangelical churches. 'Revisiting Calvin'
is in some respects similar to a church visitation of the historical roots of
the Reformed tradition, with the question in mind as to how the spiritual
life of early modern Christianity can still be inspiring today.

Calvin does not use the verb *revisitare* in his works,[3] but he knew the
verb *visitare* from his Latin Bible. Commenting on Christ's true humanity
in the *Institutes*, he turns to Psalm 8:4 where *visitare* has the meaning of
remembering. "What is man that thou art mindful of him, and the son of
man that thou visitest him?"[4] Discussing Christ's descent into hell a few
chapters later in the *Institutes*, Calvin claims that the power of Christ's
death is so great that he penetrated even to the dead; "godly souls enjoyed
the present sight of that visitation which they had anxiously awaited."[5]
Apparently, the essence of Old Testament faith is waiting for God, or more
specifically waiting the *visitation* of God in Christ. Although those who
died in this expectation did not obtain their desire, they received a glance
of Christ's victorious death. Regardless of the truth in that claim, Calvin's
explanation is a nice example of his understanding of the unity of the
Old and New Testaments. However, it also shows that the incarnation
of Christ is the core of the gospel. He became as weak and frail as all the

---

[2] W. van 't Spijker, *Calvin: A Brief Guide to His Life and Thought* (Louisville: Westminster
John Knox Press, 2009), 74.

[3] A quick search in the Calvini Opera offers no entries for *revisit** in Calvin's Latin
works. J. Calvin, *Calvini Opera database 1.0*, ed. H.J. Selderhuis (Apeldoorn: Instituut voor
Reformatieonderzoek [Institute for Reformation research], 2005).

[4] Psalm 8:4. Calvin, *Institutes* II.13.2. For references to Calvin's *Institutes* only the
numbers of the book, chapter, and paragraph are given throughout this volume. Unless
a different translation is mentioned, all direct quotes are from John T. McNeil (ed.),
Calvin: Institutes of the Christian Religion, transl. Ford Lewis Battles (Louisville: Westminster John Knox Press, 1960). A reference to the *Opera Selecta* is added only if the Latin is
important.

[5] Calvin, *Institutes* II.16.9. In chapter 8 of the present volume, Johan Buitendag examines Calvin's interpretation of this part of the Apostolic Creed and claims that it reveals
influence from Plato's dualism.

sons and daughters of Adam. He became one of us, in order that we may be reconciled with God. The true visitation, according to Calvin, is that God visits us in Jesus Christ. Any revisiting of Calvin to analyze, assess, and study the reception of his work should keep that fundamental notion in mind.

Several contributions to this volume illustrate the relationship between the *Institutes* and Calvin's commentaries, especially when he explicitly refers to Scripture. In his commentary on Psalm 8 Calvin elaborates on the meaning of the Hebrew original. On the one hand he lines up with the traditional translation of the Hebrew verb by the Latin *visitare* in the Vulgate. On the other hand, as a humanist scholar he also shows his feel for the nuances in the meaning of the verb. God's visiting of human beings should not be taken literally; it is a form of accommodation in which the Psalmist expresses the marvelous grace of God who remembers them.

> When it is said, God is mindful of man, it signifies the same thing as that he bears towards him a fatherly love, defends and cherishes him, and extends his providence towards him. Almost all interpreters render פָּקַד (*pakad*), the last word of this verse, 'to visit'; and I am unwilling to differ from them, since this sense suits the passage very well. But as it sometimes signifies 'to remember', and as we will often find in the Psalms the repetition of the same thought in different words, it may here be very properly translated 'to remember'; as if David had said: This is a marvelous thing, that God thinks upon men, and remembers them continually.[6]

According to Calvin, visiting means remembering, and thus revisiting might mean remembering something that has been forgotten. Calvin himself does not seem to have been forgotten, but some aspects of his theology deserve to be rediscovered.

Redemption and Recreation

Calvin is often careful with an immediate Christological interpretation of Old Testament texts in his commentaries, even if the New Testament explicitly relates the passage to Christ. As the use of Psalm 2 in his concept of the government's religious tasks demonstrates, Calvin sees the

---

[6] Calvin, Commentary on Psalm 51:7, *CO* 31, 91–92. Cf. J. Calvin, *Commentary on Psalms*, transl. J. Anderson (Edinburgh: Calvin Translation Society, 1846), 101. References to Calvin's commentaries offer the text from Scripture followed by the volume and column in the *Calvini Opera*. If a translation is quoted, it is mentioned in the footnotes.

Messianic prophecies as multilayered references to divine lordship.[7] His Christological understanding of Scripture does not diminish Calvin's honest and humanistic exegesis. In his commentary on Hebrews 2:5–7, where the passage from Psalm 8 is quoted, Calvin remarks that the author underlines the difference between Christ and the angels by stating that Christ ought to be obeyed because God the Father has conferred a sovereign rule over the whole world to him. The quote from Psalm 8 seems to be inaptly applied to Christ, because David is dealing with the benefits God bestows on human beings in general, turning to them, after considering God's power manifested in the heaven and the stars.[8]

Even though the Psalm in the first place applies to all humankind, there is no reason not to apply it to Christ as well. The first man, Adam, possessed the whole world as a ruler over all God's works, but lost his dominion as a punishment for sin. Adam alienated himself from God and therefore he was deprived of his rights.

> The wild beasts ferociously attack us, those who ought to be awed by our presence are dreaded by us, some never obey us, others can hardly be trained to submit, and they do us harm in various ways; the earth answers not our expectations in cultivating it; the sky, the air, the sea, and other things are often adverse to us.[9]

The rights which Adam lost are restored by Christ; the restoration of the relationship with God and the return to original righteousness hinges on Christology. As long as sin reigns, the relationship remains distorted, but through faith in Christ, the believer may enjoy the whole world with God's benediction. This is why Paul teaches that food is sanctified by faith and that to the unbelieving nothing is clean.

Hermeneutically the Psalm can be applied to Christ, because it applies to humankind according to God's original intention and because Christ restores fallen humankind to its original harmony, thereby rescuing creation from the dominion of sin. Christ is the heir of all things, thus the Psalm will only be fulfilled by the eschatological restoration through Christ. The dominion mentioned in Psalm 8 was lost to us in Adam and must be restored as a donation. That gift starts with Christ as the head and therefore the dominion of humankind over all creatures refers to Christ.

---

[7] Chapter 5 in this volume deals with the exegetical background of Calvin's view of the government and discusses his commentary on the Psalm in detail.

[8] Calvin, Commentary on Heb. 2:5–7, *CO* 55, 23.

[9] Calvin, Commentary on Heb. 2:5–7, *CO* 55, 24. Cf. J. Calvin, *Commentaries on the Epistle of Paul the Apostle to the Hebrews* (Edinburgh: Calvin Translation Society, 1853), 57.

Calvin distinguishes between the present world and the future world. The first is lost, the second will be renovated. The first is old, corrupted by Adam's sin; the second is new and restored by Christ. The eschatological world, however, is not only the future world after the resurrection, but it has begun with the start of Christ's kingdom, although it will only have its full accomplishment in the final redemption.

After his beautiful exposé of the eschatological restoration of all things Calvin in his commentary on Hebrews 2 returns to some ordinary exegetical difficulties. It is strange to him that the author interprets the words 'a little' (βραχύ τι) as a reference to time, 'a little while,' and not to Christ's humiliation, 'a little lower.' Secondly, Hebrews confines the glory with which humankind will be crowned to the day of resurrection, while in the Psalm it applies to this life. According to Calvin, the apostle did not intend to give an exact explanation of the Psalm but only some comments on it, interpreting it in a Christological framework. Calvin solves these differences, by underlining that the apostle did not intend to give an exact explanation.

Just as in his commentary on the Psalm itself, Calvin concludes with the sober remark that the verbs 'to be mindful' and 'to visit' are synonymous, although the second verb 'is fuller because it designates God's presence by its effect.' If God visits us in Christ, he is really present with us: in this *presentia realis* the heart-beat of Calvin's theology is felt. Probably the best way to revisit Calvin is by focusing on God's visitation in Christ.

Remarkably, many themes that are covered in this volume resonate with the above summary of a short random passage from Calvin's commentaries. The passage on Hebrews 2 makes clear how Calvin's whole theology hinges on Christology, but then, from that central point on, it extends to the whole creation. Believers are pilgrims in a fallen world, yet they are carried through the wilderness by the eschatological hope that is founded on God's visitation in Jesus Christ. Notwithstanding the variety of subjects, in one way or other, the contributions to this volume can be clustered around the theme of the restoration of fallen creation through the redemption by Christ. That, of course, is also the central issue of Reformed theology that views the incarnation, crucifixion, and resurrection of Christ as the center of God's revelation. Most of the chapters refer directly to one of the aspects of this redemptive visitation of Christ or elaborate on its implications for the individual, the church or society.

Analysis

The contributions that revisit Calvin by offering some new insight into the understanding of his theology, and compare him with his sources, are characterized by an historical emphasis with a systematic theological application. Gijsbert van den Brink (chapter 1) assesses Calvin's attitude towards the dogma of the Trinity and in particular to the formulation of the Creed of Nicea (325). He shows that this doctrine is very important to Calvin since God is the only one who can save us. The renewed communion with God is grounded in the redemptive work of Christ and accomplished by the Holy Spirit. Calvin's contribution to the doctrine lies in the removal of all traces of subordinationism by claiming that the Son is *autotheos*. The correction by the synod of Bern concerning Calvin's earlier plea for a loose understanding of the classical concepts of Person and Trinity, might be understood as a rare example of successful discipline.

Rinse Reeling Brouwer (chapter 2) turns to God's revelation in creation, revisiting Calvin with regard to the claim in the *Belgic Confession* that God is made known to human beings by creation and by his Word. The authors of the French and Belgic Confessions, however, deviate from the Trinitarian shaping of the two first articles in Calvin's original proposal. According to Calvin's *Institutes*, after the fall it is impossible for the knowledge of God through creation to stand on its own legs. God only makes himself known intimately in the face of Christ and therefore fallen creatures must seek redemption in Christ. The knowledge of God through creation should not be abstracted from the knowledge of Christ.

Turning from the consequences of the fall for revelation to sin itself, Nico Vorster (chapter 3) shows how Calvin modifies Augustine's concept of the doctrine of original sin by a noetic approach. Calvin shares Augustine's view that original sin is an inheritance, but shifts the focus to the knowledge of God and the self. The result is an understanding of sin as moral and religious blindness. Calvin's understanding of the transmission of sin led him to reject Augustine's view on the meaning of Christ's virgin birth. Jesus was free of sin, not because of the virginal conception, but through the sanctification of the Spirit. The doctrine of original sin would be more comprehensible if it is explained from the perspective of Christ's saving work, Vorster argues, instead of from a starting point in the past which placed history on a course of destruction. Even knowledge of sin hinges on redemption, because it is produced by the gospel that shows how much it cost God to redeem us.

Amie van Wyk, one of Vorster's colleagues in Potchefstroom, compares Augustine and Calvin (chapter 4); their writings reveal the key characteristics of their ethics. Accepting the natural virtues of the philosophers (prudence, fortitude, temperance, and justice), Augustine subordinates them to the 'infused virtues' of faith, hope, and love. Calvin follows him in many respects, but replaces virtue ethics by a Christological and Pneumatological concept of ethics. For Calvin, the Christian life centers on union with Christ and following of Christ. Self-denial, cross-bearing, and meditation on the future life color the enjoyment of the present life. Today the different context and greater challenges beg for revisiting the Christian life in terms of broader social Christian ethics.

Henk van den Belt's contribution on Calvin's concept of the civil government (chapter 5) turns to the successive editions of the *Institutes* to show the development of his thought on the task of the government to promote the Christian religion. Over the years his view appears to become less reticent and his biblical account of this view more outspoken. The Christological understanding of Psalm 2 is cardinal for Calvin's concept of the active role of the government regarding religion. The conflict with the Anabaptists shaped Calvin's growing emphasis on the religious responsibility of the magistrates. If Christ reigns as king, this must have consequences for the way Christians rule, because his kingdom is not merely spiritual.

The first part of this volume analyzes several topics in Calvin's theology, all related to the redemptive work of Christ. The study of Calvin's thought on the trinity, on the knowledge of God, on sin, on the Christian life, and on politics contributes to the historical understanding of Calvin's theology but also evokes the question how that theology can be made fruitful today.

Assessment

In the second part of the volume the emphasis on the application is even stronger. The contributions in this part revisit Calvin's theology by applying his heritage to the present situation; they are marked by a systematic theological emphasis with a historical orientation.

Ernst Conradie (chapter 6) explores the challenges of evolutionary biology to reformed theology. After assessing the nature of this challenge from the problem of natural suffering, he sketches the broad parameters in

Calvin's *Institutes* for a response to this problem and then turns to a close reading of Calvin's concept of *meditatio* on the future life. On the basis of the resurrection of Jesus Christ it is already possible now to discern where the history of the universe is pointing towards; indeed, this life can only be understood in terms of the life to come. The challenge of evolutionary biology may help to shift a theological discourse on evolution to the problem of natural suffering. Here the danger is that it explores natural suffering outside of the tension between sin and salvation. That natural suffering cannot be ignored in fact forces reformed theology to revisit the relationship between creation and salvation.

The problem of moral evil and its consequences is also addressed in Jaeseung Cha's contribution on Calvin's concept of penal substitution (chapter 7). He reviews Calvin's thoughts on the atonement, which often have been criticized for stressing the substitution too strongly. He makes a case for the idea that punishment is part of human reality and subsequently argues that Christ takes up both human sins and punishment by accepting death. The legal bond between sin, death, and punishment relates to this universal human context. Therefore Cha suggests that penal substitution should be understood collectively and intertextually.

Johan Buitendag (chapter 8) addresses Calvin's understanding of Christ's descent into hell, an article of the Apostolic Creed that Calvin interprets metaphorically. Buitendag argues for maintaining the clause because it transcends finitude and proclaims Christ's victory, including the deliverance of the whole of creation from sin. He advocates a hermeneutical understanding of the Creed that takes the original socio-historical context into account and transforms the spatial terms in accordance with the insights of the contemporary physics. After all, we are not redeemed from the earth, but with the earth that Christ visited.

Roger Haight approaches Calvin from the perspective of comparative ecclesiology (chapter 9). He takes his starting point in a theology of spirituality that may be paraphrased as 'the Christian life'. Some of the characteristics of a common ecclesial existence are expressed exemplarily in Calvin's ecclesiology. For him sanctification is the central defining element of the church. Individuals are united with God in their everyday vocational lives, in which the church mediates God's grace in the form of Word and Spirit. At the same time, however, the church has a corporate identity that transcends each single member and should lead its members into patterns also of publically bearing witness to the values of the kingdom of God.

Turning to the Lord's Supper Todd Billings (chapter 10) offers a contemporary appraisal of Calvin's eucharistic theology. Calvin's thought underwent significant developments, displaying flexibility to affirm unity among Protestants. Calvin has not weakened the importance of the Supper with his claim that believers also feed upon Christ outside of the Supper, as the practice of 'Holy Fairs,' and the imagery of 'spiritual marriage' in the later Reformed tradition show. Billings concludes his contribution by exploring the symmetry between the promise of the gospel and the promise of the Lord's Supper as a possible point of contemporary retrieval of Calvin's eucharistic theology.

The last contribution that focuses on the application of Calvin's thought is of Cornelis van der Kooi (Chapter 11). Exile and pilgrimage are important metaphors in Calvin's eschatology. The believer is on his way between the 'already' of the blessings received in Christ and the 'not yet' of the consummation. The present life of the believer is subject to tremendous tension with the 'already' of the expectation of God's presence in this life. Today the 'already' of being a child of God—being in communion with Jesus Christ, and being in a life of prayer and activity—is significant for Christians living under the cross and in a marginal situation.

Thus the second part of this volume again covers a range of issues for Reformed systematic theology: creation and natural suffering, Christ's descent into hell and physics, spirituality in an ecumenical ecclesial context and the relevance of Calvin's sacramental and eschatological theology. Here too, the unity seems to consist of the theme of the renewal of creation that hinges on redemption in Christ. God's work of salvation cannot be understood without his works of creation, continuing creation, and eschatological re-creation. Ernst Conradie compares Calvin to a juggler in the way he maintains the tensions between God the Creator and God the Redeemer. But this juggler left Reformed theology with the hermeneutical problem how to understand the relationship between creation and salvation.

Reception

The third part of the volume turns particularly to the reception of Calvin's theology in Reformed churches world-wide. Philippe Theron (chapter 12) explains how the concept of accommodation in Calvin's theology is understood and elaborated by the Dutch theologian Oepke Noordmans. While for Calvin the incarnation is the supreme form of accommodation, for Noordmans even creation itself is a deed of accommodation. In history we encounter God as Father, Son, and Holy Spirit, but to the extent that God's accommodation becomes more historical, its character of revealing-through-concealing increases. The hiddenness of God culminates in Christ's cry of God-forsakenness on the cross. The concept of accommodation is also useful to address the modern rejection of justification as a synthetical judgment of God. Answering the question of how it is possible that God simultaneously forgives sinners and expresses his hostility to them, Calvin explains that God's love and his wrath, his curse and his care, go together in an ineffable manner. God is most incomprehensible in his being incomprehensibly just and incomprehensibly good.

Koos Vorster (chapter 13) investigates Calvin's contribution to a Reformed perspective on human dignity. In the early twentieth century Calvin's views were accommodated to modern politics, by among others, Karl Barth, Gerrit Cornelis Berkouwer and Jürgen Moltmann. Calvin laid the foundations for the development of a Reformed ethics of human dignity and human rights by his concepts of the image of God and common grace: natural law, and civil authority. According to Calvin, human dignity is founded in the image of God; while the moral law is engraved in the conscience and thus a gift of creation to all people. On that ground it is the responsibility of civil government to protect the dignity of all people.

The reception of Calvin in North America is I. John Hesselink's topic (chapter 14). North American scholars have significantly added to Calvin scholarship, but most of their contributions were made after World War II, partially due to the revival of interest in Reformation theology in Europe. An impetus to Calvin studies was the reprinting of Calvin's *Institutes* and *Tracts and Treatises* in the late 40s and early 50s and the translation of some of Calvin's sermons in English. The translation of Calvin's *Institutes* by Battles was of great benefit to Calvin research, as well as the formation of the Calvin Studies Society in the early 1970s. There have also been two notable breakthroughs in Calvin scholarship in recent decades: Roman Catholic contributions to Calvin studies, and the number of women who have written important studies on Calvin. Another trend has been the move away from theological studies to historical and biblical research on Calvin.

According to Robert Vosloo (chapter 15), Calvin's reception and influence in South Africa is a multifaceted story with several interwoven and conflicting strands. After making some comments on the link between Calvinism and Afrikaner civil religion, the main body of the article revisits the ways in which Calvin was used by some theologians from the Dutch Reformed family of churches to critique the theological presuppositions associated with Afrikaner neo-Calvinism. Against this historical theological backdrop, Vosloo makes some searching remarks on reclaiming the legacy of Calvin. The challenges in the current South African context relate to the unity of the church, hospitality, and economic justice.

The host of the conference, Paul Wells, concludes the volume by commenting on French Protestantism (chapter 16). From the time of the Reformation, down through the Revolution to the present, it has been characterized by a love–hate relationship with Calvin. On the one hand Calvin is revered as a forerunner of modern liberties, because of his stand for human integrity and freedom from the tyranny of the Church, his humanism, and aspects of his economic and social thought. On the other hand, his theological intolerance, the doctrines of predestination and divine judgment are viewed as dangerous artifacts. In the typically French dream—characterized by liberty, equality, and fraternity—human life leads to the modern understanding of *laïcité* which is contrary to Calvin's ideal that God is sovereign over all of creation and human activity as show in Christ among us.

Although these chapters on the reception of Calvin naturally have less in common than the other chapters, still the theme of redemption is present. Accommodation culminates in the incarnation and crucifixion of Christ, but the atonement in Christ is also essential for the understanding of the *imago dei* to really understand human dignity as foundation of social and political justice. Among the books printed in North-America the person and work of Christ seems to be an important issue in recent Calvin studies.[10] In South Africa, Calvin is fruitful against some of the Calvinists because of his emphasis on the Lordship of Christ that applies to all spheres of life, including the social, political and economic spheres and counters pietistic escapism. According to Wells the French reception of Calvin lacks the notion of God's sovereignty and a conviction that union with Christ is the goal of Christian living.

---

[10] Hesselink mentions, among other: Peter Wyatt, *Jesus Christ and Creation in the Theology of John Calvin* (Allison Park: Pickwick Publications, 1996), Philip Walter Butin, *Revelation, Redemption and Response: Calvin's Trinitarian Understanding of the Divine-Human Relationship* (New York: Oxford University Press, 1995), and Stephen Edmondson, *Calvin's Christology* (Cambridge: Cambridge University Press, 2004).

Meditatio Vitae Futurae

One of the golden threads in this volume is Calvin's emphasis on the *meditatio* of the future life. For Calvin the verb *meditare* has the connotation of *studium* and *exercitatio*. If the literal translation with 'meditation' is understood in a passive or pietistic way, the notions of pursuit and training disappear. However, it is not an expression of pessimism, otherworldliness or asceticism, because, rightly understood, this meditation produces joy and boldness in believing. "The *meditatio futurae vitae* signifies that the elect are the standard-bearers of God."[11] Or as Cornelis van der Kooi expresses it, this contemplation implies a turning of the believer *to* eternal life, towards which everything must turn.

At Aix-en-Provence Phillipe Theron (1942–2010) was still present as a much respected member of the International Reformed Theological Institute. He studied theology at the University of Pretoria and after ministering in Pretoria and Stellenbosch he took chair in systematic theology at the University of Stellenbosch. On the 7th of July 2011 his earthly life took an end. His life was characterized by a healthy Reformed spirituality that does not shy away from the callings of the present life. In the circle of the IRTI he is remembered because of his kindness and humility and for the eye he constantly kept on the need for theology to serve the faith of the believers.

In an 'Obituary' for the IRTI community, Bram van de Beek wrote:

> When I asked what he liked that I would say in his memorial service he just answered: 'Do not speak about me but just about the three solas.' Sola fide, sola gratia, sola scriptura, bound together by solo Christo was the heart of Flip's theology and that is why he claimed to be Reformed.

Phillipe Theron was very familiar with the Reformed theologians from the Netherlands, such as Herman Bavinck (1854–1921), Oepke Noordmans (1871–1956), Kornelis Heiko Miskotte (1894–1976), and Gerrit Cornelis Berkouwer (1903–1996) and applied their theological heritage to the specific situation in South Africa. It is typical for him that he ends his contribution to this volume with a reference to a meditation by Noordmans, on the words "Peace be with you!" God's greeting, grounded in the incarnation and culminating in the cross, has the character of a blessing

---

[11] Walter Earl Stuermann, *A Critical Study of Calvin's Concept of Faith* (Ann Arbor, Mich.: Edwards Brothers, 1952), 365.

descending on God's groaning creation and forms the counterpart to the cry of God-forsakenness on the cross of Calvary.

The redemption through Christ is the only foundation for the eschatological hope for the believer and for the recreation of the world. To quote Calvin:

> let us not hesitate to await the Lord's coming, not only with longing, but also with groaning and sighs, as the happiest thing of all. He will come to us as Redeemer, and rescuing us from this boundless abyss of all evils and miseries, he will lead us into that blessed inheritance of his life and glory.[12]

---

[12] Calvin, *Institutes*, III.9.5.

CHAPTER ONE

CALVIN AND THE EARLY CHRISTIAN DOCTRINE OF THE TRINITY[1]

Gijsbert van den Brink

Sola Scriptura *as Critical Starting Point*

According to John Thompson it is a "widespread misconception that by way of the motto *sola Scriptura* Protestants wished to dispense with all post-apostolic traditions and writings."[2] Thompson is definitely right on this. Still, it was not immediately self-evident from the beginning that the *sola Scriptura* of the magisterial Reformation did not exclude the recognition of even the most authoritative writings that had gained normativity in the early church: the ecumenical creeds. Although we do not find in John Calvin a detailed theory of inspiration—as was to arise in later Reformed orthodoxy—he certainly considered the Bible as the sole norm and source for Christian life and doctrine. Today such a position is easily associated with biblicism, dogmatism and fundamentalism, but we should not overlook the great critical and emancipatory potential of the *sola Scriptura* guideline during the formative period of the Reformation. In those days, it was a progressive motto rather than a conservative one. For its direct consequence was—and still is—that everything that cannot be traced back to the scriptures does not earn a status of absolute authority in the Church. Therefore, there is no need for the Christian community to be impressed by any claim to authority or power that manifests itself in the world or the church and that goes beyond the Word of God.

In Calvin's days, of course, there were some voices and institutions that made precisely such claims, thereby almost giving a divine aura to their own interests. For example, the Reformation itself arose from a profound unease with the non-biblical pretensions of the Roman Catholic Church of

---

[1] An earlier Dutch version of this article appeared as "Geslaagde tucht. Calvijn en de drie-eenheid," [Successful discipline. Calvin and the Trinity] in: W. de Greef & M. van Campen (eds), *Calvijn na 500 jaar. Een lees- en gespreksboek* [Calvin after 500 Years] (Zoetermeer: Boekencentrum, 2009), 42–59.

[2] John L. Thompson, "Calvin as Biblical Interpreter," in: Donald McKim (ed.), *The Cambridge Companion to John Calvin* (Cambridge: Cambridge University Press, 2004), 62.

the day. Perhaps even more than the Lutheran Reformation, its Reformed counterpart was characterized by a profound distrust of every human invention and every extra-biblical claim to authority. It is no coincidence that it was John Calvin who famously called the human mind "a perpetual factory of idols."[3] In this sense, Calvinism is by nature distrustful, as Bram van de Beek puts it.[4]

It seems to me that we can understand Calvin's initial reservations with regard to the doctrine of the Trinity in this light. For some time at least, it was a difficult question for Calvin whether one may urge people to assent to formulations regarding what they should believe which cannot as such be found in the Bible. This question became especially urgent in relation to the trinitarian formulations of the ancient Creeds. For clearly these formulations had been accepted as expressing normative truth by the Church of the first centuries. At the same time, however, they could not be found in the Bible; the Bible simply does not contain concepts like 'Trinity,' 'divine person,' 'divine essence,' et cetera. Moreover, the very idea that God is one being consisting of three persons has a speculative and philosophical flavor; it easily prompts endless reflections and discussions on the make-up of God's inner being. Medieval theology had seen many examples of such abstract reflections and discussions, but the Reformation tended to break with these because they lead us astray, distracting our attention from the sole thing which must concern us: the biblical message of salvation. The criticism uttered by Philipp Melanchthon in his famous exclamation "(...) this is to know Christ: to know his benefits, and not as they teach to perceive his natures and the mode of his incarnation"[5] could with equal right be applied to the *trinitarian* distinctions. In brief, if nothing that cannot be found in the Bible is allowed to have authority in the Church, then what does this say about the doctrine of the Trinity, and the creedal formulations affirming this doctrine?

---

[3] John Calvin, *Institutes of the Christian Religion*, transl. Ford Lewis Battles (Philadelphia: Westminster Press, 1960) I.11.8.

[4] "Calvinism is by nature distrustful. It distrusts well-presented ideals. It distrusts tight systems. It distrusts idols. It distrusts the pious. It distrusts the world. It distrusts the church at least as strongly, because it consists of fallible people. (...) But a Calvinist most of all distrusts himself (...)." A. van de Beek, "Calvinism as an Ascetic Movement," in: Wallace M. Alston & Michael Welker (eds), *Reformed Theology. Identity and Ecumenicity* (Grand Rapids: Eerdmans, 2003), 220.

[5] "(...) hoc est Christum cognoscere, beneficia eius cognoscere, non quod isti dicent, eius naturas, modos incarnationis, contueri"; from the *Loci Communes* (1521), see Robert Stuperich (ed.), *Melanchthons Werke in Auswahl* 2.1 (Gütersloh: Mohn, 1952), 7.

The Caroli Case

It is remarkable that this became a real question for Calvin for quite some time. As is well-known, when in 1537 Calvin was asked to subscribe to the early Christian creedal formulations regarding the Trinity, he refused. Calvin's Lausanne colleague Pierre Caroli, who like Calvin was of French origin, had accused Calvin (as well as Viret and Farel) of Arianism, and therefore of a heretical doctrine of the Trinity. It is difficult to determine the precise background of Caroli's accusations, but it is conceivable that he still cherished the high estimation of the ecclesial and doctrinal traditions with which he had been raised (he had also defended the mass for the deceased, for instance). However this may be, Caroli saw his suspicions reinforced when Calvin and Farel, in an attempt to defend themselves, quoted from their newly written *Instruction et Confession de Foy* (Geneva 1537). Since in this document they did not use classical terms such as *trinitas* and *persona*, Caroli argued that it is the classical creeds that we must subscribe to rather than such modern texts as Calvin and Farel had written. Therefore, during a regional synod in Lausanne (May 1537), Caroli urged that Calvin and Farel without compromise ought to comply with the Nicene and Athanasian Creeds. As said, however, Calvin, who had written an extensive confession for this occasion, on behalf of his colleagues also, refused to do so.[6] Calvin succeeded in convincing the synod that his confession was perfectly orthodox and that therefore he and his colleagues stood in good faith. Because of his unfounded allegations Caroli was removed from his post, and retreated to France (from where he continued to challenge Farel and Calvin on the Trinity issue).[7]

Yet, Calvin did not leave this battle field entirely undamaged either. His refusal to adopt the classical concepts and formulations surprised many people in his environment. Therefore, at a synod that was held in Bern somewhat later that year (September 1537) Calvin is asked to account for his unwilling attitude. It is decided, then and there, that a common

---

[6] *Confessio de Trinitate propter calumnias P. Caroli*; this 'Confession on the Trinity because of P. Caroli's False Accusations' has been included twice in the *Corpus Reformatorum*: as part of the *Defensio* (1545; cf. footnote 9) in part 7 (311–314) and as a separate piece in part 9 (703–710).

[7] Cf. for a succinct account of the Caroli-affair as mirrored in Calvin's writings: Wulfert de Greef, *The Writings of John Calvin. An Introductory Guide* (Louisville: Westminster John Knox Press, 2008), 158–160; see also W. Nijenhuis, "Calvin's Attitude towards the Symbols of the Early Church During the Conflict with Caroli," in: W. Nijenhuis, *Ecclesia Reformata. Studies on the Reformation* (Leiden: Brill, 1972), 73–96.

declaration is to be drafted,[8] which Calvin and Farel (like all others) have to subscribe to. In doing so, Calvin now acknowledges that the trinitarian conceptuality which was coined by the ancient creeds is of lasting significance for the Church of Christ, and that therefore terms like Trinity and Person merit unambiguous recognition in the Church and in theology. Thereby Calvin clearly abandons his previous plea for a "free use" (*liberum usum*) of the classical terminology.[9] In so far as Calvin may have done so for pragmatic reasons, it will become clear later on that he gradually moved towards a firm inner conviction that the classical concepts were indispensable indeed. So it might be said that the synod of Bern provides us with an example of successful discipline. For here, a young theologian (Calvin was 28 years old at that time) who had displayed a somewhat liberal attitude towards the existing confessional documents allows the ecclesial community to correct him, is summoned to acknowledge the lasting significance of the classical concepts, and gradually becomes wholeheartedly convinced of their value.

But why did Calvin initially refuse to side unequivocally with the early Christian statements of faith concerning the divine Trinity? Here we can discern two reasons, both of which are mentioned by Calvin himself.[10] First of all, signing the early Christian Creeds in this situation would in his eyes amount to a confession of guilt. For in doing so Calvin would implicitly admit that his own work (and that of his fellows) could indeed raise doubts concerning the orthodoxy and reliability of its writer(s). Secondly, however, Calvin resists the literalism which is implied by Caroli's demand. It would be wrong if in the church that person would be considered a heretic, who does not speak according to the formula which is prescribed by someone else.[11] According to Calvin, this kind of "tyranny"

---

[8] *De voce trinitatis et de voce persona* (On the Concept of 'Trinity' and the Concept of 'Person'), *CO* 9, 707–708.

[9] Cf. A. Baars, *Om Gods verhevenheid en Zijn nabijheid. De Drie-eenheid bij Calvijn* [Concerning God's Loftiness and Nearness: Calvin on the Trinity] (Kampen: Kok, 2004), 114, 120. This voluminous work contains by far the most comprehensive and detailed analysis of Calvin's doctrine of the Trinity up to date. For a rendering of Calvin's conflict with Caroli, see 104–121. An evaluation of this conflict that is less in sympathy with Calvin can be found in François Wendel, *John Calvin. The Origins and Development of His Religious Thought* (New York: Harper & Row, 1963), 53f.

[10] In his *Pro G. Farello et collegis eius adversus Petri Caroli calumnias defensio* (1545) [A Defence of G. Farel and his Colleagues against the False Accusations of Peter Caroli]; cf. *CO* 7, 318f. What follows in the body of the text is a summary of these pages of the *Defensio*.

[11] Calvin, *Pro Farello Defensio*, *CO* 7, 318.

would be incompatible with the *sola Scriptura* principle. Caroli's demand had nothing to do with the Bible, but all the more with a traditionalist clinging to old terms, which presumably was a result of the conservatism Caroli had imbibed during his studies at the Sorbonne.

This second consideration is particularly interesting in connection with our theme. Bernd Oberdorfer acutely remarks that in Geneva Calvin did not take his maxim that believers should not be pressed to subscribe to any other documents than the Bible as seriously as one might have expected.[12] For clearly, in Geneva Calvin himself demanded uncompromising compliance with the Reformed confession. So why was Calvin so vehemently opposed to the enforced endorsement of the early Christian Creeds? The formal consideration that no non-biblical texts should be imposed on Christian believers is clearly insufficient as an explanation. Here one might suspect that, after all, Calvin had some concerns about the *material content* of the ancient Creeds. Did he perhaps perceive a tension between the Greek-philosophical terminology of the Creeds on the one hand and the non-speculative language of the Bible on the other?

Indeed, in the course of his *Defensio* Calvin admits that he has some problems with the text of the Nicene Creed:

> As you see we find some verbosity (*battologia*) in these words: "God from God, Light from Light, True God from True God." Why this repetition? Does it give some extra emphasis, or a greater liveliness? You see that it is more fit to be sung as a hymn than as a confessional form, in which it is preposterous when there is one syllable too much.[13]

So indeed Calvin turns out to be critical towards the text of the Creed. Still, it seems that his criticism is limited to the style of the document. As a scholar who was trained in the humanist tradition, Calvin experienced the style of the Creed of Nicea[14] as too loose for a confessional statement. Or did he have problems indeed with its material content?

---

[12] Bernd Oberdorfer, *Filioque. Geschichte und Theologie eines ökumenischen Problems* (Göttingen: Vandenhoeck & Ruprecht, 2001), 279.

[13] Calvin, *Pro Farello Defensio*, CO 7, 315–316 (my translation).

[14] It is interesting that Calvin's criticism touches the Creed of Nicea (325), but not the so-called Nicene Creed (381) of which the official Latin name is Niceano-Constantinopolitanum. According to Baars, Calvin never goes back behind the text of 381 to the confession of 325; but since the words "God from God" do not occur in the Nicene Creed of 381, it seems that he must be mistaken here. Baars, *Om Gods verhevenheid*, 641. If, as is frequently held, the Nicene Creed is an extension of the Creed of Nicea, the reason for omitting the words "God from God" may have been exactly the same as the one mentioned by Calvin: given the subsequent phrase "true God from true God" they were superfluous.

The Conflict with Gentilis

Sixteen years later, in 1561, Calvin returns once more to his reservations concerning the ancient Creeds. Again, his doubts concern the doctrine of the Trinity. But now not only the repetitions trouble him. Rather, he allows himself a critical remark about the content of the Creed, or at least its formulations.[15] Here is what he says:

> But the words of the Council of Nicea resound "God from God." This is a hard saying, I acknowledge. However, no one is better able to remove any ambiguity or a more capable interpreter than Athanasius, who dictated it. And certainly the counsel of the Fathers [like Athanasius, GvdB] was no other than that the Son in terms of origin is led out from the Father as far as his Person is concerned; it was in no way to oppose his being-of-the-same-essence and deity. And so, according to his essence, he is the Word of God without beginning; according to his person, however, the Son has a beginning from the Father.[16]

What is at stake in this quotation? The passage stems from a new polemical writing of Calvin, this time directed at Giovanni Valentino Gentilis, an Italian teacher of Latin who had settled in Geneva in 1556 and who had joined the church of the Italians there. In that church critical voices with respect to the early Christian doctrine of the Trinity had been heard before, and Gentilis associated himself with this anti-trinitarian sentiment in his own way. To be sure, Gentilis distanced himself from the radical anti-trinitarianism of Michael Servetus, but still, he as well, had difficulties with the classical doctrine of the Trinity.

Incidentally, it is difficult to determine which textual edition(s) of the ancient Creeds Calvin was acquainted with.

[15] Indeed, following Benjamin B. Warfield, "Calvin's Doctrine of the Trinity," in B.B. Warfield, *Calvin and Calvinism* [Works, vol. 5] (New York: Oxford University Press, 1931), 249, it might be argued that also in the Gentilis-case Calvin's criticisms of the Creed only affected its (inexact) formulations, not its content. Cf. Robert Letham, *The Holy Trinity in Scripture, History, Theology and Worship* (Phillipsburg: P&R Publishing, 2004), 266.

[16] John Calvin, *Expositio impietatis Valentini Gentilis* (Exposition of the Impiety of Valentino Gentilis) in *CO* 9, 368. "Sed verba consilii Nicaeni sonant, Deum esse ad Deo. Dura loquutio, fateor, sed ad cuius tollendam ambiguitatem nemo potest esse magis idoneus interpres, quam Athanasius, qui eam dictavit. Et certe non aliud fuit patrum concilium, nisi manere originem quam ducit a patre filius, personae respectu, nec obstare quominus eadem sit utriusque essentia et deitas: atque ita, quoad essentiam, sermonem esse Deum absque principio; in persona autem filii habere principium a patre." I have used (but slightly adapted) the translation of Robert Letham, *Holy Trinity*, 262, who speaks of a "crucial passage" in this connection.

In particular, Gentilis was of the opinion that the so-called Athanasian Creed detracted from the special position of the Father within the Trinity. And exactly the same criticism Gentilis had raised against Calvin. According to Gentilis, within the Trinity the Father is not at the same level with the other Persons. To be sure, the Son and the Spirit are God as well as the Father, but within the single being of God we must distinguish between a higher and a lower part. For the Son and the Spirit owe their divinity to the Father; the Father, on the other hand, owes his divinity to no other person than himself. Therefore, he is the only Person who is God in the proper sense: only the Father is *autotheos*. Gentilis appealed to the Nicene Creeds to find support for this view, since here it is held that the Son is "God from God" and/or "true God from true God."

It is in this context that we can understand Calvin's response. Calvin resists Gentilis' subordinational interpretation of the relation between the Father and the Son in the Creed. Nevertheless, he has to concede that the passage to which Gentilis refers is ambiguous indeed. For that reason, he considers the phrase "God from God" to be somewhat infelicitous. However, when we look at the interpretation of this phrase that was given by Athanasius, the problem is easily resolved; for Athanasius was quite clear that from all eternity the Son participates in the being and the deity of the Father. It is only as far as the personal relation between Father and Son is concerned that the Son is "God from God" (like a son by definition stems from his father). This is not to say, however, that the Son belongs to some inferior part in God.[17]

It may be asked why this point was so important to Calvin. In order to answer this question, we will now focus on the more systematic account of the doctrine of the Trinity that Calvin gave in his *Institutes*. From that perspective it will become clear why Gentilis touched such a raw nerve with Calvin. In any case, we can already conclude that Calvin's reservations with the early Christian creeds were not the result of a skeptical attitude towards the doctrine of the Trinity. On the contrary, it seems that in Calvin's eyes this doctrine was not yet sufficiently developed in a clear and unambiguous way. But Calvin was deeply convinced that fathers like Athanasius had made the right choices on the issues that were at stake in elaborating the doctrine of the Trinity. As a result, contemporary research has abandoned the view that the Reformers, and in particular Calvin and

---

[17] See for a more detailed account of Calvin's dispute with Gentilis: Baars, *Om Gods verhevenheid*, 242–256. Unfortunately the new monograph of Brandon Ellis, *Calvin, Classical Trinitarianism and the Aseity of the Son* (Oxford: Oxford University Press, 2012) appeared too late to be included in the research for this article.

his friends, had politely taken off their hats to the trinitarian dogma, but
lacked an inner congeniality with this doctrine so highly revered by the
early Church.[18] It is true that Calvin did not feel committed to a slavish
repetition of the literal phrasing of the ancient Creeds. For Calvin perceived that some of the creedal formulations were open to misunder-
standing, and moreover he wanted to understand them spiritually rather
than literally. With the material content of the early confessions, however, he was fully in harmony. This will become clear when we examine
Calvin's exposition on the doctrine of the Trinity in his *Institutes*.

The Institutes I: Calling into Question the Tradition

Not only in Calvin's polemical writings (as referred to above), but also
in his *Institutes*, we encounter his hesitations concerning the imposition
of non-biblical concepts and formulations. At the same time it becomes
clear that Calvin gradually became more and more convinced of their
indispensability. That was not only the result of the concessions he had
to make during the synod at Bern in 1537. No doubt, it had to do more
with the later conflicts with opponents of the doctrine of the Trinity,
the anti-trinitarians to whom, among many others, Gentilis belonged.
That the issue continued to occupy Calvin's mind appears from the fact
that in the fourth and final edition of the *Institutes*, Calvin begins the
chapter on the Trinity (I 13) with a discussion of the classical concepts
and definitions. In the previous editions, Calvin had placed this discussion at the very *end* of the chapter in question. This change may have
been partially inspired by didactical motives, but presumably it also tells
us something about Calvin's growing appreciation of a proper use and of
the importance of the early Christian terminology. In the final edition of
his *Institutes* (1559—this was one year after the difficulties with Gentilis
and other anti-trinitarians had started), Calvin deliberately incorporated
materials from his previous polemical writings, no doubt because he was
convinced that his views on what is important in the Christian religion
had matured as a result of the conflicts he had gone through.

---

[18] J. Koopmans, *Het oudkerkelijk dogma in de reformatie, bepaaldelijk bij Calvijn* [The
Dogma of the Early Church in the Reformation, Particularly in Calvin] (Wageningen:
Veenman, 1938), 38; see for this older view E. Bähler, "Petrus Caroli und Johannes Calvin,"
Jahrbuch für Schweizerische Geschichte 29 (1904), 41–169.

However this may be, in the opening section of the chapter on the Trinity Calvin speaks in a very balanced way. He still proves sensitive to the motives of those who do not want to subscribe to the traditional formulations concerning God's triunity. This sensitivity has a profound theological background in Calvin's thinking. When it comes to God, we always have to speak with the greatest possible reticence, because of God's immensity and incomprehensibility. This basic theological intuition of Calvin is not entirely unlike what we encounter in so-called negative theologies. As Paul Helm has it, "[w]e speak most sensibly about God's essence when we say what it is not (...) and when we exercise reserve and restraint in our positive statements. (...) Calvin's repeated references to God's incomprehensible essence are (...) intended to warn us against imagining what God is like, which would lead us inexorably down the road to idolatry."[19] That Calvin also applied this basic intuition to the doctrine of the Trinity is clear from the fact that he quotes with approval the famous dictum of Augustine, that we use the word *hypostasis* for the three divine persons "not to express what it is, but not to be silent on how Father, Son, and Spirit are three."[20] So when speaking about God, we easily say too much; we proceed as if God is one of us, and in fact ignore that God entirely transcends all our imaginations. It is precisely for that reason, says Calvin, that God has revealed to us his infinity and spirituality, lest we should think of Him in a limited way.

> But even if God to keep us sober speaks sparingly of his essence, yet by those two titles that I have used [viz. infinite and spiritual, GvdB] he both banishes stupid imaginings and restrains the boldness of the human mind. Surely, his infinity ought to make us afraid to try to measure him by our own senses.[21]

This also explains why in the *Institutes* Calvin does not develop any further thoughts on God's essence, "which we ought more to adore than meticulously to search out."[22]

A second reason Calvin adduces for not making the traditional formulations in the doctrine of the Trinity sacrosanct, is that the church fathers

---

[19] Paul Helm, *John Calvin. A Guide for the Perplexed* (London: T&T Clark, 2008), 39, 40.

[20] Calvin, *Institutes* I.13.5; Augustine, *De Trinitate* V 9, 10.

[21] *Institutes* I.13.1; cf. Cornelis van der Kooi, *As in a Mirror. John Calvin and Karl Barth on Knowing God. A Diptych* (Leiden: Brill, 2005), 124 (in a passage on Calvin's "anti-speculative tenor").

[22] Calvin, *Institutes* I.5.9; cf. E.P. Meijering, *Calvin wider die Neugierde* (Nieuwkoop: De Graaf, 1980).

did not use them in a single and unambiguous way. Rather, although they tried to speak very reverently on these matters, the ancients "agree neither among themselves nor even at all times individually with themselves."[23] By way of example, Calvin points to the fact that Jerome called it sacrilege to predicate three substances in God, whereas in Hilary one can find more than a hundred times precisely this view, viz. that there are three substances in God. This difference stemmed from the confusion which had arisen in the early church around the translation of Greek concepts into Latin. It clearly shows, however, that we have to be very cautious here: when we want to impose certain non-biblical concepts on each other's minds because of their rootedness in the ecclesial tradition, this tradition may on closer inspection turn out to be a bundle of contradictions. Calvin is in line with the other Reformers when suggesting that we cannot avoid a critical sifting of the tradition, at the end of which we can only uphold what is in accordance with the scriptures.

Calvin was keen to notice that some of the church fathers were themselves quite conscious of the fact that it is risky to swear to all kinds of non-biblical concepts. For example, both Augustine and Hilary themselves offered excuses for introducing new words in their theological vocabulary, and qualified their importance. Calvin concludes from this that

> (...) this modesty of saintly men ought to warn us against forthwith so severely taking to task, like censors, those who do not wish to swear to the words conceived by us, provided they are not doing it out of either arrogance or forwardness or malicious craft.[24]

In short, when believers sincerely (rather than driven by impure motives) have difficulties with the adoption of the classical concepts, for example because they want to live by the Bible alone, they should meet with our understanding. Calvin himself at least is not "a stickler as to battle doggedly over mere words." What is more: "I could wish they [i.e. the classical trinitarian terms] were buried."[25]

---

[23] Calvin, *Institutes* I.13.5.

[24] Calvin, *Institutes* I.13.5.

[25] Calvin, *Institutes* I.13.5; this exclamation follows on the final sentence of I.13.4, where Calvin had indicated that according to the *patres* the unity of God exists in a trinity of persons. So in this context as well, he has in mind classical concepts like 'trinity' (*trinitas*) and 'person' (*persona*), possibly next to 'existing' (*subsistere*) and 'unity' (*unitas*).

The Institutes II—Joining the Tradition

Did Calvin really wish to do so? Or is this a slip of the pen? It is an audacious exclamation at the least, since in the aftermath of the conflict with Caroli Calvin had been forced to acknowledge that the classical concepts could *not* be buried, since they were of lasting significance to the Church. So how could he still in 1559 wish for their abolition? In order to understand this we have to carefully place this utterance in its proper context. This will bring us to the other side of the story, namely Calvin's motives for firmly holding on to the classical doctrine of the Trinity. In order to see this, let me quote Calvin's statement once again, but this time in its direct context:

> If (. . .) these terms were not rashly invented, we ought to beware lest by repudiating them we be accused of overweening rashness. Indeed, I could wish they were buried, if only among all men this faith were agreed on: that Father and Son and Spirit are one God, yet the Son is not the Father, nor the Spirit the Son, but that they are differentiated by a peculiar quality.[26]

So if only the realities which the terms intend to express (however imperfectly) stand firm, Calvin does not want to quarrel over words and concepts. This also explains his critical attitude towards the so-called vestiges of the Trinity (*vestigia trinitatis*—examples or traces from our everyday world that may explain how something can at the same time be three and one) as he encountered them (among others) in Augustine.[27] In his own summaries of the doctrine of the Trinity, Calvin from time to time even intentionally avoided the contested classical terms, replacing them by other ones such as source and fountain, wisdom and counsel, and power and efficacy, as if he wanted to make clear that we can do without the classical concepts:

> I really do not know whether it is expedient to borrow comparisons from human affairs to express the force of this distinction [viz. between the three divine Persons]. Men of old were indeed accustomed sometimes to do so, but at the same time they confessed that the analogies they advanced were

---

[26] Calvin, *Institutes* I.13.5. Cf. Paul Helm, *John Calvin's Ideas* (Oxford: Oxford University Press, 2004), 41, who observes in connection with this quotation: "Calvin here reveals an essentially conservative, catholic spirit. He was personally content with a minimalist expression of the Trinitarian formula, the essential deposit of Patristic reflection, in order to avoid speculation (. . .)."

[27] Cf. John Calvin, *Commentary on Genesis* 1: 26 (*CO* 23, 25); cf. the closing paragraph of *Institutes* I.15.4.

quite inadequate. Thus it is that I shrink from all rashness here: lest if anything should be inopportunely expressed, it may give occasion either of calumny to the malicious, or of delusion to the ignorant. Nevertheless, it is not fitting to suppress the distinction that we observe to be expressed in Scripture. It is this: to the Father is attributed the beginning of activity, and the fountain and wellspring of all things; to the Son, wisdom, counsel, and the ordered disposition of all things; but to the Spirit is assigned the power and efficacy of that activity.[28]

Still, it was clear to Calvin that the traditional distinctions "were not rashly invented," so that we must be careful not to reject them out of hand. Calvin writes in a very pastoral tone about those who tended to do so because of their reluctance to accept the traditional concepts that have been handed down to us over the centuries: "But let these very persons, in turn, weigh the necessity that compels us to speak thus, that gradually they may at length become accustomed to a useful manner of speaking."[29]

Now what does this 'necessity that compels us to speak thus' amount to? Most of all, Calvin leaves no room for doubt that in his opinion the classical doctrine of the Trinity is in accordance with the Bible. That had been Calvin's view already in the first (1536) edition of the *Institutes*, where he had opened his treatment of the doctrine with an exegetical exposition. Calvin's point of departure here had been that on the one hand the Bible teaches that there is only one God, whereas on the other not only the Father, but also the Son and the Spirit are called God. In fact, this twofold affirmation already contains in itself the heart of the doctrine of the Trinity (whether or not one wants to give it that name). Drawing on a whole range of biblical texts, and especially discussing Matthew 28:19 and Ephesians 4:5, Calvin therefore had tried to elucidate these two biblical lines. In his subsequent systematic reflection on the question how this unity and trinity of God are related to each other, Calvin even had already cautiously adopted the early Christian terminology. Although he

---

[28] Calvin, *Institutes* I.13.18; see for a discussion of Calvin's preference for the triad Source, Wisdom and Power: Baars, *Om Gods verhevenheid*, 661–669. In his informative recent survey of "The Trinity in the Reformed Tradition", *Journal of Reformed Theology* 3 (2009), 57–76, Dirkie Smit reminds us in this connection of the fact that it is "a typical Reformed intuition, that the tradition (...), including all the terms, is not in itself authoritative, but subject to critical consideration and rejection, if necessary. It is only because the scriptures make some distinction that these should be considered necessary and useful" (61 n. 9).

[29] Calvin, *Institutes* I.13.5. If one reads these words from the perspective of the preceding polemics Calvin had been involved in, they at once receive an extra dimension: It is as if Calvin briefly summarizes his own biographical development here. As we have seen, in earlier years Calvin himself had "gradually (...) become accustomed" to the classical distinctions, getting more and more convinced of their "necessity."

had thoroughly qualified its use (i.e this should not be out of a desire for speculation, only sparingly, not at the wrong occasion, etc.), he still had argued that the traditional concepts can to some extent clarify complicated biblical texts.[30]

In fact, Caroli could have concluded already from this first edition of the *Institutes* that Calvin did not have any fundamental objections against the classical trinitarian dogma. On the contrary, in his resistance to the anti-trinitarian tendencies that had developed in his days (especially in radical circles and with Servetus), Calvin had already implicitly endorsed it. That Calvin had avoided an exposition on the trinitarian terminology in his Catechism of 1537 (i.e. one year after the first edition of his *Institutes*), was for pastoral reasons: a relatively simple, practical booklet on the heart of the Christian faith would have been such a "wrong occasion" for bothering people with complex trinitarian distinctions.[31] In general, however, Calvin is of the opinion that concepts that do not occur in the scriptures may nevertheless be very useful in explaining what is meant in the scriptures. Otherwise our sermons as well would have to consist simply and solely of biblical texts.[32] Thus, the *sola Scriptura* did not turn Calvin into a biblicist.[33] The crucial question is whether or not the relevant dogmatic concepts and distinctions help us in interpreting and understanding the Bible. And when it comes to the doctrine of the Trinity, Calvin is quite convinced that this is the case. Accordingly, in contrast to e.g. Thomas Aquinas, Calvin develops his exposition of the doctrine along strongly biblical and exegetical lines, discussing all kinds of biblical texts that put forward the unity of God and the divinity of the Son and the Spirit.[34]

---

[30] For a summary of Calvin's treatment of the Trinity in the first edition of his *Institutes*, see Baars, *Om Gods verhevenheid*, 76–92.

[31] It was no coincidence that this *Instruction et Confession de Foy dont on use en Leglise de Geneve* had been written in French, the language of the local population. Still, one may perceive a tension with what Calvin had written one year before, viz. that the classical trinitarian concepts might *clarify* the scriptures (rather than complicating the issues).

[32] "If they call a foreign word one that cannot be shown to stand written syllable by syllable in Scripture, they are indeed imposing upon us an unjust law which condemns all interpretation not patched together out of the fabric of Scripture"; Calvin, *Institutes* I.13.3.

[33] Cf. Helm, *John Calvin's Ideas*, 37; Baars, *Om Gods verhevenheid*, 78.

[34] Smit, "The Trinity in the Reformed Tradition," 61, shows that this biblical approach was to have a lasting influence in Reformed theology; he identifies as the first characteristic of Reformed trinitarian thought that (in contemporary words) "the doctrine is seen as providing the necessary 'grammar' to speak about the message of the scriptures."

For Us and our Salvation

If we now consider briefly the special character of Calvin's interpretation of the doctrine of the Trinity, this has to be found above all in his
emphasis on the full divinity of both the Son and the Spirit. As we saw
in his polemic with Gentilis, Calvin did not hesitate to call the Son *autotheos* ('God from himself'). Calvin even went so far as to apply the name
Jehovah to the Son, which was very unusual in the doctrinal tradition and
was therefore criticized not only by Caroli but also by Roman Catholic
theologians. Still, Calvin continued to insist upon it, and Paul Helm speaks
of a "basic thought" of Calvin in this connection: none of the three Persons
in God has a derived divine nature.[35] In this way, Calvin removed the
final remnants of subordinationism from the doctrine of the Trinity. As
Benjamin Warfield already suggested a century ago, it is probably here
that the unique contribution of Calvin to the doctrine of the Trinity must
be located.[36]

Why was the complete equality of Father, Son and Spirit so important
to Calvin? The answer to this question leads us to the heart of Calvin's
theological intentions: Calvin wanted Church and theology to concentrate
upon the *communion* that God seeks to have with us sinful humans. It is
in the communion with God through faith that we receive our creaturely
destination and our ultimate salvation from the powers of sin and evil.
This communion, however, can only be restored through Christ and the
Spirit, since it is grounded in the redemptive work of Christ and accomplished by the Holy Spirit. And since God is the only one who can save us
(according to Athanasius' famous argument for the *homoousios*), it follows
that the Son and the Spirit are no less God than the Father. Already in
the first edition of his *Institutes* Calvin wrote: "We are convinced that we
have no other Leader and Guide to the Father than the Holy Spirit, just as
there is no other way to Him than Christ."[37]

It is this soteriological concentration that gives not only Calvin's doctrine of the Trinity but also his complete doctrine of God its distinctive
anti-speculative flavor. In Calvin we don't find the extensive philosophical
reflections on the existence, essence, and attributes of God that were so
characteristic of medieval theology and that would become perhaps even

---

[35] Helm, *John Calvin's Ideas*, 43, 45.
[36] Warfield, *Calvin and Calvinism*, 284, and *passim* (189–284).
[37] Calvin, *Institutes* (1536), in: P. Barth, W. Niesel (eds), *Joannis Calvini opera selecta* I
(München: Chr. Kaiser Verlag, 1926), 82.

more characteristic of post-Reformation scholastic theology.[38] Nor is the Trinity an occasional final note in his doctrine of God, added only for the formal reason that the tradition forbade its total negligence. Rather, although it is an overstatement to say that for Calvin "the Trinity *is* his doctrine of God,"[39] it certainly forms the heart of it. Calvin broke away from the conventional separation of the discussion of the one God from the discussion of the triune God. When Calvin starts speaking about God, as soon as possible he also wants to point to the Son and the Spirit, in order to be able to discuss the communal work of Father, Son and Spirit for our salvation. Thus, it is not the immanent but the economic Trinity which is the primary focus of Calvin's attention.[40] "For us and our salvation"—the key sentence by means of which the Nicene Creed underlines the necessity of the incarnation—might also have been used by Calvin to explain why the Trinity is of pivotal importance for the Church. So here, in the end, Calvin is in complete harmony with the ecumenical Creed, the authority of which he at one time contested.

By way of conclusion we can side with Parker that from as early as 1536 (the year of the first edition of his *Institutes*) Calvin's view of the Trinity was "perfectly orthodox," whereas, as he went on, Calvin became more and more convinced that "the orthodox doctrine of the Trinity said precisely what he himself wanted to say."[41] We can hardly overestimate the importance of this development in Calvin from an ecumenical point of view. For as a result of the fact that Calvin and his fellow Reformers not only formally accepted, but also spiritually and theologically appropriated the doctrinal heritage of the undivided Church, the Reformed churches remained firmly within the tradition of the catholicity of the Church. The conflict between the Protestant Reformation and the Roman Catholic

---

[38] In spite of Richard Muller's unceasing efforts to prove that there is no *substantial* difference between Calvin's theology and post-Reformation Reformed dogmatics, this is still argued by e.g. William C. Placher, *The Domestication of Transcendence. How Modern Thinking about God Went Wrong* (Louisville: Westminster John Knox, 1996), 164–178.

[39] Letham, *Holy Trinity*, 253; Veli-Matti Kärkkäinen, *The Trinity. Global Perspectives* (Louisville: Westminster John Knox, 2007), 56, rightly perceives "some overstatement" in this qualification.

[40] Cf. Philip W. Butin, *Revelation, Redemption and Response. Calvin's Trinitarian Understanding of the Divine-Human Relationship* (New York: Oxford University Press, 1995). Smit, "Trinity in the Reformed Tradition," 72, even shows that "[m]any of the Reformed voices in the [contemporary, GvdB] trinitarian renaissance seem concerned that there was too little interest in Calvin in the so-called immanent Trinity" (which they themselves usually conceive of in a social or relational way).

[41] T.H.L. Parker, *The Doctrine of the Knowledge of God. A Study in the Theology of John Calvin* (Edinburgh: Oliver and Boyd, 1952), 61–62.

Church, bitter though it was and may still be at times, is mainly a conflict on ecclesiological issues.[42] It may be surmised that the soteriological differences concerning faith, justification and grace need not have been unbridgeable from the beginning if there had been a common willingness to address them from the "shared conceptual framework and (...) common theological heritage" of classical Christology and the orthodox doctrine of the Trinity. For clearly, these key theological building blocks were left firmly in their place by Protestant theology.[43] The much more divisive and tragic conflict that is humanly speaking unsolvable, is the dispute with those who do not claim any share in the Church's common theological heritage, such as the anti-trinitarians in Calvin's days and their Muslim counterparts in ours.

---

[42] Also the doctrinal controversies on the sacraments can be interpreted as being, basically, conflicts on the role and power of the church.

[43] Alan Spence, *Christology. A Guide for the Perplexed* (London: T&T Clark, 2008), 78.

CHAPTER TWO

THE TWO MEANS OF KNOWING GOD: NOT AN ARTICLE OF CONFESSION FOR CALVIN

Rinse Reeling Brouwer

In his inaugural oration as a professor at Leiden University on the 14th of December, 2007,[1] Gijsbert van den Brink argued for the relevance and the currency of the second article of the *Belgic Confession* (1561):

> We know him [the single and simple God, as mentioned in the first article] by two means: First, by the creation, preservation, and government of the universe; which is before our eyes as a most elegant book, wherein all creatures, great and small, are as so many characters leading us to contemplate the invisible things of God, namely, his eternal power and Godhead, as the Apostle Paul saith in Romans 1:20. All which things are sufficient to convince men, and leave them without excuse?
>
> Secondly, he makes himself more clearly and fully known to us by his holy and divine Word; that is to say, as far as is necessary for us to knowing this life, to his glory and our salvation.[2]

The first means, i.e. the knowledge of God through creation, Van den Brink argues, can be seen in our time as the foundation for the so-called 'anthropic principle', formulated by dr. Francis S. Collins in the following way: "God is the explanation of those features of the universe that science finds difficult to explain (such as the values of certain physical constants favouring life)".[3] As far as the history of science is concerned, it is correct

---

[1] G. van den Brink, *Als een schoon boec: Achtergrond, receptie en relevantie van artikel 2 van de Nederlandse Geloofsbelijdenis* [Like a Beautiful Book: On the Background, Reception, and Relevance of Article 2 of the Belgic Confession] (Leiden: University Press, 2007).

See www.leidenuniv.nl/tekstboekjes/content docs/oratie_van_den_brink.pdf.

[2] Belgic Confession, Article 2 'By what means God is made known unto us.' Philip Schaff (ed.), *The Creeds of Christendom with a History and Critical Notes.* Vol. III. *The Evangelical Protestant Creeds, with Translations* (New York: Harper and Brothers, 1882), 384.

[3] Van den Brink, "Als een scoon boec", 16. He refers to Francis S. Collins, *De taal van God. Prominent geneticus verzoent geloof en wetenschap* [The Language of God: A Prominent Geneticist Reconciles Faith and Science], (Kampen: Ten Have, 2006), 72. However, there is a great difference between the notion of the 'kosmos' in antiquity and medieval times, which is presupposed in the confessions of the 16th century, and the concept of the 'universe' of modern physics.

in my opinion to stress that for a long time during early modernity in the reformed world this 'first means' furnished the theological justification in the minds of the investigators of physical reality for approaching the object of their research: they were convinced that by their careful reading of the 'book of nature' God himself and God alone would receive all the honour.[4] But it seems to make no sense to maintain this part of the Confession today as a foundation for a theory that explains features of the universe in competition with other theories within the sciences. However, it is not the purpose of this paper to defend this thesis. I rather want to make a more modest case, i.e., *to dispute Van den Brink's view, that John Calvin is the theologian who has provided the underlying theological theory for this second article of the Confession.* As far as Calvin as the author of the *Institutio Religionis Christianae* is concerned, this view is subject to considerable doubt, and to the extent that he was an important source in the formation of the *Belgic Confession*, it can be shown to be incorrect. In what follows I will demonstrate both assertions, and at the same time I will show what is actually going on in these Calvin texts.

"That Knowledge Would Be Useless ..."

It is evident that Guido de Brès, the author of the Belgic Confession, was a good pupil of Calvin. Therefore one can imagine why Van den Brink wants to resist attempts to play off Calvin against De Brès: "It seems to me that *both* perceive creation as a separate scripture preceding source of the knowledge of God".[5] However, there is a difference between the way Calvin perceived this distinction as a theologian, in quiet reflection as he was writing his *Institutio*, and the extent to which he considered this issue relevant to a contemporary confession of faith. However, in his reflection Van den Brink does not take this difference into account. Let us first look at the *Institutes*.

From the second edition of 1539 onwards, Calvin starts this work with a chapter on the knowledge of God.[6] After an introduction in which he deals with the question of the relationship of the knowledge of God and

---

[4] Cf. Eric Jorink, *Reading the Book of Nature in the Dutch Golden Age, 1575–1715* (Leiden: Brill, 2010).

[5] Van den Brink, "Als een scoon boec", 12.

[6] Cf. F.H. Breukelman, *The Structure of Sacred Doctrine in Calvin's Theology*, ed. Rinse H. Reeling Brouwer (Grand Rapids: Eerdmans, 2010), 123–154.

the knowledge of ourselves in our misery,[7] he speaks about the knowledge of God as implanted in the minds of men by nature (something pagan philosophers like Cicero already knew),[8] then about the objective testimony of God contained in the set-up of the world and its continuing government,[9] and finally about the proposition that what the 'works' of God proclaim about their maker, is adequately documented in the book of scripture. The latter confirms what they are declaring and which, in order to deprive us of any excuse that we as creatures would not be able to correctly read the book of creation, is offered to us as a pair of glasses, as it were, enabling us to read in creation what we're supposed to read there.[10] At the end of this chapter, however, it turns out that all of this knowledge is still insufficient. A more intimate view of God can be given only as he makes himself known in the face of Christ and this knowing is only available to the eyes of faith.[11]

When in the winter of 1558/1559 Calvin decides to reshape the book, something strange and ambiguous happens that has confused many commentators. The duality between what can be said about God from the observation of creation on the one hand and what will have to be said later when seeing God in the face of Christ on the other hand, is strengthened by dealing with these matters in two separate books: first 'The Knowledge of God the Creator' (I) and then 'The Knowledge of God the Redeemer' (first under the Law, then in the Gospel, both in Christ, II). Faith is only mentioned at the beginning of the third book as the first and crucial gift of the Holy Spirit to people who belong to Christ. Thus the two ways of knowing, and with them the doctrine of the 'two means' of the second article of the Belgic Confession, almost seem to be doctrinally established here. And this, consistently enough, leads to the same duality in the discussion of scripture. First Calvin now speaks of a 'general doctrine of scripture',[12] in which scripture functions as the eyeglasses providing the help by which God can be recognized in his creation. One might say: scripture as a textbook for a Christian world view. Then secondly, he

---

[7] Using the section numbering of the 1550 edition: Calvin, *Institutes* I.1–3; cf. *CO* 1, 279–282.

[8] Calvin, *Institutes* 1550, I.4–10, *CO* 1, 282–286.

[9] Calvin, *Institutes* 1550, I.11–18, *CO* 1, 286–291.

[10] Calvin, *Institutes* 1550, I.19–38, *CO* 1, 292–304.

[11] As announced in Calvin, *Institutes* 1550, I.38. In 1539 faith is treated in the fourth chapter and in 1550 in the fifth chapter. Cf. Calvin, *Institutes*, III.2 (unless a different year of publication is mentioned, 'Calvin, *Institutes*' refers to the edition of 1559).

[12] Calvin, *Institutes*, I.2.1, I.10.3.

teaches a 'proper doctrine of faith',[13] in which God is acknowledged as the Redeemer in Christ, and therefore scripture is fully functioning as a doctrine of salvation.[14] One could easily suggest that with this all the crucial elements for a doctrine of the 'two means' are ready to be combined in a confession at the proper time.

Remarkably, however, another line of thought can be found in the *Institutes* in its final edition. When Calvin is working on his new second book, 'On the Knowledge of God the Redeemer', and then tries to attach the old second chapter 'On the Knowledge of Ourselves' (as the knowledge of our misery)[15] to the former chapter 'On the Law' (as a means to know our sin, but at the same time and chiefly as a witness to Christ),[16] he needs a 'glue', as it were, a short new chapter, in which he can place the preceding as well as the following materials into the context of his ongoing argument: 'that fallen man must seek his redemption *in Christ*'.[17] We read shocking sentences here:[18]

> "The whole human race perished in the person of Adam. Consequently that original excellence and nobility which we have recounted [in the earlier treatise on the fall][19] would be of no profit to us but would rather redound to our greater shame, until God, who does not recognize as his handiwork men defiled and corrupted by sin, appeared as Redeemer in the person of his only-begotten Son. Therefore, since we have fallen from life to death, the *whole knowledge* of God the Creator that we have discussed *would be useless* [Italics added] unless faith also followed, setting forth for us God our Father in Christ." "Surely, after the fall of the first man no knowledge of God apart from the Mediator has had power unto salvation."[20]

So it seems that Calvin, after having made quite a bit of progress in writing his second book, fundamentally tones down the whole gist of his first book. Apparently, after the fall it is impossible for the knowledge of God through creation to stand on its own legs. It can only stand alongside the

---

[13]   Calvin, *Institutes* 1559, I.6.1.
[14]   Van den Brink, "Als een scoon boec", 11ff., disputes the thesis that for Calvin scripture would not only function as glasses for the knowledge of God, but also for the right view of creation. However, he fails to discuss the function of the distinction *generalis Scripturae doctrina—propria fidei doctrinae* (the general doctrine of the scripture—the proper doctrine of faith) in the final edition of the *Institutes*.
[15]   Calvin, *Institutes* 1559, II.1–5.
[16]   Calvin, *Institutes*, II.7–8.
[17]   Calvin, *Institutes*, II.6.
[18]   *OS* 3, 320.
[19]   Calvin, *Institutes*, II.1–5.
[20]   Calvin, *Institutes*, II.6.1.

knowledge of God as the Redeemer. Van den Brink fails to show how he is able to base his endorsement of the lasting relevance of a relatively independent knowledge of God through creation in abstraction of the knowledge of salvation in Christ on the theology of John Calvin.[21]

Calvin's Involvement with the French Confession

After discussing the *Institutes*, we now turn to confessional texts. Calvin's involvement with them is quite a different story in which other, i.e., ecclesiastical and political factors, come into play as well.

It is evident that De Brès, in drafting the *Belgic Confession*, did have before him the *French Confession* of 1559 as an example. In many instances he applied this text to the situation in (the southern parts of) the Low Countries. In the critical edition of Bakhuizen van den Brink the French text of the *Confessio Gallicana* is therefore correctly positioned on the page to the left of the French, the (not authorized) Latin, and the Dutch text of the *Confessio Belgica*.[22] Whether Calvin was in any way involved in the composition of the *Belgic Confession* is unclear and unproven. But his involvement with the formation of the *French Confession* is certain and provable.[23]

During the fifties of the sixteenth century, an increasing number of Reformed churches emerged in France, often with ministers trained in Geneva. These churches suffered considerable repression from the side of the French state. Gradually the need grew to make themselves known to the authorities and to dare to claim a place of their own in the nation. For that purpose, the composition of a confession of their own could be helpful. A national synod was to formulate such a confessional statement,

---

[21] "God the Creator is not the object of a general knowledge of God, he is only known in the Mediator, Jesus Christ. And assuming that there was such a general knowledge of God the Creator, it would not benefit us at all; for we no longer live in the original state. One can only claim something else than this, if one has overlooked Inst. II.6.1." Werner Krusche, *Das Wirken des Heiligen Geistes nach Calvin* (Göttingen: Vandenhoeck & Ruprecht, 1957), 83.

[22] J.N. Bakhuizen van den Brink, ed, *De Nederlandse Belijdenisgeschriften. Vergelijkende teksten* [The Dutch Confessions. Comparative Texts], (Amsterdam: Holland, 1940), 58ff.

[23] Cf. Jacques Pannier, *Les origines de la confession de foi et la discipline des églises réformées de France* (Paris: Félix Alcan, 1936); Hannelore Jahr, *Studien zur Überlieferungsgeschichte der Confession de foi von 1559* (Neukirchen-Vluyn: Neukirchener Verlag, 1964); H.A. Speelman, *Calvijn en de zelfstandigheid van de kerk* [Calvin and the Independency of the Church] (Kampen: Kok, 1994), 135–152.

while at the same time it had the task of making arrangements for the
organizational structure of the churches. The meeting of this synod was
prepared in utmost secrecy. It was to meet in May 1559 in a private house
of a member of the congregation of Saint-Germain (Paris). Calvin had
been ill for many months and suggested that he was totally surprised by
the plan, although that is not very probable. At any rate,, he expressed
having the greatest possible difficulties with the undertaking. For his strategy was—and would remain until his death in 1564—to refrain from any
action that could be regarded as subversive of the legal government, however tyrannical it might be, and to patiently wait for the right moment,
when the Lord would call a member of the ruling house of the French
monarchy to reform, as a new king Josiah, the church under his jurisdiction (as the 'most Christian King of France'). The leaders of the Huguenots
did not possess this patience and were gradually developing quite a different point of view: not that of a general reform of the national church,
but that of a legal acknowledgement of a reformed minority *alongside*
the old 'papist' church. In a letter, dated May 17th, to his former pupil,
the minister Francois de Morel in Paris, Calvin is critical of this strategy:
"Are you sure," he asks, "you want to hand in" (Latin: *edere: eat, 'stomach'*)
"such a confession? Does this plan not betray too much passion, too much
zeal? And is there not actually hidden behind such haste a fear, a lack of
the confidence of faith, the wish to force an immediate end to the present
repression?"[24]

Nevertheless, Calvin was willing to prepare a text for the confession
that the synod requested. After his objections against such a text had
been overruled, he was happy to make a draft for it himself. For the main
part this draft was adopted by the Paris Synod, but not without some striking amendments. These differences came to light, when in the autumn
of 1559, under changed political circumstances (to wit: the sudden death
of king Henry II shortly after the synod had ended, the new role of Catha-
rina de Medici as regent for her under-age son François II, and her offer
to negotiate with the higher nobility among the Huguenots, who were
inclined to respond positively to her offer) Calvin and the French Reformed
leaders, independently of each other, published their draft: containing
35 articles in the case of Calvin, but 40 articles in the text that actually had been accepted by the synod. Generally, the differences did not

---

[24] The letter can be found in *CO* 17, 525.

appear to be very noteworthy,[25] with the exception of those at the beginning, particularly the introductory articles of the Confession. Here it was Calvin who had deviated from an earlier draft, perhaps drawn up in 1557 by another of his pupils, Antoine de La Roche-Chandieu, and known as 'the Confession of Paris,'[26] and it was the members of the synod who wished to maintain the earlier formulation. H.A. Speelman remarks that this formulation displays a "classical medieval composition, which would facilitate the conversation with the established church".[27] Van den Brink, for whom the continuity of the doctrine in question (that of the 'two books') with the medieval church is an important argument, fails to mention this deviation from tradition that Calvin permits himself here. Van den Brink does correctly quote Karl Barth, who expresses his astonishment "that of all churches the French martyr church would commit the kind of mischief ['Unfug'] which may now be read in article 2 of the *Confessio Gallicana*, from which it quickly spread to the *Confessio Belgica*," but he fails to quote Barth's addition at this point, i.e., that this happened "in contradiction to Calvin's proposal" ["im Widerspruch zu Calvins Vorlage"].[28]

Given all this background, it is high time to see what exactly Calvin's 'proposal' contained and on what points first the synod of the French reformed churches—and afterwards the ministers and elders in the Netherlands, who established the text of the *Belgic Confession* in common agreement ('in gemeyn accoort')—felt they had to deviate from this proposal.

Calvin's Proposal

By 1559 the reformational movement had produced two different types of introductions to a confession. The first one was supplied by Philipp Melanchthon. In the Augsburg Confession, presented to Emperor Charles V

---

[25] De Morel does not fail to stress this in the report he sent to Calvin at the end of the synod. See *CO* 17, 540.

[26] Cf. *CO* 9, 715–720.

[27] Speelman, *Calvijn en de zelfstandigheid van de kerk*, 144.

[28] Karl Barth, *Die Kirchliche Dogmatik* II/1 (Zürich: Zollikon, 1940), 141; *Church Dogmatics* II/1 (London, New York: T & T Clark International, 1957), 127; Van den Brink, "Als een scoon boec", 11. Barth may have found his information in the edition of the French Confession by Wilhelm Boudriot in W. Niesel, *Bekenntnisschriften und Kirchenordnungen der nach Gottes Wort reformierten Kirche* (Zürich: Zollikon, 1938), 65–66. The deviated text of Calvin on the articles 1–5 is quoted there in a footnote. Cf. *CO* 9, 739–52.

in 1530, the first article testifies that in Lutheran pulpits the decisions of the ecumenical councils of ancient Christianity are respected:[29]

> We unanimously hold and teach, in accordance with the decree of the Council of Nicaea, that there is one divine essence, which is called and which is truly God, and that there are three persons in this one divine essence, equal in power and alike eternal: God the Father, God the Son, God the Holy Spirit.[30]

The message is: do not fear, dear emperor, we are not heretics, we hold to the same articles that have always been taught by orthodox Christians.

One can find the second type in the Swiss Reformation. It contains the Reformed 'Scripture Principle' as the formal foundation for all doctrine. For instance, the confession that was presented by the ministers of Geneva in 1537, and was presumably drafted by William Farel, begins with the following article:[31]

> The Word of God
> First we affirm that we desire to follow Scripture alone as rule of faith and religion, without mixing with it any other thing which might be devised by the opinion of men apart from the word of God, and without claiming to accept for our spiritual government any other doctrine than what is conveyed to us by the same word, without addition or diminution, according to the command of our Lord.[32]

Here the message is: one has to know that we do not want to respect any other authority than that of scriptures.

Now, in a subtle way, Calvin joins both traditions and corrects them at the same time. Article 1 of his draft seems to follow the Swiss beginning, Article 2 that of Wittenberg. But he articulates Article 1 in such a way that it prepares the reader for understanding Article 2, and Article 2 appears

---

[29] See 'Die Augsburgische Konfession', in: *Die Bekenntnisschriften der evangelisch-lutherischen Kirche*, Göttingen 1930, 50–51. For a 'classical-medieval example' see, e.g., the 'Definitio contra Albigenses et Catharos' of the Fourth Council of the Lateran (1215). Heinrich Denzinger, and Adolf Schonmetzer, *Enchiridion symbolorum: definitionum et declarationum de rebus fidei et morum* (Freiburg: Herder, 1963), nr. 800.

[30] Augsburg Confession, article 1. Jaroslav Pelikan and Valerie Hotchkiss (eds), *of Faith in the Christian Tradition* II/4 [Creeds and Confessions of the Reformation Era] (New Haven, London: Yale University Press, 2003), 58.

[31] The text is in *CO* 22, 85 and in *OS* I, 418 recorded under the works of Calvin himself, but his authorship is extremely unlikely.

[32] Geneva Confession of 1536, in: Pelikan and Hotchkiss, *Creeds & Confessions* II, 313.

in such a way that it organically follows from Article 1. This happens as follows:[33]

> 1. Because the foundation of believing, as Saint Paul says, is (laid) by the Word of God (Rom. 10: 17), we believe that the living God manifests himself in his law and through his prophets, and finally in his gospel (Hebr. 1), and that he has given testimony of his will there to an extent that is sufficient for the salvation of mankind.
>
> And so we consider the books of Holy Scripture, the Old and the New Testament, to be the sum total of the only infallible truth that proceeds from God which is not allowed to be contradicted. Since even the perfect rule of all wisdom is contained in it, we believe that it is not allowed to add or to subtract anything from it (Dt. 4:2; 12:32; Prov. 30:6), but that one must agree with it in and through all things.
>
> Well then, since this doctrine derives its authority neither from men nor from angels (Gal. 1:8), but from God alone, we believe also (since it is a matter that transcends all human understanding to distinguish that God is the one who speaks), that he alone grants the certainty of it to his elect and seals it in their hearts by his Spirit.

The first sentence contains a variant of the Farel-type introduction: the starting point lies in the Word, as Law and Prophets plus Gospel. This Word is the 'manifestation' of the living God—the same terminology that the French Confession will use to underline the two means of knowing God in article 2. That this Word is a word of salvation, and sufficient to that end, will come back in Article 2 of the *Belgic Confession*, although there it will be related to 'God making himself known to us more openly', which is the second means of knowing God. But here Calvin remains silent with regard to the first means (and thus there is no necessity here for a comparison between the first and the second means).

---

[33] "2. Pource que le fondement de croire, comme dit St. Paul, est par la parole de Dieu, nous croyons que le Dieu vivant [c'] est manifeste en sa Loy et par ses prophetes, et finalement en l'Evangile et y a rendu tesmoignage de sa volunté autant qu'il est expedient pour le salut des hommes. Ainsi nous tenons les livres de la saincte Escripture du vieil et nouveau Testament comme la somme de la seule verité infaillible procedee de Dieu, à laquelle il n'est licite de contredire. Mesmes pource que là est contenue la regle parfaicte de toute sagesse, nous croyons qu'il n'est licite d'y rien adiouster ne diminuer mais qu'il [y] faut acquiescer en tout et par tout. Or comme ceste doctrine ne prend son autorité des hommes ne des anges, mais de Dieu seul, aussi nous croyons (d'autant que c'est chose surmontant tous sens humains, de discerner que c'est Dieu qui parle) que lui seul donne la certitude d'icelle à ses elues, et la seelle en leurs coeurs par son Esprit." The French text can be found under the siglum O in the critical apparatus in Bakhuizen van den Brink, *De Nederlandsche Belijdenisgeschriften*. See for Article 1 of Calvin's proposal the pages 58–60.

The second sentence marks the transition from the living Word of the speaking God to scripture as the written record of it. Here, again in the tradition of Farel, the commandment 'no addition, no subtraction' is included, an expression which the scriptures use to reflect on their own character. The formula of scripture as 'the perfect rule of all wisdom' is in keeping with the language of the *Institutes*. Terminology like 'one must agree with it', 'rule', 'it is not allowed to be contradicted,' points to the danger that scripture could be interpreted as a formal juridical text, and one cannot deny that this has happened many times in the reformed world. However, in the setting of a confession it rather functions as a declaration of devotion: 'this is the only one to love, only these texts communicate this love to us'.

The third sentence deals with the issue of authority. We expect to hear God's own voice in the words of the Bible. But who is able to distinguish that it is really God himself who is speaking? No human being is able to distinguish that. Only God can reveal Godself. Only the Holy Spirit can touch the spirit. The same Spirit that was working in the prophets and the apostles is also working in us. God is not only there on the objective side—God's Word that comes to us—but also on the side of the human subject: in our openness to receive the Word. The reformed liturgy testifies to this: there is no opening of scripture without a prayer for illumination by the Holy Spirit. In this particular text all this is narrowed down to the aspect of an objective truth that demands a subjective certainty.[34] The hermeneutics of later times will also pay attention to other aspects. But in essence an important mystery is touched on here: it is a miracle when these strange old words are actually still *saying* something to us, and it is an equally great miracle when human hearts open up and flourish when hearing these words. The first article of Calvin's draft for a confession testifies to both miracles, or on both sides of the one miracle of the true hearing, it is heaven itself that guarantees the veracity of this mysterious happening. Therefore God as the Word depends on the Spirit (and not on any clerical authority), and God as the Spirit shows us the way to understanding the Word (and not into a spirituality that moves away from the scriptures).[35] Now, this combination of Word and Spirit

---

[34] This is related to the typically early modern preoccupation with the question of *certitudo* that connects Calvin and Descartes.

[35] Cf. in the first Book of the *Institutes* in its final edition, the relationship between Chapter I.7—where the Word is correlated to the Spirit and therefore not to clerical

together gives Calvin the opportunity to make a transition to the second article of his draft:

> 2. Thus grounded, we believe in one single eternal God who's essence is spiritual, infinite, incomprehensible, and simple: yet there are three distinct persons in this being: the Father, his Word or his Wisdom, and his Spirit. And although sometimes the name of God is attributed in particular to the Father insofar as he is the principle and origin of his Word and of his Spirit, yet this does not rule out that the Son possesses full divinity in perfection, as also the Holy Spirit, insofar as each one of them fully possesses what properly belongs to their person without (causing) any division to the unique essence. And in this we confess what has been established by the ancient councils and we detest all sects and heresies which were rejected by the holy doctors, from St. Hilary, and St. Athanasius, to St. Ambrose, and St. Cyril.[36]

Here we see the motif of Melanchthon. But yet it functions differently than with Melanchthon himself in the *Augustana*, just as, for instance, the Swiss motif functioned differently than with Farel. For it is not only about the formal aspect here—we're not innovators, we don't deviate from the decisions of the ancient councils (which only gets mentioned in the last sentence). Rather, it fits in with the first article Calvin drafted which now receives further emphasis and elaboration here. In its intent the treatment of scripture was *already* Trinitarian. And so now the elaboration of the doctrine of the Trinity in this second article is in a certain sense *still* hermeneutical. That in reading and hearing the words of scripture we hear God himself speaking to us is the presupposition of faith with regard to reading and hearing. In the same way, the idea that our responsiveness to the text is awakened by God himself is such a presupposition.

---

authority (against Rome)—and Chapter I.9—where the Spirit is correlated to the Word and therefore not to arbitrary inspiration (against spiritual 'fanatics').

[36] "Estans ainsi fondez nous croyons en un seul Dieu eternel, d'une essence spirituelle, infinie, incomprehensible et simple: toutesfois en laquelle il y a trois personnes distinctes, le Pere, sa Parole ou sa Sagesse, et son Esprit. Et combien que le nom de Dieu soit quelque fois attribué en particulier au Pere d'autant quíl est [le] principe et origine de sa Parole et de son Esprit, toutesfois cela n'empesche point [pas] que le Fils n'ait en soy toute Divinité en perfection, comme aussi le sainct Esprit, d'autant que chacun ha tellement ce qui luy est propre quant à la Personne que l'essence unique n'est point divisee. Et en cela nous a[uo]uons ce qui a esté determiné par les anciens Conciles et detestons toutes sectes et heresies qui ont esté reiettees par les saincts docteurs depuis S. Hilaire, Athanase, iusq'à S. Ambroise et Cyrille." The French text can be found under the siglum O in the critical apparatus in Bakhuizen van den Brink, *De Nederlandsche Belijdenisgeschriften*. See for Article 2 of Calvin's proposal page 70.

Therefore the Word of God is Godself. And therefore also the Spirit of God is Godself. And thus they possess a common origin and they together with their origin are one God in mutual distinctiveness.

The dogma of ancient Christianity is quoted here, including its technical aspects: unity and trinity, the category of the person, the threefold differentiation of the infinite essence that is, however, free from division. But these mechanics are subservient to the regulative function of the Trinitarian dogma: to confess that divine action in all its aspects always remains truly an action of God himself.

What Happened to Calvin's Proposal in the French and the Belgic Confession

Let us now take a look at how the Paris Synod of May 1559 responded to Calvin's proposal.[37] Over against his two articles, it insisted on half a dozen, i.e., 1. The one God (the beginning of Calvin's second article); 2. The double form of divine manifestation, first in his works and secondly and more clearly in his Word, identified with scripture(Calvin is silent about this duality here); 3. The canonical books of the scriptures; 4. The acknowledgement of the canon as the rule of faith not so much by consent of the church, but through the inner illumination of the Holy Spirit; 5. The perfection of scripture ("it is not lawful for men, nor even for angels, to add to it, to take away from it, or to change it"). All this in articles 3–5 takes the place of Calvin's Trinitarian approach of the human encounter with scripture based on the actions of Word and Spirit; and so for the sixth article a variant of Calvin's second article on the Trinity was left.

De Brès clearly used the text of the *French Confession* as his starting-point for the *Dutch Confession*. The arrangement remains the same, although it contains several extensions. Under the doctrine of scripture he adds articles on *theopneustia* (the inspiration of the words of the Bible by the Holy Spirit) and the *apocrypha*, and under the doctrine of the Trinity three more articles. In this way Calvin's original two articles become six in Paris and eleven in Tournai:

---

[37] The French Confession of 1559. For an English translation see Pelican and Hotchkiss, *Creeds & Confessions* II, 372–386.

Table 1

Calvin's proposal	French Confession	Belgic Confession
1. Word and Spirit	1. The one and only God	1. The one and only God
	2. The twofold manifestation of God: in his works and in his Word	2. The two means (two books) of knowing God: through creation and through the divine Word
		3. The inspiration of holy men (prophets and apostles) by the Holy Spirit
	3. The canonical books	4. The canonical books
	4. The authority of scripture	5. The authority of scripture
		6. The apocrypha
	5. The perfection of scripture	7. The perfection of scripture
2. The one and triune God	6. The triune God	8. The triune God
		9. The Scriptural witness of the Trinity
		10. The Deity of the Son
		11. The Deity of the Holy Spirit

So what happened in this process of transformation? I will make three observations:

1. The connection that Calvin had made between the doctrine of God and the doctrine of scripture has been abandoned. The synthesis, attained by the reformer of Geneva, has been resolved again into its original factors: Melanchthon and Farel.
2. The doctrine of God itself also falls apart. What Roman Catholic theologians (since Karl Rahner) so disapprove of in (neo-)thomistic scholastics—the separation of the treatises *De Deo uno* and *De Deo trino*[38]—is repeated here: the existence and the attributes of the one God are spoken of first (*French* and *Belgic Confessions* art. 1), and only further

---

[38] Cf. Catherine Mowry LaCugna, *'God for us', the Trinity and Christian Life* (San Francisco: HarperSanFrancisco, 1991), 145.

on (articles 6 and 8, respectively) this one God also appears to be a triune God.

3. As we saw above, the synod of Paris could fall back on the *Institutes* of Calvin in a certain sense for its doctrine of a twofold revelation. But Calvin himself—during his illness and confronted with the necessity of making some final decisions by which a 'martyr church' (Barth) could live or die—apparently did not feel the need to include this part of theological theory in a confessional act or text. We may conclude that for him it did not involve the heart of the Christian witness. The churches in France, and later in the Netherlands, had a different opinion. Gijsbert van den Brink apparently still holds to that different opinion, when we see how he considers it necessary to use Article 2 of the *Belgic Confession* as ammunition in favour of a theistic world view competing with other world views in the current scientific debate. However, it would have been better, if he had refrained from appealing to Calvin for this undertaking.

CHAPTER THREE

CALVIN'S MODIFICATION OF AUGUSTINE'S DOCTRINE OF ORIGINAL SIN

Nico Vorster

The term *original sin* is not found in Scripture, but was developed by Augustine to articulate the biblical doctrine of the total depravity of man. He used the Latin term *peccatum originale* to explain that the whole of mankind partakes in the original sin of Adam and consequently shares a common state of guilt before God. Augustine's doctrine was accepted by both the Council of Trent and the Calvinist Reformation, though not in all its dimensions, in order to defend the doctrine of the total depravity of mankind and the undeserved nature of the grace of God against the teachings of the Pelagians.

Recent studies of Calvin's use of Augustine established that Augustine was Calvin's main source of inspiration and reference within the Christian tradition.[1] This is also true of Calvin's doctrine of sin. Calvin's discussions of sin reflect and appeal directly to key positions advanced by Augustine, particularly in his anti-Pelagian writings.[2] He followed Augustine in viewing sin as more than a mere negativity, namely as a depravity that contaminates all dimensions of human existence. Yet it would be a mistake to equate Augustine's view with that of Calvin. Though Calvin accepted Augustine's doctrine of original sin and the bondage of the human will, he also attempted to modify it in such a way that it would be logically more comprehensible. This essay discusses Calvin's attempt to modify Augustine's doctrine on original sin. In the first section, Augustine's concept of original sin is analysed. The second section discusses Calvin's attempt to modify Augustine's doctrine, while the third section reflects on the significance of Calvin's noetic approach to original sin.

---

[1] Barbara Pitkin, "Nothing but concupiscence: Calvin's understanding of sin and the *Via Augustini*," *Calvin Theological Journal* 34 (1999), 347.

[2] Pitkin, "Nothing but concupiscence", 348.

Augustine's Understanding of Original Sin

Augustine's classical doctrine of original sin was the result of his nega-
tion of both Manicheanism and Pelagianism. Against the Manicheans
he maintained that evil is not identifiable with human finitude nor an
ontological necessity, but it erupts freely and contingently. Against the
Pelagians he stated that sin is not merely accidental or contingent, but is
a corruption of human nature because of the positive propensity of the
will towards evil.[3]

The Manicheans offered a deterministic account of sin that exempted
the self from moral agency.[4] They stated that God is in no way, whether
directly or indirectly, the source of evil. Evil is rather an ontological force
that stems from Matter that opposes the divine and compels the innately
good souls of human beings to sin.[5] The Manicheans thereby eliminated
the moral dimension of evil and the personal accountability of the human
being. Augustine insisted against the Manicheans that evil is not an independent force or structural reality but the corruption of being and moral
goodness. It is committed by moral agents who are responsible for their
own actions. God is therefore not unjust when he holds humanity accountable for their sins. On the other hand he argued that, even though humans
are capable of moral evil, they were created good by God. God is in no way
the source of evil or the creator of human sin. Augustine was able to reconcile his position that man is accountable for his sins with the view that
God is not the source of evil, through the concept of the free will of man.
It provided him with a mechanism through which something that comes
forth good from God could, at the same time, be capable of evil.[6]

However, after 392 Augustine began to modify his original position on
the free will as the possession of all human beings, first in his polemic with
the Manichean Fortunatus, and thereafter in his polemic against the Pelagians. In his polemic against Fortunatus he shifted the free exercise of will
from all human beings to only the first human being, thereby abandoning

---

[3] Stephen, J. Duffy, "Our hearts of darkness: Original sin revisited," *Theological Studies*
49 (1988), 600. Augustine, *De civitate Dei* (On the city of God), 12, *PL* 41, 13–804.

[4] William S. Babcock, "Augustine on sin and moral agency," *Journal of Religious Ethics*
16/1 (1988), 30.

[5] Gerald Bonner, *St Augustine of Hippo. Life and controversies* (Philadelphia: Westminster, 1963), 317. Babcock, "Augustine on sin and moral agency," 31.

[6] Babcock, "Augustine on sin and moral agency", 33.

a crucial element in his earlier argument for human agency in moral evil.[7] As a consequence of the first man's voluntary sin the whole of humanity descended into the necessity of habit and bondage to sin and death. Man's compulsion to sin is thus caused by an initial sin. After the first sin, man sins involuntarily. Yet Augustine maintained that if there is complicity at the start, a subsequent set of forced actions can still be interpreted as the agents own. God's penalty on man's sin is therefore justly imposed.[8]

Augustine developed his argument on the nature of man's free will and original sin further in his polemic writings against the Pelagians. Pelagius understood grace to be either a natural faculty or a form of illumination after baptism has cleansed sin. Man's natural faculties are good because they are created by the good Creator, therefore man could, if he chose, be without sin. Though man's will is sound, his mind is clouded and he therefore needs the illumination of the Law and Gospel to lead a Christian life after the remission of sins through baptism.[9] Closely connected with Pelagius's view on grace went a particular doctrine of the fall which denied that Adam's sin injured his descendants or can be transmitted to subsequent generations. Adam's sin only injured himself and though he set an evil example for his descendants, he did not corrupt their nature also. Human nature cannot be corrupted by sin, because sin is an action, not a substance, and therefore cannot change our nature.[10] Every descendant of Adam possesses Adam's original innocence and thus there is no such thing as original sin.[11]

Augustine found Pelagius's reduction of sin to a conscious free choice simplistic. He held that sin not only amounts to an option for another mode of being, but to the disintegration of that nature.[12] He replied to Pelagius in his book *De Natura et Gratia* wherein he states that man originally had a free will but that the original sin darkened and flawed man's will so that human nature itself is corrupted.[13]

---

[7] Babcock, "Augustine on sin and moral agency", 40. Augustine, *Acta seu Disputatio contra Fortunatum Manicheum* (A Treatise or Dispute against Fortunatus the Manichean) (392), *PL* 42, 111–130, *NPNF* 4, 113–124.

[8] Babcock, "Augustine on sin and moral agency", 38.

[9] Bonner, *Augustine of Hippo*, 362.

[10] Augustine, *De natura et gratia* (On the Nature of Grace), xix, *PL* 44, 247–290, *NPNF* 5, 121–155.

[11] Cf. Bonner, *Augustine of Hippo*, 318–319.

[12] Stephen, J. Duffy, "Our hearts of darkness: Original sin revisited," *Theological Studies* 49 (1988), 602.

[13] Augustine, *De natura et gratia*, iii.

For his position to be intelligible, Augustine had to give some indication how the sin of the first human beings is continuous with the character of subsequent generations. Otherwise he could not maintain the position that sin is genuinely the moral agent's own. In *De Civitate Dei* he argues that the Fall differs from the ordinary daily sin of man in that it led to a shift in the orientation of the will—that is a turn from a higher state of being to a lower state of being—from God to the self, thereby making itself rather than God the principle of its existence.[14]

Augustine regarded pride, which is a longing for a perverse kind of exaltation, as the start of every kind of sin. Through his pride man decided to desert God that is the changeless Good, to follow his own desire, thereby abandoning the light and love of God. This, in turn, causes a darkening of the human will and a taking of itself rather than God as the principle of existence.[15] The Fall led, according to Augustine, to the weakening of all man's faculties so that he becomes liable to disease, impotent to rule the desires of the body and subject to death.[16]

However two questions needed to be answered, namely how does the first evil act arise, and how is the sin of the first human beings transmitted to the subsequent generations?

In *De Civitate Dei* Augustine attempts to answer the first question by stating that whereas the first evil deed had an efficient cause, evil will had no efficient cause, because nothing causes an evil will, since it is the evil will itself which causes the evil act.[17] Anything that one might suppose to cause an evil will must have a will of itself. That will must be either good or bad. If it is good it would be absurd to think that a good will can cause evil, if it is evil the question remains what caused that evil will. An evil will that is caused by an evil will cannot be the first act of evil. If it is replied that it had no cause and had always existed, the question is whether it existed in nature. If it was not in nature, then it did not exist at all. If it existed in some nature, it vitiated that nature and corrupted it. A bad will cannot exist in a bad nature, but only in a good but mutable nature that can be corrupted. Therefore an evil will could not be eternal in anything, because an evil will needs the goodness of nature to destroy it. Now if the evil will was not eternally there who created it? The only possible answer

---

[14] Augustine, *De civitate Dei*, 14.13.
[15] Augustine, *De civitate Dei*, 14.3.
[16] Augustine, *De perfectione justicis hominis* (On man's perfection in righteousness), II, *PL* 44, 291–318, *NPNF* 5, 159–178.
[17] Augustine, *De civitate Dei*, 12.6.

is: Something that had no will. However, this answer is unsatisfactory, because if such a being is equal or superior to angelic nature it must have a will, and that will must be good. A nature without will or with an evil will cannot be regarded as equal to a nature endowed with a good will. Augustine's conclusion is that evil resides not in anything else than in the will's own turn that desires the inferior thing in a perverted and inordinate manner. This turning of the will is not a matter of efficiency but of deficiency, because the evil will is not effective but defective. To defect from Him who is the Supreme Existence, to something of less reality, is to begin to have an evil will. This turning of the will is not a matter of efficiency but of deficiency, because the evil will is not effective but defective.[18] To defect from Him who is the Supreme Existence, to something of less reality, is to begin to have an evil will. To try to discover the causes of defection is like trying to see darkness or hear silence. As darkness is the absence of light and silence the absence of sound, deficient causality is the absence of cause. Whereas good will is specifically effected by God, evil will is uncaused.[19] Evil is a corruption of good, and can only be as long as there is something good to be corrupted. By definition it cannot exist on its own. The introduction of evil into a wholly good creation is thus, according to Augustine, fundamentally a negative act that is not intellectually comprehensible. Sin is the perverse manifestation of our godlike faculty of freedom.[20]

Babcock rightly observes that Augustine's explanation does not solve the problem.[21] If the first evil will is simply uncaused, it will have the status of an entirely accidental happening and will no more count as the agents own than it would be if it could be ascribed to an efficient cause. Secondly, it is difficult to see how a defection can be described as a defect if it is not an act at all.

With regard to the question on the transmission of original sin, Augustine held that original sin is both an inherited guilt (*reatum*) and inherited disease (*vitium*). The *reatus* of sin denotes its juridical aspect whereby it is a violation of God's law and therefore punishable, while the *vitium* is the

---

[18]   Augustine, *De civitate Dei*, 12.7.
[19]   Augustine, *De civitate Dei*, 12.7.
[20]   Cf. Charles, T. Mathewes, "Augustinian anthropology. Interior intimo meo," *Journal of Religious Ethics* 27/2 (1999), 205.
[21]   Babcock, "Augustine on sin and moral agency", 46.

corruption and crippling effect of sin on human nature.[22] He grounded his view on the Latin translation of Romans 5:12 which says:

> Therefore, just as sin entered this world by one man and through sin death; so death passed into all men, in whom all sinned.[23]

On the basis of this translation of Romans 5:12 Augustine posits the seminal identity of the human race with Adam. In *De Peccatorum Meritis et Remissione* he correspondingly states that the condemnation of Adam's progeny was constituted in Adam.[24] From one all men were born to a condemnation from which there is no deliverance, but in the Saviour's grace.

Augustine clearly asserts that all future generations were in some sense, present in their progenitor's loins at the time of the Fall, and therefore all mankind participated, in some mysterious fashion, in the original sin of Adam.[25]

However, Augustine made a serious mistake in his exegesis of Romans 5:12 by using a wrong Latin translation of Romans 5:12. The Greek gives *eph' hoi pantes hemarton*, and not *en hoi*. In other words, mankind does not sin *in Adam* but *because of Adam*. This mistake casts serious doubts upon Augustine's doctrine on the transmission of sin.

Augustine locates the transmission of sin from the first human beings to subsequent generations in concupiscence. Adam's disobedience to God caused him to lose power to control his body. This loss of power over the body becomes particularly evident in man's sexual desire. In *De Civitate Dei* he states that man possessed no shame over his nakedness before the fall.[26] However, after the fall man became ashamed of his nakedness, because he lost control over his members and sexual desires so that lust— that is concupiscence—arose.

For Augustine, concupiscence is that element of lust which is inseparable from fallen sexuality.[27] Though Augustine does not disparage matrimony and respects it as an institution of God, even Christian marriage contains the sickness of concupiscence because generation cannot be

---

[22] Cf. Duffy, "Our hearts of darkness: Original sin revisited", 603.

[23] Per unum hominem peccatum intravit in mundum et per peccatum mors, et ita in omnes hominess pertransiit, in quo omnes peccaverunt.

[24] Augustine, *De Peccatorum Meritis et Remissione* [On the Merits and Forgiveness of Sins], I: 13, *PL* 44, 109–199.

[25] Bonner, *Augustine of Hippo*, 372.

[26] Augustine, *De civitate Dei*, 14.17.

[27] Cf. Bonner, *Augustine of Hippo*, 377.

effected without the ardour of lust.[28] Through marriage two things are propagated, namely nature that is good; and the vice of nature that is evil. It is through and from concupiscence that the guilt (*reatum*) and disease (*vitium*) of original sin is conveyed from the parents to the children. Christ alone, who was born from the virgin Mary through the operation of the Holy Spirit, is free from original sin, because concupiscence was not involved in His conception and birth. He can therefore offer a sacrifice for the sins of humankind.[29]

Because of their inherited guilt, all men who are born by human generation form a lump of sin (*massa peccati, luti, perditionis*), justly deserving damnation, even if they commit no sins to add to the guilt they inherited, unless they are cleansed by baptism. Though baptism remits the guilt of concupiscence, concupiscence remains in the regenerate, because semination takes place through concupiscence. Yet baptism remits carnal concupiscence in the regenerate, not so that it is put out of existence, but so that it is not imputed for sin.[30]

Summary

Augustine's doctrine on original sin can be summarised as follows: Man[31] was created with a free will which means that human nature was created with the possibility, but not the necessity to sin. The fall of man led to a redirection of Man's will away from God toward the world and the latter's changeable, finite goods—causing man to lose his original free will and to become enslaved to sin. This fall-away of man's will was an unexplainable act whose cause is deficient—for there is no cause. Desire, a natural tendency, becomes after the fall an enslaving concupiscense. The original sin of Adam is transmitted to subsequent generations through sexual concupiscence, since procreation cannot take place without lust.

The Manicheans thus pushed Augustine to historize evil, while the Pelagians led him to amplify the consequences of Adam's historical act

---

[28] Augustine, *De Nuptiis et Concupiscentia* (On Marriage and Concupiscence), I: 29, *PL* 44: 413–474.

[29] Augustine, *De Nuptiis et Concupiscientia*, I: 24.

[30] "Dimitti concupiscentiam carnis in baptismo, non ut non sit, sed ut inpeccatum non imputetur." Augustine, *De Nuptiis et Concupiscentia*, I: 25.

[31] In this section, for the sake of authenticity, we will briefly follow Augustine's custom to speak of "man" in both a specific and generic sense.

to the point of making the present chain of freedom into a fatality.[32] In his effort to counter the views of both the Manicheans and Pelagians, Augustine mixed juridical and biological categories in his perspective on original sin. This made his doctrine to appear incoherent and caused an epistemological question that subsequent theologians in the Augustinian tradition had to address, namely: How can man be held responsible for his sins, if sin is an inevitable inherited condition? This question has far reaching implications, because it pertains to the relationship between human moral agency and God's sovereignty, namely how human freedom and divine sovereignty can be affirmed at the same time.

Calvin's Perspective on Original Sin

Calvin's central interest which strongly organised his theological work was to demonstrate and maintain the glory of God. In order to display this vision of the glory of God, Calvin used the human race as a foil: all human faculties are vitiated and corrupted and human works are therefore useless for salvation. The insignificance of the human being is heightens the exaltation of God.[33] Knowledge of God and of the self is therefore of utmost importance for achieving a consciousness of the glory of God. This theological premise provides the impetus for Calvin's doctrine on original sin. Pitkin rightly notes that Calvin shifts the focus of the debate on original sin to his own chief concern: knowledge of God and self.[34]

The first difference between Calvin and Augustine concerns Calvin's noetic approach to original sin. Whereas Augustine located the first sin in pride, Calvin ascribes it to human's longing for illicit knowledge. Original sin denotes a change of the mind. The sin of the first couple is best understood not as pride but as unbelief that both man and woman shared.[35] Calvin's difference with Augustine on the nature of the first sin is important. By underscoring the essentially noetic character of the first sin he shifts the focus away from the role of the will in the fall. Though the will was involved in the fall and defected with the mind, Calvin stresses the

---

[32] Christian Duquoc, "New approaches to original sin," *Cross Currents* 28 (1978), 193.

[33] Margaret, M. Miles, "Theology, anthropology, and the human body in Calvin's Institutes of the Christian religion." *Harvard Theological Review* 74/3 (1981), 304.

[34] Pitkin. "Nothing but concupiscence," 349.

[35] John Calvin, Commentary on Gen 3:6. *CO* 23, 60. The translation is from John Calvin, *The Book of Genesis* transl. J. King (Edinburgh: Calvin Translation Society, s.a), vol. 1, 152–153.

role of the mind. Original sin is, along with a misdirected will, a failure to know God and self. The mind's corruption is not only moral in nature, but it is a fundamental religious blindness. Although true knowledge of God is revealed through nature, the conscience and the sense of the divinity, the fallen mind fails to receive this knowledge and is with respect to God filled with boundless confusion.[36]

In his emphasis on original sin as a corruption of the mind and the will Calvin departs from the Augustinian tradition.[37] Augustine understands sin as concupiscence. The fallen will lacks the power to achieve the good that the intellect knows. Calvin, however, intensifies the problem of sin by stating that the mind itself no longer knows the good to be done. This dissimilar understanding of sin is largely due to a different understanding of the essence of human nature.

According to Calvin the human being consists of a body and a soul.[38] The soul is the nobler part and the primary seat of the divine image, while the body is simply the habitation of the soul.[39] The image of God is manifested in the soul by light of intellect, while the body is a reflection of the dynamics of the soul.[40]

The fall, however, lead to a weakening of the soul's capacity to maintain the integrity of body and soul.[41] Thus in contrast to Augustine who locates the effects of sin in human loss of control of physical desires, Calvin locates the crippling effects of the corruption of the image in the soul. According to Calvin the taint of sin resides in the flesh and the spirit. The flesh—which must not be equated with the human body—designates in Calvin's thought the whole human being in the condition of sinfulness. It is the governing aspect of human nature.[42] 'Flesh' is an attitude of mind in alienation from God which uses and abuses the body and the soul.[43] The soul participates in the flesh more than the body does, because when Scripture says that the human must be born again it refers to the soul not the body. The body cannot be reborn.[44] In Calvin's thought the body plays no role either in the corruption of the soul or in its own corruption, but

---

[36] Cf. Pitkin. "Nothing but concupiscence", 360, 365.
[37] Pitkin. "Nothing but concupiscence", 360.
[38] John Calvin, *Institutes* I.15.2.
[39] Calvin, *Institutes* I.15.6.
[40] Calvin, *Institutes* I.15.3.
[41] Calvin, *Institutes* I.15.3.
[42] Calvin, *Institutes* II.3.1.
[43] Cf. Miles, "Theology, anthropology, and the human body," 312.
[44] Calvin, *Institutes* II.3.1.

it is the helpless victim of the destructive hegemony of the flesh. It is the mind and its potential consciousness of the glory of God that interests Calvin. The body has no potential for consciousness—it is motion devoid of essence—in contrast to the soul which is endowed with essence and can be quickened.[45]

These different understandings of the essential nature of the human being led to different understandings of the mode of the transmission of original sin. Augustine's view on human nature led him to believe that all human beings are in a physical solidarity with Adam and hence when the first human sinned, all sinned and were guilty. Though Calvin defines sin as a hereditary corruption in all parts of the human, he does not use Augustine's biological categories to explain original sin and the transmission thereof. In his commentary on Psalm 51 Calvin states that the question on the transmission of sins from Adam to subsequent generations is not important and that it is not sensible to enter in such 'mysterious discussions' (*labyrinthos*).[46]

In his comments on Genesis 3:7 Calvin subtly rejects the Augustinian view that ashamedness and the stirrings of sexual concupiscence were the first effects of the Fall.[47] Instead he emphasizes the noetic effects of the Fall. By eating the fruit Adam and Eve's eyes were opened and they experienced a confused sense of evil. It is thus not sexual concupiscence, but rather the damage done to the human mind and will that are the first effects of the Fall.

In the *Institutes* Calvin moves away from the Augustinian notion on the role of sexual desire in the transmission of sins, by locating the reason for mankind's guilt in God's ordination that mankind would lose the gifts God bestowed upon them.[48]

Calvin's position on the transmission of sin—that it is not the mode of conception but the divine decree that accounts for the propagation of sin—necessarily led him to reject Augustine's view on the meaning of Christ's virgin birth. Whereas Augustine located Christ's sinlessness in his conception without sexual desire, Jesus was, according to Calvin, free of sin, not because of the virginal conception, but because he was sanctified

---

[45] Cf. Miles, "Theology, anthropology, and the human body", 314, 317.

[46] Calvin, Commentary on Psalm 51:7, *CO* 31, 514. Cf. J. Calvin, *Commentary on Psalms*, transl. J. Anderson (Edinburgh: Calvin Translation Society, 1846), 291.

[47] Calvin, Commentary on Gen 3:7, *CO* 23, 64.

[48] "Neque enim in substantia carnis aut animae causam habet contagio: sed quia a Deo ita fuitordinatum, ut quae primo homini dona contulerat, ille tam sibi quam suis haberet simul ac perderet." Calvin, *Institutes* II.1.8.

by the Spirit.[49] According to Calvin it is childish trifling to maintain that if Christ is free from all taint, and was begotten to the seed of Mary, by the secret operation of the Spirit, it is therefore not the seed of the woman that is impure, but only that of the man. Christ was not free of all taint, merely because he was born of a woman unconnected with a man, but because he was sanctified by the Spirit, so that the generation was pure and spotless, such as it would have been before Adam's fall.[50]

The second important difference between Calvin and Augustine pertains to the origin of evil. In Calvin's view God not only permitted but indeed ordained the fall. First he states that evil is not from nature, but from defection, and that Adam fell into sin though his own fault.[51] Yet Adam did not fall without the will and ordination of God since the created character of the first human being's will makes such a defection possible.[52] In his comments on Genesis 3:7 he states it clearly that God not only permitted, but willed that the human should be tempted.[53]

Whereas Augustine went to great lengths to explain that God was not the origin of evil, and that evil is an unexplainable phenomenon that has no cause, Calvin attributes evil and sin to God's permission.[54] According to Calvin, God's decrees of election and reprobation are not due to the Fall but were made before it, and without regard to it, while Augustine states that we are condemned because we fell in Adam, who sinned by the abuse of the free will. God foresaw the Fall but did not compel it.[55]

Summary

Calvin shares Augustine's view that original sin is an inheritance and that the whole of human nature is contaminated by it. Yet there are also substantial differences between Augustine and Calvin's view. Augustine made considerable effort to explain that sin does not find its origin in God. God foresaw the Fall but did not compel it. Calvin located sin in God's eternal decree and permission. Augustine formulated his view to counter the Manicheans and Pelagians. Calvin shifted the focus in his doctrine

---

[49] Calvin, *Institutes* II.13.4.
[50] Calvin, *Institutes* II.13.4.
[51] Calvin, Commentary on Gen 3:1, *CO* 23, 54.
[52] Calvin, Commentary on Gen 3:1, *CO* 23, 55.
[53] Calvin, Commentary on Gen 3:7, *CO* 23, 64.
[54] Cf. Calvin, Commentary on Gen 3:7, *CO* 23, 64.
[55] Cf. Bonner, *Augustine of Hippo*, 387.

on original sin to knowledge of God and the self. The result was that he emphasized the noetic character of sin as moral and religious blindness. His emphasis on the human mind—as well as his view of the body as motion devoid of essence made—made him to depart from Augustine's view that (the) original sin is transmitted biologically to subsequent generations through sexual desire. According to Calvin sin is not transmitted through conception, but because of God's divine decree. These different positions on the transmission of original sin culminated in different understanding of the meaning of Christ's virgin birth. Augustine believed that Jesus was born free of sin, because of a conception without sexual desire, whereas Calvin believed that Jesus was born free of sin because he was sanctified by the Spirit.

Problems Emanating from the Classical Position on Original Sin

The classical doctrine of original sin remains one of the most controversial doctrines in theology, because it seems to be logically inconsistent. The main critique against it pertains to its understanding of the personal accountability of the human being, specifically the notion that guilt can be ascribed to one person because of the sin of another individual. If sin is inherited and therefore an involuntarily act, human beings cannot be held responsible for their sins and God would therefore be unjust to punish them for their sins. Punishment because of an inherited guilt is not reconcilable with God's righteousness and defies the essence of justice.[56] The doctrine thus seems to be logically inconsistent. On the one hand original sin is by definition an inherited corruption, or at least an inevitable one, yet it is also regarded as not belonging to man's essential nature and therefore is not outside the realm of his responsibility.[57]

The problem with Augustine's classical doctrine on original sin is that it is based upon a historical literal interpretation of Genesis 1–3, which causes a set of related problems. These chapters were thought to yield divinely inspired and infallible literal data about creation, the state of innocence and the Fall.[58] The result of this approach was that the origin of evil was

---

[56] Cf. Gerhardus C. Berkouwer, *Sin*, transl. P.C. Holtrop (Grand Rapids: Eerdmans, 1971), 426. Geoffrey Rees, "The anxiety of inheritance. Reinhold Niebuhr and the literal truth of original sin," *Journal of Religious Ethics* 31/I (2003), 77.

[57] Cf. Reinhold Niebuhr, *The nature and destiny of man. A Christian interpretation.* (London: Nisbet, 1941), vol. 1, 257.

[58] Cf. Duffy, "Our hearts of darkness", 207.

attributed to a literal first couple, the universality of sin was grounded in the monogenistic[59] unity of all mankind and biological terms were used to explain original sin. However, modern biblical scholarship has convincingly shown that it is not the purpose of Genesis 1–11 to present us with history in the scientific sense of the word. Genesis 1, in my view, does not present itself as literal history, but contains a mixture of prosaic and poetic material. Though Genesis 1 is characterized by the absence of synonymous and antithetical parallelisms, it contains patterned repetitions, rhythm, symmetric structures and prolonged synthetical parallel sentence constructions. Days 1 and 4, 2 and 5, 3 and 6 are brought into relation with each other in a very skilled, artistic manner.

Besides the abovementioned, the Genesis narratives also have a distinctly theological and polemic purpose. They use symbols and metaphors to explain the relationship between God, the cosmos, humans and evil. They emphasize over and against Canaanite and Babylonian creation myths that God is the only God, that nothing in creation itself is divine, that humankind does not find its origin from the gods, that nature is the creation of God and are not ruled by chaotic powers. Questions on whether Adam is the physical father of all people, if his sin alone causes deprivation of grace in all and whether this deprivation were transmitted by physical generation, move far beyond the data and original intention of the creation narratives. The intention rather is to indicate that God created his creation good, that sin does not find its origin in God, but in the human being, and that the sinfulness of humankind is systemic in nature. Systematic theologians, therefore, will have to take a new look at the biblical foundations of original sin, while the classical doctrine of original sin will have to be cleansed from its literalist errors so as to retrieve it's truly profound meaning and intention.

Though Calvin's approach to the creation narratives was also literal and his understanding of particularly the origin of evil not without problems, his noetic approach to original sin, might be helpful in solving the tension—inherent in Augustine doctrine on original sin—between the inevitability of sin and man's responsibility for sin. The usefulness of a noetic approach lies therein that it enables us to stress both the historical and natural dimension of original sin. Original sin denotes a condition of religious and moral blindness. Man is by nature morally and religiously blind, and therefore unable to enter freely into a relationship with God

---

[59] Monogenism is the view that all people are the physical descendants of Adam.

and to love God by his own natural powers. This natural inability is prior to the choice of a given individual. This condition originated in the alienation that occurred between God and humankind, because of humankind's disobedience to the covenant of God. When full communion with God wanes, sin enters, in the same way that darkness enters where light is absent. A condition of perfectness can, after all, only exist where humankind stands in full communion with God. The disobedience of humankind has brought alienation and separation and with it depravity. God is not the source of sin, but humankind is, because humankind separated itself from God who is the source of all goodness. The resulting condition of blindness affects all dimensions of human existence, also the human's material and biological existence. Yet, the biological nature is not per se the locus of sin, as Augustine tends to believe. With regard to sin and generation Bavinck states the following:

> Original sin cannot be equated with what is known today as heredity. It is not, after all, a generic trait that belongs to the human essence, inasmuch as it entered human nature by a violation of God's command and can be again removed from it by regeneration and sanctification. Neither, on the other hand, is it an individually acquired trait, for it characterizes all people without exception[.][60]

Bavinck then proceeds to define sin ethically:

> Original sin, after all, is not a substance that inheres in the body and can be transmitted by procreation. On the contrary, it is a moral quality of the person who lacks the communion with God that one should and does possess by virtue of one's original nature.[61]

A fundamental insight that a modern contemporary understanding of the genre of Genesis 1–3 brings, is that man cannot exist apart from his covenantal relationship with God, because outside of God there is only chaos. The flood narrative explains the consequences of the Fall as a return to chaos—creation returns to its original watery chaos. Only through the redemptive works of God can mankind make a new beginning.

The covenantal alienation between man and God caused a condition of human and natural depravity wherein everything is led astray and therefore being threatened by a return to chaos. Despite God's redemptive

---

[60] Herman Bavinck, *Gereformeerde Dogmatiek* (Kampen: Kok, 1929), vol. 3, 96. For the English translation see Herman Bavinck, *Reformed Dogmatics* vol. 3, ed. John Bolt, transl. John Vriend (Grand Rapids: Baker Academic, 2006), 116.

[61] Bavinck, *Gereformeerde Dogmatiek* 3, 97, Bavinck, *Reformed Dogmatics* 3, 116–117.

work the effects of the Fall remain. Man's natural depravity is transmitted through procreation in the sense that it is through procreation alone that man enters into the human history that is bound in solidarity with evil. However, neither monogenism nor physical descent from Adam is a prerequisite for being procreated in sin, since sin is not transmitted biologically. To be in the world is to be in the condition of original sin—that is a condition of moral and religious blindness—since the communication of ethical and religious values is interrupted through the sins of previous generations. Original sin is not mere imitation, but is part of human nature, since our actual personal relations with others—not a common descent from one progenitor—constitute our nature.

Duffy's description of original sin, that underscores the abovementioned perspective, is in my view very adequate:

> The reality of original sin is not a static given at birth but an intrinsically dynamic historical dimension of being human in a sinful world and as an existential of our freedom grows and varies as each one's participation in sinful humanity grows. Being situated in and participating in the sin of the world is not a conscious decision. It is not *imitatione*. For sin works its shaping influence before one is capable of moral decisions. Inserted into a race and environment contaminated by corporate evil, each person is affected by the contagion before being able to offer the least resistance.[62]

The universal nature of sin implies that man's guilt is both collective and personal in nature. Collective in the sense that humankind's history of sin constitutes a collectivity of sin that has a historic dimension. Because of man's moral blindness, sin entered into the world and inhabits the world; it intervenes; it abounds and it reigns.[63] Human beings are thus bound in historical solidarity with evil and accountable to God for their disobedience to the covenant of God. The guilt of original sin is not passed down to subsequent generations through natural descent, but is attributed to subsequent generations by God because original sin is not merely a sin of one forefather, but is a collective sin continuously committed by the whole of humanity. Though sin also affects man's corporeal existence, it is not a physical inheritance. Yet it is inevitable in the sense that it is a temptation to which persons ultimately and inevitably succumb because they live outside of true communion with God and therefore in a state of religious and moral blindness. Though Christ came to restore the relationship

---

[62] Duffy, "Our hearts of darkness", 615–616.
[63] Duffy, "Our hearts of darkness", 616.

between God and the human, we still live in the tension between the *yet* and *not yet* of the kingdom of God. The reconciliation that Christ brought has restored the relationship between God and the human in part, but not completely. Full communion between God and man will only be realised at the *parousia*.

The unity of mankind in sin is not a physical unity but a theological unity. God takes all mankind as the sinner that is Adam. Mankind's sin is not the act of Adam, but the sin of Adam is the act of mankind. God is not unfair in imputing guilt upon the whole of mankind because the condition of original sin is a condition of the generic human nature. Though man cannot be held responsible for something he inherited—because inheritance designates that which precedes the individual and for which he cannot account—he can be held responsible for actions that he freely chose even if it is inevitable that he would make the wrong choice.[64] Because man lives outside of true communion with God and therefore in a state of religious blindness, he inevitably asserts his freedom in a wrong way. Since human actions can be both inevitable as well as freely chosen, man is really and truly guilty of the sin of Adam.[65] The relationship between inevitability and responsibility is thus not contradictory but rather dialectical in nature.

Romans 5 provides an important perspective in this regard. Paul explains the universal culpability of humanity in Romans 5 christologically and corporatively. His didactic purpose in Romans 5 is not to affirm the existence of a unique individual sinner, but to emphasize the universal reach—though not universal efficiency—of redemption in Jesus Christ. Paul does not see the sin of one man as the sin of all, but all as acting in the single individual who is representative of the group.[66]

This collective guilt would not have been, if sin had not a personal dimension and if every human being was not an actual sinner. Sin is personal and actual in every human being in the sense that every man lives outside of a true personal relationship with God and therefore in a moral condition of sin—because where God is not, sin is. Sin is not only potentially part of the human, but actually as well since man lives in the old aeon that is characterised by religious and moral blindness and a disturbed relationship with God.

---

[64] Cf. Niebuhr, *The nature and destiny of man*, 66.
[65] Cf. Rees, "The anxiety of inheritance", 81.
[66] Berkouwer, *Sin*, 323.

Final Remarks

The Christian doctrines of sin and grace were mostly developed in their decisive aspects from the perspective of Christology and not from the perspective of Genesis 1–3. Though the Old Testament says a great deal about sin and grace, both of these were revealed in their deepest sense in Jesus Christ.[67] The doctrine of original sin would be more comprehensible if it is explained from the perspective of Christ's salvational work, instead of from a starting point in the past which placed history on a course of destruction. Knowledge of sin is produced by the gospel, because it points us to how much it cost God to redeem us. In the act by which the Gospel announces salvation in Jesus Christ to us, it reveals to us that sin is committed by human beings.[68]

The universal nature of Christ's redemptive work can only be attributed to the universal nature of sin. The sacrificial atonement of Christ was necessary only because man is guilty before God for his sins. That man can be saved through grace alone, can only be because man is a slave of sin and incapable to salvage himself. In essence, original sin denotes mankind's break with God which makes reconciliation in and through Christ necessary.

---

[67] Cf. Bernhard Lohse, *A short history of Christian doctrine*, transl. by F.E. Stoeffler (Philadelphia: Fortress Press, 1978), 101.

[68] Berkouwer, *Sin*, 156.

CHAPTER FOUR

THE KEY CHARACTERISTICS OF A CHRISTIAN LIFE: A COMPARISON OF THE ETHICS OF CALVIN AND AUGUSTINE AND THEIR RELEVANCE TODAY

J.H. (Amie) van Wyk

Two of the greatest theologians that lived on planet earth were Aurelius Augustine (354–430) and John Calvin (1509–1564) whose 5th Centenary we celebrated recently. Hans Küng is of the opinion that "no figure in Christianity between Paul and Luther has exercised greater influence in theology and church than Augustine".[1] We may add: between Paul and Calvin. On the other hand it is a well-known fact that Calvin was profoundly influenced by Augustine,[2] especially with regard to dogmatics (sin and grace) and that he quoted Augustine 410 times in his *Institutes* of 1559.[3] No Church Father is as frequently quoted by Calvin as Augustine.[4] The question arises whether this is also true as far as ethics is concerned. Did Calvin also follow his mentor in ethics?

It is generally accepted that dogmatics deals with "what we believe" while ethics is all about "what we do". This distinction is not nuanced enough because not all human activities are ethical activities, but for the purpose of this article I will use this general distinction.

Christianity is about *doctrina* and *vita*, doctrine and daily life, orthodoxy and orthopraxy, and they form an inseparable unity. We have to

---

[1] H. Küng, *Christianity. Its Essence and History* (London: SCMPress, 1995), 288. Somebody once said that Western philosophy is nothing more than footnotes to Plato, and likewise it can be said "that theology in Western Christianity has been a series of footnotes to Augustine" (D.D. Williams, "The significance of St. Augustine today," in: R.W. Battenhouse (ed.), *A Companion to the Study of St. Augustine* (New York: Oxford University Press, 1955), 4.

[2] A.N.S. Lane, *John Calvin: Student of the Church Fathers* (Edinburgh: T. & T. Clark, 1999), 38: "Calvin held Augustine in the highest regard," and: "Calvin's teaching was to a considerable extent [...] a revival of Augustinianism..."

[3] J.M.J. Lange van Ravenswaay, *Augustinus totus noster: Das Augustin-Verständnis bei Johannes Calvin* (Göttingen: Vandenhoeck & Ruprecht, 1990), 105.

[4] R.J. Mooi, *Het Kerk- en Dogmahistorisch Element in de Werken van Johannes Calvijn* [The Church and Dogma-historical Elements in the Works of John Calvin] (Wageningen: Veenman & Zonen, 1965), 262.

believe the correct things and we have to *do* the right things. The one cannot go without the other and they are inseparably intertwined.

"A tree is recognized by its fruit", Christ taught.[5] And: "Not everyone who *says* to me, 'Lord, Lord,' will enter the kingdom of heaven, but only he who *does* the will of my Father who is in heaven."[6] The same message resounds in the letters of Paul, in Romans for example, and also in Galatians 5:6 where he writes that "the only thing that counts is faith expressing itself through love." James also very closely relates faith and deeds.[7] John writes to the congregation of Ephesus that keeping to the pure doctrine is not enough when the love for Christ and Christians is lacking.[8]

Augustine and Calvin were very keen on accepting and protecting the true doctrine. What did they teach about Christian life? Did Calvin follow Augustine in this regard? How relevant is their teaching for us today? This article starts with an exposition of some of the key characteristics of the ethics of Augustine followed by that of Calvin.

De Beata Vita: *Augustine*

When one investigates the ethics of Augustine, different approaches are possible. One could highlight his views on various ethical topics like marriage and sexuality,[9] politics[10] and war.[11] Or one could focus on the key features of his ethics like happiness, humility, truth and love.[12] In this approach I will focus on the key features without ignoring the topics.[13]

---

[5] Matt. 12:33.

[6] Matt. 7:21.

[7] James 2:14–26.

[8] Rev. 2:1–7.

[9] Cf. J.H. van Wyk, "*Venialis culpa?* Augustinus oor huwelik en seksualiteit," [Venial sin? Augustine on Marriage and Sexuality] *In die Skriflig* [In the Light of Scripture] 3 (2002), 327–348.

[10] For Augustine on state and church, cf. J.H. van Wyk, *Etiek en Eksistensie in Koninkryksperspektief* [Ethics and Existence in Perspective of the Kingdom] (Potchefstroom: PTP, 2001), 133–152.

[11] Cf. J.H. van Wyk, *Etiek van Vrede. 'n Teologies-etiese evaluering van die Christenpasifisme* [Ethics of Peace. A theological ethical Evaluation of Christian Pacifism] (Stellenbosch: Cabo, 1984), 58–61.

[12] Of course there are more, for example 'freedom' and 'peace'. See further A. Reul, *Die sittlichen Ideale des heiligen Augustinus* (Paderborn: F. Schöningh, 1928).

[13] For the ethics of Augustine see *inter alia* the following books: J. Mausbach, *Die Ethik des heiligen Augustinus* I & II (Freiburg im Breisgau: Herder, 1909); A. Reul, *Die sittlichen Ideale* (1928); B. Switalski, *Neoplatonism and the Ethics of St Augustine* (New York: Polish Institute of Arts and Sciences in America, 1946); J. Wetzel, *Augustine and the Limits of Virtue* (Cambridge: Cambridge University Press, 1992); W.S. Babcock (ed.), *The Ethics of*

Augustine never wrote a handbook on ethics in the real sense of the word. As a young theologian he reflected on *De beata vita* (386/7)[14] and *De moribus ecclesiae catholicae et de moribus Manichaeorum* (387/8)[15] and 40 years later gave a summary of the divine Biblical precepts and prohibitions in *Speculum* (427).[16] In many of his other books, commentaries, sermons and letters many suggestions and reflections on ethical matters are found. To a certain extent we find Augustine's fully developed ethics in his magnum opus *De civitate Dei* (413/427)[17]—as Carney remarks.[18]

Although Augustine accepted the natural virtues discussed by philosophers like prudence, fortitude, temperance and justice, he subordinated them to the three "infused virtues" namely faith, hope and love.[19] "These seven virtues together with the commandments of God and the Beatitudes of the New Testament constitute a seven-stage plan for Christian living in which the virtues play the decisive role" according to Lavere.[20]

St. Augustine (Atlanta: Scholars Press, 1991). See also B. Roland-Gosselin, *La morale de saint Augustin* (Paris: M. Riviére, 1925); G. Armas, *La moral de San Agustin* (Madrid: Asilo de Huérfanos, 1955). For shorter studies see the following: B. Roland-Gosselin, "St. Augustine's System of Morals," in: M.C. D'Arcy et al., *A Monument to St. Augustine. Essays on some Aspects of his Thought written in Commemoration of his 15th Centenary* (New York: MacVeagh, 1930), 225–248; T.J. Bigham and A.T. Mollegen, "The Christian Ethic," in: R.W. Battenhouse (ed.), *A Companion to the Study of St. Augustine* (New York: Oxford University Press, 1955), 371–397; G.J. Lavere, "Virtue," in: A.D. Fitzgerald (ed.), *Augustine through the Ages. An Encyclopedia* (Grand Rapids: Eerdmans, 1999), 871–874; G.W. Schlabach and A.D. Fitzgerald et al., "Ethics," in: Fitzgerald (ed.), *Encyclopedia*, 320–330; B. Kent, "Augustine's Ethics," in: E. Stump and N. Kretzmann (eds), *The Cambridge Companion to Augustine* (Cambridge: Cambridge University Press, 2001), 205–233.

[14] Augustine, *On the Happy Life* (*PL* 32, *CSEL* 63).

[15] Augustine, *On the Catholic and the Manichean Ways of Life* (*PL* 32, *CSEL* 90; *NPNF* 4).

[16] Augustine, *The Mirror* (*PL* 34, *CSEL* 12). See A.D. Fitzgerald, "*Speculum* (The Mirror)," in: Fitzgerald, *Encyclopedia*, 812.

[17] Augustine, *City of God* (*PL* 41, *CSEL* 40; *NPNF* 2). Cf. also *The Works of Aurelius Augustine, Bishop of Hippo: The City of God*, vol. I & II (Edinburgh: T. & T. Clark, 1949) (trans. M. Dods).

[18] F.S. Carney, "The Structure of Augustine's Ethic," in: Babcock, *Ethics of Augustine*, 23.

[19] Augustine, *De moribus ecclesiae catholicae et de moribus Manichaeorum* (Henceforth: Augustine, *Moribus* [Concerning Morals], 15.25, (*PL* 32, *CSEL* 90; *NPNF* 4). See also Augustine *De catechizandis rudibus* [On the Instruction of Beginners] (399) (*PL* 40; *NPNF* 3). See further Bigham and Mollegen, "Christian Ethic" in: Battenhouse, *Companion*, 15, 19–25 and Lavere, "Virtue," in: Fitzgerald (ed.), *Encyclopedia*, 872. Wetzel, on the other hand, is of opinion that Augustine heavily depends on the Stoic ethics of virtue, autonomy and happiness: "Augustine's sensibilities in ethics are fundamentally Stoic" (see Wetzel, *Augustine*, 11, 54).

[20] Lavere, "Virtue," in: Fitzgerald (ed.), *Encyclopedia*, 872. See also Switalski, *Neoplatonism*.

Happiness

I start with the notion of happiness, not because it is the most important characteristic, but because Augustine reflected on it from a very early
stage. Marrou[21] even refers to it as a central problem in the thought of
Augustine. As Cicero had done in his *Hortentius*, Augustine mentioned
many times that all persons strive to be happy.[22] Morality has to do with
the way people want to live a happy life.[23]

The central question during his short stay with friends and his mother
in Cassiciacum near Milan after his conversion was: what is a happy life
and where do we find it?[24] Against the skeptics Augustine argued that
they would never find happiness because they denied the existence
of truth. Only those who possess the eternal and graceful God can be
happy.[25] True happiness exists in knowing God and Jesus Christ.[26]
Unhappy are those who know everything, may be all facts, but not God.[27]

In the first ten books of his *De civitate Dei* Augustine refuted the pagan
approach that happiness in and after this life is possible by serving idols.
In one of his sermons he prayed that God must give us happiness, not

---

[21] H.-I. Marrou, *Augustinus und das Ende der antiken Bildung* [Augustine and the End
of the ancient Culture], Paderborn: Ferdinand Schöningh, 1981), 151. See also Mausbach,
Ethik I, 51–84.

[22] Augustine, *De beata vita* [On a Happy Life], 2.10 (PL 32, CSEL 63); *Confessiones* (Confessions) (397/401), 10.20–23 (*PL* 32, *CSEL* 33; *NPNF* 1). Cf. also *St. Augustine: The Confessions* (Peabody: Hendrickson Publishers, 2004) (ed. A.C. Outler); Augustine, *Sermo* 150,
cf. *Augustinus: Carthaagse Preken* [Augustine: Carthaginian Sermons] trans. G. Wijdeveld
(Baarn: Ambo 1988), 69; *Sermo* 1.1, Augustine, Psalm 118/119, cf. *Augustinus: Commentaar op
Psalm 118/119* [Augustine: Commentary on Psalm 118/119] trans. T.J. van Bavel (Baarn: Ambo;
1996], 26.

[23] Augustine, *Moribus* 5.8.

[24] "Quid sit beata vita." S. Lancel, *St Augustine* (London: SCM Press, 2002), 176.

[25] Augustine, *De beata vita*, 2.11, 3.19.

[26] Augustine, *De beata vita*, 4.33,34. See also: H. de N. Galvao, *Beatitudo*, in C. Mayer (ed.),
Augustinus-Lexikon, vol. 1 (Basel: Schwabe, 1986–1994), 624–638; P.J. Couvee, *Vita beata en
vita aeterna: Een onderzoek naar de ontwikkeling van het begrip "vita beata" naast en tegen-
over "vita aeterna," bij Lactantius, Ambrosius en Augustinus, onder invloed van Romeinsche
Stoa* [Vita beata and vita aeterna: An Investigation into the Development of the Concept
"vita beata" alongside and over against "vita aeterna" in the Works of Lactantius, Ambrose
and Augustine under the Influence of the Roman Stoics] (Baarn: Hollandia, 1947). Couvee
demonstrates that Augustine in the end overcame the philosophic influences.

[27] Augustine, *Confessiones*, 5.4. Augustine rejects the idea that happiness rests on virtue
(paganism) or freedom (Pelagianism). Cf. Wetzel, *Augustine*, 123.

through earthly possessions, which can be lost, but through Him whom we never can lose.[28]

In the end the highest happiness is found in eternal life where there is no fear and no delusion.[29] Ultimately a restless heart can only come to rest in God.[30]

Augustine did not advocate a cheap form of eudaemonism (i.e. happiness is the aim and measure of virtue; happiness is the supreme good).[31] Happiness without piety and adoration of the true God is cheap.[32] Therefore in his sermons and writings the bishop would always warn against the evils of this world like gambling, theatre, pub, brothel, abuse of liquor, greed, fraud, adultery, fornication and astrology.[33] A happy life is a life of close fellowship with God and the neighbour.

Humility

Another very important feature of Augustine's ethics is humility. Humility is a fundamental virtue, the virtue of all virtues.[34] It is correctly observed

---

[28] Augustine, *Sermo*, 113, Augustinus, *Als korrels tussen kaf: Preken over teksten uit het Marcus- en het Lucasevangelie* [Like Grain among Chaff: Sermons on Texts from the Gospels of Mark and Luke], trans. J. Gehlen-Springorum, et al. (Amsterdam: Ambo, 2002), 199.

[29] Augustine, *Sermo* 113; *Carthaagse Preken*, 76. See also Augustine, *De Trinitate* (399–422/426), 13.2.7–13.3.12; *Saint Augustine: The Trinity* trans. E. Hill (New York: New City Press, 1997), 347–353. Happiness is here very closely related to immortality and eternal life.

[30] "Et inquietum est cor nostrum, donec requiescat in te." Augustine, *Confessiones* 1.1. See also Augustine, *De catechizandis rudibus* [On catechism for beginners/rudimentary cathechism], 17.27.

[31] Augustine rejects the hedonism of the Epicureans as well as the apathetic approach of the Stoics, see Roland-Gosselin, "Augustine's System," 229–231.

[32] Augustine, *De civitate Dei*, 4.23.

[33] Augustine, *De catechizandis rudibus*, 7.11, 16.25, 25.48, 27.55. The bishop had no objections against the (moderate) use of wine, see Possidius, *Vita Augustini,*, 22.2 (*PL* 32, 33–66). Possidius, *The Life of Saint Augustine*, J.E. Rotelle (ed.) (Villanova: Augustinian Press, 1988).

[34] See Augustine, *Regula: Praeceptum* (397/399) [The Rule: Precepts] (*PL* 32). See also *Augustinus van Hippo: Regel voor de gemeenschap* [Precepts for the Community] trans. T.J. van Bavel (Kampen: Kok, 1991), 50. According to Mayer, *humilitas* is derived from *humus* which means 'surface of the earth', 'down to earth'; C. Mayer, *Humiliatio, humilitas*, in C. Mayer (ed.), *Augustinus-Lexikon*, vol. 3, fasc. 3/4 (Basel: Schwabe, 2006), 443–456. See further F. van der Meer, *Augustinus de zielzorger: Een studie over de praktijk van een kerkvader* [Augustine as a carefiver of souls: A Study on the Practice of a Church Father] (Utrecht: Het Spectrum, 1949), 273; Roland-Gosselin, "Augustine's System," 246 and *in extenso* O. Schaffner, *Christliche Demut. Des Hl. Augustinus Lehre von der Humilitas* [Augustine's Teaching on Humility], (Würzburg: Augustinus Verlag, 1959). O'Donnell, on the other hand, considers the *Confessiones* not as a book of humility but of personal aggrandizement: J.J. O'Donnell, *Augustine, Saint and Sinner: A New Biography* (London: Profile Books, 2005), 36.

that Augustine's great discovery was the significance of humility, as opposed to the sin of pride, and that happiness can only be experienced where reason submits itself to faith and the will to grace.[35] Happiness starts with humility.[36] For Augustine pride is the beginning of all sin and the beginning of pride is infidelity towards God.[37] Pride is the origin and highest expression of sin.[38] Pride, as the perverted imitation of God, is the beginning of all sin and it ends up in abuse of power (*libido dominandi*).[39] Perverted self-love, based on pride, is the fundamental disorder of the individual and society.[40] "For Augustine, then, pride is the root form of evil, separating the self from God and playing itself out in claims to moral self-suffiency, to religious superiority, and to political domination".[41] It is intriguing that a man who was so well-known and famous in his own time—according to Jerome[42]—put so much emphasis on the notion of humility.

Truth

Another moral value that was held in high esteem by the Church Father was truth. A life of beatitude (to him) implies a life of joy in truth, which means a life of joy in God.[43] Truth and happiness form an inseparable unity: add truth to your life and you will find happiness; only the truth can make one happy.[44] Without faith nobody will discover truth.

---

[35] E. Gilson, *The Christian Philosophy of Saint Augustine* (New York: Random House, 1960), 227.

[36] Augustine, *De sermone Domini in monte* [The Sermon on the Mount] (393/395), 1.10, Aurelius Augustinus, *Het huis op de rots. Verhandeling over de bergrede* [The House on the Rock. Dissertation on the Sermon on the Mount] trans. L. Wenneker and H. van Reisen (Amsterdam: Ambo, 2000), 81.

[37] Augustine, *De sermone Domini in monte*, 1.32; Augustinus, *Bergrede*, 81. See also Augustine, *Sermo* 198: Aurelius Augustinus, *Als lopend vuur: Preken voor het liturgisch jaar 2* [Like spreading Fire: Sermons for the Liturgical Year 2], trans. R. van Zaalen, H. van Reisen, and S. van der Meijs (Amsterdam: Ambo, 2001), 79.

[38] Cf. T.J. van Bavel, *Augustinus. Van liefde en vriendschap* [Augustine: On Love and Friendship] (Baarn: Het Wereldvenster, 1970), 43.

[39] Cf. R.A. Markus. *'Saeculum': History and Society in the Theology of St. Augustine* (Cambridge: University Press, 1988), xvii.

[40] Markus, *'Saeculum'*, xviii.

[41] J.P. Burns, "Augustine on the Origin and Process of Evil," in: Babcock, *Ethics of Augustine*, 82.

[42] Cf. E. TeSelle, *Augustine the Theologian* (London: Burns & Oats, 1970), 341; J.M. Rist, *Augustine. Ancient Thought Baptized* (Cambridge: University Press, 1999), 290.

[43] Augustine, *Confessiones*, 10.23.

[44] Cf. J. Burnaby, *Amor Dei. A Study of the Religion of St. Augustine* (London: Hodder & Stoughton, 1938), 153; Gilson, *Philosophy*, 3.

From his early writings till his more mature reflections he rejected scepticism and discovered the *summa veritas* in the Word of God presented to us by the Holy Spirit.[45]

The bishop was very much outspoken against any form of lying, without any exception whatsoever, as can clearly be seen from his studies on *De Mendacio* (394) and *Contra Mendacium* (420).[46] This radical and perfectionist standpoint prevented him from developing any notion of a so-called "necessary lie" (or "crisis truth") which we experience in critical situations in a sinful world.[47] Augustine's view on truth was greatly influenced by Neo-Platonism, but it is also true to say that in his later development he followed a more theological and Christological approach in this regard.

Love

A last, and most important, aspect that I would like to mention is Augustine's treatment of the notion of love. Augustine is described as *doctor gratiae* and *doctor pacis*, but in a very real sense he can also be referred to as *doctor caritatis*. This notion appears in almost all his writings, most explicitly in his *Enchiridion ad Laurentium de fide spe et caritate* (421/422) and *In epistulam Joannis ad Parthos tractatus* (406/407).[48]

For Augustine love is the highest value and the biggest gift. The Bible teaches nothing else than love (*caritas*) and condemns nothing else than desire (*cupiditas*) and pride (*superbia*), which results in the lust for power (*libido dominandi*).[49] Love can be described as the hermeneutical key to a correct understanding of the Bible. If someone reads the Bible and does not discover what love really means, then he has not discovered what the Bible is all about.[50] From the very beginning catechumens have to know

---

[45] Augustine, *Confessiones*, 10.24, 13.31; Augustine, *Moribus*, 29. See also B. Studer, "*Veritas Dei* in der Theologie des heiligen Augustinus" [Veritas Dei in the Theology of the holy Augustine], *Augustinianum* XLVI (2006), 411–455.

[46] Augustine, *On Lying* and Augustine, *Against Lying* (*PL* 40; *CSEL* 41). Cf. *Enchiridion ad Laurentium de fide spe et caritate* [A Handbook for Laurentius on Faith, Hope and Love] (421/422), 16–22 (*PL* 40; *NPNF* 3). See also *St. Augustine: The Enchiridion on faith, hope and love*, H. Paolucci (ed.) (Washington: Regnery Gateway, 1987). For a discussion of Augustine's views on truth and lies, see Van Wyk, *Etiek en Eksistensie*, 74–82.

[47] Cf. Van Wyk, *Etiek en Eksistensie*, 82–86.

[48] Augustine, *Tractates on the the First Letter of John* (*PL* 35; *NPNF* 7).

[49] Cf. Augustine *De doctrina Christiana* [On Christian Teaching] (396; 426/427), 3.10.15 (*PL* 34, *CSEL* 80). Cf. *Saint Augustine: On Christian Doctrine*, trans. D.W. Robertson (New York: Macmillan Publishing Company, 1958). See also Mausbach, *Ethik* I, 222–263.

[50] Augustine, *De doctrina Christiana*, 3.15.23.

that the main reason for the advent of Christ lies in the fact that God wanted to show us his love.[51]

Love is defined as "the motion of the soul toward enjoyment of God for his own sake, and the enjoyment of one's self and of one's neighbour for the sake of God."[52] Our highest bliss consists of the enjoyment of the triune God.[53] The good (people) use the world that they may enjoy God; the wicked, on the contrary, use God that they may enjoy the world.[54]

The Church Father prefers to speak of an ordered love (*ordo caritatis*).[55] "The peace of things is the tranquility of order. Order is the distribution which allots things equal and unequal, each to its own place."[56] First comes the love for God en then the love for humans.[57] We should never love the Absolute (God) in a relative way and what is relative (humans) in an absolute way. Love is the weight which orders life and keeps it in balance.[58] True religion does not exist in anger, nepotism and hate, but in love (including love for the enemy) and the imitation of God.[59] There is no more difficult assignment than to love your enemy.[60]

It is clear that for Augustine love takes priority.[61] If you want to know whether a person is good, do not ask about his faith or his hope, but what he loves. Because a person who loves in the correct way, will also believe and hope in the correct way, while a person who does not love correctly, will believe in vain (even if the contents of faith are correct) and also hope in vain (even if the object of his hope is real).[62] According to Augustine there are two cities (or kingdoms) on earth, the *civitas Dei* and the *terrena civitas*, and the difference between the two is revealed in two ways of life and two ways of love: love for God or love for the self.

---

[51] Augustine, *De catechizandis rudibus*, 4.7.
[52] Augustine, *De doctrina Christiana*, 3.10.16.
[53] Augustine, *De Trinitate*, 1.8.18. See Augustine, *Trinity*, 77. See also Mausbach, *Ethik* I, 168–221.
[54] Augustine, *De Civitae Dei*, 15.7.
[55] See N.J. Torchia, "The Significance of ORDO in St. Augustine's Moral Theory," in: J.T. Lienhard, E.C. Muller, and R.J. Teske (eds), *Augustine: Presbyter factus sum* [I became a priest], (New York: Peter Lang, 1993), 263–276.
[56] Augustine, *De Civitae Dei*, 19.13.
[57] Augustine, *De Civitae Dei*, 15.22.
[58] Augustine, *Confessiones*, 13.9.
[59] Augustine, *Sermo*, 7.4, 9.3, Augustinus, *Commentaar Psalm 118/119*, 59.
[60] Augustine, *Sermo*, 7.4 Augustinus, *Commentaar Psalm 118/119*, 59.
[61] Augustine, *Enchiridion*, 117.
[62] Augustine, *Enchiridion*, 117.

Two cities have been formed by two loves: the earthly of love of self, even to the contempt of God; the heavenly by the love of God, even to the contempt of self. The former, in a word, glories in itself, the latter in the Lord.[63]

Therefore citizens of the city of God only make use (*uti*) of earthly things, for they can only enjoy (*frui*) God and his kingdom.[64]

Augustine's sermon commentary on 1 John can be described as a song of praise on love, a song with many variations as can be seen from the following quotations: a man *is* as he loves;[65] love is the beauty of the soul;[66] love is the completion of all our work; if we have reached love, we shall find rest;[67] love, and you will do nothing else than good;[68] the practicing of love, her strength, her flourishing, her fruit, her beauty, her charm, her nourishment, her drink, her food, her embracement, know no satisfaction.[69]

It is within this context that the bishop turns to the schism between the Catholic and Donatist churches which developed during the fourth century and tragically divided the churches of Christ in North Africa.[70] There were no fundamental confessional differences between the two "denominations", although the Donatists strongly emphasized the holiness of the church. Schismatics tend to view themselves as better and more advanced and holier Christians than those who belong to the "mother church". Augustine, stressing the unity and catholicity of the church of Christ, and that the church is a *corpus permixtum*, argued that those who break the unity (albeit with good intentions) act without love. "Of the Donatists, for example, you cannot possibly say that they have love, because they have broken the unity of the church".[71]

It is also within this context that Augustine used his famous dictum: Love and do what you will (*dilige et quod vis fac*).[72] Christians must love

---

63 Augustine, *De Civitae Dei*, 14.28.
64 For a discussion of *uti* and *frui*, see Van Wyk, *Etiek en Eksistensie*, 106–132. See also K.Y. Burchill-Limb, "The actuality of Augustine's distinction between *uti* and *frui*," [...to use and enjoy], *Augustiniana* 56(2006), 183–197.
65 Augustine, *In epistulam Joannis*, 2.14.
66 Augustine, *In epistulam Joannis*, 10.9.
67 Augustine, *In epistulam Joannis*, 10.4.
68 Augustine, *In epistulam Joannis*, 10.7.
69 Augustine, *In epistulam Joannis*, 10.7.
70 See W.H.C. Frend, *The Donatist Church: A Movement of Protest in Roman North Africa* (Oxford: Clarendon, 1952). For a short overview, see J.H. van Wyk, "Faith, Ethnicity and Contextuality: An Investigation of their Relation and Relevance to Church and Christianship," in: A.J.G. Van der Borght, D. van Keulen, and M. Brinkman (eds), *Studies in Reformed Theology: Faith and Ethnicity. Vol 2.* (Zoetermeer: Meinema, 2002), 26–32.
71 Augustine, *In epistulam Joannis*, 6.2.
72 Augustine, *In epistulam Joannis*, 7.8.

everybody, even their opponents, yes, their enemies. This also applies to Catholic Christians in their relationship with Donatist Christians.[73]

As far as ecclesiology is concerned, the Church Father speaks loud and clear to us today who feel very comfortable in a never ending situation of church separation and division. The New Testament knows only of the *one* church of Christ, situated in many villages, towns and cities and nothing of divided and opposing churches and "denominations". The New Testament calls upon us to speak the *truth* in *love*.[74] When love disappears, even if there is a strong pursuit of truth, the church has no future.[75]

Eschatology plays a very important role in the theology and ethics of the Church Father as can be seen from his *De civitate Dei*. Christian life must be orientated towards and focused on the future life and the consummation of the kingdom of God:

> There we shall rest and see, see and love, love and praise. This is what shall be in the end without end. For what other end do we propose to ourselves than to attain to the kingdom of which there is no end?[76]

Comments

Did Augustine himself live up to the high standard of love which he emphasized so much? Three further questions arise in this regard: his view on war, the use of state power, and his marriage ethics (including his relationship with his concubine). Augustine was probably the first theologian to develop the theory of a just war (*bellum justum*).[77] The three preconditions are: *legitima auctoritas, justa causa* and *recta intentio*, with emphasis on the latter. However, it is unclear how the principle of love could be kept intact in a situation of war. It is obvious "that peace is the end sought for by war; for every man seeks peace by waging war, but no man seeks war by making peace".[78] What is *not* obvious is what happens

---

[73] Cf. E. TeSelle, "Towards an Augustinian Politics," in: Babcock, *Ethics of Augustine*, 151.

[74] Eph. 4:15.

[75] Rev. 2:1–7.

[76] Augustine, *De Civitate Dei*, 22.30.

[77] See Van Wyk, *Etiek van Vrede*, 58–61; J. Langan, "The Elements of St. Augustine's Just War Theory," in: Babcock, *Ethics of Augustine*, 168–189; R.L. Holmes, "St. Augustine on the Just War Theory," in: G.B. Mattthews (ed.), *The Augustinian Tradition* (London: University of California Press, 1999), 323–344; O. O'Donovan, *The Just War Revisited* (Cambridge: Cambridge University Press, 2003).

[78] Augustine, *De Civitate Dei*, 19.12.

to the commandment of love in a war situation. Is it morally acceptable for Christians to kill other Christians—even with a *recta intentio*?

The second question arises from the fact that the bishop in the end— after ten years of discussions, debates and writings with and against the Donatists—approved of state enforcement against them to join the Catholic Church. Although Augustine stated in his *Retractationes*[79] (426/427) that it was not his desire that the schismatics be forced back into the church, his approach as a whole seems to have given too much power to the state in church affairs.

Thirdly, Augustine's marriage ethics belongs to the most problematic part of his ethics, because of his degrading of the physical and sexual dimension of love in marriage life. With his strong emphasis on marriage life for the sake of procreation (*proles*), Augustine failed to arrive at a positive view on sexuality (and sexual desire) as a dimension of love in marriage (*venialis culpa*).[80] Was this one of the reasons why he later distanced himself from his concubine with whom he had lived for fourteen years, whose name he never mentioned? Indeed, "There is no way to excuse Augustine's treatment of Una" [his concubine].[81]

Summa Vitae Christianae: *Calvin*

Although the insights of Paul and Augustine form the main ingredient of Calvin's theology in book III of the *Institutes*,[82] it is intriguing that Calvin nowhere referred to Augustine when he developed his views on the life of a Christian[83]—although the undertones of the views of Augustine are clearly heard. It also is interesting that Calvin in this context nowhere gives an explanation of the Ten Commandments which he treated in book II.8 of the *Institutes*[84] where he deals with Christology. This of course does not imply that the commandments of God are irrelevant, but clearly that they should never function in an abstract way as the foundation of Christian life. Calvin's ethic is not legalistic; it is solidly built on the redeeming

---

[79] Augustine, *Retractiones*, 2.5. See Augustine, *Retractations* trans M.I. Bogan (Washington DC: The Catholic University of America Press, 1968).

[80] See Van Wyk, "*Venialis culpa?* [Venial Fault?]," 327–348.

[81] G. Wills, *Saint Augustine: A Penguin Life* (New York: Viking Penquin, 1999), 41. The name 'Una' is a nickname given by Wills and derived from *unam habebat* ['had one']. Wills, *Augustine*, 16.

[82] Lange van Ravenswaay, *Augustinus totus noster*, 111–113.

[83] Cf. Mooi, *Het Kerk- en Dogmahistorisch Element*, 389.

[84] Cf. John Calvin, *Institutes of the Christian Religion*, trans F.L. Battles (London: Westminster John Knox Press, 1960). The references in the text are to the *Institutes*.

work of Christ and the renewing work of the Spirit. It is also clear from Calvin's theology that ethics and dogmatics form an inseparable unity. Another characteristic is Calvin's aversion to philosophical ethics which he estimated inadequate if compared to the wisdom of the Bible.

Calvin deals with ethics in book 3 where he explains the work of the Holy Spirit. The section on the Christian life (III.6–10) succeeds sections which deal with faith, regeneration and repentance (III.2.3). After the section on Christian life Calvin continues with sections on justification by faith (III.9–18), Christian freedom (III.3.19), prayer (III.3.20), election (III.3.21–24) and the final resurrection (III.3.25).

The key features of a Christian life are self-denial, cross-bearing and meditation on the future life—and of course the correct use of the present life. The focus is on a theocentric life, a life of self-denial in the footsteps of Christ, a renewed life through the Holy Spirit and a life in the light of the Word of God.[85] I now turn to the *Institutes* to give a very brief overview of his ethics.[86]

---

[85] Cf *inter alia* the following books on the ethics of Calvin: P. Lobstein, *Die Ethik Calvins in ihren Grundzügen entworfen. Ein Beitrag zur Geschichte der Christlicher Ethik* (Strassburg: C.F. Schmidt's Universitäts-Buchhandlung, 1877); G. Harkness, *John Calvin. The Man and his Ethics* (New York: Henry Holt & Company, 1931); W. Kolfhaus, *Vom christlichen Leben nach Johannes Calvin* (Neukirchen Kreis Moers, 1949); R.S. Wallace, *Calvin's Doctrine of the Christian Life* (Grand Rapids: Eerdmans, 1961); W.C. Gentry, *a Study of John Calvin's Understanding of Moral Obligation and Moral Norms in Christian Ethics* (Michigan: Ann Arbor, 1970); P. de Klerk (ed.), *Calvin and Christian Ethics* (Grand Rapids: Calvin Studies Society, 1987); L. Schulze, *Calvin and "Social Ethics". His views on Property, Interest and Usury* (Pretoria: Kital, 1985); J.H. Leith, *John Calvin's Doctrine of the Christian Life* (Louisville: WJK, 1989). In my booklet *Die Etiek van Calvyn* [The Ethics of Calvin] (Potchefstroom: IBC, 1979) I gave summaries of many studies on Calvin's ethics and in my 1983 study I tried to give a short overview of his ethics, *Calvyn oor die Christelike lewe* [Calvin on the Christian Life] (Pretoria: NG Kerkboekhandel, 1983). For shorter studies on Calvin's ethics, see *inter alia*: A. Göhler, "Das christliche Leben nach Calvin," *Evangelische Theologie* 4 (1937), 299–325; J.G. Matheson, "Calvin's Doctrine of the Christian life," *Scottish Journal of Theology* 2 (1949), 48–56; A.H. van Zyl, "Calvyn oor die Christelike lewe" [Calvin on the Christian Life], *Nederduitse Gereformeerde Teologiese Tydskrif* (Dutch Reformed Theological Journal) 3 (1964), 182–200; B. Engelbrecht, "Die Etiek van Calvyn" (Calvin's Ethics), in: C.J. Wethmar and C.J.A. Vos (eds), *'n Woord op sy Tyd: 'n Teologiese Feesbundel aangebied aan Professor Johan Heyns ter Herdenking van sy Sestigste Verjaarsdag* [A Timely Word. A theological Festschrift presented to Professor Johan Heyns in Commemoration of his Sixtieth Birthday] (Pretoria: NG Kerkboekhandel, 1988) 35–42; W.H. Velema, "Ethiek bij Calvijn" (Ethics in Calvin) in: D.H. Borgers et al., *Reformatorische Stemmen—Verleden en Heden* [Reformational voices—Past and Present] (Apeldoorn: Willem De Zwijgerstichting, 1989), 193–222; D.J. Smit, "Views on Calvin's ethics: Reading Calvin in the South African context," *Reformed World* 4 (2007), 306–344.

[86] I am fully aware of the fact that Calvin's ethics could be developed in a much wider context (see my *Calvyn oor die Christelike lewe*, 1983), but for the purpose of this article I focus on the summary Calvin himself has given of the Christian life in his *Institutes*.

Calvin makes it very clear: the life of a Christian can only be described from a Biblical perspective (III.6.1–5), which implies that he is skeptical of an ethics of virtue where we should live "in accordance with nature" (Cicero, Seneca) (III.6.3). On the contrary, Christian life receives its strongest motive to God's work through the person and redeeming act of Christ. Christ, who reconciled us with God, "has been set before us as an example, whose pattern we ought to express in our life"; our life must express Christ (III.6.3). Furthermore, Christian life is not just a matter of the tongue but of the inmost heart. This expression is very Augustinian. Doctrine and daily life must go hand in hand. Calvin does not advocate perfectionism: "I do not so strictly demand evangelical perfection that I would not acknowledge as a Christian one who has not attained it. For thus all of us would be excluded from the church..." (III.6.5). But Christians should always strive and struggle for the goal ahead (namely integrity), which is the opposite of a double face.

Calvin summarizes the Christian life as a life of self-denial (III.7.1–10), of which cross-bearing forms an integral part (III.8.1–11). He then continues with meditation on the future life (III.9.1–6) and concludes with how we must use the present life (III.10.1–6).

Self-Denial

Self-denial (*abnegatio nostri*) is a key concept in the ethics of Calvin: self-denial in relation to the world (III.7.1–3), self-denial in relation to our fellow humans (III.7.4–7) and self-denial in relation to God (III.7.8–10).

We belong to God and therefore we must direct all the acts of our life to Him, glorifying Him, fleeing the (fashion of the) world. Self-denial consists therefore in obeying the will of God and glorifying Him. According to Titus 2 Christian life consists of a life of sobriety (temperance), righteousness (equity) and godliness (holiness). Self-denial also creates the right attitude towards our fellow humans.

Although there is no explicit reference to Augustine here, his views clearly reverberate in this case. Calvin refers to the fact that each one of us "wishes to tower above the rest", and to the deadly pestilence of pride and self-love. He then mentions 1 Corinthians 4:7, a text so many times quoted by Augustine: "If you have received all things, why do you boast as if they were not given to you?" Therefore Calvin appeals that, "whatever man we deal with, we shall treat him not only moderately and modestly but also cordially and as a friend" (III.7.4). It is clear that for Calvin self-denial leads to proper helpfulness towards the neighbour; we should seek not our own interest but that of others first.

Love for the neighbour—which includes all persons—does not depend upon the manner of a person, but on the fact that all are created in the image of God. As Christians we should assist every person because we look "upon the image of God in them" (3.7.6). Like Augustine, Calvin emphasizes that the outward work of love is not sufficient; it is the intention that counts.

Self-denial is also necessary for a good relation to God—it is the "main part". It is for all to see how "uneasy in mind all those persons are who order their lives according to their own plan; we can see how artfully they strive.....to obtain the goal of their ambition or avarice..." (III.7.8). People who live according to their own satisfaction are restless, only those are happy who are blessed by God and who trust in his blessing only. Self-denial also implies that we have to resign ourselves totally to the Lord, that we permit every part of our lives to be governed by God's will. In all things believers must see God's kindness and truly fatherly indulgence. In whatever happens, a believer, "because he will know it ordained of God, will undergo it with a peaceful and grateful mind so as not obstinately to resist the command of him into whose power he once for all surrendered himself and his every possession" (III.7.10).

Cross-Bearing

An inseparable part of self-denial is found in the idea of cross-bearing (*tolerantia crucis*) (III.8.1–11). As followers of Christ we have to take up our cross. Christ has given us an example of patience and we must be conformed to Him. The cross leads us to perfect trust in God's power and grace; it also permits us to experience God's faithfulness and gives us hope for the future; it furthermore trains us to patience and obedience; it prevents us from becoming proud and self-sufficient and helps us to stay humble before God. God afflicts us not to ruin or destroy us but to free us from the condemnation of the world.

There are many reasons for suffering, for instance when we defend the (truth of the) gospel or when we in any way maintain the cause of righteousness, but in all circumstances Christians find consolation in God.

Christians experience suffering as sent by God, and—unlike the Stoics' insensibility—gives expression to their pain and sorrow (III.8.9–11). It is not unchristian to groan and weep. There is a big difference between the philosophic and Christian understanding of patience. Nothing happens to believers "except by the will and providence of God. He does nothing except with a well ordered justice" (III.8.11). Therefore Christians can always be thankful, joyful and patient.

Meditation on the Future Life

Another aspect of the Christian life is the meditation on the future life (*meditatio futurae vitae*) (III.9.1–6). By our tribulations God weans us from excessive love for this present life, because all our actions are worldly. In this regard Calvin does not steer away from—may be too—strong expressions: we should despise the present life in order to meditate upon eternal life (III.9.1–2). "When it comes to comparison with the life to come, the present life can not only be safely neglected but, compared to the former, must be utterly despised and loathed. For, if heaven is our homeland, what else is the earth but our place of exile?" (III.9.4). "If the earthly life be compared with the heavenly, it is doubtless to be at once despised and trampled underfoot" (III.9.4). Calvin even uses Platonic anthropology to clarify his view: "If to be freed from the body is to be released into perfect freedom, what else is the body but a prison?" (III.9.4; see III.6.5). However, the contempt for the present life must not end up in a hatred for it or ingratitude towards God (III.9.3–4). In words that are very Augustinian, Calvin says that because to enjoy the presence of God is the summit of all happiness, and in the light of the expectation of eternal life, we can joyfully await the day of death and the final resurrection. "No one has made progress in the school of Christ who does not joyfully await the day of death and final resurrection" (III.9.5).

Use of the Present Life

Calvin concludes his treatment of the Christian life with a section on how we must use the present life (III.10.1–6). He argues that the good things of this life are to be enjoyed as gifts of God. We must try to avoid two dangers: mistaken strictness and mistaken laxity. The main purpose is to use God's gifts for the purpose He created and destined them for us— whether it is clothes, wine, oil, flowers, gold, silver, ivory or marble. We should not use these blessings indulgently or seek wealth greedily, but to serve dutifully in our calling. The fact that God is the Giver of earthly gifts, prevents our narrow-mindedness and immoderation. Our expectation of eternal life also determines our conduct in life.

Comments

Calvin's ethics can be characterized as theocentric, Christological, pneumatological, eschatological and Biblical.[87] The foundation of Christian life is (faith in) God, the realisation thereof consists of following in the footsteps of Christ through the power of the Holy Spirit on the way to eternal life.

What is striking in Calvin's ethics is his Christological presentation (self-denial and cross-bearing) and eschatological alignment (meditation on future life), all within the context of pneumatology. What is lacking, *here* at least, is an explicit explanation of a key concept namely *love*, which is so central in Biblical teaching. Not that it is totally lacking, because in his explanation of the Ten Commandments Calvin wrote: "We ought to embrace the whole human race without exception in a single feeling of love; here there is no distinction between barbarian and Greek, worthy and unworthy, friend and enemy, since all should be contemplated in God, not in themselves" (II.8.55). Even in the case of civil government and lawsuit the principle of love stays indispensable (IV.20.18).

Another question (which Calvin did not clarify) is how one should apply the central notion of self-denial in politics and civil government where self-assertion is the order of the day. We know that Calvin carefully distinguishes between Christ's spiritual kingdom and civil jurisdiction (IV.20.1), although it is true that the spiritual government of Christ is already initiating in us "certain beginnings" of the heavenly kingdom on earth (IV.20.2). Thus it is understandable that all human laws must be in conformity "with that perpetual rule of love" (IV.20.15/18). But how do you realize self-denial and love in a situation of war, even if it is a just war, which Calvin accepted (IV.20.11)?[88]

---

[87] "The work of Christ is the foundation of Calvin's ethics." Velema, "Ethiek bij Calvijn," 199.

[88] I think Calvin (IV.20.3/2) goes too far in committing to civil government "the duty of rightly establishing (true) religion", because it is not part of the government's task and cannot be applied in cases of a non-Christian government and in multi-religious countries. Theocracy is a confession of faith and not a social ideal to be realized in a sinful world.

Comparison

As far as the *foundation* of the Christian life is concerned, both Augustine and Calvin agree that faith in the triune God, as attested in Scripture, provides the final answer. Christian life is a theocentric life. This world and the form of this world are passing away and can never provide happiness, security and rest. Because sin[89] ruins individuals and societies, we need the grace of God in Christ and the renewing work of his Spirit to live a meaningful life.

Concerning the *realization* of Christian life, Augustine strongly emphasizes love as a key feature, while Calvin focuses on the notions of self-denial and cross-bearing. This does not imply that Augustine totally neglected the last two notions, and Calvin the first, but indicates where the emphasis lies for each.[90] Because Augustine views pride as the essence of sin, he could also accentuate the necessity of humility in a good life.

For both, the *consummation* of the Christian life exists in the hope for and expectation of eternal life in the presence of God. Christian life implies not only a life of faith and love but also a life of hope. The way in which both theologians develop their eschatologies is to a certain extent influenced by Greek philosophy, Augustine by Neo-Platonism and Calvin by Platonism. The consummation of the kingdom is very much a *heavenly* reality in which the dimensions of the renewed *earth* is underplayed, although not totally lacking.[91] But in the end eschatology makes the world go round. Christians live a life of hope and expectation and are looking forward towards the fulfillment of the great promises of God: the completion of the kingdom of God and the dawn of a new heaven and earth.

Relevance

I think one could conclude by saying that Augustine and Calvin succeeded in elucidating the essential notions of a Christian life:

---

[89] While for Augustine *superbia* is the origin of sin, for Calvin it is *infidelitas*. Lange van Ravenswaay, *Augustinus totus noster*, 37.

[90] Calvin remarks that Augustine correctly says that humility is the first, second and third commandment of the Christian religion. Mooi, *Kerk- en Dogmahistorisch Element*, 238.

[91] See Van Wyk, *Calvyn oor die Christelike lewe*, 42–44, as well as my article, "John Calvin on the Kingdom of God and Eschatology," *In die Skriflig* 2 (2001), 191–205.

- Christian life is not possible without the light of the Word of God.
- Christian life is not possible without putting God in the centre of it, God our Creator, Sustainer, Provider and Source of strength.
- Christian life is not possible without the redeeming and reconciliatory work of Jesus Christ and without following in his footsteps of self-denial and cross-bearing.
- Christian life is not possible without the renewing and transforming work of the Spirit of God, who teaches us how to live a life of love, humbleness and truth and to reject pride and hatred.
- Christian life is not possible without focusing on the advent of a new heaven and a new earth where God will be all in all.
- Christian life is not possible without faith and hope and love.

To this we have to add something else: For centuries Christian ethics focused on individual personal ethics, neglecting to a large extent social ethics. However, the twentieth century represents a turning point in this situation when social ethics receives more attention.[92] Social ethics is concerned with nuclear war, the world-wide energy, political, economical, and ecological crises; it tries to apply the Christian message of love and humility and self-denial as well as the principles of the kingdom of God to the structures and systems of this overpopulated, damaged, endangered and exhausted world. The world nowadays experiences new challenges of immense proportions. Communism (resp. socialism) collapsed in 1989 and since 2008 (extreme) capitalism finds itself in a severe crisis which asks for new thinking as far as economical systems are concerned. The ecological crisis (environmental pollution, energy exhaustion and global warming) has taken on such extreme proportions that any delay to deal with this problem will be fatal. The Biblical notion of caretaking (Gen 2:15) must be rediscovered and revived.

It is also evident that we are the first (or second) generation with the ability to destroy all life on planet earth several times with nuclear

---

[92] See *inter alia* J. Stott, *Issues facing Christians Today: New Perspectives on Social and Moral Dilemmas* (London: Marshall Pickering, 1990); C. Villa-Vicencio and J. de Gruchy (eds), *Doing Ethics in Context: South African Perspectives*, Claremont: David Philip Publishers, 1994); H. Küng, *Global Responsibility. In Search of a New World Ethic* (London: SCM Press, 1991); H. Küng, *A Global Ethic for Global Politics and Economics* (London: SCM Press, 1997); K. Nürnberger, *Prosperity, Poverty & Pollution. Managing the Approaching Crisis* (Pietermaritzburg: Cluster Publications, 1999); D.J. Smit, *Essays in Public Theology: Collected Essays I* (Stellenbosch: Sun Press, 2007).

weapons and that therefore the *bellum justum* theory is outdated and should be replaced by a theology of peace.

Christians are called to be the salt of the earth, the light of the world and the yeast of society. Although it will be impossible for them to transform this sinful world into the kingdom of God and the (expected) new earth and heaven, they must try to (re)direct society to that great ideal, they have to penetrate social structures and try to improve and humanise them and in doing so create small signs of the coming kingdom of God.

CHAPTER FIVE

THE EXEGETICAL BACKGROUND OF CALVIN'S VIEW OF THE GOVERNMENT[1]

Henk van den Belt

Commenting on Psalm 2, Calvin writes:

> Where David urges all kings and rulers to kiss the Son of God [Ps. 2:12], he does not bid them lay aside their authority and retire to private life, but submit to Christ the power with which they have been invested, that he alone may tower over all. Similarly, Isaiah, when he promises that kings shall be foster fathers of the church, and queens its nurses [Is. 49:23], does not deprive them of their honor.[2]

This quotation from the closing chapter of the *Institutes* shows how Calvin refers to the Old Testament to defend the task of the civil government to promote the gospel and the welfare of the church.[3] The fact that the quotation is from the final Latin edition of the *Institutes* prompts the question why he inserted it at that time and how these references relate to his commentaries, published at an earlier date.

The First Edition of the Institutes

Calvin's *Institutio* was first intended as a catechetical work. From the very start, however, it also had an apologetic character, being dedicated to

---

[1] For a more detailed assessment of this subject, see Henk van den Belt, *De Messiaanse kus: Overheid en godsdienst bij Johannes Calvijn* [The Messianic Kiss: John Calvin on Government and Religion] (Gouda: Guido de Brès-Stichting, 2009). The main ideas of this paper have also been published in Romanian. Henk van den Belt, 'Cât de Tolerant a fost Jean Calvin? Viziunea evolutivă a lui Calvin privind îndatoririle guvernării civile,' [How tolerant was John Calvin? Calvin's Developing View of the Religious Task of the Civil Government], in *Annales Universitatis Apulensis: Series Historica* XVI–XVIII (Alba Julia: Altip, 2010), 11–18.

[2] Calvin, *Institutes*, IV.20.5.

[3] The term 'theocratic' is avoided in this paper, because of its ambivalence. Calvin believed that civil authority was responsible to God, but not that the church should govern the state. Höpfl suggests disposing of the "outworn issue of whether Calvin was or was not a proponent of theocracy." H. Höpfl, *The Christian Polity of John Calvin* (Cambridge: Cambridge University Press, 1982), 184.

Francis I, king of France.[4] As the author says, it seemed worthwhile to use the instruction written for those who were hungering and thirsting after Christ, as a confession before the king, to enable him to learn the nature of the doctrine against which he was incited by 'madmen'.[5]

Important for Calvin's view of the government is his reference to confusion due to the Anabaptists at the end of the dedication. Satan, seeing that he cannot oppress the truth with violence, has now, according to Calvin, aroused disagreements and dogmatic contentions through 'his Catabaptists' and other 'monstrous rascals'.[6] Calvin assures the king that the evangelicals he represents are peaceful subjects who always remember him in their prayers.

The final paragraphs of the first edition of the *Institutes* discuss the reciprocal callings of magistrates and their subjects. It is the duty of the government to represent God and the duty of the subjects to accept, respect, and obey their authority, even if the government is ungodly and oppressive. Theologically this position is sustained by a reference to God's providence and to the high calling of the magistrates as vicars of God.[7] All authority is given by God and rebellion against the government is disobedience against him. Thus Calvin seems to confirm the status quo. At least he has an interest in demonstrating that the evangelicals in France are not revolutionary.

Two elements, however, nuance the confirmation of any given government. In the first place, the rulers—exactly because they are God's

---

[4] On the successive editions of the *Institutes* cf. W. de Greef, *The Writings of John Calvin: An Introductory Guide* (Grand Rapids: Baker Books, 1993), 195–202.

[5] J. Calvin, 'Epistle Dedicatory to Francis', in J. Calvin, *Institutes of the Christian religion: 1536 edition*, ed. F.L. Battles (London: Collins, 1986), 1–14, 1. Cf. Calvin, *OS* 1, 2. The dedicatory letter remained included in the later editions of the *Institutes*.

[6] Calvin, 'Epistle Dedicatory', in J. Calvin, *Institutes of the Christian religion: 1536 edition*, ed. F.L. Battles (London: Collins, 1986), 12. Calvin mostly uses the term 'anabaptists.' 'Catabaptist' can be translated as 'antibaptist' and was also used by Martin Bucer, Huldrych Zwingli, and Johannes Oecolampadius. For Bucer cf. the notes of Battles. Calvin, *Institutes 1536*, 243. For Zwingli and Oecolampadius cf. H. Zwingli, *Huldrych Zwinglis sämtliche Werke*, vol. VI (Leipzig: Heinsius, 1935), 21–22.

[7] Calvin, *Institutes 1536*, 210. Cf. Calvin, *OS* 1, 262. Cf. Calvin, *Institutes*, IV.20.6. In the Genevan confession of 1536 he calls the magistrates *vicaires et lieutenans de Dieu*. *OC* 9, 700. For an English translation of article 21 on the magistrates cf. Calvin, *Institutes 1536 edition*, ed. Battles, 329–330. In his Catechism of 1538 he calls them 'gods' with a reference to Ex. 22:8 and Ps. 82:1, 6. I.J. Hesselink, *Calvin's First Catechism: A Commentary: Featuring Ford Lewis Battles's Translation of the 1538 Catechism* (Louisville: Westminster John Knox Press, 1997), 38. Cf. I.J. Hesselink, 'Calvin on the nature and Limits of Political Resistance.' In: D. van Keulen and M. Brinkman, eds, *Christian Faith and Violence*, vol. 2 (Zoetermeer: Meinema, 2005), 54–74, 58.

vicars—will be called to account by God. As the Ruler of all rulers he is free to break the bloody scepters of arrogant kings and to overturn intolerable governments. "Let the princes hear and be afraid."[8] All rulers, king Francis included, must realize that God is sovereign. Next to the confession of God's supreme sovereignty, Calvin also refers to the calling of lower magistrates to restrain the licentiousness of the kings. This resistance is not merely their legal right, but also their Christian duty, because lower governors are appointed by God to protect the freedom of the people.

Later Reformed theologians have developed this position into a right of the oppressed to resist a tyrannical government, especially if they were led by the nobility.[9] Some even concluded that rebellion to tyrants was obedience to God.[10]

Although Calvin acknowledges that the civil government does have a task in religious affairs, in 1536 this task is restricted to providing the outward circumstances in which the church can flourish and in preventing blasphemy and other public religious offences. Thus he writes that the government "prevents idolatry, sacrilege against God's name, blasphemies against his truth, and other public offenses against religion from arising and spreading among the people[.]"[11] In one breath he mentions the maintenance of public peace and the protection of private property. The government takes care of the existence of a public manifestation of religion among Christians and for general *humanitas*.[12] The government positively creates and guarantees the conditions for public religion and negatively prevents and punishes public violation of what is sacred. The magistrate does not have a task regarding the doctrines or worship of the church. At least Calvin does not mention it. In general, Calvin was reticent

---

[8] Calvin, *Institutes 1536*, 225. Calvin, *OS* 1, 279. Cf. Calvin, *Institutes*, IV.20.31.

[9] One example is the anonymous Huguenot tract, titled *Vindiciae contra tyrannos* [Defences against tyrants] (1579), which answers the question if a people are allowed to resist a prince that is ruining the commonwealth to the affirmative. Still individuals should be led by a lower magistrate. On the debated authorship cf. H. Languet and G. Garnett, eds, *Vindiciae Contra Tyrannos: Or, Concerning the Legitimate Power of a Prince over the People, and of the People over a Prince* (Cambridge: Cambridge University Press, 1994), lv–lxxvi.

[10] This maxim was used by Thomas Jefferson and Benjamin Franklin, but does not originate with them. It was already used by John Bradshaw (1602–1659), the president of the parliamentary committee that sentenced Charles I of England. David W. Hall, *The Genevan Reformation and the American Founding* (Lanham: Lexington, 2003), 21, n. 1.

[11] Calvin, *Institutes 1536*, 208. Calvin, *OS* 1, 260. Cf. Calvin, *Institutes*, IV.20.3.

[12] Calvin, *Institutes 1536*, 208. Calvin, *OS* 1, 260. Cf. Calvin *Institutes*, IV.20.3. For Calvin the classical notion of *humanitas* is constitutional for the political order. J. van Eck, *God, mens, medemens: Humanitas in de theologie van Calvijn* [God, human being and fellow human being: Humanity in Calvin's theology] (Franeker: Van Wijnen, 1992), 210–211.

regarding the active role of the government in church affairs as his rejection of civil influence on ecclesiastical excommunication shows.[13]

The idea of an active role of the government in the promotion of the true religion is also absent from other early writings of Calvin, such as the *Confession de la Foy* of 1536, where he only says that the magistrates serve God and pursue a Christian calling.[14] Calvin's Catechism of 1538 is content to say that magistrates ought to keep the public form of religion uncorrupted.[15] In the commentary on Romans (1540) Calvin concludes from the fact that the government is Gods servant (*minister*) that magistrates should take care for the public interest in stead of their own. Calvin is critical of absolutism; because magistrates are God's deputies, they are debtors to their people. At this stage Calvin is remarkably silent on the magistrate's calling regarding the defense of religion.[16]

The Later Discussion with the Anabaptists

A shift in emphasis appears from a comparison of the first and the final editions of the *Institutes*. In 1536 Calvin writes that "civil government has as its appointed end, so long as we live among men, to adjust our life to the society of men, to form our social behavior to civil righteousness, to reconcile us with one another, and to promote general peace and tranquility."[17] In 1559 he inserts some religious duties before the social duties of the civil government, stating that "civil government has as its appointed end, so long as we live among men, to cherish and protect the outward worship of God, to defend sound doctrine of piety and the position of the church".[18]

This shift is not exceptional. On the contrary, all the explicit references to a positive task for civil authorities originate from the final Latin edition. Whereas Calvin, in turning to the office of the magistrates, first restricted

---

[13] The initial draft of the *Ecclesiastical Ordinances* defended the church's freedom in its own sphere. W.G. Naphy, 'Geneva II' in H.J. Selderhuis ed., *The Calvin Handbook* (Grand Rapids: Eerdmans, 2009), 44–56, 44.

[14] Calvin, *OS* 9, 700. cf. Calvin, *Institutes 1536*, 329–330.

[15] Hesselink, *Calvin's First Catechism*, 38.

[16] The commentary on Romans was one of the first published. In later publications, however, Calvin also does not mention Romans 13 to defend the particular religious tasks of the civil government. Of course an appeal to Romans would be difficult, because Paul's remarks refer to a heathen in stead of a Christian government. *CO* 49, 251.

[17] Calvin, *Institutes 1536*, 208. Calvin, *OS* 1, 259. Cf. Calvin, *Institutes* IV.20.2.

[18] Calvin, *Institutes 1536*, 208. Calvin, *OS* 1, 259. Cf. Calvin, *Institutes* IV.20.2.

it to the second table of the law; to doing justice, delivering the oppressed from the hand of the oppressor, and protecting those who are weak in society, in 1559, Calvin inserts an extensive paragraph in which he states that the office of the magistrates, extends to both tables of the Law. This can even be learned from the secular writers—Calvin possibly has Plato or Cicero in mind—who begin their treatment of the subject with the task of the civil government regarding religion and divine worship.[19]

Calvin expressly criticizes those who neglect the first table, the concern for God, and give attention only to human justice. "As if God appointed rulers in his name to decide earthly controversies but overlooked what was of far greater importance—that he himself should be purely worshiped according to the prescription of his law."[20] After this insertion, he continues with the social tasks of civil government, introducing them by the opening statement: "as far as the second table is concerned."[21]

Scripture, according to Calvin, condemns anarchy. In the French translation of the *Institutes* he explains that anarchists are "those who would have people live pell-mell like rats in straw."[22] Some turbulent people want to overthrow every order, in Calvin's opinion, because they want all vindicators of violated piety to be removed from their midst. Apparently, Calvin is writing from a polemical perspective. His opponents are the Anabaptists, who accept the government as an ordinance of God, but deny that Christians should be involved in it. The growing emphasis on the positive role of Christian magistrates for the church is caused by the developing discussion with these representatives of the Radical Reformation.

This is clear from a comparison of the *Brief Instruction for Arming All the Good Faithful against the Errors of the Common Sect of the Anabaptists* (1544) with the final edition of the *Institutes*. In one of the additions Calvin refers to three biblical passages to refute the opinion of those who deny that the civil government has a religious task and state that it is incompatible with the perfection of Christ. As the opening quotation of this paper shows, according to Calvin David urges kings and rulers to kiss the Son of

---

[19] Calvin, *Institutes* IV.20.9. For Cicero see John Calvin, *Institutes of the Christian Religion*, ed. J.T. McNeill, trans. F.L. Battles (Philadelphia: The Westminster Press, 1967), 1495. n. 23. Cf. Calvin, *OS* 5, 480. In one of his commentaries he refers to Plato, who laying down the constitution of a republic, calls the fear of God the preface to all laws. Calvin, Commentary on Deut. 18:19. *CO* 24, 354.

[20] Calvin, *Institutes* IV.20.9.

[21] Calvin, *Institutes* IV.20.9.

[22] Calvin, *Institutes* IV.20.5, Calvin, *Institutes*, ed. McNeill, 1490, n. 15. Cf. *CO* 5, 475.

God (Ps. 2:12). That means that they should submit to Christ. Isaiah fore-
tells that kings shall be foster fathers of the church, and queens its nurses
(Is. 49:23). The third and, according to Calvin, most notable reference is
to one of the epistles of Paul, where he tells Timothy to pray for kings
(1 Tim. 2:2). Paul adds as a reason that Christians may lead a peaceful life
under them with all godliness and honesty. "By these words he entrusts
the condition of the church to their protection and care."[23]

In his *Brief Instruction against the Anabaptists* Calvin replies to one of
the early Anabaptist documents, the *Brotherly Union*, or the *Schleitheim
Confession*, composed by Michael Sattler in 1525.[24] In 1544 Calvin wrote a
reaction, because at that time a French translation of the document circu-
lated in Geneva. Some of the arguments against the Anabaptist statement
that the sword is an ordering of God outside the perfection of Christ, first
found in Calvin's *Brief Instruction*, were copied in the *Institutes*. All three
biblical references appear in that context.

David does not command the kings to throw down their scepters, but
to kiss the Son. Isaiah prophesies that the kings will become the foster
fathers of the Christian church and that queens will nurse it with their
breasts. Calvin says: "I beg of you, how do you reconcile the fact that kings
will be protectors of the Christian church if their vocation is inconsistent
with Christianity?"[25] Regarding 1 Tim. 2:2, he says that "If God wills to
lead princes to the knowledge of truth, by what authority do Anabaptists
repulse them?"[26]

The polemical context of Calvin's ideas prompts the question regarding his exegesis of the three texts he mentions. To answer this question
we will turn to Calvin's commentaries to see if we can find hints to the
development of his thought and to the exegesis his concept.

Calvin's Commentaries on Role of the Government

First in chronological order is the commentary on the Pastoral Epistles
(1548). In 1 Tim. 2:2 Paul exhorts his pupil to pray for everyone, but espe-

---

[23] Calvin, *Institutes* IV.20.5.
[24] For the background of the tract cf. M. van Veen, 'Introduction' in: John Calvin, *Brieve
Instruction pour armer tous bons fideles contre les erreurs de la secte commune des anabap-
tistes*, ed. M. van Veen (Genève: Librairie Droz, 2007), 11–32. For the English translation
cf. J. Calvin, *Treatises Against the Anabaptists and Against the Libertines*, ed. B.W. Farley
(Grand Rapids: Baker Book House, 1982), 13.
[25] *CO* 7, 82. Cf. Calvin, *Treatises Against the Anabaptists*, 79.
[26] *CO* 7, 84. Cf. Calvin, *Treatises Against the Anabaptists*, 82.

cially for those who are in authority. According to Calvin, Paul mentions them because they might be hated by Christians, seeing that all the magistrates at that time were sworn enemies of Christ and spent all their power and wealth fighting against his kingdom.

Christians might conclude that it is better not to pray for them. Paul, however, finds prayer necessary in order that Christians may live in peace. According to Calvin, this prayer also implies that it is the task of the magistrates to take care for godliness. Calvin distinguishes three advantages of a well ordered government. The first is a quiet life; rulers bear the sword to keep the peace. The second advantage "is the preservation of *godliness*, that is, when magistrates undertake to promote religion, to maintain the worship of God and to require reverence for sacred things."[27] The third is the care for public decency; the government should prevent the people from filthiness and promote moderation.

The prayer implies the possibility of the conversion of the kings and therefore "we should ask God to make wicked rulers good. We must always hold to the principle that magistrates are appointed by God for the protection of religion and of the public peace and decency."[28] In other words, the prayer for the conversion of ungodly magistrates means that it is their task to promote godliness.

Calvin connects the following verses—which express that God wants all to be saved and come to knowledge of the truth—to the exhortation to pray for kings to harmonize the general statement on salvation with predestination. Paul is not speaking of all individual people, but of all kinds of people, even kings. According to Calvin, the apostle means that no one is excluded and that God wishes the gospel to be proclaimed to all: God invites all unto salvation, including princes and foreign nations. In his commentary Calvin also refers to Psalm 2 that says that the nations will be given to the Messiah for an inheritance and the ends of the earth for a possession.

"Paul's intention was to show that we should consider not what kind of men princes are, but rather what God willed them to be."[29] Christians should realize that God may extend his grace to them also. "He takes for

---

[27] Calvin, Commentary on 1 Tim. 2:2. *CO* 52, 267. The translation is from J. Calvin, *The Second Epistle of Paul the Apostle to the Corinthians and the Epistles to Timothy, Titus and Philemon*, D.W. Torrance and T.F. Torrance ed. (Grand Rapids: Eerdmans, 1996), 207.

[28] Calvin, Commentary on 1 Tim. 2:2. *CO* 52, 267. Cf. Calvin, *2 Corinthians, Timothy, Titus and Philemon*, 207.

[29] Calvin, Commentary on 1 Tim. 2:2. *CO* 52, 269. Cf. Calvin, *2 Corinthians, Timothy, Titus and Philemon*, 209.

granted that God will do so among all ranks and all nations, for so it has been foretold by the prophets."[30] Thus Calvin connects the Paulinic exhortation with Old Testament prophecies regarding the worldwide extension of the Messianic kingdom.

From the prayer that Christians may lead a peaceful life under the government Calvin concludes that Paul intends a prayer for the conversion of the governors. Converted magistrates will not only take care for honesty, but also for godliness. According to Calvin, it is not enough if magistrates restrain injustice, give each his own, and maintain peace, "if they are not also zealous to promote religion and regulate morals by wholesome discipline. The exhortation of David that they should 'kiss the Son' (Ps. 2.12), and Isaiah's word that they should be nursing fathers to the Church are very relevant. Thus they have no cause to congratulate themselves, if they neglect to give their assistance in maintaining the worship of God."[31] Apparently, the three biblical references, so foundational for Calvin's view of the task of the government in the 1559 edition of the *Institutes*, are in his mind already in 1548.

The commentary on Isaiah was published in 1551. Calvin interprets Is. 49:23 as a prophecy of the future state of the church. Commenting on the verse in question, Calvin offers a lengthy discussion of the role of rulers in the New Testament church. Isaiah compares the kings to hirelings and queens to nurses, because they shall supply what is necessary to nourish the posterity of the church. They shall acknowledge Christ as supreme king and honor, obey, and worship him. "This happened when God revealed himself by the gospel to the whole world. Mighty kings and princes not only submitted to the yoke of Christ, but also conferred their means to establish and take care of the church of Christ, as her patrons and guardians."[32] Apparently, Calvin sees the prophecy fulfilled in the *corpus christianum*.

---

[30] Calvin, Commentary on 1 Tim. 2:2. *CO* 52, 269. Cf. Calvin, *2 Corinthians, Timothy, Titus and Philemon*, 209.

[31] Calvin, Commentary on 1 Tim. 2:2. *CO* 52, 267. Cf. Calvin, *2 Corinthians, Timothy, Titus and Philemon*, 207.

[32] Calvin, Commentary on Is. 49:23. *CO* 37, 210. The translation is mine. Cf. J. Calvin, *Calvin's Commentaries*, [reprint] (Grand Rapids: Baker Books, 1999), vol. 8b, 39–40. On the influence of Calvin in the spread of this biblical image in England cf. J.H. Hutson, *Forgotten Features of the Founding: The Recovery of Religious Themes in the Early American Republic* (Lanham: Lexington Books, 2003), 45–72.

Over against the traditional interpretation of financial support of priests and monks by the royalty, Calvin insists on a spiritual interpretation, rejecting an interpretation that the kings should pamper priests and monks financially, fattening them like pigs. The financial application was not only present in medieval theology, but was also followed by some Protestants. The Wittenberg Articles (1536), written as a draft confession for the English delegates of Henry VIII, say that it is the responsibility of kings to provide for the expenses of pastors, teachers and students. That is why Isaiah calls kings nursing fathers, and queens nursing mothers.[33]

According to Calvin, the text refers to the removal of superstitions and idolatry, to the promotion of the kingdom of Christ and the maintenance of pure doctrine. This, of course, does not annul the fact that the kings should supply the pastors and ministers of the Word with all they need, install schools, take care for the financial needs of teachers and students, build houses for the poor and hospitals, and protect and defend the church.[34] Although the situation was still far from ideal, Calvin nonetheless encourages his readers to hope for the restoration of the church and the conversion of kings. Then they will be nursing-fathers and protectors of the believers and defenders of the doctrine of the Word. All people should promote the glory of God, "but as for kings, the greater power they have, the more diligently they should devote themselves to it and strive after it. For this reason David expressly mentions them, exhorting them to be wise, serve the Lord, and kiss the Son."[35]

The repeated reference to Psalm 2 makes one curious about Calvin's commentary on the Psalms (1557). In general Calvin was rather careful and reticent about applying prophecies from the Old Testament immediately to Christ.[36] In his humanist influenced approach of hermeneutics he interpreted the sacred texts from their original contexts and according to the intention of the human author. In that light, his far-reaching

---

[33] G.L. Bray, *Documents of the English Reformation* (Minneapolis: Fortress Press, 1994), 152–153.

[34] Calvin, Commentary on Is. 49:23. *CO* 37, 211.

[35] Calvin, Commentary on Is. 49:23. *CO* 37, 210. In the commentary on Is. 60:16, Calvin makes the same point. The prophet says that Israel will suck the breasts of kings and Calvin comments that the kings are reminded of their duty to be the servants of the church, lest God call them to account. Again he refers to Psalm 2. Calvin, commentary on Is. 60:16. *CO* 37, 365. Cf. Calvin, *Calvin's Commentaries*, vol. 8b, 293.

[36] The Christological interpretation of the Old Testament should not ignore the original historical context. P. Opitz, 'Scripture,' in: *Calvin Handbook*, 235–244, 244.

interpretation of the fulfillment of Old Testament prophecies in the extension of the kingdom of Christ is remarkable.

In Calvin's exposition of Psalm 2 a tension appears between this cautious humanistic approach and the Messianic application of the Psalm.
On the one hand it is David who boasts that his kingdom would be upheld
by the power of God and be extended to the ends of the earth. On the
other hand, the Psalm must be interpreted typologically, because it contains a prophecy concerning the future kingdom of Christ.

As this is the first Messianic Psalm, Calvin makes a few hermeneutical
remarks on the Messianic reading of the Psalms. According to his interpretation, David was aware of the fact that his kingdom was merely a shadow
and that he was a type of the coming Redeemer. Moreover David's temporal kingdom was a token to God's ancient people of the eternal kingdom
of Christ. Therefore, what David says of himself is not improperly, or even
allegorically, applied to Christ.[37] The Messianic meaning is the true meaning of the text. Still Calvin is careful not to exceed the limits of grammati-
cal interpretation. The New Testament references to this Psalm (Acts 4:24
and Hebr. 1:5) sustain a Christological exegesis, but the text 'This day
I have begotten you' should not be interpreted as a reference to the eternal Trinitarian generation of the Son.[38]

For the view on the task of the government, Calvin's comments on the
closing verses of the Psalm seem most important. David addresses kings
and rulers, who naturally are too proud to learn and when David tells
them to be wise, he condemns their confidence in their own wisdom. The
princes of the world are fools until they become humble scholars at the
feet of Christ. Turning to the exhortation to kiss the Son, Calvin comments
that "the legitimate proof of our obedience and piety for God is respect-
fully to embrace his Son, whom he has appointed king over us."[39] But,
remarkably, he does not refer to the task of kings and other magistrates
regarding the promotion of true religion.

The lack of the expected application leads to the question of the status
of the repeated reference to Psalm 2 in other places. Perhaps his careful
exegesis of the text prevented Calvin from drawing too farfetched applica-
tions. At any rate, the references also occur in Calvin's writings after 1557,
the year in which he published his commentary.

---

[37] Calvin, Commentary on Ps. 2:1–3. *CO* 31, 43.
[38] Calvin, Commentary on Ps. 2:7. *CO* 31, 46–47.
[39] The translation is mine. Calvin, Commentary on Ps. 2:10. *CO* 31, 50. Cf. J. Calvin, *Calvin's Commentaries*, vol. 4b, 24.

One more example from Calvin's commentaries will suffice to illustrate this. In 1563 he published his *Harmony on the Law*. After the historical part, dealing with the exodus, Calvin divides the material into four parts, the second of which is a discussion of the Ten Commandments and all the related texts. After discussing several 'ceremonial supplements' to the first commandment, Calvin turns to the 'judicial supplements.' The first thing that Calvin discusses under the heading of the first commandment is the rule that false prophecy should be extinguished (Deut. 18:19 and 13:5).

God does not need the assistance of the worldly sword for the defense of true religion, but still it is his will to use it as an instrument.[40] Some reject the sword as a means of promoting the kingdom of God, but, says Calvin, if theft, fornication, and drunkenness do not go unpunished, a judge should also not hesitate when the worship of God and true religion are violated. In a rhetorical style, Calvin asks if, when adulterers and those who poison others are punished, despisers of God who adulterate the doctrines of salvation and poison souls to eternal destruction should go unpunished.[41]

One objection might be that this law does not apply to the spiritual kingdom of Christ. Indeed, Christ said that his kingdom is not of this world. But then Calvin makes a remarkable distinction between the beginning period of Christianity and its further development.

> True, it was the will of Christ that his gospel would be preached by his disciples in opposition to the power of the whole world and he sent them like sheep among wolves, armed with the Word alone. But he did not bind himself to an eternal law that he would never subject kings unto himself, tame their violence and make them from cruel persecutors into patrons and guardians of his church.[42]

To prove this from Scripture, Calvin refers to the same three texts as in the 1559-edition of the *Institutes*. Magistrates were first tyrants against the church, because it was not yet their time to kiss the Son of God and become the nursing fathers of the Church. The prophecy of Isaiah 49:6–23 certainly refers to the coming of Christ. When Paul exhorted to pray for

---

[40] Calvin, Commentary on Deut. 13:5. *CO* 24, 356.

[41] Calvin, Commentary on Deut. 13:5. *CO* 24, 356. The discussion with Sebastian Castellio on the execution of Michael Servetus also influenced the stronger emphasis on the active role of the government in the punishment of heresy. In opposition to Castellio and other humanists, Calvin defended the duty of the government to exterminate heresy. M.G.K. van Veen, 'Calvin and His Opponents,' in *Calvin Handbook*, 156–164, 162.

[42] Calvin, Commentary on Deut. 13:5. *CO* 24, 356. Cf. J. Calvin, *Calvin's Commentaries*, vol. 2b, 77.

kings and other worldly rulers, he explained that under them we may lead a quiet and peaceful life in godliness and honesty (1 Tim. 2:2). Christ is meek and he wants us to imitate him, but pious rulers should take care for the safety of the church by their defense of godliness.

Conclusions

The development of Calvin's thought on this point is influenced by the debate with the Anabaptists. Calvin's *Institutio* of 1536 had an apologetic character. He distances himself from the Anabaptist revolt in Münster and emphasizes the calling of the government to represent God and of the subjects to accept the given order, even if the government is ungodly and oppressive. In the final edition of the *Institutes* Calvin is much more outspoken on the duties of the civil government to promote the causes of true religion. He underlines his position with a reference to three biblical texts: Ps. 2:12, Is. 49:23, and 1 Tim. 2:2, texts that already occur in the polemical *Brief Instruction against the Anabaptists* (1544) and in the commentary on the Pastoral Epistles (1548).

The commentaries on these texts reveal that Calvin sees the Messianic prophecies (Psalm 2 and Isaiah 49) fulfilled in the later development of Christianity, in the post-Constantinian *corpus christianum*. It is remarkable that the commentary on the exhortation to kiss the Son in Psalm 2 is silent on the task of kings and other magistrates regarding the promotion of true religion. It is also remarkable that Calvin does not refer to Romans 13 to defend a Christian task for the government.

Most likely the ongoing confrontation with the Anabaptists, next to the defense of the right of Geneva to execute Michael Servetus, led Calvin to a stronger emphasis on the active role of the government in the promotion of Christianity.

CHAPTER SIX

DARWIN'S AMBIGUOUS GIFT TO REFORMED THEOLOGY: THE PROBLEM OF NATURAL SUFFERING AND CALVIN'S MEDITATION ON THE FUTURE LIFE[1]

Ernst M. Conradie

The year 2009 marks the birth of John Calvin (1509) as well as that of Charles Darwin (1809). It also marks the 450th anniversary publication of the 1559 edition of Calvin's *Institutes of the Christian religion* and the 150th anniversary of the publication of Darwin's *On the origins of species through natural selection* (1859). In this contribution I will invite a conversation between Calvin and Darwin on the theme of "natural suffering".

In the next section I will briefly identify a number of challenges raised by evolutionary theory in order to focus on one of these, namely the problem of natural suffering. This raises the theodicy problem and the nature of God's relationship with the world afresh. Although the problem of suffering is thus addressed, in my view this falls outside the soteriological tension between sin and redemption that is so typical of Reformed theology. Instead, human sin is regarded as a further (and more or less natural) aggravation of the suffering already embedded in God's creation—which is often regarded as the primary problem.

On this basis I will explore Calvin's *Institutes* in search of resources within the Reformed tradition to respond to such contemporary discourse. How does Calvin understand natural suffering, if at all? How, then, should we assess the contemporary tendency to focus on such natural suffering as the primary problem that has to be addressed and the preoccupation with the theodicy problem instead of the Christian message of redemption from sin? I will explore such questions with specific reference to Calvin's famous meditation on the future life.

[1] This essay is based upon work supported by the National Research Foundation. Any opinion, findings and conclusions or recommendations expressed in this material are those of the author and therefore the NRF does not accept any liability in regard hereto.

Darwin's Gift to Reformed Theology: A Blessing in Disguise or a
Poisoned Chalice?

It is not self-evident what the precise nature of the challenge is that evolutionary biology (as distinct form evolutionism as a comprehensive metaphysics) poses to Christian theology. This has been understood in diverging ways over the last 150 years.

The challenge may be understood in terms of biblical hermeneutics, namely that biblical literalism could no longer be maintained. Although the Priestly creation narrative allows for the emergence of various species in history, Darwin's account is often regarded as a threat to the "truth" of the biblical version. The differences between these accounts, especially in terms of the timeframe involved, were emphasized on the basis of the insights emerging from the geological, biological and later the astrophysical sciences regarding the billions of years of evolutionary history. Such challenges to biblical literalism touch on more complex questions around theological affirmations of the goodness of creation (also "in the beginning"), the fall of humanity, the notion of paradise, and the deepest causes of suffering and death. Each of these could be regarded as mythical renderings of theological judgements. However, the question would remain whether such theological judgements are unrelated to the history of life as reconstructed in evolutionary biology.

Once such insights became widely acknowledged, the debate shifted to the understanding of human descent and the similarities and differences between the human and other species. This again posed theological problems related to creation theology, namely on the distinctiveness of the human species, the notion of the image of God and the significance of the incarnation of Jesus Christ as a human being (and not a horse). Although questions on human distinctiveness continue to attract theological attention,[2] the evolution of human beings from other species is by now widely accepted, also in Reformed circles.

A third debate subsequently emerged on the implications of the process of natural selection itself. If life on earth emerged through randomness instead of intelligent design, what implications does this have for faith in a Creator God? Is God on the side of order or of chaos, design or random-

---

[2] See Ernst M. Conradie, *An ecological Christian Anthropology: At Home on Earth?* (Aldershot: Ashgate, 2005) and J. Wentzel van Huyssteen, *Alone in the World?* (Grand Rapids: Eerdmans, 2006).

ness, purpose or chance?[3] Should God's action in the world be understood as a way of influencing the gaps that remain in nature (e.g. at the level of quantum mechanics) or does God act through non-interference, through waiting, by allowing for the creative potential of randomness?[4] Although the notion of a cosmic blueprint and also of intelligent design is discredited by many on theological grounds, popular debate on intelligent design is of course still widespread and emotionally charged. If such a notion of design is discredited, could one still speak of a sense of purpose? Can one detect directionality in the history of evolution, for example towards diversification and complexification (consciousness)? How should that be interpreted theologically? Does this imply progress?

A fourth debate emerged on the implications of the mechanism of natural selection through the notion of "the survival of the fittest". This led to considerable discourse on social Darwinism, noting its destructive effect in Nazi Germany and apartheid South Africa. Does this imply that God is on the side of the strong and that God regards the weak as evolutionary failures? What about the role of cooperation within and interdependence between species and the mutually beneficial functioning of the food chain? Is the "the survival of the fittest" an accurate description of evolutionary drivers or should one instead focus on the sustainability of apt ecosystems? Although social Darwinism is widely discredited, the underlying questions around natural suffering have often been glossed over. I will return to that in the discussion below.

A fifth debate is currently taking place on the implications of the concept of evolution for the phenomenon of religion. Is religion itself a function of human adaptation in order to survive in a hostile world? Did religion

---

[3] It should be noted in passing that there would be little doubt as to how Calvin would answer this question. He commented: "What then? you will ask. Does nothing happen by chance, nothing by contingency? I reply: Basil the Great has truly said that 'fortune' and 'chance' are pagan terms, with whose significance the minds of the godly ought not to be occupied. For if every success is God's blessing, and calamity and adversity his curse, no place now remains in human affairs for fortune or chance" (Calvin, *Institutes*, I.16.6, see also 8). Calvin consistently emphasized God's sovereignty and rejected any notion of chance or fate as determinative of events in history. He welcomed almost any form of order—in the cosmos, amidst non-human nature and in human history—as signs of God's work. Clearly, the 16th century was one where the threats of chaos were evident.

For this essay I used the English translation by Ford Lewis Battles in John T. McNeil (ed.), *Calvin: Institutes of the Christian Religion (2 volumes)* (Louisville: Westminster John Knox Press, 1960). All quotations are from this edition. For cross-referencing only the sections are provided and then in parenthesis in the text.

[4] See Denis Edwards, *The God of Evolution: A Trinitarian Theology* (New York: Paulist Press, 1999), 53–54.

offer some human communities an adaptive advantage?[5] Is the "decline" of religion in Western Europe to be understood along such lines, namely as something that is no longer needed? Is the emergence of religion to be explained genetically? Is there a religious gene or only a "selfish gene"?

Finally, it is important to see that discourse on evolution in the context of Christian theology has shifted over the last decade or so to the problem of "natural suffering". It may be helpful to explore this challenge in more detail.

In his work *God after Darwin: A theology of evolution* (2000), the American process theologian John Haught entitles one chapter "Darwin's gift to theology". He argues that theological reflection on evolution should be less concerned with intelligent design and more with the theodicy problem. This is now reframed in terms of the question how a powerful and compassionate God could allow all the agony, aimless wandering and waste that scientific accounts of evolution highlight. The enormity of suffering in non-human nature was already troubling for Darwin himself. Haught speaks of Darwin's gift to theology because he regards this as an opportunity for discourse on science and theology to return to a theology of the cross. He says: "In the symbol of the cross, Christian belief discovers a God who participates fully in the world's struggle and pain. The cruciform visage of nature reflected in Darwinian science invites us to depart, perhaps more decisively than ever before, from all notions of a deity untouched by the world's suffering."[6] If Darwin's idea is "dangerous" for theology (as Daniel Dennett suggests), it is only dangerous for those shallow theologies of order that ignore God's compassion and solidarity in suffering. On this basis Haught explores a kenotic understanding of God's presence in suffering. A God of love redeems the world primarily through solidarity in suffering.[7]

It is not necessary here to discuss Haught's own position in full. I do note in passing that theological interest in the suffering associated with evolutionary history is particularly strong in Catholic and Anglican circles—as

---

[5] See Cornel W. du Toit (ed.), *The Evolutionary Roots of Religion: Cultivate, Mutate or Eliminate?* (Pretoria: Unisa Press, 2009).

[6] John Haught, *God after Darwin: A Theology of Evolution* (Boulder: Westview Press, 2000), 46.

[7] This interest in the theme of kenosis is echoed in many recent publications. See especially John Polkinghorne (ed.), *The Work of Love: Creation as Kenosis* (Grand Rapids: Eerdmans, 2001). All too often, kenosis is regarded as a principle underlying the "moral nature of the universe" (George Ellis); more than as God's contingent response to human sin in history.

the work of (and on) Teilhard de Chardin, Celia Deane-Drummond, Denis Edwards, John Haught, Arthur Peacocke and Christopher Southgate, amongst others, amply illustrate. Such views have been widely affirmed in discourse on science and religion and also in Protestant circles—as the writings of Jürgen Moltmann, Ted Peters and Bram van de Beek also illustrate.

It should also be noted that such discourse on natural suffering is typically discussed under the theological rubric of the theodicy problem (sometimes the doctrine of providence) and not in terms of soteriological discourse. These two (legitimate) rubrics should not be equated with one another. The Christian gospel of redemption for the whole earth from the destructive impact of human sin has an altogether different focus compared to discourse on the justification of God with regard to the inadequacies of the created order. Here protest theodicies (e.g. in the work of Dorothy Sölle and Jürgen Moltmann) occupy some middle ground.

It is necessary, though, to explore the question that is at stake in more depth. In such discourse on evolution it is acknowledged that suffering is deeply embedded in all forms of life and that such suffering clearly cannot be understood merely as the result of sin. This poses some very serious theological challenges. Why did a loving Creator bring a world into existence where such suffering is biologically necessary? How dare God declare creation to be good? Is nature indeed evil? Does nature have to be redeemed, irrespective of the impact of human sin? What could then be meant by the "redemption of nature?" I note in passing that this set of problems is also of importance for soteriological discourse from an ecological perspective:[8] What on earth could it mean that the earth is to be "saved" (the salvation *of* the earth and not of humans *from* the earth)?

It is indeed important to acknowledge that suffering is also experienced by non-human sentient animals irrespective of human involvement. There is a rapidly expanding literature on the cosmological and biological roots of such natural suffering, the related problem of "natural evil" (as distinct from social or moral evil) and the need for the "redemption" of nature,

---

[8] For an overview of discourse in Christian ecotheology on the theme of salvation, see my essay "The Salvation of the Earth from Anthropogenic Destruction: In Search of appropriate Soteriological Concepts in an Age of Ecological Destruction", *Worldviews: Global Religions, Culture, Ecology* 14: 2–3 (2010), 111–140. This essay was written as part of Working Group 4 of the Christian Faith and the Earth project on "How is the Earth to be saved? Christian Discourse on Creation, Salvation and eschatological Fulfilment."

not only from the impact of humans but from such natural suffering and natural evil.[9]

Again, what precisely is it that nature needs to be redeemed from? Is nature to be redeemed from anthropogenic destruction only (which may be re-described in terms of the legacy of human sin) or do we as human beings have to be redeemed from the biological roots of our existence since that necessarily entails vulnerability, pain, suffering, aging, degeneration and the decay of possibilities? How does the emergence of human sin relate to the biological rootedness of our existence? Can it be regarded as the almost inevitable result of an anxiety over human finitude?

In the rest of this contribution I will investigate the ambiguities of Darwin's gift specifically to reformed theology. I will argue that the shift to a soteriological line of inquiry may be welcomed from within reformed circles. It may also provide an opportunity to investigate the relatedness of creation and redemption afresh. In this sense it is indeed a welcome gift.

However, this may also prove to be a poisoned gift (Afrikaans: gif). How can the goodness of God's creation be affirmed on this basis? One also has to consider what role knowledge from non-theological sources play in such inquiry. What are the sources of such a kenotic view (construction) of God? Is there not a danger that the redemption of nature can redirect theological interests towards interesting intellectual inquiries but away from the primary societal and ecological problem, namely suffering induced by human sin (domination, rape, oppression, killing)? Moreover, how should reformed theology respond to the Catholic assumptions on grace elevating nature, so typically at play in such theological discourse on evolution? Indeed, in what way is nature to be redeemed? Where exactly does the problem lie that has to be addressed?

From What Does Nature Need to be Redeemed? Calvin's Parameters

In order to address this set of problems I will explore some resources in Calvin's theology. Of course, it will not be possible to do that in depth, as this will require investigating core themes such as the knowledge of God

---

[9] See, for example, Willem B. Drees (ed.), *Is nature ever evil? Religion, science and value* (London: Routledge, 2003), Cornel W. du Toit (ed.), *Can Nature be Evil and Evil Natural? A Science-and-Religion View on Suffering and Evil* (Pretoria: Unisa, 2006) and Christopher C.B. Southgate, *The Groaning of Creation: God, Evolution and the Problem of Evil* (Louisville: Westminster John Knox Press, 2008).

and the knowledge of humanity, nature as the "theatre of God's glory" and Calvin's understanding of the nature of redemption and the redemption of nature. Moreover, one would need to consider the complexities of Calvin's own writings and the wealth of secondary material. In this section I will only mention some of the broad parameters within which Calvin would probably have addressed this question. In the next section I will then work within such parameters on the basis of a close reading of Calvin's so-called "Meditation on the future life".[10]

Most commentators would agree that Calvin's *Institutes* does not constitute a neat theological system. Instead, his theology is kerygmatic, polemical and, as we would nowadays add, deeply contextual. He had a remarkable ability to maintain creative tensions between contrasting insights which eludes any secondary systematization. Like an expert juggler, he managed to keep a number of cones in the air. Which cones are relevant in order to address the above question? Let me identify a few of these broad parameters (with some reference to appropriate sections of Calvin's *Institutes*).

- Knowledge of God the Creator may be derived from contemplating the beauty and order of the universe (see I.5.1).
- God created the world with incredible wisdom and artistry, if not a Platonic sense of perfection (see I.5.2).
- Nothing that happens in the world happens outside of God's sovereign will—not even the emergence of sin. There is no other force such as "chance", "fortune" or "fate" that control our lives or our destinies alongside God (see I.16.8).
- God's creative resolve is also evident from ongoing creation (*creatio continua*) and from God's well-ordered conservation (*conservatio*) despite the corruptibility of creation (*creatura*) as the work of God's hands (see I.14.20).
- The contemplation of God's goodness in creation should lead human beings (for whom all things were made) to gratitude and trust (see I.14.22).
- However, human nature has become so corrupted that we stand condemned before God (see II.1.8, II.3.5).
- Humans proceeded spotless from God's hand and may therefore not shift the blame for sins to the Creator (see I.15.1, II.1.10, II.1.11).

---

[10] Calvin, *Institutes*, III.9.

• Although humans have thus become completely corrupted, they can
  still be distinguished from "brute beasts" on the basis of an ability to
  understand and to will (see II.2.12).

Calvin's Meditation on the Future Life

Calvin's meditation on the future life was added as a last paragraph in the
1549 edition of the *Institutes*. In the 1559 edition it is placed between his
discussion of regeneration and justification in Book III of the *Institutes*,
namely in a series of four brief chapters sometimes published separately
under the title of "The Sum of Christian Life". Here Calvin argues that we
are not our own but belong to God. His meditation on the future life has
elicited considerable interest in terms of secondary scholarship. A review
of such literature is not necessary for my purposes here. This "meditation"
(better translated as a "study" or "exercise") seems to provide the clearest indication[11] that he saw Christian hope in terms of ultimate redemption from that which is earthly, bodily and material. Here we seem to find
a message of redemption *from* the earth and not the redemption *of* the
earth. From the perspective of contemporary ecotheology Calvin is here
apparently at his weakest. It would be easy to demonstrate how Calvin
seems to exemplify all the stereotypes of a Platonic disdain for that which
is material and bodily, a dualist anthropology and an escapist eschatology.
From the perspective of contemporary discourse on science and theology
these fault lines are exacerbated by Calvin's cosmological assumptions
in which he contrasts that which is earthly with that which is heavenly.
Calvin maintains the hope for the resurrection of the body but only in
order to make our ascension into heaven possible.[12] His eschatological
(and Eucharistic) vision is governed by the relationship of the faithful to
the ascended Lord.

Let me illustrate these with a number of quotations that may well shock
the sensibilities of many 21st century readers:

> For since God knows best how much we are inclined by nature to a brutish
> love of this world, he uses the fittest means to draw us back and to shake
> off our sluggishness, lest we cleave too tenaciously to that love. There is not

---

[11] I am opting here to focus only on one chapter of the *Institutes*. It would be possible
to explore Calvin's views on the suffering embedded in God's good creation with reference
to several other themes in Calvin's oeuvre, for example his sermons on Job.

[12] Calvin, *Institutes*, IV.17.29.

one of us, indeed, who does not wish to seem throughout his life to aspire and strive after heavenly immortality. For it is a shame for us to be no better than brute beasts, whose condition would be no whit inferior to our own if there were not left to us hope of eternity after death.[13]

But it is wholly unbearable that there is not in Christian hearts any light of piety to overcome and suppress that fear [the fear of death], whatever it is, by a greater consolation. For if we deem this unstable, defective, corruptible, fleeting, wasting, rotting tabernacle of our body to be so dissolved that it is soon renewed unto a firm, perfect, incorruptible, and finally, heavenly glory, will not faith compel us ardently to seek what nature dreads?[14]

Let us, then, take hold of a sounder view, and even though the blind and stupid desire of the flesh resists, let us not hesitate to await the Lord's coming, not only with longing, but also with groaning and sighs, as the happiest thing of all. He will come to us as Redeemer, and rescuing us from this boundless abyss of all evils and miseries, he will lead us into that blessed inheritance of his life and glory.[15]

Is Calvin's theology, then, still of any use in an age of ecological destruction and anxieties over the long-term impact of climate change? How could his views contribute to an understanding of the dynamism of history?[16] One may argue, in response, that his theology can still be "sanitised", for example by bracketing his pre-Copernican cosmology,[17] his "unresolved Platonism" and Stoicism, his dualist anthropology and his strong emphasis on the immortality of the soul,[18] his "pessimist" view of the "total depravity" of the human condition, his determinist notion of providence and his escapist eschatology. However, what exactly would we then be left with?

---

[13] Calvin, *Institutes*, III.9.1.

[14] Calvin, *Institutes*, III.9.5.

[15] Calvin, *Institutes*, III.9.5.

[16] See D.E. Holwerda, "Eschatology and History: A Look at Calvin's Eschatological Vision" in Donald K. McKim (ed.), *Readings in Calvin's Theology* (Eugene: Wipf & Stock, 1998), 311–342.

[17] On Calvin's cosmology, see especially Susan E. Schreiner, "Creation and Providence" in Herman J. Selderhuis (ed.), *The Calvin Handbook* (Grand Rapids: Eerdmans, 2009), 267–275.

[18] Holwerda is probably correct that the immortality of the soul was crucial in Calvin's theology as a whole but that he also moderated the Platonic notion in this regard on the basis of the Christian doctrine of creation: "The soul is not immortal in and of itself. Immortality is a gift of God and the life of the soul is continually dependant on the grace and will of God." (Holwerda, "Eschatology and History," 315). The soul is a direct creation of God and a substance independent of the body with which the image of God is primarily associated. In a similar vein Calvin's view on the immortality of the soul is coupled with the hope for the resurrection of the body—and on this basis for the ascension of the faithful to be with Christ in heaven.

Some interpreters suggest that we should perhaps regard this meditation as a function of the imitation of Christ and of bearing one's cross
in the context of persecution.[19] Accordingly, meditation of the future life
implies contempt for the present life only to the extent that it is characterized by tribulation and the discipline of the cross.[20] Others suggest that
we should concentrate on his notion of human dominion and responsibility (equally criticized as anthropocentric if not androcentric). Or maybe
we should compare Calvin with his contemporaries in order to stress the
world-affirming dimensions that are elsewhere so evident, the Calvinist
work ethic (also criticised due the association between Calvinism and
capitalism), his involvement in social issues in all areas of society or his
sense of realism in everyday affairs. Accordingly, as Heinrich Quistorp
maintains, "The aspiration towards heavenly life cannot therefore imply
any flight from the world, but rather impels us already in this world to live
another kind of life."[21] Such a strategy may be flawed though. His seemingly more attractive emphasis that "the good things of this life are to be
enjoyed as gifts of God" (III.10) follows immediately after the meditation
on the future life (III.9) in the 1559 edition and has to be understood precisely in this light.

As a scholar standing within the Reformed tradition and deeply committed towards reforming our understanding of the content and the
significance of the Christian faith in response to ecological concerns, I
cannot take these questions lightly. In the remainder of this essay I will
submit a number of observations on Calvin's legacy in the light of Darwinian sensibilities:

a) In this meditation on future life Calvin is perhaps closer to Darwin
than anywhere else in the *Institutes* in recognising the pain embedded
in creaturely life. True, he still regards adversity in terms of the cumula-
tive impact of human sin. Indeed, such adversity may well be a function
of the judgement and punishment enacted by God. Mortality is certainly
ascribed to the "wage of sin". The bondage by sin is the primary problem
that has to be addressed. However, a closer reading of the chapter reveals

---

[19] See Holwerda, "Eschatology and History," 318, with reference to Wilhelm Niesel, *The
Theology of Calvin.* (Philadelphia: Westminster, 1956).
[20] See Cornelis P. Venema, *Accepted and Renewed in Christ: The Twofold Grace of
God and the Interpretation of Calvin's Theology* (Göttingen: Vandenhoeck & Ruprecht,
2007), 127.
[21] See Heinrich Quistorp, *Calvin's doctrine of the last things* (London: Lutterworth Press,
1955), 43.

to what extent redemption is portrayed as redemption not only from sin but from the frailty, emptiness of this earthly life, this "boundless abyss of all evils and miseries", "crammed with infinite miseries" as it is. Here the "decay" (*phthora*) of Romans 8 clearly lurks in the background. This is why, for Calvin, only our ascension, admittedly a bodily ascension, can overcome the handicaps of earthly existence. He says at the very end of this meditation: "To conclude in a word: if believers' eyes are turned to the power of the resurrection, in their hearts the cross of Christ will at last triumph over the devil, flesh, sin, and wicked men."[22] The predicament is indeed not only the devil, sin and wickedness but "flesh". If Calvin is closer to Darwin here, it should be acknowledged that this may well be on the basis of residual forms of dualism that are still evident in the *Institutes*. This charge is only partially weakened by the recognition that Calvin's message has to be understood in the context of his awareness of his own frailty, of medical predicaments in the 16th century and of the plight of refugees.

b) Calvin's references to animals, plants and other forms of life are usually understood within the context of his contemplation of nature, his luscious creation theology and his notion of human dominion. In the meditation on the future life there are several references to non-human animals as well. However, here the misery of animal life is foregrounded. Calvin's rhetoric is also to emphasize the distinctiveness of human beings in comparison with "brute beasts". He finds this not so much in the soul, human reason, understanding or will, but in the hope for immortality.

> But, someone will object, there is nothing that does not crave to endure. To be sure, I agree; and so I maintain that we must have regard for the immortality to come, where a firm condition will be ours *which nowhere appears on earth*. For Paul very well teaches that believers eagerly hasten to death not because they want to be unclothed but because they long to be more fully clothed [II Cor. 5:2–3]. *Shall the brute animals, and even inanimate creatures—even trees and stones—conscious of the emptiness of their present existence*, long for the final day of resurrection, to be released from emptiness with the children of God [Rom 8:19ff.]; and shall we, endowed with the light of understanding, and above understanding illumined with the Spirit of God, when our very being is at stake, not lift our minds beyond this *earthly decay*? (italics-EMC)[23]

---

[22] Calvin, *Institutes*, III.9.6.
[23] Calvin, *Institutes*, III.9.5.

c) Viewed on their own, these comments would, in my opinion, miss the underlying thrust of Calvin's argument in Book III of the *Institutes*. After the discussion of faith and regeneration (based on repentance and satisfaction), he explores the impact of redemption on Christian life, characterised by the imitation of Christ and self-denial. In chapters 7–10 he seeks to assess the significance of Christian life, of this present life. This has to be understood in terms of the ringing declaration of chapter 7: "We are not our own." From this follows not only self-surrender and obedience to God's will, but also the activist drive to selfless service in the world and serene courage in the face of calamity. It is precisely here that Calvin introduced the meditation of the future life. Indeed, how should this life be understood? Calvin says:

> Let the aim of believers in judging mortal life, then, be that while they understand it to be of itself nothing but misery, they may with greater eagerness and dispatch betake themselves wholly to meditate upon that eternal life to come. When it comes to a comparison with the life to come, the present life can not only be safely neglected but, compared to the former, must be utterly despised and loathed. For, if heaven is our homeland, what else is the earth but our place of exile? If departure from the world is entry into life, what else is the world but a sepulcher? And what else is it for us to remain in life but to be immersed in death? If to be freed from the body is to be released into perfect freedom, what else is the body but a prison?[24]

My sense is that here Calvin is pre-empting insights that were developed more recently by Wolfhart Pannenberg.[25] His argument is that anything in life can only be interpreted within a larger frame of reference. But how could one understand the significance of life itself? Pannenberg suggests that it is only possible in terms of an understanding of "the whole". However, that whole would include the future and is therefore not yet there. For Pannenberg, as for Calvin, one may discern now already, on the basis of the resurrection of Jesus Christ, where the history of the universe is pointing towards. One can therefore only truly understand the significance of this life in terms of (constructions of) that which transcends it, namely the life to come. Likewise, one may understand the earth in terms of "heaven" and this world in terms of that which transcends the

---

[24] Calvin, *Institutes*, III.9.4.
[25] See, especially, his *Anthropology in Theological Perspective* (Edinburgh: T & T Clark, 1985).

world, namely God.[26] For Calvin, of course, this is not a merely cognitive or hermeneutic insight but the sum of all piety. A failure to fathom this hope would have to come to terms with the vanity, the transitoriness of this earthly life. This can only lead to despair.

However, there is more at stake. As Holwerda argues, the reference to the present life has to be understood not merely in a context of suffering but of the church under the cross and the persecution of Protestants in the 16th century.[27] It is because this life is nothing but struggle that meditation on the future life may strengthen one's resolve. When faced with imminent death on the stake, a trust in God's faithfulness may be one's only hope. Calvin is thus not merely interested in the cognitive problem of understanding the significance of this life, but with the pastoral problem of responding to the plight of persecuted refugees.

One may also wish to explore the impact of such hope for the future on this life. From the meditation on the future life it is evident that the vision for the future unleashes a dynamic of Christian action and obedience in this world. Is this a proleptic eschatology in the making where we are pulled towards God's future (Pannenberg)? This question may be explored further, but it is at least clear that for Calvin such a vision is not merely significant for the sake of struggles in this world. It is because this life is "nothing but misery" that Calvin turns his eyes towards the future life.

d) A vision of eternal life leads us towards a right estimate of the present life. Actually, Calvin has it the other way round: A right estimate of the present life—present life which is transient and unsatisfying—leads us to meditate on the life to come. For Calvin, the focus is not on the instrumental value of Christian hope to transform this life, but on the right longing for eternal life.[28] Nevertheless, he has much to say about the significance of Christian hope for this life.

---

[26] This is also the gist of the argument in my book *Waar op dees Aarde vind Mens God? Op Soek na 'n Aardse Spiritualiteit* [Where on earth can one find God? In search of an earthly spirituality] (Wellington: Lux Verbi.Bm, 2006). An earthly *spirituality* is born from the recognition that an appreciation for God's transcendence is necessary in order to grasp the meaning of that which is material, bodily and earthly precisely since it is not self-evident.

[27] Holwerda, "Eschatology and History," 320.

[28] This point is missed by McKim who regards the meditation on the future life as a prescription to help us set priorities for life here and now. See his essay "Calvin: A theologian for an age of limits" in *Readings in Calvin's Theology*, 309–310.

Firstly, longing for eternal life would lead us to despise this life but not towards hatred. Indeed, "in comparison with the immortality to come, let us despise this life and long to renounce it, on account of bondage of sin."[29] He adds:

> If to enjoy the presence of God is the summit of happiness, is not to be without this, misery? But until we leave the world "we are away from the Lord" [II Cor. 5:6]. Therefore, if the earthly life be compared with the heavenly, it is doubtless to be at once despised and trampled under foot. Of course it is never to be hated except in so far as it holds us subject to sin; although not even hatred of that condition may ever properly be turned against life itself.[30]

Calvin's use of the word "despise" here may be contrasted with that of Thomas à Kempis' famous work *On the imitation of Christ and contempt for the world*. Whereas Thomas à Kempis recommends that the world be avoided and rejected in order to focus exclusively on that which is interior, spiritual, eternal, Calvin's view of such contempt precisely does not lead to a withdrawal from this world but to gratitude for this world.[31]

Secondly, longing for eternal life should foster gratitude for earthly life:

> But let believers accustom themselves to a contempt of the present life that engenders no hatred of it or ingratitude against God. Indeed, this life, however crammed with infinite miseries it may be, is still rightly to be counted among those blessings of God which are not to be spurned. Therefore, if we recognize in it no divine benefit, we are already guilty of grave ingratitude toward God himself. For believers especially, this ought to be a testimony of divine benevolence, wholly destined, as it is, to promote their salvation. For before he shows us openly the inheritance of eternal glory, God wills by lesser proofs to show himself to be our Father.[32]

In Chapter 10 of Book III on "How we must use the present life and its helps" Calvin explores the significance of such gratitude. He warns against mistaken moral strictures giving the impression that Christians should abstain from all things that they could do without.[33] Since no one can abide by that, this paves the way for licentious indulgence and immoderate desires (or a guilty conscience). Calvin's rhetoric here is to avoid

---

[29] Calvin, *Institutes*, III.9.4.
[30] Calvin, *Institutes*, III.9.4.
[31] Holwerda, "Eschatology and History," 321.
[32] Calvin, *Institutes*, III.9.3.
[33] Calvin cites the example of Crates the Theban who is said to have thrown all his goods into the sea. He thought that unless they were destroyed, they would destroy him (*Institutes* III.10.1).

moralism and laying down too many rules. He emphasized freedom of conscience in things that are indifferent (*adiaphora*).[34] Instead, Calvin argues, God provided not only for necessity but also for delight and good cheer.[35] The good things in life are therefore to be enjoyed as gifts from God.[36] Calvin clearly gives no licence here for contemporary hedonism or consumerism or anything remotely sounding like the prosperity gospel. These blessings should be used frugally and in moderation in order to serve in our calling dutifully. We are not to use these blessing indulgently or to seek wealth greedily.[37] He commends "abstinence, sobriety, frugality, and moderation" and abominates "excess, pride, ostentation, and vanity". He approves of "no other distribution of good things than one joined with love" and condemns "all delights that draw man's spirit away from chastity and purity, or befog his mind".[38] Calvin is here much stricter than any of us in the consumer class would contemplate, but in age of anxiety over anthropogenic climate change we would do well to invite Calvin's counsel in this regard.[39]

Thirdly, it is important to add here that Calvin describes the clue to such moderation in III.10.4 as "contempt for the present life and meditation upon heavenly immortality". In some remarkable phrases Calvin argues that such an orientation will enable us "to bear poverty peaceably and patiently" but also "to bear abundance moderately." With reference to 1 Corinthians 7:29–31 Calvin observes that such an orientation would preclude "the intemperance of gluttony in food and drink, and excessive indulgence at table, in buildings and clothing, ambition, pride, arrogance, and overfastidiousness, but also all care and inclination that either diverts

---

[34] Calvin, *Institutes*, III.19.7.

[35] Calvin, *Institutes*, III.10.2.

[36] Calvin observes: "To conclude once for all, whenever we call God the Creator of heaven and earth, let us at the same time bear in mind that the dispensation of all those things which he has made is in his own hand and power and that we are indeed his children, whom he has received into his faithful protection to nourish and educate. We are therefore to await the fullness of all good things from him alone and to trust completely that he will never leave us destitute of what we need for salvation, and to hang our hopes on none but him! We are therefore, also, to petition him for whatever we desire; and we are to recognize as a blessing from him, and thankfully to acknowledge, every benefit that falls to our share. So, invited by the great sweetness of his beneficence and goodness, let us study to love and serve him with all our heart" (*Institutes* I.14.22).

[37] See also Calvin, *Institutes* III.7.9, also III.20.44.

[38] Calvin, *Institutes*, III.10.5.

[39] See also McKim, "Calvin: A Theologian for an Age of Limits," 291–310.

or hinders you from thought of the heavenly life and zeal to cultivate the soul."[40]

Again, it would simply not do to focus on the wise counsel expressed in Chapter 10 of Book III without reference to the meditation on the future life in Chapter 9. As Heiko Oberman observes,[41] Calvin's intention is not to establish a contrast between life and death, between present and future. Instead, to reflect on God's future is a form of prayerful meditation on the hidden rule of God in order to discover how the experience of this life and the future life are embedded in God's mysterious plan. The meditation of eternal life helps to put this life into perspective, precisely because this life is not eternal, but temporal, frail, limited. It is a loan entrusted to us, but not belonging to us. It is to be affirmed, but not in itself and absolutely.

Conclusion

From the perspective of reformed theology the legacy of Darwin may be regarded as a welcome gift. It serves as a call to return to a soteriological line of inquiry when contemplating the knowledge of God in creation— whether in the form of a theology of nature or natural theology. This is crucial in order to avoid theological speculation over the evolutionary drivers of God's ongoing creation that becomes independent of the suffering experienced by humans and other forms of life. Apartheid theology may serve as a notorious example of such speculation over God's original intentions around diversity in creation. Moreover, discourse on the suffering embedded in evolution seems to undermine any deist notion of God's omnipotence and to invite a kenotic understanding of God's presence in creation. Indeed, Darwin's gift may help reformed theology to hold creation and salvation as two dimensions of God's economy together.

However, for Reformed theology to accept this gift is a risk since it may well prove to be a poisoned chalice (gif). Perhaps the primary problem is not that it undermines an affirmation of the goodness of God's creation. God's creation is said to be "good" without assuming a sense of Platonic perfection. Given its ambiguity, it is only where threats to creation's goodness are faced and overcome that it can be appreciated. Indeed, it is crucial to acknowledge the problem of natural suffering, that illness, decay,

---

[40] Calvin, *Institutes*, III.10.4.
[41] Heiko O. Oberman, *The Two Reformations: The Journey from the Last Days to the New World* (New Haven: Yale University Press, 2003), 134.

death and extinction form part of life on earth. To distinguish between different sources of suffering—anthropogenic and otherwise—may help to appreciate the specific content of the Christian gospel of redemption. Instead, in my view the danger of Darwin's gift is that it may direct theological interests towards interesting intellectual inquiries (on the possible roots of human sin in natural suffering) but away from the primary problem, namely the destructive impact of human sin (domination, rape, oppression, killing). Then even a kenotic theology can easily revert to a theology of glory instead of a theology of the cross.

From the perspective of Christian ecotheology it is crucial to focus on the anthropogenic roots of ecological threats. Species come and go as a result of natural processes, but the current loss of biodiversity is clearly anthropogenic. The earth's climate has changed continuously throughout geological history (due to variations in the sun's radiation, volcanoes, asteroids or other variables), but current Christian discourse on climate change should focus on the danger of anthropogenic climate change.

The primary problem that we are faced with is not the unmistakable inadequacies of God's otherwise good creation, but the roots of various forms of evil in human sin. To channel all one's energies to explore the rootedness of human evil in "natural evil" may easily become an elitist way of avoiding responsibility for the task of addressing anthropogenic ecological destruction—although it may be equally treacherous to adopt a romanticised view of nature and to blame all planetary suffering on the fall of humanity. Here Reformed theologians will have to draw from Calvin selectively. They can affirm with Calvin that the plight of all creatures is bound up with humanity and that humanity has dragged all other creatures into a pit of corruption. This is the primary predicament that has to be addressed, even if it now seems obvious that the mortality of creatures cannot be attributed to humankind.

These observations may help us to see that God's work of salvation cannot be understood without reference to other aspects of God's work, including creation, continuing creation, providence and eschatological re-creation. There can be little doubt that Calvin maintained a soteriological focus in the *Institutes*. Like a juggler he maintained the tensions between God the Creator and God the Redeemer in a remarkably fruitful way that could do justice to both these aspects of God's work. However, since he did not explore the nature of the relationship between creation and salvation in the *Institutes* except in terms of a few cryptic comments about the structure of the *Institutes*, he had left Reformed theologians with an enormous hermeneutical problem, namely to figure out how this relationship has to be understood. In the South African context this remains a crucial and unresolved debate. The South African followers of Kuyper, Bavinck, Noordmans, Barth, Van Ruler and Moltmann occupy quite different positions in this regard even though they each claim some continuity with Calvin's legacy. In a future contribution I hope to address this problem in more depth.

CHAPTER SEVEN

CALVIN'S CONCEPT OF PENAL SUBSTITUTION:
ACKNOWLEDGEMENT AND CHALLENGE

Jaeseung Cha

After he had attended a conference on the theme 'Theologies of the Cross,'
Steve Holems reported that all the participants were both united and certain on what they didn't believe in, namely, the traditional Reformed and
Evangelical idea of penal substitution.[1] It cannot be denied that John Calvin holds a full-fledged view of penal substitution in which Christ is punished on the cross in our place.[2] "For by dying in this manner he was not
only covered with ignominy in the sight of God, but was also accursed in
the sight of God [coram Deo maledictio]."[3] The idea that Christ is punished
in our place can be subtly distinguished from the idea that Christ takes up
our punishment. The former stresses the direct reality of the punishment
whereas the latter focuses more on a substitutionary aspect of Christ's
death as the *redemption* from punishment that lies upon humanity in
general. The indirect aspect of penal substitution can be seen in patristic
and medieval theologians.[4] In comparison with the indirect aspect found

---

[1] Steve Holems, "Can Punishment bring peace? Penal substitution revised," *Scottish
Journal of Theology* 58/1 (2005), 104.

[2] "Calvin has been represented as holding the theory of penal substitution 'in its harsh-
est form'..." Robert S. Paul, "The Atonement: Sacrifice and Penalty," in *Readings in Calvin's
Theology*, ed. Donald K. McKim (Grand Rapids: Baker, 1984), 142.

[3] Calvin, Commentary on Phil. 2:8, CO 52, 27.

[4] In Athanasius, death had been laid down by God because of the transgression (*Incarnation of the Word* 6.2, NPNF2 4.39), Christ came down because of our transgression (4.2,
NPNF2 4.38), and Christ took up the curse laid upon us (25.2, NPNF2 4.49). Augustine, after
softening the meaning of God's wrath into 'indignation [*indignatio*]' in Psalm 88:7, directly
relates it to the death of the Cross (*On the Psalms* 88.6, NPNF1 8.426). Yet, his stress falls on
the indirect aspect by viewing the anger of God as the calm fixing of righteous punishment
[*justi supplicii*] and understanding Christ's work as that of Mediator in whom believers are
absolved from the guilt of all their sins [*soluto reatu omnium peccatorum*] and might be
delivered from perpetual condemnation [*liberarentur damnatione perpetua*] (*On the Gospel
of St. John* 124.5, NPNF1 7.449–450). Paul van Buren finds the idea of compensation rather
than substitution in Thomas Aquinas. Paul van Buren, *Christ in our Place: The Substitutionary Character of Calvin's Doctrine of Reconciliation* (Grand Rapids: Eerdmans, 1957), 53, n5.
It is, however, to be noted that Aquinas embraces the seed of penal substitution: "He who
knew nothing of sin, he was made to be sin for us, that is because of the punishment of

in those theologians as a seed of penal substitutionary ideas, clearly both
indirect *and* direct aspects of penal substitution are manifested in Calvin.[5]
Moreover, this substitutionary punishment, which Christ bears, is viewed
by Calvin as appeasement of God's wrath.[6] This idea of penal substitution
creates three serious problems: for humanity, for the nature of the very
notion, and for God. It thus is to be considered that (1) human morality
can be seriously harmed by the fact that the idea of punishment propa-

---

sin [*poenam peccati*]" (*Summa Theologiae* 3a.46.4). Moreover, Aquinas further relates the
idea of substitutionary punishment to the attribute of God: "*God's severity* is thus manifested; he was unwilling to remit sin without punishment [*peccatum sine poena dimittere
noluit*]...for as man was unable to make sufficient satisfaction through any punishment
he might himself suffer..." (3a.47.3). Even so, other motifs and notions such as satisfaction,
example of virtue, and restoration of what Adam has stolen, are more frequently used than
the idea of penal substitution. When the redemption from sins is dealt with in relation to
the pain and suffering of Christ, Aquinas puts two aspects together: vicarious repentance
from love and the bearing of sins rather than substitutionary punishment: "This pain of
Christ surpassed any pain ever felt by a penitent, first because it proceeded from a greater
wisdom and love, by which the pain of contrition is increased, and second, because he
suffered for all sins at once" (3a.46.6). Furthermore, answering the question of whether
Christ's passion is violence, Aquinas moves his focus to the idea of substitutionary endur-
ance, quoting from Chrysostom: "...Christ came to overcome, not his own death—for he is
life—but that of men. Hence he did not lay his body aside by a natural death, but endured
a death inflicted upon him by men..." (3a.46.3). Thus, it can hardly be argued that the idea
of penal substitution is one of the major atonement motifs in Thomas Aquinas.
   [5] Clearly, punishment implies in Calvin that Christ bears punishment in our place:
"But the Prophet openly declares that the punishment of our sins was transferred to him"
[*poenam in eum translatam esse*] (Calvin, Commentary on Is. 53:5, *CO* 37, 258), and, in this
case, it is natural that an accent falls on substitutionary aspect rather than punishment:
The guilt that held us liable for punishment [*poenae*] has been transferred [*translatus*] to
the head of the Son of God and we must remember this substitution [*compensatio*] Calvin,
Institutes, II.16.5. Not ignoring that this indirect aspect of penal substitution is magnified in
Calvin, we also admit that Calvin includes a more direct and intensified sense of punishment: "But Peter...means that not only guilt was imputed to him, but that he also suffered
its punishment [*sed poena quoque defunctum*], that he might thus be an expiatory victim [*expiatrix victima*]" Calvin, Commentary on 1 Pet. 2:24, *CO* 55, 252. More importantly,
punishment is argued as God's wrath and curse [*ira Dei et malediction*] retaining justice:
God's wrath and curse always lie upon sinners; and, since he is a righteous Judge, he does
not allow his law to be broken without punishment [*non sinit impune legem suam violari*]
Calvin, *Institutes* II.16.1, *CO* 2, 368.
   [6] Christ took upon himself and suffered the punishment [*poenam*] that threatened all
sinners, and as intercessor, he has appeased God's wrath [*intercessore iram eius fuisse pla-
catam*] (Calvin, *Institutes* II.16.2, *CO* 2, 369). Even when he comments on the phrase 'peace
through the blood of his cross' in Colossians 1:20, Calvin does not hesitate to relate it to
the necessity of punishment and appeasement: "For it was necessary that the Son of God
should be an expiatory victim [*victinam expiatricem*], and endure the punishment of sin
[*peccati reatum sustinere*], that we might be *the righteousness of God in him*. The *blood of
the cross* therefore, means the blood of the sacrifice which was offered upon the cross for
appeasing the anger of God [*ad placcandum iram Dei*]" Calvin, Commentary on Col. 1:20,
CO 52, 88.

gates violence or the idea of substitution deteriorates the moral impetus of humanity, (2) the nature of penal substitution in its essential logic of righteousness is self-contradictory (customarily with respect to this idea of substitution in such a way that one—the Innocent—takes up the other's sins, and (3) God is violent (mostly related to the idea that God is the subject of punishment and the object of appeasement), and that Jesus is passively a victim of his Father's abuse.[7]

This article intends neither to recklessly defend Calvin's view against above-mentioned criticisms nor to be blindly sympathetic with modern sentiments of revisionism of the atonement views with emphasis upon a loving and merciful God. Instead, it will explore the core logic and arguments of penal substitution and make three points of suggestions. First, this paper will deal with the scope of the penal substitutionary perspective in light of the hermeneutical difficulty. Second, it will discuss the most essential reality of the cross, considering that the difficulties are deeper than hermeneutical issues, and further relate it to the affirmative value of the idea of penal substitution. Third, it will suggest that the understanding of the nature of God revealed on the cross should be balanced with ideas and concepts collected from the scriptures' own world. At the end of each section Calvin's view will be discussed.

Human Reality: Sin and Punishment

One of the strategies that Calvin's defenders take is to demonstrate that the idea of penal substitution is neither the only atonement paradigm nor even the central idea in Calvin.[8] It is without a doubt that theological giants seldom narrow the profundity of the cross into a single framework. In his reply to Sadoleto Calvin writes,

---

[7] J. Denny Weaver, "Violence in Christian Theology," *Cross Currents* 51/2 (2001), 157. Christiana A. Baxter categorizes major criticisms of the penal substitutionary view of the atonement in five ways: (1) real change is not capable of demonstration by it so that a subjective view of the atonement is sufficient, (2) it is unethical for God to punish an innocent victim instead of the guilty sinner, (3) it is either untrinitarian or tritheist to envisage a loving Son set over against a wrathful Father as mediator on our behalf, (4) it is self-contradictory that the Father acts with Christ and against Christ, and that the beloved is also simultaneously cursed, and (5) scripture lacks the reference that God punished the Son. Christiana A. Baxter, "The Cursed Beloved," in *Atonement Today*, ed. John Goldingay (London: SPCK, 1995), 68–69.

[8] Holems, "Can Punishment," 109–110. Trevor Hart, "Humankind in Christ and Christ in Humankind: Salvation as Participation in our Substitute in the Theology of John Calvin," *Scottish Journal of Theology* 42/1 (1989), 74.

Then we show that the only haven of safety is in the mercy of God, as manifested in Christ, in whom every part of our salvation is complete. As all
mankind are, in the sight of God, lost sinners, we hold that Christ is their
only righteousness, since, by His obedience, He has wiped off our transgressions; by His sacrifice, appeased the divine anger; by His blood, washed away
our sins; by His cross, borne our curse; and by His death, made satisfaction
for us.[9]

Several different motifs are present in this brief passage: the mercy of God,
righteousness, obedience, sacrifice, appeasement, sin-cleansing, curse-
bearing, and satisfaction. Even so, this holistic view regarding the characteristics of God (in which penal substitutionary perspective is included)
creates an implication that the major language field and its concern of
penal substitution should represent the attributes of the one who punishes the sins and the sinners. This impression gets worse when it is linked
to a cultic idea of victimization: "It has been blotted out by the death of
Christ, in which he offered himself to the Father as an expiatory victim
[*se parti obtulit hostiam expiatricem*]."[10] Therefore, it is our suggestion that,
despite the fact that God is deeply involved in the event of the cross and
that the judgment is God's,[11] the primary concern that penal substitution
must represent ought to be Christ's work for the sake of humanity, not
for the sake of God. Two further points are to be discussed in defense of
the above-stated suggestion. The idea of penal substitution—representing
who God is—remains provisional because of (1) the lack of biblical basis
and (2) the lack of human contexts.

    First, the lack of biblical basis is critical provided that we understand
the difference between the argument 'Christ is punished in the place
of human beings' and the idea that 'God punished Christ.' It is logically
invalid to argue that penal substitution theory, by assuming the violence of retribution or justice based on punishment, naturally results in

---

[9] Calvin, *A Reformation Debate: Sadoleto's Letter to the Genevans and Calvin's Reply*,
ed. John C. Olin (Grand Rapids: Baker, 1976), 66–67. This holistic perspective is repeatedly
maintained: punishment [*poenam*], expiation [*expiare*], satisfaction [*satisfactum*], sacrifice
[*litatum*] appeasing God's wrath [*iram eius placare*], and peace [*pacem*] in his *Institutes*
II.16.2, reconciliation, appeasement, payment, satisfaction, and penal substitution in his
commentary on Is. 53:5 (*CO* 37, 258), and redemption, satisfaction, atonement, cleansing,
pardon, and righteousness in his commentary on Gal. 2:21, *CO* 50, 200–201.
[10] Calvin, Commentary on Eph. 2:16, *CO* 51, 172.
[11] Deut. 1:17. This will be further explored when the twofold aspect of the atonement,
namely external and internal principles, is discussed later. Yet at this stage, it is of importance to distinguish between the idea of punishment laid upon humanity and the idea of
God's nature in punishment.

the God-directed violence.[12] Such reasoning without biblical references concerning the transition from human reality to God's attributes would be a false type of *analogia entis* between God and humanity. In fact, the idea that God actually punished Christ on the cross can hardly be found in scripture, even though God is portrayed as the very activator of the cross.[13] Instead, it is noticeable that we are under the curse and that Christ became a curse for us.[14] Interestingly, Isaiah 53:4 specifically points out this misconception: "We accounted him stricken and struck down by God, but he was wounded for our transgressions."

Second, a hermeneutical distinction between the statements concerning God and concerning humanity needs to be observed in the atonement view because human contexts lack the parallels of a Christian God who forgives sinners in punishment. Therefore, a cautious reservation should be made when biblical language is applied to God with regard to Christ's crucifixion. Christ is the mystery of God and all the treasures of wisdom and knowledge are hidden in him.[15] The mystery of the cross, however, never implies a doubt about the *actuality* of God's revelation in Christ's crucifixion. Apparently, God is revealed on the cross as Christ declares, "Whoever has seen me has seen the Father"[16] and "When you have lifted up the Son of Man, then you will realize that I am he."[17] The limitation

---

[12] Weaver, "Violence in Christian Theology," 158.

[13] The passages in which we read about the wrath of God are not so much about God's action of punishment at the moment of the cross as they are about the reality of humanity under God's justice in general (Rom. 1:18; 4:15; Eph. 2:4; 5: 6; Col. 3:6; 1Thess. 2:16). The only place where the wrath of God is related to the cross is Romans 5:9. Yet, this verse is in the literal context of verse 8 (one of the most significant verses regarding the love of God), and verses 10–11 (where the notion of reconciliation is declared). 1 Peter 2:23 can be seen to contain a link between God as the judge and Christ's entrusting to him on the cross: "When he was abused, he did not return abuse; when he suffered, he did not threaten; but he entrusted himself to the one who judges justly" (*NRSV*). The text, however, is principally about Christ's voluntary suffering for us rather than about God who punishes Christ.

[14] Gal. 3:13.

[15] Col. 2:2–3. Calvin also expresses the human limitation in understanding the cross using the word 'mystery' as he interprets Christ's crucifixion as it is included in the Apostles' Creed, both in his *First Catechism* and *Institutes*: "The form of Christ's death also embodies a singular mystery" (Calvin, *Institutes* II.16.6) and "But there is nothing without mystery in that redemption" Calvin, *First Catechism* 20.vi, I. John Hesselink, *Calvin's First Catechism: A Commentary* (Louisville: Westminster John Knox, 1997), 23. J.I. Packer defines mystery as something more of God in the created order than what we can grasp, highlighting *mysterium crucis* in his article on the idea of penal substitution: "Now the atonement is a mystery in the defined sense, one aspect of the total mystery of God." J.I. Packer, "What did the Cross Achieve? The Logic of Penal Substitution," *Tyndale Bulletin* 25 (1974), 7.

[16] John 14:9.

[17] John 8:28.

is rather about our human capability to understand the nature of God as we attempt to convey the profundity of the cross using such human devices as metaphor, imagination, inference, and causality. The possibility to make a single, definitive, and declaratory statement on any attribute of God, not in general but in relation to the cross, collapses if we consider the problem of analogy in a 'single case alone,' something David Hume points out against the teleological argument for God's existence in his *Dialogues concerning Natural Religion*:

> When two *species* of objects have always been observed to be conjoined together, I can *infer*, by custom, the experience of one wherever I *see* the existence of the other; and this I call an argument from experience. But how this argument can have a place, where *the objects, as in the present case [the universe], are single, individual, without parallel, or specific resemblance*, may be difficult to explain.[18]

The core of Hume's logic is that the universe is not analogous to objects because it is one single object without anything paralleled within itself. If his attack on the teleological argument can be applicable to the analogy between the universe and objects in it, more cautious reservation must be kept when it is meant to apply to God who created the universe and did not withhold his own Son but gave him up for all of us.[19] In essence, there is seldom a parallel between God's self-sacrifice revealed on the cross on the one hand, and a divine being imagined and worshiped in diverse cultural contexts of human societies. The Christian message fundamentally broke apart the customary conception of atonement in the ancient world, and it has challenged human ideology since the day of Christ.[20] The cross is unique and not so much about 'who we are' as about 'who God is.' Thus how the idea of penal substitution meaningfully reveals human reality therefore needs to be distinguished from an inference about God's reality that is based on human contexts when the parallel to the divine self-sacrifice can hardly be found.

Calvin does not undervalue the burden of the problem that the idea of penal substitution may harm God's image. He presents his well-known concept of accommodation for his atonement view. Raising a question of 'how the merciful God should be our enemy until he was reconciled with

---

[18] Emphasis is mine. David Hume, *Dialogues Concerning Natural Religion*, Part II, ed. Richard H. Popkin (Indianapolis: Hackett, 1980), 20–21.

[19] Rom. 8:32.

[20] Martin Hengel, *The Atonement: The Origins of the Doctrine in the New Testament*, tr. John Bowden (Philadelphia: Fortress, 1981), 31.

us through Christ,' Calvin concludes, "Expressions of this sort have been accommodated to our capacity [*Humus generis locutions ad sense nostrum sent accommodate*] in order that we may better understand how miserable and ruinous our condition is apart from Christ."[21] What we must not fail to notice from this statement is his emphasis on the miserable human limitation in comprehending the nature of God. It may imply that one of the reasons Calvin employs such controversial terms as appeasement, propitiation, and wrath, is not so much because he intends to uncover the attributes of God by them but because he recognizes that they provide convenient ways for a better understanding of the cross, especially for a humanity that suffers from its interpretative limitation before the cross.[22]

Narrowing down the idea of penal substitution to humanity and at the same time having a reservation in pointing out God's nature related to the cross due to the biblical reality of God's own accommodation does not mean that the view of penal substitution cannot produce any meaningful knowledge of God's nature. Who God is in relation to Christ's substitutionary punishment will be discussed after dealing with the nature of the penal substitutionary view of the atonement and its relevance to human reality.

Reality of the Cross: Death!

The primary issue with which penal substitution is concerned is neither the morality nor the rationality of God's ways.[23] What penal substitution represents is that all human beings are under punishment and that Christ bears it on the cross. The irony is that we either find an excuse for our

---

[21] Calvin, *Institutes* II.16.2, *Co* 2.368.

[22] Calvin's concept of accommodation covers a wide range: from the ontological lowering down of God in Christ's incarnation (Calvin, *Institutes* II.6.4, Calvin, Commentary on 1 Pet 1:20) to a method of edification (Calvin, Commentary on Gen. 1:11). One of most common expressions related to the words *accommodare, attemperare, and submittere* is 'accommodated to our capacity.' Ford Lewis Battles, "God Was Accommodating Himself to Human Capacity," in *Readings in Calvin's Theology*, ed. McKim, 35. This interpretative incapability of humanity is the totally other side of the same coin in order to illuminate that the words and expressions employed to reveal God must not be literally accepted at face value. Jane Dempsey Douglass finds that the origin of the idea that the wrath of God is not to be taken literally in Augustine and Erasmus. Jane Dempsey Douglass, "Calvin's Use of Metaphorical Language for God: God as Enemy and God as Mother," in *Articles on Calvin and Calvinism: A Fourteen-Volume Anthology of Scholarly Articles* vol. 6, ed. Richard C. Gamble (New York & London: Garland, 1992), 91–92.

[23] Packer, "What did the Cross Achieve?" 27.

violence in God or falsely worry about God's violence. Christ takes up this humanity. Obviously, what matters is deeper than this. Its nature is still undeniably violent *per se*, even with the suggestion that it applies to human reality within a limited range. The theological scope of penal substitution is less significant than the very nature of what the cross ought to reveal: What is this essential nature of the cross as such?

There is no doubt that death is the bare reality of the cross. All lines of thought concerning the atonement must begin with this true reality of the cross, namely, death. The theological and hermeneutical burdens of any atonement views are rooted in the problem of how to find converting paths from this death to its relevance of what happens in death and of how death does not have the final say but can produce any results at all through which God speaks. As for the penal substitutionary theory, the substantial conversation focusses on a 'mechanism' of the conversion from death to punishment: How does this transition work? How can death be a type of punishment? A solution to this question can be given by combining three ideas held together by a legal bond and context: sin, punishment, and death. In this legal 'mechanism' two aspects need to be further explored: (1) positively, the idea of punishment as the result of sin can be closely linked to the actuality of death and (2) negatively, in that it creates a danger of reductionism in which the cross is viewed as a retaliatory transaction between sin and punishment. The latter trajectory will be discussed in the next section, as we will focus on the former connection first.

The positive value of the notion of penal substitution lies in its relatively tighter connection with the actuality of death than other atonement views. It has been argued, for example, that love is the ultimate actuality of the cross. Robert Daly goes further as he prefers *love* to suffering:

> In the suffering of Christ there is, undeniably, a transcendent sacredness. But there is no unconditioned absoluteness there in the suffering of Christ. For Christ did not *have to* suffer. There is no absolute divine necessity there; but there is absolute divine necessity in the *love* with which Christ suffered. For ultimately, it is not suffering but love that saves.[24]

What is clearly biblical here is that love is the supreme reality of the cross. The strangeness of Daly's argument described above is, however, that he confuses necessity and reality, viewing the cross in light of neces-

---

[24] Emphasis is the author's. Robert Daly, "Images of God and the Imitation of God: Problems with Atonement," *Theological Studies* 68 (2007), 47.

sity. But death is primarily reality rather than necessity. Can the fact that Christ did not have to suffer eliminate the whole reality of his suffering on the cross?

Love cannot camouflage the reality of death in Christ's crucifixion. On the contrary, the cross is love precisely because Christ lays down his life for the sake of love.[25] God's love was proven by Christ's death.[26] A critical question here is not as to whether love is without death or with death, since death actually happened, but as to how death can be linked to love: love certainly, but why in a death?[27] Undeniably, death in general could not be love without any connecting notion or conceptual link between death and love, considering that various types of death such as accidental, suicidal, and natural deaths that can hardly be understood in terms of love. A death must have its own specific characteristic. Only after that, can one such specific death be viewed as love.

'Punishment' is relatively closer to 'death' than 'love' when the path from 'death' to 'punishment' is based on a legal framework with two presuppositions: (1) sins and sinners must be punished and (2) death is a punishment. Although not self-evident, the idea of penal substitution within the legal bond between sin, death, and punishment must be accepted as one (if not the only one) of various interpretations of the cross for these reasons: (1) sin is one of the most critical and universal limitations of humanity Christ must take up on the cross, (2) the central idea is not about violence or victimization but about justice that any legal system must demand, and (3) the externality of death is close to the execution of punishment.

Notwithstanding the limitations of a legal bond between sin and punishment, it is clear that death is at best a type of a *quid pro quo* transaction and thus that its superficial mirror but dimly reflects the cross on the basis of human ideology. Nevertheless, it unfolds the crucial reality of sin and sinners. Sin, along with death, is one of the most critical (and thus *crucial*) human limitations that must be taken up by Christ. Steve Holems claims that penal accounts are a way of making sense of the biblical language of guilt and sin bearing substitutionary sacrifice in a context where sacrifice itself is what has been called a dead metaphor.[28] What is

---

[25] John 10:11; 15:13; 1 John 4:10.

[26] Rom. 5:8.

[27] Paul S. Fiddes, *Past Event and Present Salvation: The Christian Idea of Atonement* (Louisville: Westminster/John Knox, 1989), 155.

[28] Holems, "Can Punishment," 110.

to be noticed here is, however, that even the mechanism of a cultic and substitutionary idea of victimization, as far as sin and guilt offerings are concerned, embraces the idea that sin must be punished in such ways that sin is transferred to victims and that those victims are executed.[29] For this reason, it would be a seriously naïve misconception if a legal understanding of the cross were considered simply a culturally colored perspective of the western world.

The reality of human sinfulness and an aching for its resolution, including punishment, is one of the universal struggles of humanity in history and extends beyond any specific cultural boundaries. The non-western world has been full of its own cultural devices and codes to cope with the problem of sins and sinners. The power of tribal chiefs is often tightly related to how effectively they can handle criminals by punishing or forgiving them by varying degrees. The wisdom and knowledge that King Solomon asked for was meant for being able to judge (שָׁפַט-*vindicate, govern, and punish*) God's people appropriately.[30] Without a causal connection between sin and punishment—regardless of whether it is sophisticated or minimized, and whether it is oral or statutory—a society could not be sustained at all. Concerns about how to treat human sin are as universal as the reality of sin. The causality between sin and punishment is the very seed of all the mechanisms of sacrificial ritual, commercial satisfaction by payment, and forensic substitution. We sin, and therefore our sins must be sacrificed, paid for, forgiven, or punished.

A critical question remains in this causal relation between death and punishment: Why must we interpret Christ's death as punishment rather than sacrifice, forgiveness, or payment? Considering death as the essential starting point of the cross, a commercial idea of payment is too metaphorical to point out the cruciality of death. The concept of forgiveness demonstrates the internal principle of the cross in relation to sin, but it has the same problem as the idea of love: why is death necessary for forgiveness? Only two notions are still relevant to the externality of death: sacrifice and punishment.

Interestingly, these two concepts are complementary to each other. The idea of sacrifice is more holistic than punishment if it can be viewed as self-sacrifice of Christ and not as victimization offered by humanity directed toward a divine being. It incorporates the expression of thanks-

---

[29] Lev. 4:1–6:7.
[30] 2 Chr. 1:10–11.

giving, resolution, and reconciliation. It brings in the images of cleansing sins or of executing their effective outcomes. The idea of punishment is faithful in revealing righteous, responsible effect caused by sin and is more direct in touching the extreme reality of the way to death of the cross as suffering, abandonment, and termination of life. All three elements previously described, causality between sins and death, fulfillment of justice, and externality of death, are incorporated more evidently in an extreme way of punishment than in the ritual practice of sacrifice.

Death is an extreme way of punishment in the sense that it allows no second chance to be reformed by punishment. Biblical texts authentically describe this extremity of punishment in the case of Christ's death. Christ's own proclamation itself details the way to death of the cross: The Son of Man must undergo great suffering, and be rejected by the elders, the chief priests and the scribes, be killed,[31] be betrayed into human hands,[32] and they will mock him and spit upon him and flog him, and kill him.[33] Moreover, Christ was betrayed by his disciples, and forsaken by God. The whole sentiment of the way to the cross does not simply evoke the specter of a natural death but rather the unimaginably painful and shameful death of betrayal, rejection, abandonment, mockery, and suffering. All the more importantly, his death becomes the most intensified punishment when Christ shares and bears all human sins, crying out why God has forsaken him. The biblical reality of death as result of sins is once and for all manifested in the abandonment by God and in Christ's substitutionary taking up of human sin.

This intensified punishment is taken up by Christ for the sake of humanity. Christ's substitution is essential in his work on the cross in diverse motifs of the atonement thought.[34] The way Christ bears humanity is to share himself with us. Yet, this sharing has been viewed as the authenticity of Christ' incarnation rather than of Christ's including humanity into himself. Even when it is declared that Christ unites himself with us, it has been ignored that we are united with Christ's crucifixion as well. Without Christ's full inclusion of humanity, substitution would be nothing but a replacement. When Christ died on the cross—we were crucified with

---

[31] Mark 8:31.
[32] Mark 9:31.
[33] Mark 10:34.
[34] "So substitution is not a 'theology of the atonement.' Nor is it even an additional image to take its place as an option alongside the others. It is rather the essence of each image and the heart of the atonement itself" John R.W. Stott, *The Cross of Christ* (Downers Grove: Intervarsity, 1986), 202–203.

Christ.[35] One has died for all; therefore all have died.[36] This inclusiveness sends us back to the clearer idea of punishment: punishment upon Christ is the very punishment upon all of humanity. A legal bond between sin, punishment, and death can be ultimately deepened by the idea of sub-stitution, however not as a 'replacement' but as a living bond of dying together. It is not so much about an inner conflict between the Father and the Only Son as it is about an external declaration of the reality that *we* are under sin and punishment and that *Christ* is abandoned into this humanity by becoming a curse. Hence, there is no place for the criticism as explained in the beginning of this article that the essential logic of righ-teousness is self-contradictory in such a way that the Innocent takes up others' sins. That is because Christ's death is not a death of the innocent but that of the sinners.

Conclusively we have seen that the penal substitutionary view of the atonement has a unique value that no other motif can deliver: It proclaims the miserable and sinful reality of humanity most strongly and holds the external character of death, including the painful and shameful way to the cross, as long as it can be upheld by the legal inner workings of causality between sin and punishment and is fully assisted by the biblical concept of substitution.

Now, turning to Calvin's view of penal substitution, we want to examine whether or not his exposition has this affirmative value. Calvin's comment on Galatians 3:13 can be summarized in two points: curse as a harsh causal reality between sin and punishment and curse as a substitutionary death. Calvin writes:

> Now, he does not say that Christ was cursed, but, which is still more, that he was *a curse*—intimating, that the curse "of all men was laid upon him" (Isa. Liii, 6). If any man thinks this language harsh, let him be ashamed of the cross of Christ, in the confession of which we glory. *It was not unknown to God what death his own Son would die, when he pronounced the law, "He that is hanged is accursed of God." (Deuteronomy xxi. 23.) But how does it happen, it will be asked, that a beloved Son is cursed by his Father?* We reply, there are two things which must be considered, not only in the person of Christ, but even in his human nature. The one is, that he was the unspotted Lamb of God, full of blessing and of grace; the other is, that *he placed himself in our room, and thus became a sinner, and subject to the curse, not in himself*

---

[35] Gal. 2:19; Rom. 6:6,8, Col. 2:20.
[36] 2 Cor. 5:14.

indeed, but in us, yet in such a manner, that it became necessary for him to occupy our place.[37]

The harsh reality that Christ is a curse, which is revealed by the mode of his death, is nothing but the reality of human sin because Christ placed himself in the place of humanity. Thus, substitution fulfills the actuality of Christ's bearing of humanity, which is other than a separation between the Father and the Son. Unfortunately, the idea of the union of Christ with humanity is not sufficiently emphasized with respect to the idea of penal substitution in Calvin.[38] At one point it is pregnant when Calvin claims that God's indignation remains in us until Christ's death but that we can be fully and firmly joined with God only when Christ joins us with him.[39] But in general it seems that Calvin magnifies the notion of replacement by his idea that our sin is transferred to Christ.[40] Calvin even argues that "...the whole curse was lifted from us while it was transferred to him."[41] The idea of transferring may create the implication that *we* are not crucified with Christ, which results in the exclusion of humanity from the cross. Then, a serious doubt remains as to whether 'substitution' in Calvin is similar to 'replacement' or to 'dying together.'[42]

The mystical union of Christ with humanity may be initiated with Christ's incarnation. But it must go through his crucifixion and resurrection, for only then it can culminate in his *parousia*. Without dying together

---

[37] Emphasis is mine. Calvin, Commentary on Gal. 3:13.

[38] The idea of Christ's union with us is one of the most evident features in Calvin's Christology, Pneumatology, Christian morality, and Ecclesiology: Christ himself makes us in-grafted into his body, not only in all his benefits but also in himself (Calvin, *Institutes* III.2.24), Christ unites himself to us by the Spirit alone (III.1.3), ever since Christ engrafted us into his body, we must take special care not to disfigure ourselves with any blemish (III.6.3), and Christ unites himself with the church (II.12.7) as we put on Christ in baptism (IV.15.6) and are secretly united with Christ in the Lord's Supper (IV.17.1). Calvin even understands the Lord's Supper as sending us to the cross of Christ (IV.17.4). Calvin does mention the cross in relation to the idea of the union: "The love of Christ led him to unite himself to us, and he completed the union by his death" (Calvin, Commentary on Gal. 2:20). Yet, what is not fully evident in Calvin is the idea that humanity is united with Christ on the cross. As Christ was crucified *in nobis*, we were also crucified *in Christo*.

[39] Calvin, *Institutes* II.16.3.

[40] Calvin, *Institutes* II.16.5.

[41] Calvin, *Institutes* II.16.6.

[42] Paul van Buren also views Calvin's idea as substitution, not as identity, even after he quotes Calvin's brief mentioning in his Commentary on Gal. 3:13 that Christ completed his union with us by his death. Van Buren, *Christ in Our Place*, 53. Interestingly, Van Buren's writing about Christ's union with us does not touch on this issue. Instead, the question of how far and authentically *Christ* becomes incarnated is brought into focus. Paul van Buren, "The Incarnation: Christ's Union with Us," in *Readings in Calvin's Theology*, ed. McKim, 123–141.

on the cross, a living together wouldn't be possible. If we are united with Christ in death, we will certainly be united with him in resurrection.[43] Where else can a closer union between Christ and humanity be found than when they die together? Christ includes us on the cross as he takes up what we cannot bear. It is unambiguous that Calvin's penal substitutionary view effectively uncovers the critical actuality of punishment, focusing on the profound reality of human sin and guilt and its harsh result of punishment. Yet, he seems to fail to fully clarify the biblical concept of substitution, which provokes some reserve and doubts concerning the nature of his concept of penal substitution.

Divine Reality: Punishment and Forgiveness

Even with its unique value, the idea of penal substitution at best reflects human ideology of a *quid pro quo* transaction. If we want to address the question of who God is in relation to the cross, we must go further than our own legal and social ideologies.

The last suggestion of this paper is that the nature of God in reference to the cross should be viewed collectively and intertextually within the Bible. Furthermore. This will be explored with an emphasis of the balance between the external reality of punishment and the internal reality of forgiveness.

Scripture produces a new paradigm by combining various motifs that consist in its own world. According to Paul Ricoeur, biblical texts reveal a certain parallelism between texts themselves, which is called 'intertextuality.'[44] The intertextuality is best in accord with understanding the unique God when the inter-animating conjunctions and dislocations between various motifs can explain the complexities of the meaning of the cross within the Bible.[45]

Considering God's attributes with respect to sin-oriented perspectives of the atonement, we must understand a sharp distinction between human legal mechanisms and biblical portrayals of God's attributes in

---

[43] Rom. 6:5.
[44] "It is this parallelism instituted by the text—by the 'texture' of the text—that makes a place for the process of mutual parabolization of the encompassing narrative and the embedded ones" Paul Ricoeur, *Figuring the Sacred: Religion, Narrative, and Imagination*, tr. David Pellauer (Minneapolis: Fortress, 1995), 162–163.
[45] Mark I. Wallace, "Introduction" in *Figuring*, 24.

dealing with sin and sinners. In the former, only one legal verdict can be delivered for a single legal case, whereas God shows various forms of judgment toward identical cases of sin and sinners. God's everlasting love is the true face of God's overflowing wrath,[46] since God's anger is but for a moment; his favor is for a lifetime.[47] God who tears and strikes us down is the same God who heals and binds us.[48] God forgives us all our trespasses, erasing the record and nailing it to the cross.[49]

In God's court, three different ways of judgment—such as punishment, forgiveness, and cancellation/nullification—can be made for a single case. Because of this unique configuration, any theological view of God's nature with a one-dimensional mind derived from human ideology is a caricature, specifically with respect to the cross. That is, in as much as the love of God cannot be absolutized in any atonement paradigm because of the externality of death, so punishment must not be considered as a single reality of the cross because of the internal reality of God's self-sacrifice.

Several different motifs in the Bible can be combined to produce a new paradigm regarding the nature of God. Sticking to sin-oriented perspectives, to which penal substitution belongs, we may examine which actions toward sins and sinners are more appropriate in explaining the nature of God. A neutral idea between punishment and forgiveness such as absorption,[50] erasing, cancellation, or nullification of sin can be considered in as much as we can find a clue in Psalm 51:1,9, Colossians 2:14, and Jeremiah 18:23. Understanding the cross as a sharing of sympathetic sadness would be another way to neutralize two extreme ways between punishment and forgiveness.[51] But these ideas of nullification and sympathy can hardly make it clear whether a certain action toward sin happens in its

---

[46] Isa. 54:8.

[47] Ps. 30:5.

[48] Hos. 6:1.

[49] Col. 2:14.

[50] "I answer: He who so responds to the divine wrath against sin ... is necessarily receiving the full apprehension and realization of that wrath, as well as of that sin ... and, so receiving it, He responds to it with a perfect response ... and *in that perfect response He absorbs it.*" J. McLeod Campbell, *The Nature of the Atonement* (Grand Rapids: Eerdmans, 1996), 118.

[51] "Actually some sadness is praiseworthy ... when for example it proceeds from a holy love; this occurs when a man is saddened over his own, or another's sins.... Christ, then in order to atone for the sins of all men, suffered the most profound sadness" (Thomas Aquinas, *Summa* 3a.46.6). "As the sacrificer, however, He is active and His suffering can be only an accompaniment, and can have its ground solely in sympathy with sin." Friedrich Schleiermacher, *The Christian Faith*, vol. II, eds. H.R. Mackintosh and J.S. Stewart (New York: Harper & Row, 1963), 452.

completed manner, and whether one who erases sins is entirely involved in one's action. Instead, this point of view can create a false impression that God is so detached from all the interactions that God's attributes may not be truly revealed. Death, however, is too costly for God to be removed from the scene.

One of the most observable natures of God among the sin-oriented notions with respect to Christ's work is forgiveness. It is the very opposite of punishment in that, whereas punishment signifies that the result of sins is laid upon sinners, forgiveness implies that the one who forgives takes the burden of sin upon himself or herself. Ten thousands talents are put on the king's own shoulder when he forgives the debts of his slaves.[52] For this reason, forgiveness is itself substitutionary and is self-sacrificial, which unveils the very nature of the cross. In addition, forgiveness is relational, and much more dimensional than what legal transaction can accomplish. Romans 3:25 is a critical text where we find a more extended scope of God's forgiveness than legal implication can reach. God shows God's righteousness in ἱλαστήριον and at the same time God's own righteousness is proven through the remission (*KJV*) of the previous sins (τὴν πάρεσιν τῶν προγεγονότων ἁμαρτημάτων).[53] In God's court, righteousness cannot overcome forgiveness that compensates all the weakness of a legal execution of punishment.

Several important texts in scripture show us that God forgives us in Christ on the cross. The sacramental union of Christ with us centers in the concept of forgiveness in Mathew's account of the Last Supper.[54] The

---

[52] Matt. 18:23–27.

[53] 'παρίημι,' the verb form of 'πάρεσις' means 'to let drop beside,' 'to pass by,' and 'to remit punishment or to forgive' in classical Greek according to *An Intermediate Greek-English Lexicon*, 7th edition of Liddell and Scott's Greek-English Lexicon (Oxford: Oxford University Press, 1997), 609. *A Greek-English Lexicon of the New Testament and other Early Christian Literature* explains that the verb is used of 'remitting debts and other obligation.' *A Greek-English Lexicon of the New Testament and other Early Christian Literature* ed. Frederick William Danker (Chicago: The University of Chicago, 2000), 776. Thus, it is apparent that it has connotation of 'to forgive.' But it is used in Luke 11:42 as 'to neglect' and in Hebrews 12:12 as 'to weaken.' The noun form, πάρεσις occurs only once in the New Testament, here in Romans 3:25, which creates various translation, 'unpunished' in *NIV* and 'pass over' in *NRSV*. Since the verb form clearly has meaning of 'to forgive' and the major focus of the verse lies on God's action toward the previous sins, it may be translated as remission of sin following *KJV*. More importantly, despite the fact that 'παρίημι' denotes remitting of commercial and legal obligation the actual meaning of the noun 'πάρεσις' in the context of Romans 3:25 clearly goes beyond legal boundary as it is related to God's forbearance (ἐν τῇ ἀνοχῇ τοῦ θεοῦ).

[54] ἄφεσις, Matt. 26:28.

apostles summarize Christ's work as forgiveness.[55] In Hebrews, the sacrificial purification of blood is depicted as forgiveness.[56] More straightforward connections between the cross and forgiveness can be found in the Pauline writings.[57] What is more important in the concept of forgiveness is that scripture is very clear in revealing the subject of forgiveness: Christ himself interprets his death as forgiveness in Matthew's account[58] and God is the one who forgives us.[59] Therefore, we can conclude that the internal principle of the cross is forgiveness precisely when God reveals God's own attribute on the cross.

Calvin is one of the theological thinkers who develop the comprehensive understanding of the cross. He has a balanced view between sin and death,[60] between objective and subjective views,[61] and between commercial, sacrificial, and forensic views.[62] It is nevertheless not clear whether Calvin balances his sin-oriented perspective with the idea of forgiveness as the internal nature of God. Calvin writes,

---

[55] ἄφεσις, Acts 10:43; 13:38.

[56] ἄφεσις, Heb. 9:22.

[57] πάρεσις in Rom. 3:25, ἄφεσις in Eph. 1:7; χαρίζομαι in Col. 1:14; 2:13–15. According to *Theological Dictionary of the New Testament,* ἄφεσις is etymologically rooted in the verb αφιέναι which literally means 'to send off' and is used from an early Greek period in every nuance from 'to hurl' to 'to release.' It also means 'to pardon' even early from Plato and almost always means forgiveness of God in the use of post-apostolic fathers. *Theological dictionary of the New Testament,* ed. Gerhard Kittel, tr. Geoffrey W. Bromiley, vol. 1 (Grand Rapids: Eerdmans, 1964), 509–511. In the New Testament, ἄφεσις mostly means forgiveness except for in Luke 4:18 where it signifies release or liberation. The primary connotation of χαρίζομαι is 'to show pleasure' in word or deed, which is related to the noun χάρις. *Theological Dictionary,* 375. In the New Testament, it often means 'give' (Acts 3:14; 25:11; Phil. 2:9). It also signifies 'give a certain favor' (sight in Luke 7:21; payment back in Luke 7:42; safety in Acts 27:24; graciously in Rom. 8:32; freely in 1 Cor. 2:12; a certain favor in Gal. 3:18). It definitely means 'to forgive,' (4 times in 2 Cor. 2:7–13, twice in Eph. 4:32 and Col. 3:13).

[58] Matt. 26:28.

[59] Rom. 3:25; Col. 2:13. "The forgiveness denoted by ἄφεσις (αφιέναι) and πάρεσις is almost always that of God." *Theological Dictionary,* 511. God and Christ are the subject of χαρίζομαι when it means forgiveness in Ephesians 4:32 and Colossians 3:13.

[60] "... clothed with our flesh he vanquished death and sin together that the victory and triumph might be ours" Calvin, *Institutes* II.12.3.

[61] "The second effect of Christ's death upon us is this: by our participation in it, his death mortifies our earthly members so that they may no longer perform their functions; and it kills the old man in us that he may not flourish and bear fruit" Calvin, *Institutes* II.16.7.

[62] "This readily shows that Christ's grace is too much weakened unless we grant to his sacrifice the power of expiating, appeasing, and making satisfaction.... For unless Christ had made satisfaction for our sins, it would not have been said that he appeased God by taking upon himself the penalty to which we were subject" Calvin, *Institutes* II.17.4.

In another passage, to be sure, Paul extends the basis of the pardon [*veniae*] that frees us from the curse of the law to the whole life of Christ: "But when the fullness of time came, God sent forth his Son, born of woman, subject to the law, to redeem those who were under the law" [Gal. 4:4–5].[63]

Here, the idea of forgiveness is stated as Christ's work for the curse of the law. Yet, an emphasis falls on the holistic aspect of Christ's whole life. Criticizing the Roman Catholic idea that after guilt has been remitted there remains the penalty that God's justice demands to be paid, Calvin moves on to distinguishing between Christ's bearing the punishment due for sins and God's judgment as chastisement.[64] He holds that there are two kinds of divine judgment, punishment and correction, the one which is the act of a judge and the other which is of a father.[65] Then, he concludes: "For the saints these are, after forgiveness [*remissionem*] of sins, struggles and exercises; for the wicked, without forgiveness of sins, the punishments [*supplicia*] of iniquity."[66] Here are two ideas, forgiveness and punishment, paralleled with each other. Yet, they seem to be two distinctive actions of God that are respectively applied to the saints and the wicked. If we accept this idea in a strict sense, the essential nature of penal substitution will be weakened as if Christ's death were not a substitutionary punishment for the saints.

Calvin uses expressions that denote erasing [*delevit*] and abolishing [*abolendis*], but both occur in the context of Christ's works as sacrifice for sin.[67] Calvin does relate the idea of erasing to the penal substitutionary view in his *Institutes* II.17.5:

> For this reason the apostle defines the redemption in Christ's blood as "the *forgiveness* of sins" [Col. 1:14]. It is as if he were saying, "We are justified or *acquitted* before God, because that blood corresponds to satisfaction for us." Another passage agrees with this: "In the cross he *canceled* the written bond which stood against us" [Col. 2:14 p.]. He notes there the payment or compensation that *absolves* us of guilt (emphasis mine).

What draws our attention here is that—even though he quotes Colossians 1:14 where the idea of forgiveness [ἄφεσιν] is clearly expressed, and Colossians 2:14 right before which Paul declares forgiveness [χαρισάμενος] from sins in verse 13—Calvin fails to develop the idea of forgiveness. He uses

---

63 Calvin, *Institutes* II.16.5.
64 Calvin, *Institutes* III.4.29–30.
65 Calvin, *Institutes* III.4.31.
66 Calvin, *Institutes* III.4.33.
67 Calvin, *Institutes* II.15.6 and II.12.4.

'acquitted [*absolvi*],' 'canceled [*deletum*],' and 'absolves [*absolvit*]' rather than employs more common vulgate words *remissio* for ἄφεσις and *donare* for χαρίζομαι. The word *absolvere* has commercial and legal connotation to signify 'to release or pay off,' and the meaning of *delere* is close to 'to erase or destroy' rather than 'to forgive.'[68] As for Calvin's commentaries on the texts where the cross is directly connected to forgiveness of God, Calvin translates πάρεσις in Romans 3:25 as *delere*, and stresses justification by imputation without any further discussion of forgiveness as God's inner reality.[69] Unfortunately, there is no concrete clue that Calvin's view of atonement relates to the idea of forgiveness in such biblical texts as Ephesians 1:7; Colossians 2:13–14, and Hebrews 9:22.

In sum, despite the fact that Calvin's view of the atonement is tremendously diverse and holistic, it seems that his view lacks a balance between externality and internality of the cross, not in general but regarding the sin-oriented perspectives.

Conclusion

The penal substitutionary view of the atonement has a unique value when its primary focus falls on its relevance to the serious reality of sin. So deeply is creation—and humanity supremely—enmeshed in sin that there is no inherent way to get out of the accumulation of sins, guilt and inherited punishment.[70] What Christ takes up on the cross must be broader than punishment and deeper than replacement. Nevertheless, the entirety of the crucifixion event never guarantees that the penal substitutionary perspective can be contradicted and refused. Nor can its legal paradigm prove that a stress on punishment is a culturally colored bias of the western context. The causal correlation between sin and punishment is clearly one of the human fundamentals that is sustaining societies, and is much more universal than the western ideology.

Death is the bare reality of the cross. Campbell's lamentation of how we can see it as a punishment that "The sufferer suffers what he suffers just through seeing sin and sinners with God's eyes and feeling in reference

---

[68] *A Latin Dictionary: Founded on Andrews' Edition of Freund's Latin Dictionary*, revised by Charlton T. Lewis and Charles Short (London: Oxford, 1975), 11, 537.

[69] Calvin, Commentary on Rom. 3:25, *CO* 49, 63.

[70] Alister E. McGrath, *What was God doing on the Cross?* (Grand Rapids: Zondervan, 1992), 56–57.

to them with God's heart"[71] is as naïve and sentimental as the misconceptions that death on the cross never happened, or that nothing but death happened on the cross. If we accept that legal causality between sin and punishment is one of the human universals, the idea of punishment is one of only a few ways to begin the theological discussions of the cross with its bare reality. Christ's crucifixion is even more faithful to the extremity of punishment that consists of abandonment, betrayal, suffering, and shameful contempt. The sense of punishment culminates when Christ cries out the abandonment from God, taking up all the human sins and sinners once for all. To this utmost extent Christ unites himself with us as we are crucified with him.

The idea of punishment goes beyond a human consciousness of social structures, since sin in Christianity is sin *coram deo* and thus sin cannot be handled by sinners alone. God is costly involved in the cross to the extent that God's only son was abandoned. Yet this is not to say that God's attribute with regard to this is violent and retributive. On the contrary, the internal reality of the cross is forgiveness, specifically when it is closely related to the genuine nature of God. Unlike the lack of straightforward biblical support for the idea of a punisher, scripture declares that God is the one who forgives in Christ on the cross.[72] *Mysterium crucis* is that the ultimate reality of God is the forgiving God who embraces even those who turn to other gods and other lovers,[73] while the same God did not spare God's only Son in order for sins and sinners to be punished in Christ's crucifixion. Justice is not annulled but is practiced allowing mercy to triumph over judgment.[74] The externality of punishment executed on the cross needs to be balanced with the internality of God's forgiveness.

Calvin's concept of penal substitution is to be revisited with acknowledgement as well as challenge. His idea of punishment, along with that of substitution, is most faithful and undeviating to the harsh, costly reality of Christ's death: Christ suffered, was abandoned, and became a curse because of our sin. It is even more worth noting that in Calvin the idea of punishment is not sacrificed for all his other views of the atonement wherein he convinces us of his marvelous balance between objective and subjective perspectives, between sin-oriented and death-oriented paradigms, and between commercial, sacrificial, and legal metaphors, as well

---

[71] Campbell, *The Nature*, 107.
[72] Rom. 3:25; Col. 2:13.
[73] Hos. 3:1.
[74] James 2:13.

as of his unique contribution of the threefold office of Christ in relation to the cross. In addition, his notion of accommodation may alleviate critical criticisms targeted to potential distortions of God caused by the penal substitutionary view of the atonement.

Even so, Calvin's view can be challenged in three ways. First, his perspective is often conveyed along with statements about God, which creates the misconception that punishment is what happened between God and the Innocent. Secondly, his take on substitution is closer to replacement than to inclusive substitution. Justice can be harmed if the Innocent *only* is punished and we are excluded from Christ's crucifixion. Thirdly, although his point of view clearly includes the idea of God's love and mercy, he seems to fail in linking Christ's death to the forgiveness that is one of God's ways to sins and sinners. While clarifying these weak points, Calvin's view of penal substitution must not be overwhelmed by modern sentimentalism in which Christ's death caused by human sins and guilt is distorted into fears of weakening morality, or into justification of human violence in God's cause. Calvin's concept of penal substitution will continue to refresh and challenge us as long as we are enslaved by our sinful humanity.

CHAPTER EIGHT

JOHN CALVIN'S UNDERSTANDING OF CHRIST'S DESCENT INTO HELL[1]

Johan Buitendag

John Calvin had the ability in his theology to catalogue new horizons—
some of whose implications he apparently did not necessarily fathom or
even understand personally. This is clear, for example, from his reflection
on the phrase 'descended to hell', which, by means of Rufinus (ca. 345–
410), found a place in the fourth century in the *Symbolum Apostolorum*,
and which was accepted at the Council of Ariminum in 359. For Calvin
this article was part of the 'accomplishment of redemption' (*in quo ad
redemptionis effectum*) and therefore also part of the 'summary of doctrine' (*doctrinae summa*) of the redemption.[2] Consequently, he steadfastly
wanted to maintain this particular article in the *Apostolicum*. But what is
particularly striking, is the almost intuitive subtext and attunement which
Calvin allows to filter through in his discussion of this. Christ's descent
(hereafter *descensus*) was to him a profound 'mystery' (*mysterium*), but
at the same time a matter which spelled out the redemption through the
cross (*ex mortis Christi fructus depereat*).

By now discussing the impression that Calvin formed of the importance
of this phrase for salvation in a slightly creative way and trying to develop
it along the lines of the contemporary Systematic Theological debate,
I wish to attempt to show that Calvin's intuition about the special meaning of this article was indeed right on target. That is why I do not wish to
follow Van Rensburg's solution of regarding the article as tautological and
therefore simply one to be scrapped.[3]

---

[1] This article was read in a condensed form at the IRTI conference in Aix-en-Provence,
3–5 July 2009 and published as J. Buitendag, *"Descendit ad [in] inferna*: 'A matter of no
small moment in bringing about redemption'," *HTS Theological Studies* 65(1), Art. #273,
8 pages. DOI: 10.4102/hts. v65i1.273.

[2] Calvin, *Institutes* II.16.8. *OS* 3, 492.

[3] Fika Van Rensburg and Elma Cornelius, "Die aanvaarbaarheid en vertaling van
'katelthonta eis ta katotata' in die Apostolicum Symbolum" [The acceptability and translation of katelthonta . . .], *In die Skriflig* 34/3 (2000), 397–422.

I wish to highlight two matters pertinently, matters which Calvin already handled embryonically almost 500 years ago and which seem to hold enormous meaning for theology today. On the one hand, it concerns the role that *time and space* play in this argument about the *descensus* and, on the other, the *cosmic victory* of Christ which is expressed through this. By appreciating the data through a temporal-spatial lens, the topicality of the *descensus* is realised anew. I therefore plead, in effect, for both a socio-historical reading of the text and for a post-Newtonian interpretation of space-time.

In building my argument, I first examine the background and intention of this addition to the *Apostolicum*, then briefly indicate the *Wirkungsgeschichte*—in particular Calvin's interpretation thereof—and, in conclusion, I place it within a Systematic Theological cadre and framework which takes into account insights gained from, among others, the views of contemporary physics concerning time and space. The essay concludes that this article in the *Apostolicum* can, indeed, catalogue special contours in theology and therefore ought justifiably to be part of the summary of doctrine—as Calvin felt to be true, but did not effectively demonstrate—and about which note ought to be taken increasingly.

But the topicality of this phrase also lies in the need for an appropriate *translation*. In past decades, particularly in Reformed circles, a continuous debate has been dealing with the translation of the *descensus*. The *Reformed Churches in South Africa* (RCSA), for example, have had problems with the translation of the 'underworld' reflected by the Latin word *inferna* since 1964.[4] Different reports also indicate that many Reformed churches worldwide have the same problem with the translation. In South Africa, the RCSA therefore entered into discussion with the other Reformed churches to bring the translations of the *Apostolicum*, the *Athanasium* and the *Heidelberg Catechism* in line with Calvin's interpretation.

In the midst of objections to the article, especially such as concerning the defective Biblical substructure,[5] or it being too strongly mythological,[6] it is my assessment, given my chosen view, to support maintaining the article as a function of the following dogmatic challenge:

---

[4] Van Rensburg and Cornelius, "Aanvaarbaarheid en vertaling van 'katelthonta eis ta katotata'," 398.

[5] Wayne Grudem, "He did not descend into hell: a Plea for following Scripture instead of the Apostle's Creed," *JETS* 34/1 (1991), 103–113.

[6] Randall Otto, "Descendit in Inferna: A Reformed Review of a Creedal Conundrum," *WTJ* 52 (1990), 143–150.

- A linear understanding of time compels the question about what happened to Jesus from the Friday afternoon of the crucifixion up to and including the Sunday morning of the resurrection.[7] This, in turn, leads to the issue of the so-called intermediate state and of purgatory[8] as also interpreted later, by Pope Benedict XII, in 1336.[9] Is it at all possible to speak of the course of time after death? The issue of time, and eternal time in eternity, will therefore have to be reconsidered.
- Calvin and the Heidelberg Catechism (Question & Answer 44) avoided this spatial aspect of the term 'underworld' by substituting the anachronistic concept of 'hell' for it. As such, 'hell' is seen as the *Gehenna* that, according to Matthew 25:41, for example, is the place of the accursed, the place of the 'eternal' fire that was prepared for the devil and his angels. The *descensus* is, in other words, interpreted figuratively and is taken merely as an experience of Godforsakenness. If this would be the case, a translation such as 'He suffered the torment of Hell' becomes a passable translation. Spatiality also concerns physicality. Did the *total* person of Christ, God and man, as Luther judged, then descend into the underworld or was it solely the *Logos*?[10] And then, thirdly, is the temporal able to contain the eternal (*finitum capax infiniti*)? Could God have entered the underworld at all? Had God then died, as Nietzsche did, in fact, ask?

The above-mentioned temporal-spatial interpretation means, on the one hand, that a linear view of time is replaced by a punctual one, where sequence or course is drawn into one existential point and, on the other hand, again, that the topography of the underworld was subsumed into abstraction and what could be seen as a Platonic recognition of the Ptolemaic world view with its 'concept of separation' between the 'sensible world' and the 'intelligible world'.

Although this is no exegetical study, a comment about hermeneutics should be made, as regards the understanding of both the *Apostolicum* and the Bible. The important issues are, on the one hand, whether people should dare to ignore the socio-historical context of a text and, on

---

[7] Hans Küng, *Ewiges Leben?* (München: R Piper & Co. Verlag, 1982), 163.

[8] John Kelly, *Early Christian Creeds.* 3rd. (New York: Continuum, [1960] 2006), 382.

[9] Jürgen Moltmann, "Is there Life after Death?" in John Polkinghorne and Michael Welker, *The End of the World and the Ends of God. Science and Theology on Eschatology* (Harrisburg: Trinity Press International, 2000), 247.

[10] David Scaer, "He did descend to hell: in defense of the Apostles Creed," *JETS* 35/1 (1992), 97–98.

the other, whether we may apply the church's doctrines prescriptively to determine the exegesis of a Bible verse and prescribe a translation. Biblical scientists deem these options unacceptable. A hermeneutics of suspicion is necessary, moreover, to deconstruct any interests in the process of understanding.

The importance of the *descensus* in the *Apostolicum* is that it can offer certain contours to the Systematic Theological debate, in that it can be the catalyst for the limitations to which we can so easily subject God. By relinquishing a 'receptive concept' of space and, instead, turning it around and understanding space as a predicate of the occupant in accordance with his/her nature, we demystify the problematic of Christ's presence in the underworld. Spatial terms are therefore to be retained in the interpretation of this article.

Origin in the Apostolicum

The text of the *Apostolicum* has its origins in the *Roman Creed* which, as the name indicates, originated in Rome and was already in use in the year 150 AD. It undoubtedly grew out of the confession of Peter (Matt. 16:16), which formed the nucleus for the article on Jesus Christ, as well as out of the old baptism liturgy, which gave the text its Trinitarian foundation.[11] The *Apostolicum* had no individual author, nor is it the collaboration (*symbolum*) of the twelve apostles, but is the product of an organic process[12] of the Western church (as opposed to the *Creed of Nicea*, which originated in the Eastern church). For this reason it is also not as much 'apostolic' as *ecclesiastical*, which bears testimony to the church's understanding of the Scriptures.[13] The pre-Nicene patristic fathers esteemed it highly and also regarded it as 'the rule of faith', 'the rule of truth' and later called it 'the symbol of faith'.[14]

What is also important, however, is that no single text prevailed initially. The respective churches in Aquileia, Milan, Ravenna, Carthage and Hippo each used different texts—some were longer and others were shorter. Each church therefor did as it liked with the text, without prejudicing the nucleus of Jesus's crucifixion and resurrection, or the Trinitar-

---

[11] Philip Schaff, *The Creeds of Christendom* (London: Harper & Brothers Publishers, 1931) vol. 1, 16.
[12] Kelly, *Creeds*, 23–29.
[13] Scaer, "He did descend," 92.
[14] Schaff, *Creeds*, 17.

ian foundation of the baptismal formula. The creeds were committed to memory, but not to writing. The first writer in the West who gives us the text of the Latin creed, with a commentary, is Rufinus, towards the close of the fourth century. Owing to the central role that Rome played in the West and its intrinsic excellence, Rufinus's text increasingly found general favour. Although the Greek version is older than the Latin one, the existing Greek text nevertheless is a translation from the Latin. Amongst other additions ('catholic', 'the communion of saints' and 'life everlasting'), the article 'descended into Hades' equally was a later addition. Schaff[15] dates the establishment of the text of the *Apostolicum* no further back than the end of the fifth and beginning of the sixty centuries, and the present form probably first appeared in the eighth century. By the ninth century, the *Textus Receptus* had become established and by the twelfth century it indubitably was the official creed of Rome itself.[16]

As regards the *descendit ad inferna*, it is commonplace that it appeared for the first time in the West in the Aquileian text of 309 AD, although it also appears in three other synodal resolutions, namely in Sirmium, Nicea and Constantinople.[17] The expression *descendit ad inferna* was derived from the Septuagint version of Job 38:17.[18] We also probably find something of it in Ezekiel 37:7–12 (and to some degree also in Matthew 27:52–53) where mention is made of a series of earthquakes, the opening of the graves and the resurrection of those who had been buried. There are variations of the expression, in that the preposition ('in' or 'ad') of the singular and plural are interchanged. The *Athanasianum* rather refers, for example, to the 'inferos' which indicates the denizens of the underworld. It is important to add that Rufinus initially saw the article merely as a replacement of *sepultus* (buried).[19] The Aquileian Creed omitted the clause 'was buried' and substituted for it the new clause, *descendit in inferna*. Someone like Briggs[20] has a different opinion, however, and thinks it is not a repetition of what is already said in *sepultus*. He points out, for example, that the Pastor of Hermas states that the apostles and teachers continued their work in the underworld and baptised the converted there.

In summary, the following variant readings can now also be offered with regard to the addition of the *descensus*:

---

15 Schaff, *Creeds*, 19.
16 Kelly, *Creeds*, 427.
17 Charles Briggs, *Theological Symbolics* (Edinburgh: T&T Clark, 1914), 63.
18 Otto, "Descendit," 144.
19 Otto, "Descendit," 143.
20 Briggs, *Symbolics*, 66.

I	Absent	Forma Romana Vetus	< 341 AD
II	*Descendit in inferna*	Ecclesia Aquileiensis	± 390 AD
III	*Descendit ad infernum*	Venantius Fortunatus	± 570 AD
IV	*Descendit ad inferna*	Sacramentarium Gallicanum	± 650 AD
V	*Descendit ad infer(n)os*	Athanasium	± 500 AD

Taxonomy

The *Apostolicum* has a most refined composition, even though it has
more than one author and has come into existence by an organic process extending from the third to the eighth centuries. Barth[21] takes the
first word, 'credo', as the point of departure for the full exposition of the
Apostolicum. It is the individual and ecclesiastic appropriation of the revelation of God in faith. By contrast, Du Toit[22] wants to recover the basic
forms of prayer, creed, doxology and learning in the *Apostolicum*.

As mentioned above, the Trinitarian foundation of the *Apostolicum*
is the outstanding feature. The juxtaposition of 'believe in' (Father, Son
and Holy Spirit [dative]) as opposed to the 'believe' without a preposition
(the church [accusative]) is an example of this. What is striking, too, is
the mythological cosmology of the three-storey world view. One sees the
course of the *Apostolicum*, almost like the curve of a parabola, being determined by beginning with the heavens above, going down to the earth and
then returning to the heavens. The relevant phrase is also pivotal in the
movement. The *descendit* therefore finds in the composition a pendant in
the *ascendit (in coelos/coelum)*. As the *descent into Hell* gives expression
to a mythical cosmology, the same naturally applies to the *ascension into
Heaven*.[23]

The soteriological offer in the *Apostolicum* can consequently not be
ignored. Together with creation, redemption must be confessed; together
with the first coming is the second coming; with the crucifixion is the
resurrection; with the humiliation is the glorification, with the curse is
the exoneration. Article 1 confesses that God is 'the Father, the Almighty',

---

[21] Karl Barth, *De Apostolische Geloofsbelijdenis* [The Apostolic Confession] (Nijkerk:
Callenbach, 1935), 15–16.

[22] Danie Du Toit, *"Neergedaal ter helle" Uit die geskiedenis van 'n interpretasieprobleem*
["Descended into hell." From the history of a problem of interpretation] (Kampen: Kok,
1971), 195.

[23] Scaer, "He did descend," 92.

a sequence which clearly gives precedence to the love of God. Briggs[24] also sees in the composition of the *Apostolicum* six clear successive redemptive acts or states of Jesus the Saviour and adds to this that the Creed undoubtedly means that Jesus Christ descended to *Hades* as an important part of his work of salvation; for all the acts mentioned in the Creed are saving acts. This is indeed what Calvin spotted too.

Wirkungsgeschichte

Kelly[25] argues that the insertion of this phrase was not motivated by an anti-Apollinarian bias. The only possible polemic motive was its opposition to Docetism, inasmuch as the reality of the death of Jesus is emphasized. This is confirmed by the origin of the article in the Syrian church. At the Council of Ariminum (359), the issue of the concepts of *homoousios* (one substance) and the Arian *homoiousios* (similar substance) came to a head.[26] The formulation *descendit ad inferna* was then proposed as a compromise by Marcus of Arethusa.[27] It was also so accepted at the Council of Constantinople (360). Du Toit[28] is emphatic that the dismissive attitude to the docetic and Platonic fields among some of the earliest patristic fathers led directly to the adoption of the *descensus* in the *Apostolicum*. This granted credibility to both the death and the resurrection of Jesus.[29]

Rufinus plainly explains in his *Commentary on the Apostles' Creed* (ca. 404) that, as regards the *descendit ad inferna*, 'its meaning...appears to be precisely the same as that contained in the affirmation 'buried" (cited by Kay).[30] For this he invokes Psalms 16:10, 22:15, 30:3, 9 and 69:2. This initially was meant to reinforce the meaning that Jesus really did die. But then Rufinus also added later that Christ was not just another deceased being, but also the *conqueror* of death. The *descensus* is then transposed by Rufinus from a gloss on the burial of Jesus to a thematic scène of his resurrection—and in direct relation to human redemption.

---

[24] Briggs, *Symbolics*, 52, 65.

[25] Kelly, *Creeds*, 382–383.

[26] Otto, "Descendit," 140.

[27] L. Doekes, *Credo: Handboek voor de Gereformeerde Symboliek* [Credo: Manual for Reformed Symbolics] (Amsterdam: Ton Bolland, 1975), 17.

[28] Du Toit, *Neergedaal*, 177.

[29] Kelly, *Creeds*, 383.

[30] James Kay, "He Descended into Hell," in Roger E. Van Harn, *Exploring and Proclaiming the Apostle's Creed* (Grand Rapids: Eerdmans, 2004), 119.

Jesus is not only the victim of death, but also the victor over death. Jesus's presence in hell is meant to be understood from the outset as evidence of an already accomplished redemption. It is therefore, according to the one interpretation, identical to *sepultus* and according to the other, an actual self-manifestation of Christ after the crucifixion to all departed spirits. This in particular includes those who died without a body being found who, therefore, according to tradition, could have no hope of the resurrection. Kelly[31] regards this emphasis on the victory as a clear shift in meaning and that 'the doctrine was coming to be interpreted as symbolizing His triumph over Satan and death, and, consequently, the salvation of mankind as a whole'.

Van Rensburg[32] is of the opinion that this shift in meaning is also specifically the reason why the article was incorporated in the *Apostolicum*. When the meaning was seen as simply another repetition, there was no need to incorporate it, but the moment it had something *more* to say, it was indeed incorporated in the *Apostolicum*. Not that this new content merely had been grasped out of fresh air. It was based essentially on a particular tradition which, like a rivulet, was incorporated into a river.[33] So the perennial challenge about the *descensus* concerns how to relate the respective scriptural traditions about *sheol* to those about *gehenna* and to connect them to the saving work of Jesus Christ.

Clement of Alexandria seems to be the first to have linked 1 Peter 3:19 with the descent of Christ and he interpreted it in such a way as to see this preaching as offering salvation to the souls of Noah's unbelieving contemporaries. Some authors broadened it to include other souls in prison. By the time of Augustine (354–430), the view that Christ had liberated from *Hades* any persons other than those who had foreseen his coming and kept his precepts by anticipation, was branded heretical.[34] The possibility of a conversion after death was in total disapproval. It was, therefore, the *pre-existent* Christ who preached to these contemporaries of Noah, during their lifetime. This standpoint waned in the course of time, until Wayne Grudem revived it again recently in certain circles:

---

[31] Kelly, *Creeds*, 243.

[32] Fika Van Rensburg, "The Acceptability and Translation of 'katelthonta eis ta katotata' in the Apostolicum Symbolum," *Ekklesiastikos Phafros* 70 (1989), 51–53.

[33] Hall Harris, *The Descent of Christ. Ephesians 4:7–11 & Traditional Hebrew Imagery* (Leiden: Brill, 1996), 2–3.

[34] Augustine, "Letter CLXIV. To Evodius," *NPNF1* 1. 515.

'The verse does not refer to something Christ did between his death and resurrection but something he did 'in the spiritual realm of existence' (or 'through the Spirit') *at the time of Noah.* When Noah was building the ark, Christ 'in Spirit' was preaching through Noah to the hostile unbelievers around him.'[35] However, the most popular line of interpretation of this verse, today, is that Christ proclaimed his ultimate victory to evil spirits in prison at some time between his death and his ascension.[36]

Harris points to the use of the expression *descensus* among certain post-apostolic patristic fathers: Ignatius (110 CE), Polycarp (156 CE), Irenaeus (202 CE) and Tertullian (200 CE). Van Aarde[37] suggests that, historically and exegetically, traditions such as those in 2 Maccabees 7, 1 Henoch 51:2 and the Gospel of Peter 9:35–10:42, are probably the oldest roots of 1 Peter 3:19 and reflect its 'mythical motive'. Rowland,[38] however, makes the important remark that the geography of the places visited by Henoch is presented in real terms and not in mythological contours. Apocalyptic literature had an interest in the world as it was. After Enoch ascended to heaven, he embarked on a journey which took him to the various parts of the world and at the end to the *gehenna* (1 Enoch 24–27). It was notorious as a place of punishment and torment.

In summary, it can be stated that, during the first centuries, there was no question of an extensive theory about the *descensus*. Nowhere does it appear as credal material or create the impression that it is material critical to faith.[39] Initially, therefore, it was only concerned with underlining the truth of Christ's suffering and death and thus emphasising his true humanness. The *descensus* was manifest in the liturgy of the church from the fourth century only; still not as a doctrinal precept, but as the affective experience of the greatness of Jesus's victory over death.

---

[35] Grudem, "He did not descend," 110.

[36] D.N. Campbell and Fika Van Rensburg. "A History of the Interpretation of 1 Peter 3:18–22," *Acta Patristica et Byzantina* 19 (2008), 82–83.

[37] Andries Van Aarde, "Op die aarde net soos in die hemel": Matteus se eskatologie as die koninkryk van die hemel wat reeds begin kom het"On earth as in heaven. Matthew's eschatology as the kingdom of heaven that already has begun] *HTS Teologiese Studies* 1, no. 64 (2008), 541.

[38] Christopher Rowland, *The Open Heaven: A Study of Apocalyptic in Judaism and Early Christianity* (Eugene: Wipf & Stock Publishers, [1982] 2002), 125.

[39] Du Toit, *Neergedaal*, 97–121.

Cosmology

Wyatt[40] points out that the worldview of people in antiquity basically comprised three main levels: heaven, earth and the underworld. The series of binary representations of the first story of the creation in Genesis eventually provides for a third, the inhabitable earth. Psalm 89:11–12 powerfully puts this triad into words. To people of antiquity, the underworld was simply a spatial concept. Everyone who died went to the bosom of Abraham or to the place of pain. Gemser[41] is very emphatic that the underworld in the Old Testament is used only in a 'general sense' and the apocalyptic meaning of hell is completely excluded. Naturally, this also has a direct relation with the understanding of the word *inferna*. This word is taken from Ephesians 4:9 and corresponds to the Greek word *Hades*, which occurs eleven times in the New Testament and is often incorrectly translated as *hell*. *Hades* signifies, like the Hebrew word *sheol*, the unseen spirit-world, the abode of all the departed, both the righteous and the wicked.

A hundred years ago, however, Bousset observed already that Christian belief in the descent of Christ into the netherworld represents the assimilation and spiritualisation of a much more primitive myth.[42] The theological interpretation is therefore a spiritual elaboration of a popular and archaic myth. The more mythological emphasis, however, survives only in ambiguous allusions and apocryphal expansions of the *descensus* like those that occur in the *Acts of Thomas* and the *Gospel of Nicodemus*. Gemser,[43] among others, points out that an understanding of the Old Testament view of the underworld as a fortress and a town with portals and bars (Is. 38:10; Ps. 9:14, 107:18; Job 17:16; and Matt. 16:18) was based on an antique Babylonian myth. What are spoken of are seven portals or two times seven portals on the way to the underworld, along which the goddess Ishtar had to get rid of a piece of her clothing at every portal in order to meet death naked. Wyatt[44] points out that parallels of this story also

---

[40] Nicolas Wyatt, *Space and Time in the Religious Life of the Near East*. (Sheffield: Sheffield Academic Press, 2001), 76–77.

[41] Ben Gemser, "Die Belydenis van Christus "Neerdaling ter Helle" in die lig van die gegewens van die Ou Testament" ["Descending into Hell," in light of the evidence of the Old Testament], *HTS* 1/2 (1944), 117.

[42] Joseph Hoffman, "Confluence in Early Christian and Gnostic Literature. The 'Descensus Christi ad Inferos'," *JSNT* 10 (1981), 42–45.

[43] Gemser, "Belydenis" [Confession] 122.

[44] Wyatt, *Space & Time*, 77–90.

existed in Egypt and Sumeria. The number seven refers to the influence of the seven planetary spheres on human beings.

The people in Old Israel therefore had accepted a clear stratification of the supernatural reality: Deut. 10:12 ('heaven of heavens'); 1 Kings 8:27 (plural); Ps. 148:4 (plural); 2 Cor. 12:2 (at least three); Eph. 6:12 (plural); and Heb. 4:14, 7:26 (plural). Eph. 4:8–10 also sheds special light on the stratification of the underworld. In non-canonical material the following examples exist: 3 Baruch (five heavens); Testament of Levi (seven); 2 Enoch 20:1 28:1 (ten); 3 Enoch 19:7, 34 (seven); Ascension of Isaiah (seven); Chagigah 12 (seven). The same applies to the underworld. Wyatt indicates a very early adaptation of the *Enuma Elish* story of creation (eleventh century BC) which distinguished both three levels of heaven and three levels of the underworld:

> The upper heavens are of *luludanitu*-stone, of Anu. // He settled the three hundred Igigi therein. // The middle heavens are of *saggilmut*-stone, of Igigi. // Bel sat therein on the lofty dais in the chamber of // lapis lazuli. // He lit a lamp of *elmesu*-stone. // The lower heavens are of jasper, of the stars. // He drew the constellations of the gods thereon. // On the base of the upper-earth he made frail mankind // lie down. // On the base of the middle earth he settled his father Ea. // On the base of the lower earth he shut in // the six hundred Anunnaki.[45]

Greek allusions are evidently from the same conceptual background as the Mesopotamian material, with a mixture of Egyptian thought.[46] Du Toit[47] also points out the duality in Greek mythology by which *Hades* was the opposite pole of *helios*, alluding to the darkness as opposed to the light. With Homer, a more complicated view of *Hades* comes to the fore. Owing to Hellenism and the development of astronomy, the concept of the flat disc of the earth made way for the concept of a spherical universe in which the freely orbiting earth is encompassed by the seven planets. The souls of the dead were now to be found in the uppermost sphere of pure ether, light and fire. Only in the Greco-Roman time was *Hades* seen as place of punishment (*tartaros*) and this was powerfully developed during the Middle Ages.[48] *Hell* signifies the state and place of eternal damnation, like the Hebrew word *Gehenna* (the dale or valle of *Hinnom*), which

---

[45] Wyatt, *Space & Time*, 76.
[46] John Cooper, *Body, Soul & Life Everlasting.* (Grand Rapids: Eerdmans, 1989), 55.
[47] Du Toit, *Neergedaal*, 49.
[48] Du Toit, *Neergedaal*, 52–55.

occurs twelve times in the Greek New Testament.[49] In 1 Henoch 22 one also encounters a clear stratification of hell. There are separate regions for the just, for martyrs, for sinners who were not fully punished on earth and for sinners who were fully punished. The locality of the underworld systematically became abstract as the place of punishment and fire.

Time and Space

It is particularly important to highlight the spatial concepts of the *Apostolicum*. We have already referred to the movement from heaven downwards to the earth and back again. What is also striking is the chronological order of the course of God's work. It begins at creation and ends with the recreation. The 'second' article dealing with Jesus's person and work in particular plainly follows this historical sequence of events. It applies to both his humiliation and his elevation. The relationship between Creator and creation is not, however, a spatial or temporal relationship. This mythological synthesis of God and cosmos, with its confusion between the presence of God and upper space, is to be found in the anonymous *De Mundo* (falsely attributed to Aristotle) that gained currency in the second and third centuries.

Thomas Torrance especially is honoured for the pioneering work that he did in analysing the concepts of time and space in the Patristics and making them serviceable to a *Christian* natural theology.[50] Torrance's analysis of Plato's spatial concept is important for our purposes.[51] He shows that Plato's concept of space is a third, along with archetype and copy. It appears that Plato thought of space as helping in some way to bridge the chasm between the intelligible and sensible realms. Yet space is not the 'receptacle' of the archetype but of the *copies*. Were it not for space, we would not be able to penetrate to the rationality lying behind sensible events. Therefore spatial elements have to be used when we speak of what is beyond the separation, as if we could speak of there being a 'place' over there.

---

[49] Schaff, *Creeds*, 17.
[50] Thomas Torrance, *The Ground and Grammar of Theology* (Edinburgh: T&T Clark, 2001), 107.
[51] Thomas Torrance, *Space, Time and Incarnation* (Edinburgh: T&T Clark, 1997), 5.

According to Torrance[52] Aristotle misunderstood Plato in the sense that he misconstrued the Platonic separation as a local or spatial separation and mistook the Platonic 'receptacle' or 'matrix' for the substrate from which bodies are derived. Aristotle listed space among the categories, with the implication that space was regarded as the actual way in which things exist. Space then, is the vessel in which things exist and which exercises a certain force or causal activity in relation to them. It is the immobile limit within which a body is contained. This demands a point of absolute rest as the centre of reference for an understanding of change and transition.

Torrance consequently opted for the approach of the Stoics in terms of space. The notion of space must be thought out, not as much from the side of any container as from the side of the body being contained.[53] The principle is that the body opens space for itself. The concept of space must be formed in accordance with the nature of the occupying agent. The material universe is not held together, as Aristotle thought, by an upper sphere which forces the parts to stay together, but by immanent reason. In terms of creation theology, God is not contained by anything; rather He contains the entire universe, not in the manner of a bodily container, but by his power. Torrance paid tribute to Origen who was the first to discern the philosophical significance of this reversal of Aristotelian and Stoic concepts. This holds that God comprehends all things, giving them beginning and end, thus making them determinate and comprehensible. In short, "space has become here an epistemological as well as a cosmological principle."[54]

Dogma History: The Middle Ages and Thereafter

The iconography of the *descensus* developed particularly strongly in the Eastern Church. Böcher[55] states that the first relic of this in Syria dates from about 700 AD. It portrays the Christ, victorious over hell, with Adam and Eve following Him. In approximately 800 AD the Western Church produced a fresco with a similar theme—probably due to the fact that the

---

[52] Torrance, *Space*, 7.
[53] Torrance, *Space*, 9.
[54] Torrance, *Space*, 12.
[55] Otto Böcher, "Höllenfahrt Jesu Christi" [Jesus Christ's Journey to Hell], In *RGG4* 3, 1858–1860.

pope, John VII (705–707) came from the East. Since the eleventh century, the victory motif has had the ascension motif added to it, namely the *ascensus*. John the Baptist and purgatory (*limbus*) also come to the fore as motifs and baptism is pertinently linked to hell (cf. 1 Peter 3:18–20). Albrecht Dürer used the same theme in about 1515 in his series of paintings on the Easter cycle. Küng[56] expresses appreciation for the German Renaissance painter, Matthias Grünewald, who depicted the resurrection as a cosmic event, not against a golden background, but against the black night sky with a few shining stars. The risen Christ does not dissolve, but remains a concrete, definite person. Dante Alighieri, in his *La Divina Commedia* (1319), also described hell imaginatively in the three poems (*Inferno, Purgatorio* and *Paradiso*) and relied very strongly on the post-exile apocalyptic tradition. He believed there were nine circles in hell, but the church recognised only three spaces in the underworld: purgatory (*purgatorium*), the foyer for the patristic fathers (*limbus patrum*) and for the unbaptised children (*limbus infantum* or *puerorum*).[57]

Du Toit[58] sees the thought complex against which the Reformers protested as being precisely in the locative aspect of the *descensus*. This encompasses a special theology of incarnation which used ontological concepts in an attempt to solve the different aspects of Jesus's *descensus*. He believes it congealed the homiletic and doxological character of the *descensus* in dogma. He also traces this argument back to Luther, who rejected such scholastic assumptions. In his preaching, Luther could aptly put into words the multicoloured images and dramatic scenes of the mediaeval artists to paint the victory of Christ over death. In his well-known Torgau sermon of 16–17 April 1533, to which Article IX of the *Formula of Concord* also refers, he states: "That is the power and usefulness of this article, the reason for its happening, being preached and believed, namely, that Christ destroyed the power of hell and took away all power from the devil."[59] What is remarkable is that Luther did not reach back to the classical verse in 1 Peter 3:19 in this sermon, but used the example of the strong man who is tied up by an even stronger man (Matt. 12:29). "It was not simply that Christ's soul left heaven to join his body in the resurrection but that he appeared in both body and soul in hell to announce

---

[56] Hans Küng, *Credo. The Apostles' Creed Explained for Today.* (London: SCM Press, 1993), 96.
[57] Hans Küng, *Ewiges Leben?* [Eternal Life?] (München: Piper & Co. Verlag, 1982), 162.
[58] Du Toit, *Neergedaal*, 220–221.
[59] Otto, *Höllenfahrt*, 146.

victory prior to his resurrection appearances on earth."[60] This doctrine preserves, therefore, a double-sided view of Christ's glorification as not only involving our world, but also the supernatural world occupied by the souls of the deceased and the angels. On the basis of the Lutheran interpretation, Scaer[61] concludes that, if we scrap the article about the *descensus*, the lowest and probably the base of the three-level world-view would be discarded. The descent, the resurrection appearances and the session at the right hand belong together as a unified proclamation of Christ's victory over hell, earth and heaven.

Calvin

The most significant Reformatory interpretation of the *descensus* would only take place with the second generation of Reformers. At that time, Calvin's understanding formed the point of departure for the Heidelberg Catechism (1563), Question and Answer 44. It offers no dogmatic explanation of the *descensus*, but, true to the point of departure of Question 1—"What is your only comfort in life and in death?"—is presented as a comforting message of Christ's substitutive death: "That in my greatest temptations I may be assured that Christ, my Lord, by his inexpressible anguish, pains, and terrors which he suffered in his soul on the cross and before, has redeemed me from the anguish and torment of hell."[62]

Althaus prefers to take note of the interfaces rather than of the differences between Luther and Calvin and thinks that, as regards this matter, they tend to agree rather than to differ. The paths of their respective traditions only diverged when the debate about the time of Christ's humiliation and elevation developed. Was the *descensus* the last event of the humiliation (Calvinism) or the first of the elevation (Lutheranism)? The absolute suffering of Godforsakenness on the cross, however, is the point of departure for the confession of faith about the *descensus* for both. But as Küng[63] rightly comments, the *descensus* is not needed to express this; the *mortuus* and *sepultus* already say it.

---

[60] Scaer, "He did descend," 97.
[61] Scaer, "He did descend," 99.
[62] Schaff, *Creeds*, vol. 3, 321.
[63] Küng, *Ewiges Leben?*, 165.

In spite of Calvin's[64] statement that he takes cognisance of the sequence of events from *suffering → death → burial → descent*, and that he states roundly that this addition does say something new and is therefore essential, it carries little weight in the development of his argument. Nevertheless, to him the *descensus* shifts back two places in the continuum of events of the article of the *Apostolicum* and rightly comes between the events of suffering and death. The linearity in fact is elevated in terms of Jesus's suffering. Even the faithful Calvinist, Grudem[65] concedes that Calvin's reasoning leaves him in the lurch here. But it does not bother Du Toit[66] at all, although he immediately concedes that Calvin wants to present a material and not a chronological interpretation.

Calvin believes that the crucifixion events are for Jesus the culminating point of Godforsakenness. From the concept of the sovereignty of God, Calvin understood the atonement in terms of punitive judgment. Christ not only died a bodily death but it also "was expedient at the same time for him to undergo the severity of God's vengeance, to appease his wrath and satisfy his judgment." The *sepultus* explains what Christ endured in the sight of man: his body was offered up as the price of redemption. With the *descensus*, however, the meaning of invisible and incomprehensible judgment which he endured before God, in order that we might know, not only that Christ's body was given as the price for our redemption, but also that he paid a greater price by suffering in his soul the terrible torments of a condemned and forsaken man. With this, Calvin therefore offers a psychological explanation of Jesus's experience. "But how do [Luther and] Calvin know that?" asks Hans Küng, "There is certainly no scriptural evidence for it."[67] As a result, Van Rensburg could say that Calvin "interprets the clause purely dogmatically."[68] The real reference of the *descensus* is not to a mythological netherworld, but to the suffering of Christ on the cross. Hell is a "theological gloss on the cross"[69] and not a mythological scène following after the resurrection.

---

[64] Calvin deals fullest with the *descensus* in the 1559 edition of his Institution (II.16.7–12). In the 1556 edition, he handled it as still merely the satisfaction of the Divine penal justice. The rest of the paragraph is derived without reference from the said five chapters of the Institution (1559).

[65] Grudem, "He did not descend," 106.

[66] Du Toit, *Neergedaal*, 34.

[67] Küng, *Credo*, 98.

[68] Van Rensburg, "Katelthonta," 54.

[69] Kay, "Descended," 125.

After his investigation of Thomas Aquinas's views on this, Calvin comes to the conclusion that it is 'childish' (*puerile*) to judge that 'the souls of the dead' are confined to a kind of limbo under the earth. Calvin therefore also invokes 1 Peter 3:19 and takes the trouble to read this verse in context, but nevertheless follows Aquinas's symbolic interpretation: "Peter extols the power of Christ's death in that it penetrated even to the dead; while godly souls enjoyed the present sight of visitation which they had anxiously awaited. On the other hand, the wicked realized more clearly that they were excluded from all salvation."[70]

In his commentary on 1 Peter 3:18–22, Calvin[71] argues that there is no possibility of salvation after death. The spirit of Christ went, some time after his resurrection, to preach deliverance from the unbelievers to the souls of the faithful of the old covenant who were in their own confinement of anxiety. Only the confirmation of their judgement was proclaimed to the godless. In this sense the imagery of *Gehenna* replaces that of the *Sheol* as more aptly describing the depths of anguish. Hell in the *Apostolicum* is therefore defined by the cross. Hell is Godforsakenness. To enter into that state is to descend into hell. But it spells out victory too. Christ died on the cross and in this way brought us eternal salvation. Our Saviour grappled hand to hand with the armies of hell and the dread of everlasting death. On the cross, death has been overcome. The cry from hell simultaneously is Jesus's cry of victory.

Calvin internalised Plato's dualism so uncritically that he did not spot the non-metaphysical nuances of the anthropological terminology of the Bible. In his *Institutes* (I.15.6), for example, he states as follows: 'Indeed, from Scripture we have already taught that the soul is an incorporeal substance; now we must add that, although properly it is not spatially limited, still, set in the body, it dwells there as in a house; not only that it may animate all its parts and render its organs fit and useful for their actions, but also that it may hold the first place in ruling man's life, not alone with respect to the duties of his earthly life, but at the same time to arouse him to honour God.'[72] Soul/spirit and body are not two separate substances, but inseparable aspects or capacities. Some, such as Cooper, criticise Calvin (see e.g. *Institutes* I.15.2), who clearly interpreted texts such

---

[70] Cited by Kay, "Descended," 124.
[71] John Calvin. *The Epistle of Paul the Apostle to the Hebrews and the First and Second Epistles of St Peter* (Grand Rapids: Eerdmans, 1963), 293.
[72] Cited from Cooper, *Body*, 13.

as Matt 10:28 and Luke 23:46 dualistically, in that the soul/spirit is separated from the body at the time of death.

In summary, therefore, it can be said of Calvin that he attributed an infinite meaning to the *descensus* which fundamentally underplayed both the temporal-spatial aspects and the inclusiveness of the redemption. For this reason, it can be deduced that Calvin inadequately showed his feelings regarding the contribution and central role that the *descensus* can play in salvation.

Hermeneutic Points of Departure

Du Toit makes the following important statement in *Tenet VII* of his doctoral thesis on the *descensus*: "The true responsibility for maintaining the continuity of the confession of faith in the church is not in the first place situated in taking over or rejecting certain formulas, but in a search for their sense in view of the original basic form and religious intention and content of each separate judgement about them."[73] It seems to me that the following perspectives are essential to the way a Biblical-Reformatory theology concerns a Bible text in general and the *descensus* in particular:

- *Respect for the original text.* This means that the most accurate reading will have to be found. This also encompasses appreciating the composition, genre and reference of a text.[74]
- *Respect for the frame of reference of the people of that time.* Whereas the people of antiquity worked, for example, with a three-tiered worldview, we today do not even have a heliocentric understanding of reality and, according to astrophysics, do not even have a universe, but a multiverse.
- *Respect for the Scriptures as the normative norm.* To us, elevating the Scriptures above the confessions of faith it is an epistemological point of departure. Naturally, one is caught up in a kind of circular reasoning in that the Scriptures determine the confession of faith and the confession of faith conversely interprets the Scriptures, but this may never take place in such a way that we try to hear the message of the Scriptures impartially.

---

[73] Du Toit, *Neergedaal*, addendum.
[74] Paul Ricoeur, *Essays on Biblical Interpretation* (Philadelphia: Fortress, 1980), 99–100.

- *Respect for continuing tradition.* We may never have given, or may not give the impression that we can leap across two thousand years of wrestling today and can hear the 'actual message' of that time purely. God's revelation in Christ resulted in a tradition of events and interpretations which must be captured and translated. Tradition is never a source on its own, but always conveys other people's wrestling with Truth and therefore links back continuous with the *Sache Jesu*. Only in this way can the Scriptures be the *explicans* (the interpreter) and tradition be the *explicandum* (that which must be interpreted).
- *Respect for the global frame of reference of the recipients today.* The message should always be present, so that contemporary people with all their knowledge (including scientific knowledge) can address judgements and prejudices.
- *Respect for God's creation.* 'Heaven and earth' have intrinsic worth and all the earth's inhabitants are dependent upon specific biotopes. This leads to an interconnectedness of the whole of creation.

Contours of Contemporary Systematic Theology

It is worth mentioning that the theologians of the *Formula of Concord* could indeed have had an overview of the temporal-spatial aspects of the problematic of the *descensus*: "When and how...did Christ go to hell? Did it happen before or after his death? Did it occur only according to the soul, or only according to the deity, or according to body and soul, spiritually or corporeally?"[75] Nevertheless, these theologians flinched in view of their own insights and eventually treated it as merely an issue of faith, and so they let it remain unreasoned: "With our reason and five senses this article cannot be comprehended...We must only believe and cling to the Word." Although a contemporary Lutheran such as Pannenberg[76] is correct when he asserts that the underworld cannot be placed within temporal-spatial co-ordinates because of our modern experience of nature, it does not resolve the problem; instead, it avoids it. People of antiquity *did* think about the underworld in temporal-spatial terms. With our post-modern understanding of time and space, by which we have done away

---

[75] Theodore Tappert, *The Book of Concord: The Confession of the Evangelical Lutheran Church* (Philadelphia: Fortress, [1959] 2000), §96.

[76] Wolfhart Pannenberg, *The Apostles' Creed in the Light of Today's Questions* (London: SCM, 1976), 91–92.

with Newton's—and Aristotle's—understanding of constants (absolute time and space), we can indeed make this article serviceable in theology without spiritualising it.

We know today that time is more than movement or certain courses of events which can be placed on a one-dimensional continuum.[77] Time is understood rather as the horizon which surrounds all that is. All that is, is *in* time.[78] "For now it can be seen that time not only *has* a structure, but *is* itself the structure." Because the past necessarily has been, the present really is and the future is possible, the future has precedence in time. It is not an extension of the past, but the origin or source of the past. Potentiality therefore has ontological precedence.[79] By contrast, space is a function of time and therefore a dimensional category.[80] Compare for this purpose the striking metaphor of a 'Flatland' (Abbot)[81] which indicates that perspective determines more or fewer dimensions: in one-dimensionality reality is to me a point, in two-dimensionality a line, in three-dimensionality a cube. Creation is aimed eventually at a cosmic Sabbath and does begin with time, but ends with space.[82] It is God who comes to stay with us.

Although Du Toit[83] indicates that the *intermediate state* and *purgatory* cannot apply as the motif for incorporating the *descensus* into the *Apostolicum*, Briggs nevertheless asserts that it was precisely the formal beginning of the later Roman Catholic dogma about it.[84] Dogmatics will have to consider the so-called intermediate state about time and space further, in view of the latest developments in Systematic Theology. Moltmann does want to make room for such a space: "So I conceive of that 'intermediate state' as a wide space for living, in which the life that was spoiled and cut short here can develop freely. I imagine it as the time of a new life, in which God's history with a human being can come to its flowering and consummation."[85] An ecological theory of creation together

---

[77] For this, see my article, J. Buitendag, "Binne of buite die blokkie? 'n Poging om iets oor tyd en ewigheid te sê" [Within or without little boxes? An attempt to say something about time and eternity], in *Verbum et Ecclesia* 29(2), 320–344.

[78] Christian Link, "God and Time. Theological Approaches to the Problem of Time," *Humanities Series 72.* (Aarhus: Aarhus University Press, 1999), 191.

[79] Jürgen Moltmann, *The Coming of God* (Minneapolis: Fortress Press, 1996), 286–290.

[80] Karl Heim, *Das Weltbild der Zukunft* (Wuppertal: Aussaat Verlag, 1980), 78.

[81] Edwin Abbot, *Flatland* (London: Penguin Books, 1998).

[82] Moltmann, *Coming*, 266.

[83] Du Toit, *Neergedaal*, 178.

[84] Briggs, *Symbolics*, 67.

[85] Moltmann, *Life*, 252.

with a cosmic eschatology will have to form the contours of our reflections on God's salvation in Christ. After all, we are not redeemed from the earth, but with the earth. Put negatively, I think that the *descensus* is the overcoming of limitations, and put positively, it is the cosmic victory of Christ that is being proclaimed. There are several manifestations of finitude (see Conradie).[86] We experience restrictions to the spatial territory on which we can have an influence and so, too, the restrictions of time, because we know our lives are limited. The sting of finitude is the impact of human sin (1 Cor. 15:55). The most obvious one is that of mortality. Finitude implies a limited life span. For Moltmann, the *eschaton* has to overcome, not only the suffering caused by sin, but also the suffering resulting from the predicament of finitude.[87] Only a radically new creation can provide a solution to the predicament of transience. However, Pannenberg distinguishes clearly between death and restriction.[88] The finite life of creatures is a life in time. To be in time is to be a sinner. Death is not an implication of human finitude, it rather is sinners' non-acceptance of their finitude. The sinner's lack of recognition of his or her restrictions is what leads to death. For precisely this reason, our perspective on life after death is limited.

I want to endorse Volf [89] who wishes to give up the notions of the end of time and the end of space. The world to come is not the 'fullness of time', but the 'reconciliation of times'. For joy to be complete, he argues, it cannot be possible to pursue total simultaneity and total possession. Joy lives from the 'movement in time' qualified by a reconciled past and future in all presents.[90] The following indicators derived from Conradie[91] are worth noting:

- Eternity implies neither timelessness nor spacelessness;
- There is a stratification in our understanding of reality;

---

[86] Ernst Conradie, *Hope for the Earth* (Oregon: Wipf & Stock Publishers, 2000), 41–86.

[87] Moltmann, *Coming*, 276.

[88] Wolhart Pannenberg, *Systematic Theology*. Vol. I. (Grand Rapids: Eerdmans, 1991), 561.

[89] Miroslav Volf, "Enter into Joy!" in J. Polkinghorne and Michael Welker, *The End of the World and the Ends of God* (Harrisburg: Trinity Press International, 2000), 272.

[90] Volf, "Joy," 275.

[91] Ernst Conradie, "Resurrection, Finitude, and Ecology," in Ted Peters, Robert John Russell, and Michael Welker, *Resurrection. Theological and Scientific Assessments* (Grand Rapids: Eerdmans, 2002), 287–295.

• Eternity is a 'depth' dimension beyond the edges of the space-time continuum;
• Heaven is a dimension of creation (not of God), a dimension that is open to God, where God dwells and where God's presence may be discerned;
• Nothing that is past can pass away (Georg Picht);
• If the whole history of the cosmos is materially inscribed, then every moment would be together in God's presence in the *eschaton*.

In short, 'afterlife' is not a property of humanity, as Plato thought, but is a divine gift, divinely enacted. Amid discontinuity, the continuity lies in a sort of 'relational ontology' which is the reconciliation of all things grounded in Christ and accomplished by the Spirit.[92]

What Calvin felt embryonically and Luther pointed out forcefully, is that the *descensus* clearly spells out the victory of Christ, too. Gemser[93] still asks hesitantly whether we might not detect here, too, a universal concept of God of the prophetic religion "which does not come to a halt before the portals of the underworld." But it is Pannenberg[94] who sees the *descensus* as a 'demonstration of triumph' and, in fact, that it should be taken as a *universal understanding of salvation.* "It asserts that men outside the visible church are not automatically excluded from the salvation."[95] Pannenberg[96] and Moltmann[97] both see the *descensus*, not as the lowest point of the humiliation, but as the first point of the elevation. I prefer Küng's[98] view, however, who regarded this as a false question, since it makes too much of the linearity or succession of points. Conversion before or after one's death is not the point then, but the all-encompassing love of God for all the dead. The words of Rom 14:9 are clearly applicable here, as is the last part of Ps 139:8. Moltmann[99] moreover, reasons that the Bible never gives the same quality to the 'eternal death' as to the 'eternal life' and that it

---

[92] Joel Green, *Body, Soul and Human Life. The Nature of Humanity in the Bible* (Grand Rapids: Baker Academic, 2008), 180.
[93] Gemser, "Belydenis," 120.
[94] Pannenberg, *Creed*, 92–95.
[95] Wolfhart Pannenberg, *Jesus—God and Man* (London: SCM Press, [1964] 2002), 307.
[96] Pannenberg, *Jesus*, 308.
[97] Jürgen Moltmann, *Der Weg Jesu Christi. Christologie in messianischen Dimensionen* (München: Kaiser 1989), 213.
[98] Küng, *Credo*, 99.
[99] Moltmann, *Coming*, 91.

is indeed the case that God will eventually and literally be everything in everyone. This applies to the whole of creation, yes, to the whole cosmos. Universal reconciliation is not a heresy. It is rather the expression of hope and trust in God's goodness.[100] In the so-called 'transitional state', Christ is therefore solidly with the dead, not in the sense that it is final, but in the sense that they are nevertheless with Him (*Christologia Viae*) on the way. Küng[101] agrees and believes that the 'eternal' of the punishment "auf keinem Fall absolut gesetzt werden."

Conclusion

It is evident that the word *infernum* in the *Apostolicum* cannot be adequately reflected in the word 'hell'. The later apocalyptic tradition simply made it too heavily loaded. The word *Hades* used in the Greek version of the *Apostolicum* clearly does not contain the Hebrew meaning of *Gehenna*. A more neutral word such as 'underworld' therefore renders the historical meaning better. It naturally requires explanation in the church's preaching and catechism, but it will not serve now to want to adapt the *Apostolicum*, the Heidelberg Catechism and also the *Athanasium* to suit our Reformed dogmatics.

A strong objection to Calvin's metaphor of the *descensus*, is that he did not respect the syntactical sequence of the text. According to the wording of the *Apostolicum*, 'hell' after all occurred after his death, not before it. Using the *Institutes* of Calvin or the Heidelberg Catechism as a heuristic tool to interpret the *descensus* feeds at least the following fallacies:

- The socio-linguistic niche (Lindbeck) of the *descensus* is misjudged;
- The valuable Christian perspective on victory in 1 Peter 3:19, including victory in the underworld, is not seen;
- Contemporary *scientific theological* insights into time and space are ignored.

---

[100] Jürgen Moltmann, *In the End—the Beginning* (London: SCM Press, 2004), 150.
[101] Küng, *Credo*, 181.

Together with Calvin we know that this phrase contains an important part of our 'summary of faith', without really differing from Küng,[102] who speaks of a 'hierarchy of truth' and thus does not place it at the centre. Something of this 'mystery' should be increasingly exposed by Systematic Theology. The *descensus*, asserts Van Ruler,[103] is indeed a 'multi-coloured palette.'

---

[102] Küng, *Ewiges Leben?*, 166.
[103] Arnold Van Ruler, *Ik Geloof. De Twaalf Artikelen van het Geloof in Morgenwijdingen* [I Believe. The Twelve articles of Faith in Morning Devotions] (Nijkerk: Callenbach, 1968), 102.

CHAPTER NINE

CALVIN'S CONTRIBUTION TO A COMMON ECCLESIAL SPIRITUALITY

Roger Haight, S. J.

This paper examines John Calvin's theology in order to raise up univer-
sally relevant ecclesiological themes that are essential to a common ecclesiology which all Christians share. The method of this effort is generally
ecumenical. More precisely, it is guided by principles of the subdiscipline
of comparative ecclesiology. One phase of comparative ecclesiology examines the history of the discipline of ecclesiology and by comparison notices
the differences that mark the understandings of the Christian churches
across its history.[1] Another phase of comparative ecclesiology proposes a
description of the living ecclesiology that all Christians share in common,
if not together. It strives to find those dimensions of an understanding
of the church that are operative in most—if not all—understandings of
the church. On the assumption that ecclesiologies reflect the actual life of
the churches, a comparison of various ecclesiologies allows one to discern
certain foundational dimensions of ecclesial existence as such.[2]

While this is not an explicitly comparative essay, it arises out of the
background of a quest for what Christians share in common. It turns to
Calvin because of the comprehensive and integral character of his ecclesiology and the wide authority and influence that it still enjoys across many
denominations. The search for the foundations of ecclesiology in an ecclesial existence means that the first priority of this essay is not to reproduce
Calvin's ecclesiology as he addressed it to Genevans and the wider church
in the sixteenth century. Generally speaking Calvin did not do ecclesiology 'from below,' although some aspects of his ecclesiology were adapta-
tions of practices already in place. Rather, the primary intent of this essay
is to draw Calvin's thought forward into the twenty-first century and to

---

[1] Roger Haight, *Christian Community in History*, I–II (New York: Continuum Interna-
tional, 2004–2005).
[2] See Roger Haight, "Comparative Ecclesiology," in *The Routledge Companion to the
Christian Church*, ed. by Gerard Mannion and Lewis S. Mudge (New York and London:
Routledge, 2008), 392–393; Idem., *Ecclesial Existence: Christian Community in History, III*
(New York: Continuum International, 2009).

propose ways in which it is relevant to all the churches in the present-day
context of Western societies.

Doing this clearly in a short space will require some definitions of
terms, an introduction to the language employed, and more explanation
of the method. Thus the chapter will have two distinct parts. The first,
entitled 'Presuppositions,' lays down the assumptions and concepts that
are being employed. For example, the term 'spirituality' is not typical of
Calvin's theology and this raises the question of its appropriateness when
discussing his thought. These considerations, then, will set up the second
constructive part entitled 'Three [Ecclesiological] Themes from Calvin.'
This part represents the heart of the thesis, namely, that an appreciation
of some central convictions about the church that were Calvin's are uni-
versally relevant and essential for any understanding of a common ecclesial spirituality.

Presuppositions

The most important presuppositions of this discussion lie imbedded in
the phrase that appears in its title: 'a common ecclesial spirituality.' A
good place to begin is with the term 'spirituality.' There is no common
agreed meaning of 'spirituality,' and thus it becomes incumbent on anyone using it to explain what it refers to. In this essay spirituality means
the way persons or a group lead their lives in relation to what they consider ultimate truth and reality. Christian spirituality consists in human
lives lived before God as God is revealed in Jesus Christ. The closest term
for this meaning of 'spirituality' in Calvin's *Institutes* may be paraphrased
as 'the Christian life' as that is described in Book III.[3] Spirituality embraces
the whole of Christian life, not just prayer, worship, and sacrament. It
includes the internal discipline described by a theology of the cross, the
use of creatures and the things of this world according to God's creative
intent, and Calvin's formula for stewardship.[4] For example, he believes
that scripture regulates human use of earthly things. "It decrees that all
those things were so given to us by the kindness of God, and so destined

---

[3] John Calvin, *Calvin: Institutes of the Christian Religion*, ed. by John T. McNeill (Philadelphia: Westminster Press, 1960), III.6–10.

[4] See Günther H. Haas, "Ethics and Church Discipline," in Herman J. Selderhuis ed.
The Calvin Handbook (Grand Rapids: Eerdmans, 2009), 332–344 for a brief overview of the
Christian life in Calvin's theology.

for our benefit, that they are, as it were, entrusted to us, and we must one day render account of them."[5] Thus care of the earth helps define a spirituality.

From this broad understanding of the term 'spirituality' one can see that it represents fairly well Calvin's concept of the Christian life and makes it relevant to a world of many Christians today who self-define as being more spiritual than religious. Christian spirituality refers to the way Christians live, as individuals and as a group, not only in church, but also in the family, at work, in society, and more generally in the world. This is the existential reality; the discipline of spirituality studies it.

This conception of spirituality as referring to Christian existence itself is so broadly defined that it forms a framework, or large topic, or area of attention that contains within itself other more specific subject matters. For example, one can see how the study of ethics, and practical theology of prayer and everyday life all come together in the area of spirituality as it has been construed here. By analogy, Calvin's theology of God and providence, his christology and conception of salvation, and his ecclesiology as well, all converge in his theology of the Christian life, his spirituality. This then is the first plank in the platform for the constructive reflections that will follow: they emerge from within the arena of a theology of the Christian life or spirituality.

The second large premise operative in this discussion states that being a Christian and a member of a Christian church defines a spirituality. While that is obvious enough, more needs to be said. Beneath the distinctive spiritualities that mark different churches, one can discern a common ecclesial existence shared by all Christians across denominational lines. This points to what may be defined as a common ecclesial spirituality. This may at first sight seem contentious, but what such a common Christian ecclesial spirituality entails can be illustrated with a simple thought experiment.

Suppose a traveling seminar of nine or ten Christians, all of widely different denominations or churches, is visiting sites of other religions. While in India, when a Hindu host asks the members of the group, "Are you all of the same faith?" they would say, "Yes, we are all Christians," even though all of them know that their churches are not the same and in fact may be quite different from each other. How or on what basis are they allowed to say that they share the same faith? No one answers that question more

---

[5] Calvin, *Institutes* III.10.5.

directly or better than Paul in Ephesians when he urges his readers, who are us, to a spirituality of patience and the forbearance of love that is worthy of our Christian calling: "There is one body and one Spirit, just as you were called to the one hope that belongs to your call, one Lord, one faith, one baptism, one God and Father of us all, who is above all and through all and in all."[6] These core elements define a unity among Christians that is infinitely more important, essential, defining, and true than all the many other smaller things that divide them. This, then, begins to define the common ecclesial existence, the common ecclesial spirituality, that is shared by all Christians.

Why is this conception important? What does it contribute to a discussion of the church? There may be several responses to these questions, but two things that this idea of a common ecclesial spirituality opens up to the imagination seem to bear relevance for our time. First, the idea of a common Christian ecclesial existence or spirituality focuses attention to something so deep in Christian existence that it provides a single groundwork for the church beneath the differences among the churches. This opens up a generative idea of pluralism. Pluralism in this context does not equal sheer plurality and difference, but precisely differences that exist together within a common field, or differences that are all parts of some greater thing that holds them together and unites them. In this case the one single reality is defined by Paul as a unity in one Father, one Lord, one Spirit, one faith, one Baptism. Second, because of this greatest common denominator, a common ecclesial existence or spirituality provides a space within which Christians can talk across differences about what they share in common. It provides a place or focal point for talking as a "we" about what both unites and differentiates us.

On the basis of these ideas of spirituality and a common ecclesial existence the following discussion will not attend to the differences among Christians but to what they share or should share in common. In other words, the point is to parse some of the characteristics of the ecclesial existence of all Christians. Some of these are expressed in Calvin's ecclesiology in an exemplary way. Therefore the goal here is to raise up and underline some characteristics of what may contribute to a common ecclesial existence as these are articulated by Calvin. But these dimensions of the Christian life will not be described for a sixteenth century audience; the point is not to reproduce Calvin's thought as he expressed it in his

---

[6] Eph. 4:4–6.

context. This essay is explicitly hermeneutical and seeks to interpret Calvin from the perspective of a present-day evolutionary, historically-conscious, and religiously pluralistic world. Underlying this essay is a method of correlation which puts Calvin's texts in dialogue with our world today. Such an interpretation therefore involves subtlety and ambiguity. The reader may be seeing and hearing 'Calvin,' but the intended audience is not the church in Geneva. Rather one will actually be reading about three themes drawn from Calvin that have a universal relevance, one that all Christian churches today who are willing to learn from Calvin could and should internalize.

Three Themes from Calvin

Thus this second part takes up the larger constructive discussion of three themes from Calvin's ecclesiology that transcend Calvinist churches and have a universal Christian ecclesiological relevance. These three themes are put forward in the form of theses. In each case the thesis is generalized, but one could affirm it about Calvin's ecclesiology from which it is drawn.

1. *[Calvin's] Ecclesiology rests theologically on a trinitarian foundation that opens up the imagination today to a narrative account of the role of the Christian church in history.*
    This first thesis about the church is drawn from Calvin as Calvin has been interpreted by Benjamin Milner.[7] Milner's book intends to get at the theological foundations of the church in Calvin's thought. In doing so he essentially moves Calvin's ecclesiology away from a narrow christocentric understanding of the church to a larger trinitarian view. This shift in focus provides a comprehensive theology of history and thus addresses present-day self-consciousness and an historicist worldview. We turn first to an abbreviated presentation of Milner's view and then the riff on it that applies to ecclesial spirituality.
    Milner believes that a way to uncover the theological foundations of the church in Calvin's theology lies in an understanding of the structure of the *Institutes* themselves. Frequently theologians construe the kernel

---

[7] Benjamin Charles Milner, *Calvin's Doctrine of the Church* (Leiden: E. J. Brill, 1970). I do not read Milner's work as polemical but as opening up a broad understanding of the church that can accommodate other emphases in Calvin's ecclesiology.

of Calvin's theology as lying in the sovereignty of God, or in its christo-centrism; some see the *Institutes* as simply following the creed. The point here is not to dispute these interpretations. But Milner suggests another structural framework for the *Institutes* that does not dismiss the others but integrates the four books books of the *Institutes* quite neatly. The coherence of the whole work lies in Calvin's idea of order and the restoration of the order of creation after the Fall through the correlative functions of the Word and the Spirit of God. After the doctrine of creation is acclaimed as order, and the Fall as a disruption of order, restored order is called for by the Word and brought to us by the Spirit through the external means of the church. This scheme displays a deep cosmic grounding for the church and locates his ecclesiology in the context of the doctrine of the Trinity.[8]

In Calvin's theology, according to Milner, the church represents the historical restoration of the way things should be in a relationship to God that is going forward in history. This implies three things. First, the church is a historical movement, a history, effected by God as Spirit in human lives. By contrast, the church is not primarily a static structure or institutional form, although that dimension is not at all neglected with Calvin. Secondly, sanctification presents itself as the central defining element of the church: this is what the church is for. Its essence does not lie in doctrine, creed, tradition, ritual, or polity, but in spirituality, or, in Calvin's terms, corporate and individual Christian life. All of the other structural elements serve the restoration of the order of human existence, the *imago Dei*, in history. But this also means, thirdly, that the church bears within itself an essential orientation towards the world and history. It does not exist apart from society but exists precisely to play a role in human society and history.[9]

This conception has a certain appeal to the consciousness of our time, and the reason for this may be found in the way Calvin employs the doctrine of the Trinity. It is the economic Trinity that he is referring to, and the economic doctrine of the Trinity represents God dealing with human existence historically, that is, interacting with human existence in the course of history and through the media of history. This framework thus provides what may be called a narrative theology of the relationship between God and human beings, a theology that tells the Christian story of God interacting with the world: first through creation, then through

---

[8] Milner, *Calvin's Doctrine of the Church*, 193.
[9] Milner, *Calvin's Doctrine of the Church*, 194–195.

various agents in history such as Abraham, Moses, the kings, and the prophets, and finally in Jesus Christ the very Word of God. But the story continues as the church mediates the Spirit of God's ongoing interchange with human beings in an explicit, self-conscious way.

This fundamental vision is both dynamic and cosmic. It portrays God working within the created process. As such it can be extended and expanded to absorb our present evolutionary worldview. God as Spirit who hovered over the deep in the dramatic image of Genesis represents God's creative Spirit who creates not all and everything at once but through time as the ongoing dynamic power of the being of reality and the movement of history. The church, as an extension of Jesus in history, and animated by God as Spirit as the power of faith and regeneration, has its grounding precisely in this dynamically energizing divine presence. This expansive cosmic view of God's work and presence in the world, revealed in Jesus and actual today in the Spirit, opens the Christian imagination out into the world in positive creative ways that will be developed further in the next theses.

2. *[In Calvin's ecclesiology] The church mediates to each member an ecclesial existence or spirituality by which the individual may be united with God morally and ontologically by the way he or she leads her everyday vocational life.*

The second and third theses will address directly the question of spirituality as that which defines the immediate goal of the church. This second thesis focuses upon the spirituality of the individual Christian; the next thesis takes up the corporate spirituality of the church as a community.

The role and purpose of the church is to mediate to people God's grace in the form of Word and Spirit. Calvin is explicit about this as the title of Book IV indicates: the church is "the external means or aids by which God invites us into the society of Christ and holds us therein."[10] God could have arranged things in such a way that God appealed internally to each individual person by a private inspiration. But, in fact, God did not do so, but deals with human beings historically through historical means and agents. The church is God's institutional agent through which God's saving power in Jesus Christ and the Spirit are channeled to human consciousness and spirit. As an institution the church provides ministry, that is, service empowered by the Spirit of God for delivering the benefits of

---

[10] Calvin, *Institutes* IV. title of the book.

Christ to the Christian community and through it to society. Thus church ministry is cooperation with God's action in society, the actualization of the church's being an instrument of God's salvation in history.[11]

This is explained by Calvin in his doctrine of redemption through Christ and more pointedly through the working of God as Spirit who opens up faith in the individual to regeneration and sanctification. Calvin incorporates into his own theology Luther's insistence on justification by grace through faith. But his more distinctive move lies in his reverence for the law as a positive guide for the spiritual life of sanctification.[12] Ethics thus becomes a part of this spirituality. It is true that we are related to God by our faith. This faith, according to Calvin, consists in an internal recognition and appropriation of God's forgiving love for us, a "firm and certain knowledge," that is "both revealed to our minds and sealed upon our hearts through the Holy Spirit."[13] But the true character of that firm and certain knowledge, its authenticity, displays itself in an ethical life. A concern for ethics is drawn into the response of faith to God's promise in the power of the Spirit. Law and ethics then become the guide of sanctification and the Christian life.

One's active relationship to God, one's spirituality, must also be celebrated in worship of God in Word and Sacrament. Stressing the Christian life does not entail minimizing expressly religious or prayerful and worshiping activities that have God as their direct and intentional object. In a way this goes without saying because these activities are thoroughly associated with the church. But they so strongly tend to encompass the whole of Christian spirituality that one has to remind oneself that the other ninety percent of one's time and activity also determine or measure our being united with God. Thus Calvin included in his conception of ecclesial spirituality some positive rules and maxims for governing one's life in the world: one should use creatures in moderation, in a way that Aristotle would call virtuous, avoiding extremes, and in a way that helps rather than hinders our journey through life towards its goal.[14] We should use all the things of this world, which are creatures of God and thus good, in the manner that God intends, according to their purpose.[15]

---

[11] Alexandre Ganoczy, *Calvin: Théologien de l'Église et du Ministère* [Calvin: Theologian of the Church and of Ministry] (Paris: Édition du Cerf, 1964), 221–243, 295–297.

[12] Calvin, *Institutes* II.7.12–14.

[13] Calvin, *Institutes* III.2.7.

[14] Calvin, *Institutes* III.10.1.

[15] Calvin, *Institutes* III.10.2.

As stewards, human beings are responsible to God for creation insofar as it is in our hands.[16] In this way Calvin incorporates the whole life of the person, one's whole spirituality as it has been defined, into the orbit of the church's concern for mediating God's grace in Word and Spirit. One's professional vocation, one's calling or station in life according to one's talents and one's actual work are drawn together into the ecclesial spirituality of each individual.

Finally, what exactly is the character of the union with God that the church thus mediates? On the one hand it is a moral union, a union of wills, a union of two freedoms that address and respond to each other. The Christian is united with God by doing God's will in his or her own life. But while he includes this, Calvin's conception of the union with God that is negotiated in ecclesial spirituality is much deeper and should be called ontological and mystical. People who live out Christian faith are empowered by the true presence of God as creator that holds them in existence. They are transformed by the forgiving and accepting Word of God that is sealed in baptism. And most dramatically of all, the Spirit of God is actually operative in their lives as an internal enlightening presence to the mind and an empowering presence to the will. The Spirit of God actually causes the knowledge given through faith and gives it the affective appeal that moves human beings to act.[17] The Spirit of God refers to God present and at work in a way that transcends creative sustenance in being. It suggests an interpersonal bonding on an ontic level that transcends mere objective obedience to the will of another. Christian spirituality in Calvin's construction, then, consists of active cooperation with the power of God within history.

3. *[In Calvin's ecclesiology] The church mediates a corporate ecclesial existence and spirituality by which the church plays a role (along with other religious bodies) in public social life and the history of the world.*

It is very important not to reduce the idea of spirituality to the level of the individual. The spirituality that makes up ecclesial existence is precisely the life of the whole community. As individuals Christians internalize a spirituality of members of the community; an individual's spirituality has a dimension that is shared with—because learned from and practiced in concert with—the community. Calvin is distinguished as a theologian

---

[16] Calvin, *Institutes* III.10.5.

[17] See note 13.

who developed both individual and corporate grounds for a spirituality of engagement in history. The social dimension of spirituality thus means two things: first, the individual is called to live in and contribute to society; second, the whole community shares a common task of being present and active in society.

The first level of a social spirituality develops out of the personal spirituality developed in the last thesis. God's providence for each person is displayed in the talents and capacities, even the external circumstances of birth and growth, that define the identity of each one. These 'givens' with creation are the signs of each one's vocation. Even though we might understand providence a bit differently than Calvin in the later contexts of an evolutionary world and history where randomness plays such a central role in our self-understanding even as a human race, still these qualities that are given to each one by God in our creation are the indicators of God's general will for our vocation in history. Ordinarily, people go in the direction their talents and capacities lead them. In virtually every case, they lead people out of themselves into community and society. Christians as such have a role in society and history.

A second level of a corporate ecclesial spirituality refers the role of the whole community in society. Here one can distinguish, as Calvin did at least implicitly in his actions, between two distinct mandates. These may be called 'witness' and 'practice,' and they correlate roughly with what are often called 'proclamation' and 'developmental practices' relative to society.

The task or mission of witness and proclamation of course goes on within the church. But the church is also called to be a witness of the values of the kingdom of God as revealed by Jesus in society outside the church. The church as the continuing agent of Jesus Christ in history has a role of continuing Jesus' ministry in history. For Calvin "the church is elected by God to serve as a tool of God and to make community with Christ possible and real. This functional meaning of the church dominates all other aspects of Calvin's ideas on the church...."[18] This includes proclaiming the values of the kingdom of God as they come to bear on the social issues of our time. This may mean backing those movements in history that foster kingdom values, or it may consist in prophetic discourse against policies that contradict the humane and healing values and practices of Jesus.

---

[18] Georg Plasger, "Ecclesiology," in *The Calvin Handbook*, 323.

On the level of practice, it is clear today that the church as a community cannot be satisfied with sending individuals out into the world to practice Christian values as private citizens who are also Christians. The churches in their congregations and in larger synodal or denominational public presences are actors in society who sometimes give dramatic witness by their silence when they do not address certain social issues. Calvin's whole career in Geneva is itself an example of a leadership of a church engaged in society. It is clearer today than it could have been in Calvin's time that there must be some kind of separation between church and state. That is a given in modern democratic and pluralistic societies. Calvin in his own way was quite clear about the distinct roles of Church and city government.[19] But these two lines of authority overlapped, and they overlap today. No one can completely separate Christian faith from citizenship, the responsibilities of one from the responsibilities of the other. The church's corporate spirituality will never be one of wanting to be or do what secular authority does, but it must play a role in secular life and do so as a community however delicate this process must be. In principle, Calvin would have favored the liberation theologies that have developed over the past few decades.

Conclusion

The goal here has been to raise up dimensions of a common ecclesial existence or spirituality that can be drawn from the ecclesiology of John Calvin; 'common' means 'ecumenical,' that is, reflective of and applicable to all churches. These are aspects of the church that transcend the sixteenth century and particularly fit our self-understanding in the twenty-first century.

The first of three dimensions lies in the foundations of the church in a God who approaches human beings across history as creator, redeemer, and sanctifier. This dynamic 'economic' view of God gives the church an identity that has a role in a narrative of God's dealings with human existence. This self-understanding coheres with a historically self-conscious humanity and a new evolutionary consciousness of the world and the cosmos. It also fits with the narrative understanding of spirituality that is

---

[19] Haight, *Christian Community in History*, II, 121–131.

proposed here. The same God as Spirit that hovers over the deep animates the church as the people of God as they live their lives.

Second, spirituality consists in a person's whole pattern of life in relation to ultimate reality. The common spirituality of all Christians that includes faith, regeneration, sanctification, ethical decisions, and religious responses of prayer and worship constitute the union with God of each member of the church. In response to grace, people's everyday behavior establish their relationship to God. Ecclesial spirituality, especially as described by Calvin, constitutes the members of the church in a moral and ontological union with God that embraces and absorbs all their weakness and sin, on one side, and their positive actions, on the other.

Third, because every church is always also a public institution or entails one, it also has a corporate identity that transcends each single member. Calvin was sensitive to the church as a moral body and how, as such, it should behave in the public arena of society. The norms for this behavior lie in Jesus' ministry to the kingdom of God. By internalizing these norms churches should lead their members into patterns of bearing witness to and practice of the values of the kingdom of God in a public way.

CHAPTER TEN

JOHN CALVIN AND THE SACRAMENT OF THE LORD'S SUPPER: A CONTEMPORARY APPRAISAL

J. Todd Billings

How are we to assess the contemporary significance of John Calvin's theology of the sacraments, and the Lord's Supper in particular? This question leads to several closely related ones. According to some, Calvin's account of the Lord's Supper caused schisms rather than healed them—thus how can it have any ecumenical value for today? Others worry that Calvin's sacramental theology is overly preoccupied with the Word, demoting the sacraments to an inferior role of something analogous to a sermon illustration. Such critics point to the deficiencies in contemporary Reformed practice of the Lord's Supper, and attribute it to Calvin's 'Word-centered' approach. If Calvin's theology is to be retrieved today, how should these alleged deficiencies be overcome?

Addressing these questions intersects three lines of inquiry that are interrelated, but distinct.[1] First, a historical question: what is a plausible historical-reconstruction of Calvin's teaching on the Lord's Supper? Second, a history-of-reception question: to what ends have Calvin's writings on the sacrament of the Supper been used, particularly in the Reformed tradition? Third, a question of contemporary relevance: what retrieval from Calvin's eucharistic thought might be possible and desirable for today? These are important questions if insights from Calvin's work are to be retrieved for today. There are enigmas within Calvin's eucharistic

---

[1] There is danger in conflating these three types of inquiry, although all three are necessary to assess and appropriate Calvin for contemporary contexts today. For example, it is tempting to put expectations on Calvin's sacramental theology that it should give a systematic statement of the Reformed tradition's beliefs on the sacraments—providing the framework for generations of Reformed Christians after him. But that is not how Calvin viewed his own project, nor how later generations of Reformed Christians viewed him. Calvin saw himself as one among a number of significant second-generation Reformational theologians, and the centuries following Calvin saw him as one among *several* key early Reformed theologians. See Richard Muller, "Demoting Calvin: The Issue of Calvin and the Reformed Tradition," in *John Calvin, Myth and Reality: Images and Impact of Geneva's Reformer* (Eugene: Cascade Books, 2011), 3–17.

theology and its reception, which also lead to difficult questions related to the contemporary reception of his work. Identifying and appropriating Calvin's insights requires textual, historical, and systematic lines of inquiry brought into tandem.

This essay pulls together these approaches in examining three topics related to Calvin's theology of the sacrament of the Lord's Supper. First, I explore Calvin's eucharistic theology in relation to the possibility of finding commonality with other Christian traditions. Second, I explore whether Calvin's sacramental theology in general, and eucharistic theology in particular, involves—and necessarily leads to—a word-centered faith that displaces a key role for the sacraments. Finally, in light of the inquiry on the previous two topics, I explore Calvin's account of the Lord's Supper as an icon of Gospel, a sacrament of union with Christ, as an account worthy of contemporary retrieval.

Calvin's Eucharistic Theology and Agreement with Churches of Other Traditions

Polemical disputes about the nature of the Lord's Supper are central to the origins of the continental reformations. By the time Calvin begins to develop his sacramental theology, unity had been fractured not only with Rome, but between early French, Swiss and German strands of the magisterial Reformation. Thus, contextually considered, it may be surprising to claim that Calvin's eucharistic theology—with all of its polemics, and the twists and turns of its development—displays a concern for Christian unity, and a search for commonality with Christians of other traditions. But there is strong evidence to think that Calvin's eucharistic theology does just that, even if it is in very different terms than modern notions of what it means to be 'ecumenical.'

As both Christopher Ellwood and John W. Riggs have argued in distinct ways,[2] as a second generation evangelical thinker, Calvin sought to combine elements from both Zwingli and Luther in his sacramental theology. Riggs points out that in the 1536 *Institutes*, Calvin's definition of the sacrament leans toward Luther, as "an outward sign" which "never lacks a preceding promise, but is rather joint to it ... to confirm and seal the promise

---

[2] Christopher Ellwood, *The Body Broken* (Oxford: Oxford University Press, 1999); John W. Riggs, *Baptism in the Reformed Tradition* (Louisville: Westminster John Knox, 2002), chapter 2.

itself."[3] By 1539, Calvin adds a secondary, more Zwinglian, sense to this: to "attest to religion in the sight of others."[4] Elwood shows how from early in his career, Calvin was profoundly influenced in his sacramental theology by Guillaume Farel and Antoine Marcourt—representing a Zwinglian strand of the Reformation, and using a theology of the ascension as a polemic against transubstantiation, and any idea of the local presence of Christ at the Supper.[5]

Yet, on the other hand, Calvin appropriates Luther's own criticism of a Zwinglian position as that which presents an "empty sign," failing to communicate God's promise. Against this, Calvin claims that sacramental signs truly exhibit the reality signified.[6] Moreover, eating Christ at the Supper is not simply the same as believing in Christ—but that in receiving the Supper by faith, Jesus Christ as the "substance" of the sign is truly communicated to the recipient.[7]

> Now, that sacred partaking of his flesh and blood, by which Christ pours his life into us, as if it penetrated into our bones and marrow, he also testifies and seals in the Supper—not by presenting a vain and empty sign, but by manifesting there the effectiveness of his Spirit to fulfill what he promises. And truly he offers and shows the reality there signified to all who sit at that spiritual banquet, although it is received with benefit by believers alone, who accept such great generosity with true faith and gratefulness of heart.[8]

---

[3] John Calvin, *Institutes of the Christian Religion: 1536 ed.*, trans. F.L. Battles (Grand Rapids: Eerdmans, 1986), 87.

[4] See Riggs, *Baptism in the Reformed Tradition*, 42–47.

[5] Ellwood, *The Broken Body*, 63.

[6] *Genevan Catechism*, 1545. "Have we in the Supper a mere symbol of those benefits you mention, or is their reality exhibited to us there? Since our Lord Jesus Christ is the truth itself, there can be no doubt but that the promises which he there gives us, he at the same time also implements, adding the reality to the symbol. Therefore I do not doubt but that, as testified by words and signs, he thus also makes us partakers of his substance, by which we are joined in one life with him." Translation from *Calvin: Theological Treatises*, ed. J.K.S. Reid (Philadelphia: Westminster Press, 1954), 137.

[7] On the "substance" language, see the previous note. On the difference between "believing" and "eating:" "For there are some who define the eating of Christ's flesh and the drinking of his blood as, in one word, nothing but to believe in Christ. But it seems to me that Christ meant to teach something more definite, and more elevated, in that noble discourse in which he commends to us the eating of his flesh. It is that we are quickened by the true partaking of him; and he has therefore designated this partaking by the words "eating" and "drinking," in order that no one should think that the life that we receive from him is received by mere knowledge. As it is not the seeing but the eating of bread that suffices to feed the body, so the soul must truly and deeply become partaker of Christ that it may be quickened to spiritual life by his power." Calvin, *Institutes* IV.17.5. Unless otherwise noted, references to the *Institutes* are from *Institutes of the Christian Religion*, ed. John T. McNeill, trans. Ford Lewis Battles (Philadelphia: Westminster Press, 1960).

[8] Calvin, *Institutes* IV.17.10.

Calvin seeks to articulate a mediating position between the Lutheran and Zwinglian divide, and also seeks to affirm doctrinal commonality with the two groups when possible. Thus, in seeking commonality with the Lutheran tradition, Calvin can subscribe to Melanchthon's revised Augsburg Confession which states that "the body and blood of Christ are truly exhibited with the bread and wine."[9] Calvin not only subscribes to this formulation, he repeatedly uses the term *"exhibere,"* meaning "to exhibit" or "to present," in his various writings on the Lord's Supper. The term itself has a conciliatory sense, as it was a term used by Melanchthon and Bucer in the Wittenburg Concord in 1536.[10] Yet, on the other hand, Calvin is willing to make considerable compromise in his preferred language about the Lord's Supper in order to sign the Agreement of Zurich with Bullinger (the *Consensus Tigurinus*).[11] In both cases, Calvin sought to harmonize the language of differing Protestant traditions with his own.

Seen in his historical context, Calvin not only sought to consolidate a limited Protestant unity by statements of agreement, but also with his strong rhetorical attack upon the Mass. In the context of quite fragile early Protestant unity, a common enemy in the doctrine of transubstantiation provided an area with considerable common ground for early Protestants. The bulk of Calvin's negative polemic against the Mass was likely to be broadly agreed upon among the early Protestant readers of the *Institutes*. While I do not consider this feature of Calvin's thought to be a promising direction for ecumenism today, in a historical account of Calvin's eucharistic theology, one should recognize that agreement upon what constitutes a reprehensible error is still a form of agreement.[12]

So, in both his constructive work and negative rhetoric, Calvin displays concern for a limited form of Christian unity on the sacraments. Yet, as

---

[9] See Timothy George, "John Calvin and the Agreement of Zurich (1549)" in *John Calvin and the Church*, ed. Timothy George (Louisville: Westminster John Knox, 1990), 44–45.

[10] See Sue A. Rozeboom, "Calvin's Doctrine of the Lord's Supper and Its Early Reception," in *Calvin's Theology and Its Reception*, ed. J. Todd Billings and I. John Hesselink (Philadelphia: Westminster John Knox, 2012).

[11] See J. Todd Billings, *Calvin, Participation, and the Gift: The Activity of Believers in Union with Christ* (Oxford: Oxford University Press, 2007), 96–100.

[12] I am not suggesting that contemporary appropriations of Calvin's sacramental theology continue this practice of forging agreement through a common polemic against the Mass. Rather, as a historical and contextual observation, I want to point out how many points of Calvin's polemic rhetoric against the Mass would have a type of unifying function for Protestant readers of his eucharistic theology.

the recent essay by Wim Janse points out,[13] precisely because he seeks to stretch between the traditions of Zwingli, Bucer and Luther in his theological and polemical approach to the sacraments, Calvin's eucharistic theology undergoes considerable development as he "was able to make compromises and be conciliatory in his formulations," while still holding strongly to his favored formulation on other points.[14] As Thomas Davis had pointed out, Calvin moved "from denying the Eucharist as an instrument of grace to affirming it as such, [while developing] a notion of substantial partaking of the true body and blood of Christ over his career."[15] Davis is correct, but Janse shows how the development continues even late in Calvin's career, for identifiably Lutheran, Bucerian, and Zwinglian strands of Calvin's theology persist in his "mature" eucharistic thought.[16] Calvin "did not envisage phrasing his eucharistic doctrine in a permanent timeless form," Janse argues.[17] Instead, Calvin, as a theologian seeking to give a biblical and theological account of the sacraments that could help nurture the church and forge some form of Christian unity, speaks differently about the sacraments depending upon his particular interlocutors, and the context of the particular theological question. Yet, as Janse argues, this observation suggests that at times Calvin seeks a form of Christian unity ("a desire for consensus") so deeply that he is willing to modify his eucharistic theology over the course of his career, and seek to incorporate insights from competing schools of sacramental thought.[18]

Has Calvin's eucharistic theology—in its reception—forged a way toward a limited form of Christian unity, in the way that he sought in his own context? The question is a complex one as it relates to the history of reception. Certainly, polemics between Lutheran and Reformed—and various strands of the Reformed tradition—have continued for centuries. At times, the points of disagreement have centered on areas in which there may be internal tensions in Calvin's theology. For example, Calvin's sense that part of the role of the sacrament is to display the piety of believers

---

[13] Wim Janse, "Calvin's Eucharistic Theology: Three Dogmatic-Historical Observations," in *Calvinus sacrarum literarum interpres: Papers of the International Congress on Calvin Research*, ed. Herman J. Selderhuis (Göttingen: Vandenhoeck and Ruprecht, 2008), 37–69.

[14] Janse, "Calvin's Eucharistic Theology," 68–69.

[15] Thomas Davis, *The Clearest Promises of God: The Development of Calvin's Eucharistic Teaching* (New York: AMS Press, 1995), 7–8.

[16] Janse, "Calvin's Eucharistic Theology," 60–61.

[17] Janse, "Calvin's Eucharistic Theology," 40.

[18] Janse, "Calvin's Eucharistic Theology," 51–67.

before God, while yet the sacraments are an instrument of divine grace, first and foremost a promise that God holds forth through a sign. The history of reception is further complexified on this point, however, because Calvin has never been the sole progenitor of Reformed sacramental theology. As Howard Hageman shows in his history of the Reformed liturgy, Calvin's influence was often overshadowed by others in the liturgical forms used by Reformed churches.[19] Moreover, as Brian Gerrish has shown, the Reformed confessions contain a range of perspectives on the sacraments reflecting the favored language of various Reformed thinkers; they do not reflect Calvin's sacramental theology in a direct or unmixed way.[20]

In the history of reception, however, it is striking to observe how in cases where limited Protestant ecumenical agreement has taken place, Calvin's eucharistic theology has often had a mediating role—opening the possibility to newly formulated statements that differ from Calvin, but are nevertheless indebted to his eucharistic theology. For example, consider the declaration emerging from Lutheran, Reformed and Union churches in Germany, in the face of the threat of National Socialism in 1937. Michael Welker summarizes key points of this common declaration, including that Jesus Christ is the giver and the gift in the Supper,[21] communicating himself to those with faith; the Lord's Supper is "a communal meal, a meal that grounds community."[22] Negatively, in light of the declaration, "two misplaced concentrations have been increasingly edged out of the picture"—a "concentration on 'the elements' in themselves," and a "concentration on an abstract 'ubiquity' of Christ."[23] For those with familiarity with Calvin's sacramental theology, it is easy to see reflections of his thought in ecumenical declarations like this one[24]—a declaration that

---

[19] Hageman claims, for example, that "to whatever extent theology is shaped by liturgy, to that extent Zurich has been of greater influence than either Strasbourg or Geneva." See Howard Hageman, *Pulpit and Table* (Louisville: John Knox Press, 1962), 33.
[20] Particularly significant on this point is Gerrish's typology of symbolic parallelism, symbolic instrumentalism, and symbolic memorialism. See Brian A. Gerrish, "Sign and Reality: the Lord's Supper in the Reformed Confessions," *The Old Protestantism and the New* (Chicago: University of Chicago Press, 1982), 118–130.
[21] Michael Welker, *What Happens in Holy Communion?*, trans. John F. Hoffmeyer (Grand Rapids: Eerdmans, 2000), 92, 99.
[22] Welker, *What Happens in Holy Communion?*, 92.
[23] Welker, *What Happens in Holy Communion?*, 100.
[24] Welker's account has significant parallels with Gerrish's portrait of the Calvin's eucharistic theology in the use of the language of gift, the role of faith and the community, as well as the critique of a preoccupation with the elements themselves and a doctrine of the ubiquity of Christ's body. See B.A. Gerrish, *Grace and Gratitude: The Eucharistic Theology of John Calvin* (Eugene: Wipf & Stock, 2002), especially chapter 5.

was instrumental in bringing Reformed, Lutheran, and a limited range of other Protestants into full communion in the Evangelical Church in Germany.

The fresh mining of Calvin's sacramental theology for ecumenical purposes continues today. For those seeking to forge a limited-range ecumenical agreement through the use of Calvin, George Hunsinger in *The Eucharist and Ecumenism* presents a substantive and provocative proposal.[25] While I am less optimistic than Hunsinger on the prospect of reaching broad agreement in the area of Eucharistic metaphysics and the issues he clusters with the eucharist related to polity, Hunsinger's account draws upon Calvin and other Reformed thinkers like Bucer, Vermigli, and Cranmer in a way that makes a case for the ecumenical potential for Calvin's sacramental theology, particularly when Calvin's theology is supplemented with that of other early Reformed theologians.

Is Calvin's Sacramental Theology Word-Centered in a Way that Displaces a Key Role for the Sacraments?

It is relatively common to claim that Calvin's sacramental theology and early Reformed worship suffer under the word-centered orientation of Calvin's overall thought, diminishing the significance of the bodily, material sign-action of the sacraments. For example, in James White's *Protestant Worship*, he describes the worship in Calvin's Geneva as "prolix and verbose, never lacking a chance to instruct." "So great was the imperative to teach that each service contains a condensed course in theology and ethics. This became a lasting characteristic of Reformed worship, contributing to its overall cerebral character."[26] In this cerebral context, the sacraments themselves can seem like didactic lessons of doctrine. Yet, in a recent study, Martha Moore-Keish argues that—in spite of the didactic character of parts of the Genevan liturgy—Calvin generally maintains a remarkable balance and complementarity between the preached word and the sacraments.[27]

---

[25] See George Hunsinger, *The Eucharist and Ecumenism* (Cambridge: Cambridge University Press, 2008).

[26] James White *Protestant Worship: Traditions in Transition* (Louisville: Westminster John Knox, 1989), 65.

[27] Martha L. Moore-Keish, *Do This in Remembrance of Me: A Ritual Approach to Reformed Eucharistic Theology* (Grand Rapids: Eerdmans, 2008), chapter 2.

While Calvin's liturgy for Geneva may be wordy and didactic by modern standards, I think that Moore-Keish is correct in her assessment of the broad complementarity of word and sacrament in Calvin's overall corpus of writings. There is a certain type of priority to the word, but it is not an abstract word, but the living presence of Jesus Christ. For Calvin, "the sacraments have the same office as the Word of God: to offer and set forth Christ to us, and in him the treasures of his grace."[28] As Calvin explains in his *Short Treatise on the Lord's Supper*,

> What is said of the word applies as well to the sacrament of the Supper, by means of which the Lord leads us to communion with Jesus Christ. For seeing we are so weak that we cannot receive him with true heartfelt trust, when he is presented to us by simple doctrine and preaching, the Father of mercy, disdaining not to condescend in this matter to our infirmity, has been pleased to add to his word a visible sign, by which he might represent the substance of his promises, to confirm and fortify us by delivering us from all doubt and uncertainty.[29]

The preached word and the sacraments are God's chosen means to lead believers into communion with the living Christ. The complementary of word and sacraments goes in two directions. Apart from the word of the gospel, we look to earthly elements or rites rather than God in Christ for our nourishment. For the word is "not as one whispered without meaning and without faith, a mere noise, like a magic incantation, which has the force to consecrate the elements. Rather it should, when preached, make us understand what the visible sign means."[30] Yet, on the other hand, the promise of the gospel—Jesus Christ himself—is most fully held forth when it is not just the preached word, but when the preached word is accompanied with sacramental signs. For the sacraments "convey the clearest promises" of God for sustaining faith,[31] displaying God's "good will and love toward us more expressly than by word."[32]

Remarkably, Calvin does not attribute this need for a material, sacramental sign simply to "humanity's fallen condition" as is sometimes

---

[28] Calvin, *Institutes* IV.14.17.

[29] John Calvin, *Tracts Containing Treaties on the Sacraments, Catechism of the Church of Geneva, Forms of Prayer, and Confessions of Faith*, vol. 2, trans. Henry Beveridge (Edinburgh: Calvin Translation Society, 1849), 166.

[30] Calvin, *Institutes* IV.14.4.

[31] From the 1539 *Institutes*, see Thomas Davis, *This is My Body: The Presence of Christ in Reformation Thought* (Grand Rapids: Baker Academic, 2008), 87.

[32] Calvin, *Institutes* IV.14.6.

assumed.[33] In his Genesis commentary, Calvin suggests that pre-fallen human beings had a need for a material sign of God's love to know and live in fellowship with God. In his comments on Gen. 2 and 3, Calvin interprets the Tree of Life as God's accommodation to unite Adam to himself, an external sign of God's promise. For by these signs God "stretches out his hand to us, because, without assistance, we cannot ascend to him. He intended, therefore, that man, as often as he tasted the fruit of that tree, should remember whence he received his life, in order that he might acknowledge that he lives not by his own power, but by the kindness of God alone." Before the fall, humanity needed not only God's word but the physical, external signs of God's promise to "seal his grace to man."[34]

Thus, when Calvin speaks of the sacraments as being necessary because of our "weakness" in apprehending God's promise, this "weakness" is not a contingent handicap, a crutch for immature Christians. The "weakness" is, at least in part, a dimension of the created goodness of humanity. We were created to know God by means of physical, material signs. We were also created to hear God's word, as with God's speech in the garden. But part of the created structure for a human way of knowing God, according to Calvin, involves not just hearing, but seeing, touching, and tasting.

What are we to make of the history of reception on the complementarity of Word and Sacrament in Calvin? This is a complex question, as Calvin is only one of many liturgical as well as theological sources for the sacramental theology of the Reformed tradition. For Moore-Keish, the decline from this complementarity coincides with Reformed Scholasticism.[35] This general narrative of decline overlaps with Howard Hageman's assessment that seventeenth and eighteenth century Reformed Christianity represented the "dark age of Reformed Protestantism," the age in which "most of the liturgical patterns that separate us from the Reformation came into being."[36] While this is a common narrative, it is incomplete on its own, as I will point out in the course of my final point.

---

[33] For example, Moore-Keish writes "Although Calvin implied that our need for the visible and tangible is a symptom of humanity's fallen condition, we do not have to agree with his negative judgment in order to affirm with him this fact of human nature as we know it." See Moore-Keish, *Do This in Remembrance of Me*, 29.

[34] Calvin, Commentary on Gen. 2:9, 3:22, *CO* 23, 38, 79. Cf. John Calvin, *Commentaries on the First Book of Moses Called Genesis*, vol. 1, trans. John King (Edinburgh: Calvin Translation Society; reprint, Grand Rapids: Baker, 1979), 117, 184.

[35] Moore-Keish, *Do This in Remembrance of Me*, 45–49.

[36] Hageman, *Pulpit and Table*, 36.

Retrieval: The Lord's Supper as the "Icon" of the Gospel,
the Sacrament of Union with Christ

The feature of Calvin's sacramental thought that I would like to focus upon as promising for retrieval is the relation between the sacrament of the Lord's Supper and the gospel, the good news of salvation. As noted above, Calvin formulates a complementary relationship between the promise of the Word proclaimed and the promise held forth through signs at the Supper. This complementarity is ultimately rooted in symmetry between the gospel promise and the promise of the Supper: the content of both promises is Jesus Christ himself, who is received in union with Christ by the Spirit, through faith. This symmetry is further exemplified in Calvin's exegesis of Christ's sermon in John 6:28–59 with its focus upon feeding upon the flesh and blood of Christ.

> It is certain, then, that he now speaks of the perpetual and ordinary manner of eating the flesh of Christ, which is done by faith only. And yet, at the same time, I acknowledge that there is nothing said here that is not figuratively represented, and actually bestowed on believers, in the Lord's Supper; and Christ even intended that the holy Supper should be, as it were, a seal and confirmation of this sermon.[37]

Humans feed upon Christ by faith both in the Supper and also in a "perpetual and ordinary manner" outside of the Supper in their whole Christian life. Why? Because while believers truly feed upon Christ through the Spirit with material signs in the Supper, salvation itself is a feeding, participation, and union with Christ by the Spirit. Specifically, according to Calvin in Book 3 on salvation and the Christian life, the "sum of the gospel" is the double grace of justification and sanctification, received as one comes to "possess Christ" by faith.[38] In salvation, as in the Supper, coming to "enjoy Christ and all of his benefits" happens by "the secret energy of the Spirit," for "the Holy Spirit is the bond by which Christ effectually unites us to himself."[39]

At this point, we should face an objection to Calvin's approach on this question. With the symmetry between the Supper and the nature of Salvation as union with Christ, does that not make the celebration of the

---

[37] Calvin, Commentary on John 6:54, *CO* 47, 155, Cf. John Calvin, *Commentary on the Gospel According to John*, vol. 1, trans. William Pringle (Edinburgh: Calvin Translation Society; reprint, Grand Rapids: Baker, 1999), 266.

[38] Calvin, *Institutes* III.3.1.

[39] Calvin, *Institutes* III.1.1.

Lord's Supper superfluous? As Francois Wendel poses the question, "what exactly does the Supper give us that we cannot obtain otherwise?"[40] Part of the response to this question can be inferred from the exposition of the last point on the complementarity of word and sacrament— that human beings were created to need material signs of God's promise in order to fully know and commune with God. Humans were created not only to hear the preached word, but to see, smell, and taste the word through signs. To this, I would add the insight of the present point about the symmetry of the gospel and the Supper. Calvin, and seventeenth century Reformed thinkers after him, speak about the Supper as the "icon" of the gospel.[41] The material signs and acts of the Supper are to be valued precisely because the gospel promise that they hold forth is to be valued. Thus, the Lord's Supper is God's chosen means for clearly communicating Jesus Christ and the multivalent gospel promise that is contained in union with Christ. In terms of contemporary retrieval, this approach would seek to renew the Supper not by focusing directly upon the elements and the ritual actions of the eucharist in themselves, but upon the multivalent gospel that the eucharist holds forth. Without doubt, the cultural and material context for the celebration of the eucharist deserves our careful attention, along with reflection on the ritual actions in the Supper. But conceiving of these dimensions of the Supper in light of the central reality of the eucharist as an "icon" of the gospel can provide a God-centered focus that enriches our reflection upon the concrete actions performed in celebrating the Lord's Supper.

While some think that Calvin has weakened the importance of the Supper with his claim that believers feed upon Christ both in and outside of the Supper, I sense that the reception-history has often suggested otherwise.[42] Some of the richest counter-examples to this "weakening" thesis are

---

[40] Wendel, *Calvin: The Origins and Development of His Religious Thought*, trans. Philip Mairet (London: Collins, 1963), 353.

[41] A sacrament "represents God's promises as painted in a picture and sets them before our sight, portrayed graphically in the manner of icons." Calvin, *Institutes* IV.14.6, trans. from John D. Witvliet in *Worship Seeking Understanding* (Grand Rapids: Baker Academic, 2003), 140. For more on the Reformed tradition of the Lord's Supper, in particular, as icon, see Witvliet, *Worship Seeking Understanding*, 139–141.

[42] For a critical account, see Kilian McDonnell, *John Calvin, the Church and the Eucharist* (Princeton: Princeton University Press, 1967), 378ff. More recently, Moore-Keish suggests that "this theme in Calvin is certainly part of the reason that Reformed theologians have often de-emphasized rituals or sacraments: these are simply not seen as necessary, given the importance of faith. Such a focus does not encourage careful attention to the ritual dimension of the eucharist" *Do This in Remembrance of Me*, 33–34.

found in post-Reformation Reformed communities before the nineteenth century—the "dark age of Reformed Protestantism," for Hageman. Consider the Scottish and early American practice of 'Holy Fairs,' for example. These were large gatherings spanning around four days—complete with various forms of conviviality and vigorous religious affections —all centered around the celebration of the Lord's Supper. Historical analysis of this phenomenon shows that the language of "union with Christ" is key for the participants (who often wrote spiritual journals), as well as the preachers.[43] Why did this theme have such power? It is not because of a particular eucharistic metaphysic, a theory about the elements after a prayer of consecration, or even a preoccupation with the physical, ritual action of the Supper as an end in itself.[44] Arguably, the Supper took on enormous significance precisely because it enacted a reality central to the entire Christian life, indeed, of the gospel itself: union with Christ by the Spirit, received in faith.[45]

In this tradition, as well as in the writings of the Dutch "further Reformation," the imagery of "spiritual marriage" between believers and Christ the groom becomes very prominent.[46] This imagery owes a peculiar debt to Calvin. On the one hand, Calvin is quite modest in his development of this theme in an explicit way; while he draws upon Bernard of Claurvauix and his *Canticles* commentary, he usually avoids a direct treatment of the marital/erotic imagery underlying Bernard's work. In contrast, these Scottish, American, and Dutch Reformed traditions give emphatic and often quite elaborate development of the spiritual marriage motif.[47] But the point of dependence upon Calvin seems to be the precise point in which Calvin is often criticized: that believers feed upon Christ by faith in the

---

[43] See Leigh Eric Schmidt, *Holy Fairs*, 2nd ed. (Grand Rapids: Eerdmans, 2001), 14–15, 158–168.

[44] As noted above, the cultural and material context is significant for the celebration of the Supper—and it was certainly significant for the Holy Fairs. Nevertheless, it is worth observing that these the concrete ritual actions were not approached as ends in themselves; precisely because their link with the gospel, the ritual actions took on special significance.

[45] See Schmidt's exposition of the notion of the Supper as the "visible Gospel" at the Holy Fairs in Schmidt, *Holy Fairs*, 69ff.

[46] See Arie de Reuver, *Sweet Communion: Trajectories of Spirituality from the Middle Ages Through the Further Reformation*, trans. James A. De Jong (Grand Rapids: Baker Academic, 2007) 105–280.

[47] For examples of the extensive development of this motif, see material surveyed in the doctoral thesis of Timothy Hessel Robinson, " 'Be thou my onely well belov'd': Exegesis and the spirituality of desire in Edward Taylor's 'Preparatory Meditations' on the Song of Songs" (PhD diss., Graduate Theological Union, 2006).

Christian life generally, as well as in the Supper. In the exploration of the Spiritual Marriage motif in these traditions after Calvin, these preachers and writers were energized not simply by a reflection upon the Supper itself and 'what happens in the Supper.' Rather, their vibrant reflection on the Supper presupposes that the Supper is brought up into the larger drama of salvation, an instrument of the bridegroom to give his bride a taste of the communion which constitutes the whole Christian life. The Supper took on great significance precisely by refracting the heart of the gospel itself.

While these episodes in the history of reception do not give us a direct 'roadmap' for contemporary retrieval, I think they are suggestive of how a distinctive theme in Calvin's sacramental theology can help to revitalize not only the practice of the sacraments, but the gospel-centered life of the Christian community. Indeed, this gospel-centered focus holds promise for overcoming certain deficiencies in recent ecumenical formulations of the eucharist, such as in BEM (*Baptism, Eucharist, and Ministry*). For Calvin, union with Christ always involves the double grace, of justification (focused on forensic images for salvation and forgiveness) and sanctification (focused upon organic and transformational images for salvation). In Calvin's account, these graces must be distinguished, and yet they are inseparable. This account of the double-grace penetrates his eucharistic theology, as I have argued elsewhere.[48] But precisely this non-reductive combination of forensic *and* transformational imagery is missing in statements like "Baptism, Eucharist, and Ministry" (BEM), as Michael Welker has argued. Specifically, the Supper "as pledge of eternal life substantively suppresses the aspect of the forgiveness of sins" in BEM.[49] When the Supper is framed in terms of salvation as union with Christ and the double-grace, we can move toward a non-reductive account which incorporates such biblical themes together.

Ironically, precisely because union with Christ is received both in the Supper and in salvation more generally, the Supper takes on great significance. The Supper can develop a rich, multifaceted character because it is an icon of the gospel itself.

In sum, when we consider Calvin's sacramental thought in light of historic and contemporary efforts for Christian unity, we should avoid construing

---

[48] Billings, *Calvin, Participation, and the Gift*, chapter 4.
[49] Welker, *What Happens in Holy Communion?*, 152–154.

his account as a 'timeless' formulation, or seeing him as the sole progenitor of the Reformed theological and liturgical tradition. Instead, we should
see how, as one among several early Reformational leaders, he showed
considerable flexibility in his sacramental thought as he sought commonality with a limited group of Protestant traditions. Moreover, while
Calvin's sacramental thought—like any doctrinal formulation—can be
used in a way that downplays the commonality of Protestant sacramental
traditions, in the history of reception it has shown facility in playing a
mediating role between competing Protestant alternatives.

In our second and third points, we have seen how, in Calvin's overall
sacramental theology, he does not privilege an abstract word over all else
in worship and ecclesiology. Instead, he develops a high degree of complementarity between the preached word and the sacramental sign and
action. Indeed, Calvin grounds the need for a material, sacramental sign
in pre-fallen humanity—meaning that humans were intended not simply
to hear God's word, but to see, smell, and taste it. With our third point, we
explored how this complementarity is rooted in symmetry between the
promise of the gospel, and the promise of the Lord's Supper, in particular.
This is accompanied with the claim that humans feed upon Christ by faith
both within and outside of the Supper itself. Key episodes in the history
of reception demonstrate that this symmetrical relationship between the
gospel and the Supper does not necessarily lead to a neglect of the sacramental act. Instead, it can lead to its revitalization, since the Supper is
seen as that which exhibits and holds forth what salvation itself is—union
with Christ by the Spirit, involving a double grace of justification and
sanctification, received by faith. Precisely because Calvin's sacramental
theology is so closely tied to his multifaceted account of the gospel itself,
it holds promise for those today who desire for the church to recover a
gospel-centered identity.

CHAPTER ELEVEN

LIFE AS PILGRIMAGE: THE ESCHATOLOGY OF JOHN CALVIN

Cornelis van der Kooi

Exile: A Contemporary Experience

The apostle Peter addresses his hearers and readers as "aliens and exiles."[1] Something similar can be read in the letter to the Hebrews where it is said of the saints: "They confessed that they were strangers and foreigners on the earth, for people who speak in this way make it clear that they are seeking a homeland. They desire a better country, that is, a heavenly one."[2] Christians hope for a kingdom, a city, a place to live or a context, where Gods rules, where his righteousness and love dominate. In light of this hope everything else that precedes the arrival in this homeland becomes something preliminary, a section of a pilgrimage. For many contemporaries the language of being an exile or alien, of looking for a better country, is not only figurative but describes their very life and circumstances. We live in a time with large currents of migration. Millions of people have immigrated from the old countries of Europe to the United States, to Canada, to "Down Under" in pursuit of a better life for themselves and particularly for their children. In the last twenty years, a vast stream of migration has flowed from the Mediterranean to the countries in Northern Europe, in order to get work and make use of economic opportunities and prosperity. And in recent years we heard of people from Zimbabwe, desperately seeking a place in the Republic of South Africa. Our newspapers tell us at times of vast groups of children who are driven back and forth between armies in combat with each other, and who are forced to take part in the military. One could also mention the numerous youngsters in the countries of the western world, who sometimes feel lost in their own culture and society, involved as they are in the pressure to find a place, to get a job, to meet all the challenges and claims that are put on them by their society: one has to be successful, independent, smart, and popular,

---

[1] 1 Pet. 2:11.
[2] Heb. 11:13–14.

in short, to develop a personal identity, a self that should function as the mainstay of the whole business. In The Netherlands the number of victims in car-crashes has diminished substantially—a wonderful achievement. The number of suicides has, however, doubled. And the suicide rate in many countries in Europe is even much higher.

Eschatology discusses what believers are hoping for—for them personally and for the world—and what carries them through life. It decides the relation of church and faith with this world or culture through times ahead. What is the relation of the pilgrims with the world they still live in? Is the pilgrim only an alien and therefore an outsider? Or does the pilgrim also have his or her responsibilities, because Christ is Lord, not only of the coming, but also of this world? What does the eschatology of Calvin say with respect to these questions and this modern world, with its challenges, its pursuit of happiness and, at the same time, its forms of estrangement—which is featured in movies, plays, novels? What are the essential characteristics of this doctrine of the last things and what does this older theology of a famous deceased reformer mean when we search for a living Reformed theology that looks toward the future?

Let me start with some essentials: Essential for Calvin's theology is the distinction between heaven and earth, the fundamental otherness of this world and the coming world. The identity of the believer is fundamentally determined by his adoption as a child by God the Father. It is therefore, in the words of the apostle Paul, a heavenly citizenship, which forms the hidden identity of the pilgrim. Yet we will also see that this identity has a bearing on this present life and the way this life must be lived in times to come. In Calvin's view the civil authorities have a fundamental task for the earthly pilgrim on the way to his eternal destiny. The civil government has to take care that society will be a place where the pilgrim can make progress and will not be seduced to go astray.

The old medieval idea of a Christian society, a *societas christiana* and a goal of Christianization of society, is very clear in Calvin's thought. Before addressing the question of what we can learn from Calvin, let me first give an outline of several aspects of his eschatology.

Tension between the "Already" and the "Not Yet"

Calvin knew personally what it means to be an exile. For many years he lived in Geneva as an exile. And from that place he looked at his beloved homeland, France. An important reason for the first edition of Calvin's *Institutes* (1536) lay in the danger that the conduct of the Anabaptist radicals produced for Reformation sympathizers in Calvin's home country of France. Towards those outside his own circle he wanted to protect his fellow believers against 'the evil odor or bad reputation' which clung to them according to the government.[3] In his "Prefatory Address to King Francis I of France" Calvin attempted to nullify, with all his rhetorical talent, the threatening identification of evangelicals with Anabaptists. He asks the king to take note of the content of his writing, and warns the king not to listen to the counselors at the court who put the Reformation sympathizers in the same category with the Anabaptists.[4] Even so, Calvin also sees a different danger from inside the Reformed circles. There is a frightful amount of ignorance and lack of knowledge, and Calvin probably wants to counteract such ignorance by writing a simple statement of faith. It appears that he wants to direct himself especially against the ideas current in Anabaptist circles. It is important for our purposes to note that his critique provides insight in the manner in which he wants to handle the tension in our faith between "already" and "not yet."

Distinguishing Correctly

The main thread of Calvin's critique of the Anabaptists in the first edition of the *Institutes* is that they do not know how to distinguish properly between the revealed and the hidden, and consequently go to an extreme. Thus they do not accept that the communion in Christ in the present dispensation comes first of all from God and therefore bears a spiritual character that is sometimes hidden or invisible. It is a premature intrusion on God's eschatological action when they demand of the church in her earthly existence that she must be without spot or wrinkle. However, the church, according to God's design, now lives between the ascension and Christ's return. According to God's plan, weeds and grain are now intermixed and Christ's reign has a spiritual nature and in many ways a hidden one. The Anabaptist denial of this truth leads to two positions— seemingly opposite, but in reality arising from the same source. On the one hand they have the inclination to despise everything that serves the

---

[3] W. Balke, *Calvin and the Anabaptist Radicals*, transl. William Heynen (Grand Rapids: Eerdmans, 1981), 39–72.

[4] J. Calvin, "Prefatory Address to king Francis I of France," in J. Calvin, *Institutes of the Christian Religion*, tr. F.L. Battles (Philadelphia: Westminster Press, 1960), 9–31.

maintaining of life in this broken dispensation and want to pull away from it, and thus they pull back into their own holy group and despise the state. Whatever is left of God's creation is so unworthy that the breach with salvation is total, and that salvation can be considered only in terms of re-creation in the sense of a new and different creation. The complete opposite inclination is to consider the present a time for revolutionary liberation, of God's unveiled lordship, and church and state becoming one, as in Münster. However, says Calvin, between the ascension and the return of Christ the believer lives in two domains; both domains have their source in God, but we have to distinguish between the two. According to his spiritual state, man lives in the presence of God's grace and is under God's rule (*regimen spirituale*). But he is also a part of this visible world, and here his citizenship is determined by an earthly ordinance and regulation (*regimen politicum*).

This basic pattern, sketched here briefly, surfaces already in the first edition of the *Institutes*, and reoccurs in later editions.[5] This dual existence is a distinctive mark of the world according to a Christian believer. The believer already lives in communion with Christ and this communion is of a spiritual nature. His heart is "above." Here we find the heart of Calvin's faith and theology—the communion between the human and God, which is created by the Holy Spirit and bound to the Word. Thus, the heart of his theology is not first of all to be sought in the doctrine of election, even though election says something about salvation being rooted in God himself, and even though election eventually received more weight in his theology because of polemics. Thus in the beginning of the third book of the *Institutes* we read:

> First, we must understand that as long as Christ remains outside of us, and we are separated from him, all that he has suffered and done for the salvation of the human race remains useless and of no value to us. Therefore, to share with us what he has received from the Father, he had to become ours and to dwell within us. For this reason he is called our Head (Eph. 4:15), and 'the first-born among many brothers' (Rom. 8:29). We also, in turn, are said to be 'engrafted into him' (Rom. 11:17), and to 'put on Christ' (Gal. 3:27); for, as I have already said, all that he possesses is nothing to us until we grow into one body with him.[6]

---

5 Calvin, *Institutes* III.19.15.
6 Calvin, *Institutes* III.1.1.

These words demonstrate that for Calvin the core of our faith is communion with Christ, with whom man is united through the hidden work of the Holy Spirit, and of which he is reminded in the *sursum corda* at the Lord's Supper.

Continuing Relationship with Christ

The intent and passion with which Calvin holds on to the reality of this communion shows that this is for him "already" of existential importance. In his views concerning the essence of faith in *Institutes* III.2 this prevenient grace comes to light. This emphasis is opposed to the medieval views, in which bowing before the authority of the church and observing its rituals is counted as a form of implicit faith for the illiterate masses. Step by step Calvin explains that faith certainly is a form of knowledge, and specifically knowledge of God's favor towards persons, but that this leans on the promises granted to us in Christ. It is noteworthy in Calvin's explanation that the core and basis of faith is found when and where the human creature begins to see Christ. God has granted God's benefits in the person of Jesus Christ. This knowledge rests on the work of the Holy Spirit. The Spirit has the role of an inner teacher[7] and gives the human spirit a new perception through which the divine secrets can be discerned. The inner nature of the work of the Holy Spirit also means that the knowledge of faith itself is of an inner nature also, and knows its own certainty.

This does not deny that Calvin readily admits that humanity in life on earth is subject to all kinds of temptation. We see ourselves surrounded by all kinds of ignorance which gives way only slowly. Calvin compares the way of the believer on earth with living in a dark dungeon where the light of the sun shines only through a small opening. Much is still dark, but the believer does notice the light, and in the darkness that light is most important. In the same way for the believer, a small measure of God's light and mercy is sufficient to find certainty.[8] Thus Calvin does not at all deny that faith can be faint, weak and harassed and obstructed. On the contrary, Calvin describes life as one long battle from which one should not want to flee. With love he describes the life of the believer as an advance to greater light, but this advance, based on seeing God's mercy, is completed in the manner of perseverance. This perseverance can, however, be learned, because

---

[7] Calvin, *Institutes* III.2.34.
[8] Calvin, *Institutes* III.2.19.

the "already" of Christ's mercy always prevails against the experience that that mercy has not yet become the object of unconcealed observation. The word docility or teachableness (*docilitas*) plays a central role in the meager hint that he gives elsewhere about his own faith development: "He brought my soul by an unexpected conversion to teachableness";[9] here he indicates that every believer must be ready throughout life to learn in the school of the Holy Spirit. And Calvin adds that experience teaches us that as long as we are not free from the flesh, we understand much less than we would like or need.

The eschatological direction of Calvin's thought becomes visible here in the manner in which he closely relates faith and hope. He calls hope the firm guide of faith and states that faith emanates from it. Faith and hope often form a terminological duality, joined at the hip, and are at times interchangeable. Hope is nothing else than the expectation of things that, according to the conviction of faith, have been truly promised by God. In faith we trust that God is our Father, in hope we expect that he will prove himself to be our Father. In faith we trust that eternal life has been given to us, and in hope we expect the disclosing of that eternal life.

Turning to the Future Life

Calvin himself has described thinking about life in terms of this relationship with Christ as *de meditatione vitae futurae* (on the contemplation of the future life).[10] Actually this translation does not say nearly enough. Contemplation does not so much mean a silent pondering; it rather means that each person in his existence in its entirety must have an orientation to heavenly things. It is the turning *to* eternal life. Everything must turn towards that. In the liberal theology of the 19th century this has sometimes led to the idea that Calvin was in fact an advocate for an attitude that turns away *from* the world. To this point, it is true that Calvin can speak of a "needed contempt of life." It is not strange, on the basis of what has been called the cosmological heritage in Calvin's thought, that especially in his anthropology we notice that earthly life and its related

---

⁹ "animum meum...subita conversione ad docilitatem subegit." Preface of the commentary on the Psalms. Calvin, *CO* 31, 21. See for an extensive discussion of the meaning of *subita conversio* Alexandre Ganoczy, *The Young Calvin*, Translated by Dave Foxgrover and Wade Provo (Philadelphia: The Westminster Press, 1986), 252–266. According to Ganoczy conversion essentially means for Calvin repentance and 'subita' unexpected.
¹⁰ Calvin *Institutes* III.9.1–6.

physicality are situated low on the hierarchical ladder, and that the impression of its underestimation is unavoidable.[11] But we must also note that on this point the willingness to learn from the Holy Spirit has produced fruit. The confession that God is the creator of heaven and earth appears to be a correction of the Platonic slant in Calvin's thought.

Calvin's intent is not a turning away from the earthly, but rather (and here he stands in the Augustinian tradition of the distinction between *uti* and *frui*) to the right use of things. It is striking that he goes further than what Paul says in about the use of things as if one does not use them.[12] The concentration on future life means that the eye may indeed rejoice in the beauty of flowers, and our sense of smell may delight in pleasant aromas. There is room for the enjoyment of things and in the explanation of Colossians 3:1—"Seek the things that are above, not the things that are on earth"—there is a clear distance from what one sometimes encounters in monastic rules of life. In Calvin seeking the things that are above does not decrease the freedom to let one's eye rest on the things below. The *perspectio* does not lead to a prohibition of the *circumspectio*.[13]

The enormous relativization of earthly life flows from the fact that the believer has come in touch with something better. The great deal of suffering that a person can experience in this life is a tool in God's hand to keep man free from too much attachment to this life. To cite Calvin:

> The heart also, occupied with avarice, ambition, and lust, is so weighed down that it cannot rise up higher. In fine, the whole soul, enmeshed in the allurements of the flesh, seeks its happiness on earth. To counter this evil the Lord instructs his followers in the vanity of the present life by continual proof of its miseries. Therefore, that they may not promise themselves a deep and secure peace in it, he permits them often to be troubled and plagued either with wars or tumults, or robberies, or other injuries. That they may not pant with too great eagerness after fleeting and transient riches, or repose in those which they possess, he sometimes by exile, sometimes by barrenness of the earth, sometimes by fire, sometimes by other means, reduces them to poverty, or at least confines them to a moderate station. That they may not too complacently take delight in the goods of marriage, he either causes

---

[11] W.J. Bouwsma, *John Calvin. A Sixteenth Century Portrait* (New York/Oxford: Oxford University Press 1988), 69–85.

[12] 1 Cor. 7:29–31.

[13] Cf. H.A. Oberman, *Contra vanam curiositatem. Ein Kapitel der Theologie zwischen Seelenwinkel und Weltall* [Against vain curiosity. A Chapter of Theology relating perspectives of Soul and Space] (Zürich: Theologischer Verlag 1974), 26.

them to be troubled by the depravity of their wives or humbles them by evil offspring, or afflicts them with bereavement.[14]

The concentration on eternal life, and the emphasis Calvin puts on the salvation that the believer has in Christ, do not lead to a flight into the spiritual world, however. If there is one word that appropriately describes the life of the Christian on earth, it is the verb *peregrinari*. The human being is a rambler, a pilgrim, on the way to the promised land. In fact, "if heaven is our homeland, what else is the earth but our place of exile?"[15] When Calvin uses such words and images, he knows what he is talking about. These are words and thoughts which, as is well-known, belong in his biography. He spent most of his time outside of France, and even in Geneva he was and remained a stranger, who received his citizenship in the city only in 1559. The life of the believer is spent under the cross; he does not see his glory, but knows his glory only insofar as he sees Christ. In his commentary on Hebrews 11:1 Calvin therefore writes:

> The Spirit of God shows us hidden things, the knowledge of which cannot reach our senses. Eternal life is promised to us, but it is promised while we are mortals; we are told of the resurrection of the blessed, but meantime we are involved in corruption; we are declared to be just, and sin dwells within us. We hear that we are blessed, but meantime we are overwhelmed by untold miseries. We are promised an abundance of all good things, but we are often hungry and thirsty; God proclaims that he will come to us immediately, but seems to be deaf to our cries. What would happen to us if we did not rely on our hope, and if our minds did not emerge above the world out of the midst of darkness through the shining Word of God and by his Spirit?[16]

The tension between the "already" and the "not yet", that which is given in faith and the shape of our current existence under the cross, is here pushed to the extreme. The present of salvation, which is embraced in faith, lies in Christ, but that also means a strict distinction between what the believer is in him- or herself and what they are in Christ. Note well, Calvin applies the earthly invisibility to the believer. For the believer also, salvation has a hidden character.[17]

We want to underline the eschatological structure of Calvin's thought by pointing to what Neuser has put forward about Calvin's use of the con-

---

14 Calvin, *Institutes* III.9.1.
15 Calvin, *Institutes* III.9.4.
16 Calvin, Commentary on Heb. 11:1, *CO* 55, 143–144.
17 Calvin, Commentary on Col. 3:3, *CO* 52, 118–119.

cept of promise (*promissio*).[18] In current discussions "promise" and "fulfill-ment" form a duality. Christ is seen as the fulfillment of Old Testament promises. However, Calvin's proposition is that the promises of the Old as well as the New Testament (in terms of their content) remain the same. In both dispensations God gives the promise of his presence. This promise has not quite yet come to our own fulfillment in Christ, but has become more clear than in the Old Testament dispensation. The nature of the promise is maintained.[19] One can speak of complete fulfillment only at the resurrection from the dead when the body is reunited with the soul which was already near to Christ, and God grants each person his eternal communion and nearness.

In conclusion, we can say that the eschatological direction of Calvin's thought is determined by two tracks. First, for Calvin a correct distinc-tion between the "already" and the "not yet" is of the greatest signifi-cance. Humanity lives in two domains and God is actively involved in both domains. The current world which has the shape of the "not yet," is not empty and deprived of God's involvement. A flight from the present to the future is therefore against God's intent. The second contour that keeps reappearing is that, spiritually viewed, the center of gravity is found in the "already" of the blessings of God received in Christ. The concrete life of the believer in this life, in the shape of the "not yet," is subject to tremen-dous tension, but does not remove the prevalence of the "already."

The Thousand-Year Reign and Soul-Sleep

This basic two-fold structure also returns in Calvin's treatment of several eschatological themes that were important in his time. First we must consider Calvin's battle against the doctrine of the thousand-year reign (millennium): he does not say a single favorable word about it. In fact, he considers it a naïve and wild idea that is barely worth the honor of battle. But the passion and the harshness that he exhibits show that, according him, a genuine element of faith is attacked in this doctrine. The idea of an earthly kingdom of peace before the return of Christ, in which the saints

---

[18] W.H. Neuser, "Theologie des Wortes" in W.H. Neuser (ed.) *Calvinus Theologus* (Neu-kirchen: Neukirchener Verlag, 1976), 24.

[19] On the systematic importance of this insight see also G. Sauter, *Gateways to Dogmat-ics: Reasoning Theologically for the Life of the Church* (Grand Rapids/Cambridge: Eerdmans, 2003), 225–227.

will reign for a full thousand years, he judges to be a serious curtailment of Christian hope. This idea robs the elect of the comforting power of that hope, because of the temporal boundaries placed on Christ's kingdom.

In the interpretation of the scriptural passage that has always played an important role, Revelation 20: 1–6, Calvin follows Augustine. In Book 20 of the *City of God*, Augustine disputes the correctness of the eschatological interpretation of these texts.[20] He relates the passage to all of church history, and thus he delivers support for a spiritualist explanation to this passage. This is completely in agreement with his inclination not to interpret Old Testament promises in terms of the remaining promises for the people of Israel, but in the framework of a replacement theory to apply these instead to the "spiritual" Israel, the church. In this explanation the first resurrection is seen as a description of being born again. Because they are born again, the saints are no longer under the power of Satan, but Christ reigns over them. In spiritual terms they have become invulnerable to the power of darkness. The thousand years must obviously not be taken literally, but represent, as mentioned above, a very long time.

Calvin's comments line up with this explanation.[21] The first resurrection is being born again, the second is the resurrection of the dead, and between those events lies the interim. During that time the devil can rage, and can even reduce the church to ruins, but he cannot destroy it. Moreover, Calvin does not stand alone in his vision on the millennium. He simply follows Luther and the "Augsburg Confession," which, with an eye on the ever-increasing Anabaptist movement, declared in article XVII: "They condemn also others who are now spreading certain Jewish opinions, that before the resurrection of the dead the godly shall take possession of the kingdom of the world, the ungodly being everywhere suppressed."[22] The *Confessio Helvetica posterior* (1566) follows this condemnation in Article 11.[23] During the late Middle Ages there was a widespread and tremendous desire for a peaceful kingdom that would happen in this dispensation; however, that idea was so compromised by the fiasco in Münster that that banner could not be raised for the time being. The idea can only be

---

[20] Augustine, *De civitate Dei* (On the city of God), 20, *PL* 41, *CSEL* 40. Cf. also *The Works of Aurelius Augustine, Bishop of Hippo: The City of God*, trans. M. Dods.

[21] Calvin, *Institutes* III.25.5.

[22] *Die Bekenntnisschriften der evangelisch-lutherischen Kirche* (Göttingen: Vandenhoeck, 1998[12]), 72.

[23] *Die Bekenntnisschriften der reformierten Kirche* (Leipzig: Bohme, 1903), 185. For the English translation see S.B. Ferguson and J.R. Beeke, *Reformed Confessions Harmonized* (Grand Rapids: Eerdmans, 1999), 176.

brought in relation to rebellion and unholy mingling of God's promises and human desires, that is, by a deficiency of the belief in God's promises. In his commentary on Acts 1: 8 Calvin declares that such a dream of an earthly kingdom arises out of human nature. The apostles also had to learn that it is not right to imagine those things of God's kingdom that seem most natural to our senses. The prophecies of the Old Testament describe God's reign as an earthly reality. It is therefore necessary that the apostles turn their attention on high, and learn that Christ's reign has a spiritual character, and not the form of this world.[24] But the deepest ground for the rejection of the millennium is that the bond between Christ and his people becomes delimited by a certain period of time.

A second example about the doctrine of the last things, in which the emphasis on the "already" plays a prominent role, concerns the immortality of the soul; Calvin wrote about this very early on (1534), but the work was not published before 1542 as the *Psychopannychia*.[25] This writing has the same context as the first edition of the *Institutes*. It is intended to provide clarity about a theme that preoccupied Calvin and the still young evangelical movement. To modern ears it is perhaps strange to write in favor of the immortality of the soul and against the doctrine of soul-sleep, but it obviously is of existential significance. Calvin himself recalls the struggle in the 14th century (involving Pope John XXII) about the intermediate state of the soul. In his explanation of Revelation 6, Pope John had come to the conclusion that the souls of the dead had not yet come to a full vision of God (*visio Dei*).

It is remarkable that Calvin's content hardly departs from Pope John, who was at his time strongly criticized by William Ockham.[26] Calvin, however, does show a different accent. Pope John emphasized the "not yet," while Calvin underlines the "already" of the spiritual enjoyment of the soul. If the soul would be sleeping or destroyed at death, then, as far as Calvin is concerned, the heart of the blessing of our faith would be cut out, because the communion of the soul with Christ would be destroyed or at least interrupted. The situation of the soul between death and resurrection may be seen as "not yet;" even so, there still is an expectation in as much as this prospect takes place in a situation of rest and enjoyment

---

[24] Calvin, commentary on the Acts 1:8 *CO* 48, 10–11.

[25] J. Calvin, *Psychopannychia*, [Quellenschriften zur Geschichte des Protestantismus, vol. 13] ed. W. Zimmerli ed. (Leipzig: Deichert, 1932).

[26] J. Pelikan, *The Christian Tradition. A History of the Development of Doctrine Vol. 4: Reformation of Church and Dogma (1300–1700)* (Chicago: Chicago Press 1984), 108.

with God, and a clearer vision of things that we possessed only in hope during our time on earth. When we think of the situation after the first Reformation of Luther, we can imagine the importance of Calvin's early writing. Calvin has his fellow believers in mind, who, just as he did, have broken with the church and who must now continue without the mediation of priests, without absolution, without the last rites of the sick. The confrontation with God is immediate.[27] Calvin passionately defends the immortality of the soul. We feel the trembling for a God whom nobody can escape, not even in death. The death of the soul is not that it ceases to exist, but that it misses the presence of God, and is deserted by God. The death of the soul is to want to flee from the severity and majesty of God, but not being able to.[28] The immediate and remaining bond with Christ is of vital importance, which is already experienced now and of which one expects the complete fulfillment and unveiling in the future. The prayers with which he closed his Scripture readings reflect the eschatological emphasis of his thought. The word "until" always plays a key role in these prayers, as for instance in the following sentence: "Until we have gained the final victory, and finally come to that blessed rest, which your only Son has gained for us through his own blood."[29]

Evaluation

It is not a sign of living Reformed theology to duplicate an older theology and this will also apply to our situation. We live in another time, with more technical possibilities, but not for all; with the expectation of a longer life, but not for all; with more checks and balances for our governments, but not in all the countries we know. What is significant, however, in Calvin's theology and with Christians living under the cross and in a marginal situation, is the strong emphasis on the already: the 'already' of being a child of God, the communion with Jesus Christ, in a life of prayer and activity. In Jesus Christ God speaks his 'yes' and confirms the promises. Fulfillment does not mean the filling of a void, but the penetration

---

[27] H.A. Oberman, "Initia Calvini: The Matrix of Calvin's Reformation" in: W.H. Neuser (ed.), *Calvinus Sacrae Scripturae Professor. Calvin as Confessor of Holy Scripture* (Grand Rapids: Eerdmans, 1994), 141–143.

[28] Calvin, *Psychopannychia*, 6.

[29] See A.G. Barkey Wolf, *Gebeden van Calvijn*, [Prayers of Calvin] (Den Haag: D.A. Daamen, 1940), 26. Similar phrases occur in Calvin's prayers after his lectures on Jer. 1:6–7 and Jer. 2:23–24, *CO* 37, 477, 525.

of all things by the fullness of God in Christ. Living with this "already" of God means that this life is not only 'just-a-passing-through,' but that it also becomes the place and space where God wants to meet us, addresses us by his Word, supports his children, makes them responsible, asks for an answer. This is decisive for their relation to their culture, to politics also. It is a lifetime and course where God by his Holy Spirit grants his gifts, his gifts of grace. What these gifts of grace are must be discovered by every new generation. The stories of the New Testament and the stories of the church in her pilgrimage on earth provide us with examples which can make us open and attentive to what God wants to give. What are our responsibilities in the 21st Century; how will Reformed theology react in a cultural context in which the human responsibility has become so different compared to the world of Calvin?[30]

What are the contours of such a Reformed approach? In four statements I will give a brief outline.

1. A human being may live godless, but God chooses not to live without him or her. That choice can be called election or salvation. The core element in these descriptions of what is going on between God and humanity is the reversal of direction. Salvation starts with God's decision. Not we choose, but God chooses. In life, cross and resurrection the initiative comes from God. This is the revolution of the gospel. With Calvin this is articulated in terms of adoption. With Calvin the pilgrim is an adopted child, a chair is added at the dinner table, and a life-long hospitality is imprinted on him by God. Through Christ the child of faith learns to call God his Father. On the one hand this communion with Christ provides security when under pressure and in suffering, while on the other hand it awakens courage not to be overawed by the figures of power of our societies. In gratitude to the gift of this adoption "we are called to obedient activity in a world that is God's world, though indeed, God's fallen world."[31]
2. Life is a gift. This remains true even for each pilgrim and each pilgrimage. This can be called creation. The notion of gift is not without ambivalence. It puts us in the position of a recipient, who is dependent

---

[30] See for example, N. Wolterstorff, *Until Justice and Peace Embrace* (Kampen: Kok 1983), 3–22.
[31] N. Wolterstroff, *Hearing the Call. Liturgy, Justice, Church, and World* (Grand Rapids: Eerdmans 2011), 341.

of the Giver. We are not the owners. But the notion of gift also blocks the door to cynicism and the image of an empty world, in which man lives alone, by himself. The knowledge that this life, this creation, this ongoing history is a gift, also opens the eyes of the pilgrim for what is outside. The world is God's world, as Psalm 24: 1 expresses. That is why we can meet God in that world and other human beings. Time and the world are not empty, but a place where Christ sends his Spirit, sustains and awakens people to life. That means that one enters life with hope and expectation.[32] Our answer cannot be that we turn our back to society, politics and questions of justice.

3. The world is God's world. Therefore God has given his Son and therefore God also has sent out his Spirit, the Spirit of Jesus Christ, so that people on the way to the promised land can share in the fruits of healing and renewal. Spirit means life, restoration, transformation and perseverance. We call this sanctification. It is not the fulfillment of the promises; the gifts of the Spirit are a confirmation of God's promises, first fruits, not the final harvest. There is a strong difference between our timeframe where we see still in a mirror and the full fulfillment. But this difference is not a reason to refrain from questions of social justice, migration and the struggle of the young generations to find a place in life. On the contrary, the knowledge of God's fulfillment challenges our prayers and thoughts, and puts our activities in the right perspective.

4. The sanctification of the life of the pilgrim can take the form of mortification, but also that of vivification. This also means that Reformed theology is challenged not to despise modernity with its complexities, but to approach it critically and loyally as a space-time in which God meets people through his Spirit and challenges them to an answer. The challenges of the modern world, with its technological achievements, with its globalization, ecological questions and growing populations and despair are facts of life, which God wants us to address in obedience.

---

[32] Cf. G. Sauter, *Gateways to Dogmatics*, 226.

CHAPTER TWELVE

ACCOMMODATION AND INCARNATION: A FAVOURITE CONCEPT OF CALVIN IN THE THEOLOGY OF OEPKE NOORDMANS

Phillipe (Flip) Theron

"God-Talk" as "God's Talk"

During the later part of the previous century there was a lot of talk in theological circles about "God-talk" in the sense of human talk about God. In contrast, the idea of *accommodation* in Calvin's theology deals primarily with God's talking to us.[1] As Paul Helm puts it: "God accommodates himself to us: we do not accommodate God to ourselves."[2] While the latter amounts to idolatry, the former accords with the opening words of Hebrews: "In the past God spoke to our forefathers through the prophets at many times and in various ways, but in these last days God has spoken to us by the Son, whom God appointed heir of all things, and through whom God made the universe."[3]

In Christ, the Son, the Creator-Father has bridged the "epistemic gap"[4] between Self and his alienated creation. Consequently, Sallie McFague's statement, "When we try to speak of God there is nothing which resembles what we can conceive when we say that word,"[5] provokes Carl Braaten to counter in the spirit of the Reformers: "Then what on earth is the incarnation for? Then what was Jesus all about?"[6] He insists that the *descriptive* task—speaking *about* God—as well as the *prescriptive* task—speaking *for*

---

[1] Calvin can also insist that we accommodate ourselves to God's justice, integrity and righteousness. See, Paul Helm, *John Calvin's Ideas* (Oxford University Press, 2006), 186.

[2] Helm, *Calvin's Ideas*, 196.

[3] Heb. 1:1.

[4] Helm, *Calvin's Ideas*, 31.

[5] Sallie McFague, *Metaphorical Theology: Models of God in Religious Language* (Philadelphia: Fortress Press, 1982), 194.

[6] Carl E. Braaten, "Introduction: Naming the Name," Carl Braaten (ed.) *Our Naming of God. Problems and prospects of God-talk today* (Minneapolis: Fortress Press, 1989), 5.

God—is rooted in God's speaking *to* us in prophecy and proclamation, creating in us the *ascriptive* act of prayer and praise.[7]

Even though the principle of accommodation is a recurring theme throughout the theology of Calvin, it has only recently become a focal point of theological research. In the introductory chapter to his work *The Knowledge of God in Calvin's Theology* (1952), Edward Dowey has a section on "The accommodated character of all knowledge of God,"[8] but it was Ford Lewis Battles' article 25 years later, "God was Accommodating Himself to Human Capacity,"[9] that really sparked off the discussion. As recently as 2006 Jon Balserak's study, *Divinity Compromised: A study of divine accommodation in the thought of John Calvin*,[10] was the first monograph in any language dedicated to this topic.

It is sometimes intimated that since Schleiermacher until the middle of the previous century the idea of accommodation has more or less disappeared from the theological scene. That, most definitely, is not the case within Dutch Reformed theology. J. de Jong submits that in Herman Bavinck "it functions as a central principle governing all revelation."[11] With regard to Klaas Schilder he sees accommodation as a persistent "background theme" in all his works.[12]

I would like to add another name to the list: Oepke Noordmans (1871–1956). In his *Collected Works* (published 1978–2004) we come across this subject on a number of occasions, often in contexts where it is clear that it functions as a key concept having a bearing on significant notions in Noordmans' oeuvre. In accordance with Calvin, Noordmans sees the suffering Servant as the climax of God's accommodation.[13]

---

[7] Carl E. Braaten, "The problem of God-language today," Carl Braaten (ed.) *Our Naming of God. Problems and prospects of God-talk today* (Minneapolis: Fortress Press, 1989), 11.

[8] Edward A. Dowey, *The Knowledge of God in Calvin's Theology* (New York: Columbia University Press, 1952).

[9] Ford Lewis Battles, "God was Accommodating Himself to Human Capacity," *Interpretation* 31 (1977), 19–38.

[10] John Balserak, *Divinity Compromised: A study of Divine Accommodation in the Thought of John Calvin* (Dordrecht: Springer, 2006).

[11] J. de Jong, *Accommodatio Dei; A Theme in K. Schilder's Theology of Revelation* (Kampen: Dissertatie-Uitgeverij, 1990), 62.

[12] De Jong, *Accommodatio Dei*, 63; see also 9.

[13] Calvin had an important forming influence on the thought of Noordmans as is clear from his first finger exercises to his final volume of meditations. Of course, being Noordmans, he deals with Calvin in a manner that is very much his own. As always, his focus is not primarily historical but theological. The *living* Word, as the unity of form and Spirit, is decisive. In this regard Noordmans has coined the concept, "historical spiritualism," that stands over against mere "antiquarian" historicity. O. Noordmans, *Verzamelde Werken* (Collected Works) (Kampen: Kok, 1978–2004) (henceforth: Noordmans, *VW*) vol. 1, 99.

Accommodation as Condescension

First we must take a look, albeit brief, at accommodation in Calvin. Following the early fathers[14] he sees accommodation as closely related to God's gracious condescension in revealing Himself. Calvin makes so bold as to claim in his commentary on John 21:24 that God "accommodates himself to the ordinary way of speaking on account of our ignorance, and sometimes, if I may be allowed the expression, stammers (*balbutiat*)."[15] After all, the Holy Spirit "would rather speak childishly (*quodammodo balbultire*) than unintelligibly to the humble and unlearned."[16] Calvin also uses "baby-talk"[17] as a figure of speech against the *Anthropomorphites*, who take the Bible's references to God's limbs literally when he retorts:

> For who is so devoid of intellect as not to understand that God, in so speaking, lisps (*balbultit*) with us as nurses are wont to do with little children? Such modes of expression, therefore, do not so much express what kind of being God is, as accommodate the knowledge of him to our feebleness. In doing so, he must of course stoop far below his proper height.[18]

Calvin concurs with Irenaeus "that the Father who is boundless in himself, is bounded in the Son, because he has accommodated himself to our

---

[14] The principle of accommodation was not an invention of Calvin for it had a long pre-history in Philo Judaeus, Latin rhetoric, as well as the Church Fathers. See Battles, "God was Accommodating Himself," and Balserak, *Divinity Compromised*, Chapter 2. John Chrysostom, whom Calvin considers a lesser theologian but a better exegete than Augustine, is a prime example. John H. Leith, "Calvin's Doctrine of the Proclamation of the Word and its Significance Today," Timothy George (ed.), *John Calvin & the Church* (Louisville: Westminister/John Knox Press, 1990), 209: "It was from John Chrysostom, whom Calvin judged a poorer theologian than Augustine but a better exegete, that Calvin and the others learned much about preaching." He relies John R. Walchenbach, whose dissertation of 1974 was recently published. John R. Walchenbach, *John Calvin as Biblical Commentator: An Investigation into Calvin's Use of John Chrysostom as an Exegetical Tutor* (Eugene: Wipf & Stock, 2010). Chrysostom closely links accommodation with the terms *katabasis* (God's condescension) and *astheneia* (our limitations) See De Jong, *Accommodatio Dei*, 21f. Due to the importance of accommodation in Chrysostom's thought, he was dubbed "le docteur de la condenscendance" by Henry Pinard. Balserak, *Divinity Compromised*, 13 n1.

[15] Calvin, Commentary on John 21:24, *CO* 47, 458.

[16] Calvin, Commentary on Psalm 136, *CO* 32, 365. See Herman J. Selderhuis, *Gott in der Mitte. Calvins Theologie der Psalmen* (Leipzig: Evangelische Verlagsanstalt, 2004), 125. Cf. also Calvin, Commentary on Genesis 1:6, *CO* 23, 18.

[17] Dirk W. Jellema, "God's 'baby-talk': Calvin and the 'errors' in the Bible," *Reformed Journal 30* (1980), 25–27. See also Edward A. Dowey, *The knowledge of God*, Appendix 1 "A note on anthropomorphism."

[18] Calvin, *Institutes* I.13.1. John Calvin, *Institutes of the Christian Religion* transl. Henry Beveridge (Grand Rapids: Michigan, 1962), vol. 1, 110.

capacity, lest our minds be swallowed up by the immensity of his glory."[19] That does not imply that God *in se* (in Godself) casts a shadow on God *quoad nos* (towards us)[20] but should rather discourage all improper, empty speculation with regard to God's incomprehensible being and inscrutable counsel. Certainty of salvation does reside neither in us nor in God the Father apart from the Son, but only in Christ as the "mirror" of election.[21]

Paul Helm convincingly argues that Calvin creates no contrast between God's essence and God's revelation but rather poses a disparity between God's perfect knowledge of Godself and our partial, accommodated knowledge.[22] God's incomprehensible essence is not comprehensively revealed due to our infirmity. This is borne out by Calvin's own conclusion: "Wherefore, let us willingly leave to God the knowledge of himself. In the words of Hilary (De Trinit. lib.i), 'He alone is a fit witness to himself who is known only by himself'." Thus Calvin cautions that we should "in our inquiries make application to no other quarter than God's word."[23]

It is worth noting that Calvin never uses the noun, *accommodatio* but prefers the verb, *accommodare*[24] (or *attemperare*) that expresses the dynamic character of revelation. God "adapts different forms to different ages, as He knows to be expedient for each."[25] This may explain Calvin's preference for Plutarch's metaphor of the *theater* rather than Plato's partiality for the temple. Battles observes:

> As a stage play is itself an accommodated representation of the playwright's inspiration and insight into human existence to the more limited vision of the audience, so in the vast theater of heaven and earth the divine playwright stages the ongoing drama of creation, alienation, return, and forgiveness for the teeming audience of humanity itself.[26]

---

[19] Calvin, *Institutes* II.6.4.

[20] Calvin, *Institutes* I.10.2.

[21] Calvin, *Institutes* III.24.5.

[22] Helm, *Calvin's Ideas*, 30.

[23] Calvin, *Institutes* I.13.21.

[24] Battles, "God was Accommodating Himself," 19. See also Jon Balserak, *Divinity Compromised*, 15, n13.

[25] Calvin, *Institutes* II.11.13. D.F. Wright, "Accommodation and Barbarity in John Calvin's Old Testament Commentaries," in A. Graeme Auld (ed.), *Understanding Poets and Prophets. Essays in honour of George Wishart Anderson* (Sheffield: Academic Press, 1993), 413–427, draws attention to the five differences between Old and New Testament, "relating not to substance but to mode or form of administration," (*Institutes* II.10.1), 416ff.

[26] Battles, "God was Accommodating Himself," 32.

Revealing as Concealing

Even though God's hiddenness is a fundamental theme in the theology of Calvin it attracts very little scholarly attention.[27] While Calvin is less prone to paradox than Luther and the consequent contrast between the hidden and the revealed God is less pronounced,[28] the concept of *Deus absconditus* is not absent from his vocabulary. As in the case of Luther, *theologia crucis* is also an apt description of Calvin's theology.[29]

God's "bending down" is much more than merely a rhetorical tool with which the "Great Orator"[30] avails Godself to reveal Godself, for the act of lowering as such reveals God's very being as holy love. Form (stooping down) and content (God's gracious love) are one in the act of revelation. In Calvin's commentary on Genesis 35:7 we read that God "in a certain sense abases (*extenuat*) Godself, and stammers (*balbultit*) with us."[31] Babbling like a child, means becoming a child. God's disclosing of Godself means sharing Godself, culminating in incarnation and cross.

The form of his revelation, however, prevents us from getting a hold on the Revealer. God's response to Moses' question regarding his Name, I AM WHO I AM, or I WILL BE WHAT I WILL BE, is as much an answer as a refusal to answer. Accordingly, Franklin Sherman describes it as a "nameless name".[32] Also in Origen accommodation (*symperiphora*) cuts both

---

[27] Herman J. Selderhuis, *Gott in der Mitte*, 172. He refers to Brian Gerrish as an exception to the rule. Gerrish distinguishes between God's hiddenness in God's revelation, and God's hiddenness outside God's revelation. Brian A. Gerrish, "To the unknown God: Luther and Calvin on the Hiddenness of God," in Brian A. Gerrish, *The Old Protestantism and the New: Essays on the Reformation Heritage* (Edinburgh: T. and T. Clark, 1982), 131–149, 134.

[28] See J. de Jong, *Accommodatio Dei*, 42. Randall C. Zachman, "Calvin as analogical theologian," *Scottish Journal of Theology* 51 (1998), 162 argues that accommodation in Calvin involves *analogia* as well as *anagoge*. "Analogy stresses the similarity amid difference between sign and the reality it signifies, whereas anagoge stresses the elevation from the temporal sign to the spiritual reality it represents." Also Randall C Zachmann, *John Calvin as Teacher, Pastor, and Theologian: The Shape of his Writings and Thought* (Grand Rapids: Baker Academic, 2006), 210.

[29] Selderhuis, *Gott in der Mitte*, 180.

[30] Jon Balserak, "The God of Love and Weakness: Calvin's understanding of God's accommodating relationship with his people," *Westminster Theological Journal* 62 (2000), 195: "Calvin's accommodating God appears not so much as a Grand Orator but as a Grand Shepherd (or even a Grand Parent), one who, with respect to each of his own, "treats it according to its capacity." Also Battles warns against making the whole Christian gospel a mere exercise in rhetoric. Battles, "God was Accommodating Himself," 37.

[31] Calvin, Commentary on Genesis 35: 7, *CO* 23, 469.

[32] Franklin Sherman, "Reticence and Exuberance in Speaking of God," Carl E. Braaten (ed.) *Our Naming of God. Problems and Prospects of God-Talk Today* (Minneapolis: Fortress Press, 1989), 39.

ways in revealing as well as concealing.[33] Accommodation is a double-edged sword, similar to God's Word in Hebrews 4:12, involving simultaneously judgment and justification.

On the one hand Calvin claims that the death of Christ "not only obscures his glory, but removes it altogether from our sight."[34] On the other hand, in the cross of Christ God's judgment, God's grace and God's glory coincide. The climax of concealing is concurrently the apex of revealing:

> For in the cross of Christ, as in a splendid theater, the incomparable goodness of God is set before the whole world. The glory of God shines, indeed, in all creatures on high and below, but never more brightly than in the cross, in which there is a wonderful change of things—the condemnation of all men was manifested, sin blotted out, salvation restored to all men; in short, the whole world was renewed and all things restored to order.[35]

Incarnation as Accommodation Par Excellence?

In his influential article, Ford Lewis Battles describes the incarnation as "the accommodating act *par excellence*."[36] Since then, scores of commentators have followed suit. Noticeable exceptions are David F. Wright and, in particular, Jon Balserak.[37] Balserak agrees that Calvin considers the incarnation as "the center and culmination of divine salvation."[38] He quotes Calvin's rhetorical question: "At what time did God descend lower than when Christ emptied himself?"[39] Futhermore, he concedes that Calvin describes incarnation as accommodation on many occasions.[40] Therefore, he deems it necessary to qualify his reservations.

All depends on what *par excellence* means. If it merely refers to "the simple quality of greatness or magnificence"[41] Balserak would agree with

---

[33] Battles, "God was Accommodating Himself," 23.
[34] Calvin, Commentary on John 12: 23, *CO* 47, 288.
[35] Calvin, Commentary on John 13: 31. *CO* 47, 317.
[36] Battles, "God was Accommodating Himself," 36.
[37] For instance, David F. Wright, "Calvin's Pentateuchal Criticism: Equity, Hardness of Heart, and Divine Accommodation in the Mosaic Harmony Commentary," *Calvin Theological Journal* 21 (1986), 33–50. Especially, Jon Balserak, "The Accommodating Act Par Excellence?: An Inquiry into the Incarnation and Calvin's Understanding of Accommodation," *Scottish Journal of Theology*, 55 (2002), 408–423. See also Balserak, *Divinity Compromised*, 64–67; 91–93.
[38] Balserak, "Accommodating Act par excellence?" 410.
[39] Balserak, "Accommodating Act par excellence?" 409.
[40] Balserak, *Divinity Compromised*, 161. For instance *Institutes* II.6.4.
[41] Balserak, "Accommodating Act par excellence?," 421.

the statement of Battles. However, he suspects that "par excellence" claims more. He rejects an understanding which by implication turns the incarnation into the archetypal or quintessential instance of accommodation. That would amount to a reduction of the multifarious forms, purposes and character of God's accommodation in Calvin. For sure, "incarnational accommodation" does pertain to God's revelatory descending in order to save, but this is not the sole form of accommodation. He is willing to describe God's sending of the Son, as the "zenith"[42] of self-disclosure, but revealing is only one form of accommodation.[43] Balsarak blames the tendency to equate accommodation with condescension for fostering the fallacy of considering incarnation as the accommodating act *par excellence*.

Undoubtedly, the varied forms of accommodation which Balserak identifies are extremely valuable for a fuller understanding of Calvin, but his clear-cut distinctions between accommodation as condescension, tolerance, and compromise, seem less than convincing. This also holds for the sharp contrast he posits between accommodation as revealing and concealing as well as between incarnational accommodation and providential accommodation.

If the diverse forms of God's accommodation have nothing in common, then the word is used in an equivocal manner that makes it senseless to speak of a *diversity* of forms. On the other hand, if the various forms do have something in common, I fail to see why anyone should waver to call the incarnation, not merely a great and magnificent example, but rather the supreme form of accommodation.

I am willing to accept De Jong's contention that although Calvin perceives Christ's work as accommodation, he understands the explanation and application of Christ's redemptive acts as accommodation *per se*, and the redemptive acts themselves as the fullest expression of God's grace and love.[44] I would like to suggest that, as fulfillment of the diverse forms of accommodation, Calvin is in fact somewhat reticent to use the same figure he employs for the preceding prophetic forms also for the fulfillment

---

[42] Balserak, *Divinity Compromised*, 64.
[43] He refers to God's purpose in providence that has nothing to do "with the dispensing of revelation" for "God not only speaks but behaves in an accommodated way." Balserak, "Accommodating Act par excellence?," 413, n17. See also Jon Balserak, "The God of Love and Weakness," 79.
[44] De Jong, *Accommodatio Dei*, 43.

itself. As Roland Frye phrases it: "The incarnation was God's ultimate accommodation; as such it was historical and not figurative..."[45]

Act as Word in the Theology of Noordmans

As in the case of Calvin, we can but scratch the surface of the relevant material as regards accommodation in the theology of Noordmans. Of special interest is his emphasis on the unity of word and act in God's gracious accommodation.

God knows us in all eternity but since we, as created beings, are limited to space and time, "we would not have known God, if God had not in the beginning created heaven and earth."[46] Therefore, Noordmans claims that not only the creation narrative, but also creation itself is a deed of accommodation.[47]

He concurs with Faust's contention that all passing reality is but a parable[48] but disagrees with his declaration, *Im Anfang war die That* ('In the beginning was the deed') in favor of John 1: 1 "In the beginning was the Word."[49] The Hebrew *dabar* means "word" as well as "object," Psalm 33:9: "For He spoke, and it came to be; He commanded, and it stood firm." Taking heed of God's deeds means listening to God's speech.[50] Created reality points beyond itself to the Creator who addresses us through created forms. Psalm 19:1 says: "The heavens declare the glory of God; the skies proclaim the work of God's hands". These accommodated forms and their literary reflections in the letters of Scripture, are transcendental vessels in which God pours his gracious revelation. Our faith lives by these forms even though they impart to us "but a poor reflection as in a mirror." Only

[45] Roland M. Frye, "Calvin's Theological Use of Figurative Language," Timothey George (ed.), *John Calvin and the Church: A Prism of Reform* (Louisville: Westminister/John Knox Press, 1990), 175. Paul Helm puts it as follows: "Accommodation is a divine activity, and since the ends that God seeks to secure by the use of such language are ultimately soteric in character, we must see the idea of God's accommodation of himself in his language about himself as integral to his grace, an accommodation that has its end-point in the accommodation of God the Son in the Incarnation, although Calvin does not seem to use the term in developing his account of the Incarnation... For although the Word clothed himself in our flesh, he nevertheless remained what he is, fully divine." Paul Helm, *John Calvin's Ideas*, 197.
[46] *VW* 8, 344.
[47] *VW* 8, 344.
[48] *VW* 2, 82.
[49] *VW* 1, 160.
[50] *VW* 1, 159.

in the final consummation, when believing God's Word is transformed into seeing his face (1 Cor. 13:12), these "earthen pitchers are broken at the spring" (Eccl. 12:6)[51] but in the meantime they are indispensable.

When we see creation predominantly as *act*, it is up to us to discover the Doer behind the deed; if, however, creation is primarily understood as *word*, the Speaker as such addresses us directly. To be sure, also the word remains a *medium* between the speaker and the listener that differs drastically from knowing *per essentiam*.[52] Nevertheless, while a deed is like a closed door that we have to open to discover the doer, the word is like a window through which the encounter is much more immediate.

The expression "mediated immediacy" coined by John Baillie to describe Luther's view of God's word in the Bible,[53] would also be an appropriate portrayal of Noordmans' position. While the philosopher tries to discover a deeper meaning behind the text or form, faith finds the *arcana Dei* (mysteries of God) within the "enclosure of the letter" through the illumination of the Spirit.[54] Like the *clair-obscur* Noordmans observes in the paintings of Rembrandt, our knowledge of God through the "mediated immediacy" of the Word, is not perfect, for it corresponds with our "knowing in part" in the present dispensation.[55] Even so, it is an authentic foretaste of the future that awaits us "when I shall know fully, even as I am fully known."[56]

On more than one occasion Noordmans narrates an account given by Goethe in *Dichtung und Wahrheit* of a day he spent as a student in Dresden looking at the paintings of the Dutch masters. That night he could not sleep. The old furniture in his room took on a *magische Haltung* (magic disposition) since they seemed alive with spirit. Bridging the gap between object and subject the dumb furniture was transformed into living language.[57]

The form of creation in itself is a dead letter, ambiguous, confusing, and even frightening. Looking at the blooming blossoms of a cherry tree bursting forth in summer, the poet, Paul Celan, hears the crushing sound

---

[51] *VW* 8, 344.
[52] *VW* 1, 139, 161.
[53] See De Jong, *Accommodatio Dei*, 33, who refers to Baillie who used this expression with regard to Luther's view of revelation.
[54] *VW* 2, 13.
[55] *VW* 2, 259.
[56] 1 Cor. 13:9–12.
[57] *VW* 1, 136; *VW* 4, 435.

of soldiers marching out to war.[58] Noordmans relates an experience one beautiful autumn afternoon during the Second World War in the vicinity of his hometown not far from the German border. While cycling through the woods he gradually fell under the spell of his enchanted environment. The rays of the sun and the leaves of the trees united to form a mystical unity inviting him to join in the dance. The apotheosis of his surroundings, surrendering to the caress of the sun, captivated his senses to such an extent that all sound subsided and every word died down.

Reaching a certain point where everything stood in red all around him his mood changed dramatically. All of a sudden nature seemed ominous and bewitched as if any moment a red-veined demon might appear next to a tree and an abyss might open up in front of his feet dragging him alive down into hell. The spell was only broken when he reached an opening in the trees from where he could clearly see the little church of Almen with its enormous baptismal font dating from the Middle Ages.[59]

The Incarnation as Culmination of Accommodation

The most important medium of knowledge of God is not nature but history. God can use nature as sign and sacrament to seal the historical covenant when, for instance, God takes Abraham outside his tent and shows him the countless stars in heaven as "visible words" underscoring his promises.[60] God's more common way of speaking, however, is when God stoops to enter Abraham's tent to talk to him almost as an equal, like a friend to a friend. This is the form of the Word made flesh that we encounter in the manger.

In the broken light of history we encounter God as Father, Son and Holy Spirit. When talking is not enough, He comes; when coming is not enough, He comforts.[61] This progressive history is grounded in eternity. Behind the Lamb slaughtered on Calvary, stands "the Lamb that was slain from the creation of the world,"[62] but this latter knowledge is more hid-

---

[58] Theo de Boer, *De God van de Filosofen en de God van Pascal: Op het Grensgebied van Filosofie en Theologie* (The God of the Philosophers and the God of Pascal: On the Border of Philosophy and Theology) (The Hague: Meinema, 1989), 41.

[59] *VW* 8, 147–149.

[60] Gen. 15:5.

[61] *VW* 2, 223.

[62] Rev. 13:8.

den than what transpires in history.[63] The same applies to our understanding of God's gracious election in Christ[64] through the Holy Spirit,
for God's council has nothing to do with an abstract eternity. As Noordmans puts it rather pointedly, God takes his eternal decisions at the very
last moment.[65]

Like nature, historical forms *per se* are silent. Actually, the border
between nature and history is blurred. Creation is no *fait accompli* but
creatio continua. To the extent that God's accommodation becomes
more historical, revealing through concealing increases. The darkness
deepens from creation to incarnation, which Noordmans calls "complete
accommodation,"[66] that again increases from Christ's birth to his burial
to such an extent that the imagination of faith cannot keep up any longer. In Christ prophet and word,[67] priest and sacrifice (*hostia*),[68] King and
Kingdom,[69] coincide. In Christ the Old Testament forms find their fulfillment. In Christ as "God's form"[70] in human flesh, we encounter the eternal Word clad in this "parable" that awaits the coming of the Paraclete to
explain the mystery it conceals.[71]

As God's Kingdom (respectively, Kingship) comes closer it becomes
more obscure. Since God stoops so low in incarnation and cross, we are
more in need of the Holy Spirit to recognize this God in the likeness of
sinful humanity,[72] than to see God's glory manifested in the magnificent
night sky, which Immanuel Kant so mightily admired.[73] In his cry of God-
forsakenness on the cross one gets the impression that Christ can hardly
recognize himself. It sounds like an echo of John the Baptist's frightening
question, now put in the first person: "Am I the One who was to come?"[74]
The resurrection is God's answer in the affirmative. But were such extreme
measures a necessity? Was dying on the cross inescapable? In short, *Cur
Deus homo?*

---

[63] *VW* 1, 162.
[64] See his brilliant article, "Predestinatie," *VW* 2, 124–134.
[65] *VW* 2, 493. See also 542.
[66] *VW* 2, 90.
[67] *VW* 2, 289.
[68] *VW* 2, 417.
[69] See the meditation "The King Comes," *VW* 8, 237–239.
[70] *VW* 8, "Form and Spirit," part II,1, "God's Form".
[71] *VW* 2, 290.
[72] Rom. 8:3.
[73] *VW* 8, 187.
[74] *VW* 8, 255.

Noordmans on Accommodation as Reconciliation in Calvin

The offensiveness of the cross for modern humanity is, according to Noordmans, twofold in character. The first annoying feature is more intellectual; the second more ethical. Both imply a heavenly Logos that exceeds not only subjectively our knowledge of this world but also objectively the order of this world. Noordmans often refers to a few lines from a poem by Nicolaas Beets (1814–1903): "O sing me once more the lovely old rhyme ... Of heavenly happenings occurring in time."[75] It involves a "metaphysical drama" in which the divine persons act as *dramatis personae*, in a transcendent (in the sense of transmanent, superhuman)[76] *pactum salutis* comprising a divine transaction that seems to the modern mind as nothing but mythology.[77] The *Credo* narrates this drama comprising creation, virgin birth, descending into hell, ascending into heaven, sitting at God's right hand, and coming again to judge the quick and the dead.

Noordmans deems the second objection as much more serious than the first: the modern mind takes umbrage at the doctrine of justification of the sinner, as a synthetical judgment of God executed *extra nos* on the cross.[78] In an analytical doctrine in which the *believer* (not the sinner) is justified, there is no need for atonement originating from beyond as revealed in the cross.

Reconciliation is at the center of the theology of the Western church. It is not a new dogma added to the Greek doctrines of Trinity and Christology, but their further unfolding.[79] Especially in the churches of the Reformation the doctrine of the Holy Spirit comes to the fore. In the apostolic creed no mention is made of wrath, satisfaction, sacrifice, love, grace, justification, inclusive-substitution (*Stellvertretung*), reconciliation, but in Calvin's exposition of the *Credo* everything centers upon reconciliation with justification as its epicenter.[80] Calvin himself quotes 2 Corinthians 5:

---

[75] *VW* 1, 144.
[76] Noordmans refers to J.D. Bierens de Haan, *Levensleer naar de beginselen van Spinoza* [Doctrine of life according to the principles of Spinoza] (The Hague: Nijhoff, 1900), 59. "Transmanent" stands over against "transcendent" as used by Spinoza where it is located within the human personality. *VW* 1, 301.
[77] *VW* 2, 403, also *VW* 1, 287f.
[78] *VW* 2, 403f.
[79] *VW* 2, 410.
[80] *VW* 2, 404.

19–21 where Paul "uses righteousness and reconciliation indiscriminately, to make us understand that the one includes the other."[81]

Paul's explanation of the "foolishness of the cross" clearly involves a logic that is beyond our pale. According to Romans 5:8–10 Christ demonstrates God's love by dying for us when we were God's enemies thus saving us from God's wrath by reconciliation through the death of his Son. This clarification is miles removed from the modern confidence with which Ritschl declares that the cross cures us from the impression that God is our foe.[82] Within the constraints of the immanent logic of the modern mind reconciliation through an alien atonement is nothing but foolishness.

Noordmans refers to Calvin, who poses the question how it is possible that while God is saving sinners He can simultaneously be hostile to them as the curse of the cross proclaims. Since God in his love is the author of the atonement, there can be no question of the pagan idea of the *Umstimmung Gottes* (God's change of mind) namely that a change is effected in God's attitude due to the sacrifice of his Son.[83] Characteristically, Calvin appeals to God's *accommodatio ad vivum* (accommodation to life) in which God's love and his wrath, his curse and his care, go in an ineffable manner together.[84]

Noordmans recalls that Augustine in his *Enchiridion* describes Christ's death as a parable of forgiving and remarks that one is tempted to suspect a certain symbolism in Calvin that might put the objective character of Christ's work in jeopardy. That, however, is not his intention[85] for Calvin hastens to add: "Though this is said in accommodation to the weakness of our capacity, it is not said falsely."[86] Denying the objective character

---

[81] Calvin, *Institutes* III.11.22.

[82] *VW* 2, 402.

[83] See Emil Brunner, *The Mediator: A Study of the Central Doctrine of the Christian Faith* (Philadelphia: Westminister Press, [1947]), 470 m.

[84] "ineffabili quodam modo" *VW* 2, 404f. To quote Calvin himself (*Institutes* II.16.2): "The mode in which the Spirit usually speaks in Scripture is, that God was the enemy of men until they were restored to favor by the death of Christ (Rom. 5:10); that they were cursed until their iniquity was expiated by the sacrifice of Christ (Gal. 3:10, 13); that they were separated from God, until by means of Christ's body they were received into union (Col. 1:21, 22). Such modes of expression are accommodated to our capacity, that we may the better understand how miserable and calamitous our condition is without Christ... We are so instructed by divine truth, as to perceive that without Christ God is in a manner hostile to us, and his arm raised for our destruction. Thus taught, we look to Christ alone for divine favor and paternal love."

[85] *VW* 2, 416.

[86] "non tamen falso" Calvin, *Institutes* II.16.3.

of reconciliation amounts, for Noordmans, to the same confusion as the naive realists who reckon they have lost all objective reality the moment they learn that form and colour are located in our minds.[87] Although Calvin is fond of the figure of the theater he nevertheless insists that no fiction or play-acting prompts the complaint in the cry of God-forsakenness on the cross.[88]

God's forgiving is not a matter of course. Grace is not cheap, especially for God, since it involves, *quodam modo* (in a certain sense), paying a price.[89] God's righteousness as love and his love as righteousness necessitate the sending of his Son. The "necessity" of the curse incurred by humanity and the "cost" involved for the Father, does not reside outside Himself in an absolute law with which He has to comply but in his sovereign will, and thus forms part of his Holy Love that blots out his wrath[90] when Christ's righteousness is "by some wondrous way" communicated to us through imputation.[91]

Although the Biblical articulations of reconciliation are *ad sensum nostrum accommodatae* (accommodated to our frame of mind), they are not false, for Christ truly is as we encounter him clothed in his Gospel (*Evangelio suo vestitum*).[92] This corresponds with Calvin's emphasis on the clarity of the letter of Scripture in which the "holy darkness" of the *arcana Dei* is revealed. "Calvin listens to the Spirit while focusing his attention on the letter."[93] Hence, Noordmans describes the clarity of revelation as a "clear mystery".[94] This explains why Calvin's "monumental" commentaries are as profound as they are sober.[95] His emphasis on the word differs drastically from Noordmans' own teacher, professor J.M.S. Baljon (1861–1908), who bans the Holy Spirit as the *auctor primaries* (primary author), "from

---

[87] *VW* 1, 299.
[88] Calvin, Commentary on Matthew 27:46, *CO* 45, 779. See Randall C. Zachman, "Calvin as analogical theologian," 182–184.
[89] *VW* 2, 405.
[90] Brunner, *Mediator*, 471. In a footnote on page 472 Brunner criticizes Anselm's view that this "necessity" is something absolute. On the other hand he also rejects the idea that this choice of God was an incomprehensible arbitrary act. He concludes that Calvin's idea of "relative necessity" is the correct option. See Calvin, *Institutes* II.12.1. Noordmans refers to Emile Brunner in this regard.
[91] Calvin, *Institutes* III.11.23.
[92] Calvin, *Institutes* III.2.6. Noordmans, *VW* 1, 298.
[93] *VW* 2, 12.
[94] *VW* 2, 402.
[95] *VW* 2, 10.

the exegetical synagogue declaring every meaning that rises above the mere *gramma* as gibberish."[96]

In Calvin's "pastoral dogmatics"[97] assurance of salvation is essential. This is not meant in an individualistic manner, for God's word of forgiveness is nothing less than a new creation,[98] a *civitas Dei* (city of God). God's words are acts creating the reality his promises confer. They are not merely informative but first and foremost performative. His Word judges and justifies whilst addressing us personally. God's speaking to us through his Word and Spirit is really and truly a "speech-act" *par excellence* reconciling sinners to Himself.

In Conclusion: God's Gracious Greeting

Many years ago, trying to allay my fears by browsing through a periodical in the waiting room of a dentist, I came across an article on analytical philosophy. The author started with an anecdote about two philosophers strolling the university grounds arguing vigorously over an astrophysical issue. Says the one: "What do you mean by saying that space is curbed?" Replies the other: "What do you mean by saying it isn't?" Counters the first: "What do you mean by *mean*?" A senior colleague, who was passing by, could not refrain from greeting them rather cheerfully: "Good morning gentlemen—if that means anything to you?"

This little story gives pause to ponder. If the perimeters of created time and space are mind-blowing, what are we to say about the eternal Creator of the universe? As Calvin puts it: "For God is infinite; and when the heavens cannot contain him, how can our minds comprehend Him?"[99] Since our minds are curbed it should be quite comprehensible that God is incomprehensible. In Article 1 of the *Confessio Belgica* God's simplicity (trustworthiness) is mentioned in the same breath with God's incomprehensibility. In addition the *Belgica* confesses that God "is perfectly wise, just, good, and the overflowing fountain of all good." Obviously, God's incomprehensibility does not cancel the rest but underscores it: God is incomprehensibly just and incomprehensibly good. God's incomprehensible essence

---

[96] *VW* 2, 13.
[97] *VW* 2, i.a. 236, 241.
[98] *VW* 2, 417.
[99] Calvin, Commentary on Ezekiel 1:28, *CO* 40, 60.

overflows in a fountain of incomprehensible favor towards the work of God's hands.

The cheerful greeting of the old professor during the merry meeting with his younger colleagues, reminds me of a meditation by Oepke Noordmans. He refers to the words of the angels to the shepherds the night of the nativity, also uttered by Christ to his disciples the morning of the resurrection, "Peace be with you!" The title of the meditation reads, "God's greeting".[100]

This greeting, which is grounded in the incarnation culminating in the cross, has the character of a blessing descending on God's groaning creation. This greeting is a promise that is imparted by Word and Spirit that is able to discard sin and repel sorrow. This greeting forms the counterpart to the cry of Godforsakenness on the cross of Calvary.

---

[100]   *VW* 8, 282–284.

CHAPTER THIRTEEN

CALVIN AND HUMAN DIGNITY

J.M. Vorster

The concept of "human dignity" has become a major directive in modern ethics. This concept underlies the modern constitutional state and has become an important guideline in the development of medical ethics, bio-ethics and the ethics of human rights. Since World War II Christian theology has shown an increasing interest in human dignity as the leading principle in Christian anthropology, and in the way in which human dignity can be founded in Scripture and in the Christian tradition. It is a very popular theme in current philosophical, juridical and theological debates.[1]

Reformed theology, with its strong emphasis on the social calling of Christians and the divine calling of the state, is also deeply involved in these debates. Since the Reformation several theologians enunciated the implications of human dignity with reference to Calvin. Reformed theology emphasizes, like Calvin, the total depravity of humankind in its soteriology. It is fair to conclude that because of this angle of approach in its theology, it does not depart from a totally pessimistic view of humankind in its anthropology. Even so, Reformed theology also developed implications of human dignity for human relations and holds the view that Scripture teaches as well the inherent human dignity of all people, which should be respected by fellow human beings and social institutions. Human depravity does not inhibit the inherent human dignity of persons in the eyes of fellow-humans and social institutions.[2]

Can the idea of human dignity be found in Calvin's anthropological teachings? It is clear that Calvin did not use the term "human dignity" as the concept is interpreted today. Moreover, this concept as a constitutional principle was not in view during his time. Yet, although the term "human

---

[1] J.M. Vorster, *Ethical Perspectives on Human Rights* (Potchefstroom: Potchefstroom Theological Publications, 2007), 18.

[2] J. Witte, *The Reformation of Rights, Law, Religion, and Human Rights in Early Modern Calvinism* (Cambridge: Cambridge University Press, 2007), 10.

dignity" in this later sense does not feature in Calvin's social teachings, the vestiges of this idea are intertwined throughout his teachings about humankind and society, and especially so in his view about the calling of civil authority as a servant of God. The influence of Calvin's theology on modern democracy, in the sense of government *by* the people, has been discussed for a long time, although Calvin, with the exception of one part in his *Institutes*, wrote no extensive treatise on politics and related matters.[3] However, various references to the issues can be found in his huge corpus of writings, which was written over a period of 25 years.[4]

This fact becomes evident when Calvin's legacy regarding the rights of people is examined. In a recent book, John Witte, Jr. (2007) provides authoritative material about the influence of Calvin in the development of modern constitutionalism. He says the following in the introduction of this book:

> Building in part on classical and Christian prototypes, Calvin developed arresting new teachings on authority and liberty, duties and rights, and church and state that have had an enduring influence on Protestant lands. Calvin's original teachings were periodically challenged by major crises in the West—the French Wars of Religion, the Dutch Revolt, the English Revolution, American Colonization, and the American Revolution. In each such crisis moment, a major Calvinist figure emerged—Theodore Beza, Johannes Althusius, John Milton, John Winthrop, John Adams and others—who modernized Calvin's teachings and converted them into dramatic new legal and political reforms. This rendered early modern Calvinism as one of the driving engines of Western constitutionalism.[5]

This article investigates Calvin's contribution to the current Reformed perspective on human dignity and the way his ideas determined modern-day Reformed ethics in this regard. The central theoretical argument of the article is that Calvin laid the foundation of the modern-day Reformed reflection on human dignity as the concept can apply to human rights and bio-ethics. When his ideas of the image of God and common grace, natural law and civil authority are outlined his vision becomes especially clear. In conclusion, the heritage of Calvin's views on these particular issues in the Reformed ethical reflection in the post-World War II era will be described.

---

[3] J.H. Leith, *An Introduction to Reformed Tradition: A way of Being the Christian Community* (Atlanta: John Knox, 1977), 20; Witte, *Reformation of Rights*, 41.

[4] J.T. McNeil, "John Calvin and Civil Government" in G.L. Hunt, *Calvinism and the Political Order* (Philadelphia: Westminster, 1965), 24.

[5] Witte, *Reformation of Rights*, XI.

The Image of God and Common Grace

Calvin's view on the creation of the human in the image of God (*imago dei*), and the concept of common grace, lie at the root of his view that humans have an inherent God-given dignity.[6] God created humans in his image. The gift of God's image is present in every person. This creational principle highlights and stresses the worthiness of the human being. In Calvin's view the creation of humankind on the "sixth day" is especially important to note because God first created a dwelling place for people, and then the angels to act as protectors of humankind. These actions were a prelude to the creation of humankind. Humankind was bestowed with a certain status. Humans are the noblest of the works of God and this fact is proof of God's justice, wisdom and goodness.[7] Humans are the mirror of his divine glory. The most distinguishing quality of humankind is its likeness to God, which seats in the intellect and in the abilities of the "soul".[8]

What happened to this created dignity of humankind after the fall? Here, the reader should differentiate between what in modern terms can be termed Calvin's soteriology and his anthropology. Due to the Fall of Adam, humankind lost its free will and any capability to rectify its destitute state. Seen from a soteriological angle of approach, humankind fell into total depravity. This depravity is an "inherited corruption, which the church fathers termed 'original sin'—meaning by the word 'sin' the depravation of a nature previously good and pure."[9] Adam was not merely a progenitor, but a root, and thus through his corruption the whole human race was deservedly vitiated. Original sin, then, may be defined according to Calvin as a hereditary corruption and depravity of our nature. This extends to all parts of the soul, which first makes us obnoxious toward the wrath of God and then produces the deeds which in Scripture are termed the "works of the flesh".[10] The only way to salvation is the free grace of God as expressed in the atoning sacrifice of Christ, which is applied by the Holy Spirit and received through faith and repentance by the helpless sinner.[11]

However, in his anthropology Calvin bases his teaching on morality, and the moral law on the dignity of the human person as a result of the

---

[6] A. van Egmond, "Calvinist Thought and Human Rights," in A.A. Adullai (ed.) *Human Rights and Religious Values. An uneasy relationship?* (Grand Rapids: Eerdmans, 1990).

[7] Calvin, *Institutes* I.15.1.

[8] Calvin, *Institutes* I.15.4.

[9] Calvin, *Institutes* II.1.5.

[10] Calvin, *Institutes* II.1.8.

[11] Calvin, *Institutes* III.1.1.

imago dei. Although humankind's alienation from God due to the Fall and its total depravity lead to the corruption of the *imago dei,* the creational dignity/nobility (*nobilitas*) of humans expressed by the *imago dei* has not been destroyed.[12] When discussing humankind's depravity, Calvin adds: "Yet God would not have us forget our original nobility, which he had bestowed upon our father Adam, and which ought truly to arouse in us a zeal for righteousness and goodness."[13] People maintain the dignity of their creation, and all the responsibilities flowing from this inherent dignity remain intact.

In his exposition of the extent of Christian love, Calvin also refers to the *imago dei* when he says:

> Assuredly there is but one way in which to achieve what is not merely difficult but utterly against human nature: to love those who hate us, to repay their evil deeds with benefits, to return blessings for reproaches [Matt. 5:44]. It is that we remember not to consider men's evil intention but to look upon the image of God in them, which cancels and effaces their transgressions, and with its beauty and dignity allures us to love and embrace them.[14]

A violation of one's fellow human is a violation of God. The fall did not destroy the *imago dei,* and this characteristic of human existence became the foundation of the spiritual and civil liberties of the individual.

In conjunction with the concept of the human being created in the image of God lies the concept of the common grace of God upon all mankind. In addition to his providence and care God bestows upon us certain inherent gifts. Calvin, says in this regard:

> Whenever we come upon these matters in secular writers, let that admirable light of truth shining in them teach us that the mind of man, though fallen and perverted from its wholeness, is nevertheless clothed and ornamented with God's excellent gifts.[15]

In this sense, the whole human race can be regarded as one body reflecting the *imago dei* with creational gifts under the common grace of God.[16] As such, humans have an inherent value and people should regard each other as people with value in the eyes of God.

---

[12] Calvin, *Institutes* I.15.4. "Quare etsi demus non prorsus exinanitam ac deletam in eo fuisse Dei imaginem, sic tamen corrupta fuit, ut quicquit superest, horrenda sit deformitas." *OS* 3, 179.
[13] Calvin, *Institutes* II.1.3.
[14] Calvin, *Institutes* III.7.6.
[15] Calvin, *Institutes* II.2.15.
[16] J.H. Leith *John Calvin's doctrine of Christian Life* (Louisville: Westminster, 1989), 184.

The image of God and the gift of God's grace to humankind constitutes the foundation of Calvin's view of the responsibilities of individuals to each other, as well as the rights which people have in inter-personal relations and over-and-against social institutions. It is the duty of all humans to see their fellow beings as creations of God with certain gifts and rights bestowed on them by the Creator. A true understanding of another person comes only as one looks to God and sees God's reflection in that other person. God is seen reflected in all creation, even in unworthy sinners.[17] It is therefore also the responsibility of the believer to act on behalf of others in order to promote justice.[18] All people must be neighbourly. All people have a mutual responsibility, which entails mutual servitude.[19] This responsibility and servitude must come to light in the protection of other people's rights.

In his thorough study of Calvin's viewpoint on the rights of individuals Witte compiled an interesting list of the rights Calvin had in mind, especially in his later writings. He indicates—with authoritative references to Calvin's *Institutes* and his commentaries on various books in Scripture— that Calvin speaks at times about the subjective "rights" (*iuria, droits*) of individuals, in addition to their "liberties" or "freedoms" (*libertates, libertés*). Sometimes, he used such general phrases as "the common rights of mankind" (*iura commune hominum*), the "natural rights" (*iura naturali*) of persons, the "rights of a common nature" (*communes naturae iura*), or "the equal rights and liberties" (*pari iura et liberates*) of all. Usually, he referenced more specific rights.[20]

Furthermore, Witte explains that Calvin spoke, for example, about the "rights of Christian liberty," the "rights of citizenship" in the Kingdom of God or in heavenly Jerusalem, and, one of his favourite expressions, the "right of adoption" that Christians enjoy as new sons and daughters of God and brothers and sisters in Christ. He referenced "the right to inhabit," "the right to dwell in," and "the right and privilege to claim the territory" that Yahweh gave to the chosen people of Israel. He mentioned "Paul's rights of Roman citizenship." He spoke frequently, as a student of Roman law would, about property rights: "the right to land, and other property",

---

[17] J.A. Templin, "The Individual and Society in the Thought of Calvin," *Calvin Theological Journal* 23/ 2 (1988), 165.
[18] N. Wolterstorff, "Can a Christian be progressive?," *Gereformeerd Theologisch Tijdschrift* 88 (1988), 168.
[19] Templin, "Individual and Society in the Thought of Calvin," 168.
[20] Witte, *Reformation of Rights*, 57.

the right to enjoy and use what one possesses," the "right to recover" and the "right to have restored" lost or stolen property; the "right to compensation" for work; the right "to sell," "to bequeath," and to "inherit" property, particularly in accordance with the "natural rights of primogeniture."[21]

Witte further indicates that Calvin spoke of the "right to bury" one's parents or relatives. He also spoke frequently of the "marital" or "conjugal" rights of husband and wife, and the "sacred," "natural" and "common" rights of parents over their children—in particular, the "right" and "authority" of a father to "name his child" "to raise the child", and to set the child up in marriage. Calvin spoke in passing about the "sacred right of hospitality" of the sojourner, the "right of asylum" or of "sanctuary" for those in flight, the "right of redemption" during the year of Jubilee, and the "natural rights" and "just rights of the poor, the needy, the orphans, and the widows."[22]

According to Calvin, all of these rights are founded in the dignity of human beings due to their creation in the image of God. The concept of the image of God is the guiding principle of Christian love and in inter-personal relations. This guiding principle comes to the fore when approaching the view of Calvin from yet another angle and that is his view on the natural law.

Natural Law

The concept "natural law" (*ius naturalis or lex naturae*) is—together with the abovementioned principles—the foundation of Calvin's understanding of civil authority. In his distinction between the heavenly and the earthly kingdoms, Calvin refers to the moral law that God uses to govern both the kingdoms. This moral law is engraved in the conscience, repeated in the Scripture and summarized in the Decalogue. It is a gift of creation to all people, and therefore is the reason why unbelievers can also act morally in order to maintain order and discipline in society. Witte explains that Calvin uses a variety of terms to describe this moral law such as: "the voice of nature"; "the engraven law"; "the law of nature"; "the natural law"; "the inner mind"; "the rule of equity"; "the natural sense"; "the sense of divine judgement"; "the testimony of the heart"; "the inner voice" and others.[23] In

---

21 Witte, *Reformation of Rights*, 58.
22 Witte, *Reformation of Rights*, 58.
23 Witte, *Reformation of Rights*, 59.

this respect he agreed with his predecessors in the Reformation era who used the concept *lex naturae* (natural law).[24]

According to Calvin the natural law of God is more than the Ten Commandments given to his chosen people. In his introduction to his discussion of the Ten Commandments he speaks about the law given to all people. "Now that inward law, which we have above described as written, even engraved upon the hearts of all, in a sense asserts the very same things that are to be learned from the two Tables."[25] In the same discussion he refers to this law as the natural law. In his commentary on Rom. 2:14–15 he states clearly that a certain conception of justice is engraved in the minds of all men.[26] The same idea is developed in his sermons on Deut. 4:44–6:4 and 19:14–15.[27]

These terms, as Calvin used them, were well researched and explained by Bohatec. He explained the concept as follows: "Die lex naturae ist vornehmlich der Inbegriff der praktischen, dem Menschengeist angeborenen rechtlichen und sittlichen Prinzipien (*iustitiae ac rectitudinis conceptiones*) die die Griechen als *proletheis* bezeichnet haben".[28] Every person has a sense of justice and civil authority has the obligation to develop this sense of justice. This sense of justice is an indication of the dignity of people and their ability to maintain good order in society, but also of their responsibility to keep these God-given laws in high regard.

In governing humanity God has three uses for the natural law. Firstly, God uses the law theologically. In this respect the law is used to condemn all persons in their conscience and to compel them to seek the liberating grace. Secondly, he uses the natural law civilly in order to restrain the sinfulness of non-believers who have not accepted his grace. In the third place, he uses the natural law educationally to teach believers the means and measures of sanctification and spiritual development.[29]

---

[24] McNeil, "John Calvin and Civil Government", 168; J. Grabill, *Rediscovering the Natural Law in Reformed Theological Ethics* (Grand Rapids: Eerdmans, 2006), 70.

[25] Calvin, *Institutes* II.7.1.

[26] Calvin, Commentary on Rom. 2:14–15, *CO* 49, 38.

[27] *CO* 26, 235–432 and *CO* 27, 565–576.

[28] J. Bohatec, *Calvin und das Recht* (Vienna: Bohlhaus, 1934), 3; J. Bohatec, *Calvins lehre von Staat und Kirche, mit bisonderer Berucksichtigung des Organismus gedankens* (Breslau: Scietia Aalen, 1962), 19. ["The lex naturae is primarily the quintessence of practical, legal, and the human spirit's moral and innate principles, which the Greeks designated as *proletheis*"]. This principle has also been developed in the subsequent Reformed jurisprudence. See J.D. Van der Vyver, *Die beskerming van menseregte in Suid-Afrika* (Kaapstad: Juta, 1975), 17.

[29] Witte, *Reformation of Rights*, 59–60.

However, the natural law is openly written in the Ten Commandments
for the clearer understanding of the believers. On the basis of the Ten
Commandments the magistrate is the custodian of both tables of the
Decalogue.

> [W]e ought to explain in passing the office of the magistrates, how it is
> described in the Word of God and the things in which it consists. If Scrip-
> ture did not teach that it extends to both Tables of the Law, we could learn
> this from secular writers: for no one has discussed the office of magistrates,
> the making of laws, and public welfare, without beginning at religion and
> divine worship.[30]

The rulers have specific responsibilities to administer justice among men,
and in this regard he refers to Jer. 22:3 and Ps. 82:3, 4. Natural law as it is
precisely summarised in the Ten Commandments determines the responsibility of the civil authority in protecting the dignity of people.

Calvin's concept of the natural law was very influential in the post-
Reformation development of jurisprudence and the emerging Reformed
view on the authority and task of the civil authorities. His idea was introduced by Johannes Althusius of the Dutch Republic in the development
of Roman Dutch Law. Just as Calvin, Althusius maintained that God has
written his natural law on the hearts, souls, minds, and consciences of
all persons. This natural law teaches persons higher ideas that appeal
uniquely to human reason and conscience. Through the natural law, God
commands all persons to live a life that is at once pious and holy, just and
proper. Witte quotes Althusius and indicates that he said that God teaches
people the: "natural duties of love that are to be performed toward God
and one's neighbour".[31] Furthermore, Althusius said:

> God teaches and writes on human hearts the general principles of good-
> ness, equity, evil and sin, and He instructs, induces and incites all persons
> to do good and avoid evil. He likewise condemns the conscience of those
> who ignore these things and excuses those who do them. He thereby directs
> them to goodness and dissuades them from evil. If they follow the path of
> goodness, he excuses them. If they do not He condemns them.[32]

The idea of the *lex naturae* as it featured in the teachings of Calvin and
his followers, especially Beza and Althusius, is a further indication that

---

[30] Calvin, *Institutes* IV.20.9.
[31] Witte, *Reformation of Rights*, 157.
[32] J. Althusius, *Politica Methodice Digesta* (Politics methodically set forth) (Cambridge:
Harvard University Press, 1932), xxx.16, 19–20.

Calvin nurtured the idea of the basic *dignitas* of people in his anthropology and his social teachings. Any modern ideology that rejects the idea of the basic dignity of all people with reference to the soteriology of Calvin and the Reformation, does not understand this important guiding principle in Reformed anthropology. Besides his teachings on the effect of the *imago dei* and common grace and his point of view regarding the *lex naturae*, Calvin applied the principle of the *dignitas* of people in his ideas about the responsibility of the civil authority.

Civil Authority

On the basis of the above-mentioned principles, Calvin formulated his views on the responsibilities of the civil government, not only to maintain the good order and to honour God, but to protect the dignity of people. The government is exhorted in this age "to cherish and protect the outward worship of God, to defend sound doctrine of piety and the position of the church, to adjust our life to the society of men, to form our social behaviour to civil righteousness, to reconcile us with one another, and to promote general peace and tranquillity."[33] In the execution of this task the civil authority should first of all be obedient to God because they represent God's tribunal on earth, but they are also accountable to the people in their exercise of power.[34] "For they rule not for their own cause, but for the common profit; neither are they endued with an infinite or unlimited power, but such as is tied to the health of their subjects."[35]

It is the task of the civil authority to maintain law and order because the sin of human nature creates the need for civil order. In his commentary on Jer. 30:9, Calvin says: "It would, indeed, be better for us to be wild beasts and to wander in forests, than to live without government and laws; for

---

[33] Calvin, *Institutes* IV.20.2. McNeil reveals another angle of approach in the social thinking of Calvin. He argues that Calvin defined his political ideas about the task of the civil government on the basis of his views of the perfections (*vistudes*) of God according to Jer. 9:24. These are *misericordia* (mercy), *iudicium* (judgement) and *iustitia* (righteousness). In the execution of righteousness the civil government should take care of the poor and the needy and protect the dignity of people. McNeil, "John Calvin and Civil Government," 168.

[34] Calvin, *Institutes* II.8.46.

[35] "sed quae subditorum saluti sit obstricta" Calvin, Commentary on Romans 13:4, *CO* 49, 252. For the translation see J. Calvin, *Commentary on Romans* (Edinburgh: Calvin Translation Society, 1864), 367. See in this regard also the interpretation of P.J. Strauss, "God's Servant Working for Your Own Good: Notes From Modern South Africa on Calvin's Commentary on Romans 13:1–7 and the State," *Hervormde Teologiese Studies* 54 (1998), 28.

we know how furious the passions of man are."[36] In the maintenance of morality the king should be an example to the people, because: "it is especially notorious, that the anger of God is provoked against the whole body of the people, in the person of the king."[37]

The government should not exploit the people and must not entice them to worship idols.[38] This is another example of Calvin's emphasis on the fact that the government is responsible to God and accountable to its subjects. The latter aspect has to date largely been neglected in research on Calvin's view of the civil authority. Calvin did not enter into an extended explanation on the kind of government which will be the ideal for a Christian. He took a very strong stand against any form of tyranny because he regarded it as a violation of human dignity. His view is clearly evident in his discussion of the conduct of the Pharaoh as it is described in Exodus 5:9.[39] He criticised the monarchy because monarchy is prone to tyranny. On the other hand, aristocracy can lead to the tyrannical rule of a few and a popular government can lead to anarchy. His well-known option is for an "aristocracy, either pure or modified by popular government".[40] Here also, he is adamant that the freedom of people should not be betrayed.[41] The dignity of the people should always be respected.

Church and state are separate entities. The state should, however, defend the true worship and take care of the well-being of the Church as long as this intervention does not lead to disturbance of the order and discipline in the church.[42] Both church and state are subjected to the authority of God, as this authority is expressed in God's written Word.[43] Calvin

---

[36] Calvin, Commentary on Jer. 30:9, *CO* 38, 617. For the translation see J. Calvin, *Commentaries on the Book of Jeremiah and the Lamentations* (Edinburgh: Calvin Translation Society, 1851), vol. 4, 15.

[37] Calvin, Commentary on Gen. 20:9. *CO* 23, 291. For the translation see J. Calvin, *Commentary on Genesis* (Edinburgh, Calvin Translation Society, 1852), 528.

[38] Calvin, Commentary on Dan 3:2–7. *CO* 40, 77–80.

[39] A thorough discussion of Calvin's view is presented by W.J. Bouwsma, *John Calvin, A Sixteenth-Century Portrait* (Oxford: University Press, 1988), 208.

[40] Calvin, *Institutes* IV.20.8.

[41] Calvin, *Institutes* IV.20.31.

[42] Calvin, *Institutes* IV.11.16.

[43] See J.H. Leith, *John Calvin's Doctrine of the Christian Life* (Louisville: Westminster, 1989), 199. On the same issue Witte remarks: "Within this unitary society, the church and the state stand as co-ordinate powers. Both are ordained by God to help achieve order and discipline in the community, a successful realisation of all three uses of the moral law. Such conjoined responsibilities inevitably required church and state, clergy and magistracy to aid and accommodate each other on a variety of levels." See J. Witte, "Moderate Religious Liberty in the Theology of John Calvin", *Calvin Theological Journal* 31 (1996), 398.

does not devalue the civil authority to the sphere of the secular. In this respect he differed from Augustine in his influential *City of God*. Augustine was of the opinion that the earthly city seeks an earthly peace and entails the merging of human wills with regard to the things that are useful for this mortal life.[44] Calvin's views also differed from those held by Luther and the subsequent Lutheranism.[45] Lutheranism disengaged church and state completely. In the Calvinist tradition of the early twentieth century Calvin's views were also altered to accommodate modern politics. This was particularly the case in the neo-Calvinism of the twentieth century and in the social critique of Karl Barth.[46] This fact is important to note because of the modern-day tendency to read Calvin from a modern political perspective and to criticize him without taking cognisance of his views that were enlightened in his time and context.

It is also important to stress the fact that Calvin did not regard the state as neutral. The modern-day concept of a neutral or secular state cannot be found in Calvin's ethics and the claims of modern Reformed theology in this respect are not valid. For him each community "is a unitary Christian society, a *corpus christianum* under God's sovereignty and law".[47] Still the civil authority had to respect and protect the dignity of all people, irrespective of religion or creed. Within the context of the above-mentioned explanation of Calvin's view of the authority of the civil government, the conclusion can be reached that Calvin had a high regard for the innate dignity of human beings and that this fact, inter alia, determined his view on the responsibilities and obligations of civil authorities.

Calvin's Heritage in the Modern Reformed Tradition

In his expansive book, Witte indicates that Calvin's view was highly influential in the three centuries following the Reformation.[48] This article will not repeat his findings, but will focus sbriefly on this heritage as it featured

---

[44] A. Augustine, *De Civitate Dei Contra Paganos* (London: William Heineman, 1960), 65.
[45] M. Luther, *Lectures on Romans* (St. Louis, Concordia, 1962), 473.
[46] For the Neo-Calvinist view see A. Kuyper, *Calvinism. Six Stone Lectures* (Grand Rapids: Eerdmans, 1943), 82. Barth placed his view of the authority of the civil government on a christocentric foundation. See K. Barth, *Community, State and Church* (New York: Double Day, 1960), 102. Both influential theologians drew heavily on Calvin's ideas in their respective social critiques.
[47] Witte, *Moderate Religious Liberty in the Theology of Calvin*, 398.
[48] Witte, *Reformation of Rights*, 81ff.

in the post-World War II Reformed ethical reflection.[49] This debate can now move on to the question: Do Calvin's ideas on the dignity of people have any bearing on the modern-day concept of human dignity and human rights? Could modern theologians find any foundation in Calvin's theology for their contribution to the development of a modern Reformed ethics of human dignity and human rights? Ritschl answers this question positively, but says that human rights and Calvinism may seem a *contradictio in terminis*, because in the modern democracies concepts of human rights and liberty of conscience are important, while it seems that Calvin emphasized order and punishment for heresy. He also warns against the temptation to read the modern-day concept of human rights into Calvin. In spite of this proviso he concludes that Calvinism contributed constructively to the modern-day concept of human rights.[50]

Another historical fact should also be taken into account in the study of Calvin's heritage regarding the modern-day concept of human dignity and human rights. What Schild says about Luther is also applicable to Calvin:

> Luther was a child of his time. And while humanism, in contact with earlier sources, was herald of a wider, more generalising and optimistic concept of humanity, rights in Luther's day mostly remained special to, or determined by, the medieval estates, orders and social classes into which people were born and moved.[51]

However, modern research indicates that the root of an ethics of human dignity and human rights can be found in Calvin's theology. Reformed theologians after the Reformation furthered his argument of the dignity

---

[49] Other earlier authors reached the same conclusions. McNeil, "John Calvin and Civil Government," 20, argues that the political ideas of Calvin influenced the jurist Hugo Grotius (1583–1645), who is widely regarded as the founder of modern international law. He also states that influential leaders who adhered to the Calvinist view of political order promoted the concept of democracy, for example, Stephen Bocsky (–1606) and Gabriël Bethlen (1580–1629) in Hungary, Oliver Cromwell (1599–1658) in England, Johan de Witt (1625–1672) in the Dutch Republic, William Penn (1644–1718) in New England and Rabant de St. Étienne (1743–1793) and François Guizot (1787–1874) in France. According to him they all promoted the concept of democracy in the sense that the leader is accountable to the people and may be deposed by the people. Leith, *John Calvin's doctrine of Christian Life*, 206, is of the opinion that Calvinism as it took shape in English Puritanism contributed to political democracies it developed in England and later to the colonies.

[50] D. Ritschl, "Der Beitrag des Calvinismus für die Entwicklung des Menschenrechtgedankens in Europa und Nord Amerika" [The contribution of Calvinism to the development of human rights in Europe and North America], *Evangelische Theologie* 40 (1980), 333, 345.

[51] M.E. Schild, "Being a Christ to the Neighbor: Luther and the Development of Human Rights," *Lutheran Theological Journal* 23 (1989), 11.

of humankind—especially in the twentieth century with the emergence of the idea of human rights against the background of the human rights abuses in World War II. The contributions of three prominent Reformed theologians can be mentioned in this respect namely Karl Barth, Gerrit Cornelis Berkouwer and Jürgen Moltmann.

Barth emphasized the relational aspect of the *imago dei*.[52] The *imago dei* is an expression of God's willingness to enter into a relation with humankind. Man has become a relational being and in his expression of relations of love and care, a person expresses his basic dignity. In other words, people's ability to express humaneness is a sign of the *imago dei*.[53] For what reason does God forbid manslaughter and why is the preservation of life so important in the Old Testament laws, asked Barth?[54] The purpose of human conduct is to preserve and protect life and everything it entails, such as humaneness, compassion, caring and social concern. On this basis Barth designed a Christian anthropology that revived Calvin's ideas and resisted the individualism and rationalism of the Aufklärung.[55]

At the same time, the prominent Dutch theologian Berkouwer reflected on the relevance of the *imago dei* for modern ethics and social concern. He also maintains that the doctrine of *imago dei* is essential for the development of a relevant Christian anthropology. Through the *imago dei* and the atonement in Christ, a human being becomes *"man of God,"* and receives as such the ability to strive after the justice of the kingdom of God. However, the main ethical implication of the *imago dei* is that it sets out the possibility for humans to be free from any form of slavery and lack of freedom due to the blemishes of sin and feelings of guilt. Therefore, any person who uses the *imago dei* as an angle of approach should support a people's call to freedom, and the Christian Church should also support their desire for freedom.[56] The consequence of Berkouwer's view within the framework of the topic under discussion is that the *imago dei* sets the stage for people to seek liberation by way of repentance and forgiveness. This doctrine says that in a world of suffering and hardship, people can achieve peace by respecting human dignity, seeking the kingdom of

---

[52] K. Barth, *Church Dogmatics, Volume III. The Doctrine of Creation. Part 4* (Edinburgh: T & T Clark, 1961), 116.
[53] See also C. Westermann, *Forschung am Alten Testaments. Gesammelte Studien Band II* (München: Kaisar Verlag, 1973), 344.
[54] Barth, *Church Dogmatics* III/4, 344.
[55] See also D.J. Price, *Karl Barth's Anthropology in light of Modern Thought* (Grand Rapids: Eerdmans, 2002), 97.
[56] G.C. Berkouwer, *Man: The Image of God* (Grand Rapids: Eerdmans, 1962), 330.

God and embodying forgiveness. Just as Barth, Berkouwer applied Calvin's ideas about the social relevance of the *imago dei* to a relevant Christian ethic for modern society.

The same is true of the influential public theology of Moltmann, who developed the ethical implications of the *imago dei* even further.[57] He also maintains that the concept is a theological concept with clear ethical implications. The concept should be explained in its close relationship with the *imago Christi* and *Gloria Dei est homo*. It says something about God, who created an image and then entered into a close relationship with that image. Therefore, the *imago dei* is all about relationships—the relation between God and humankind and the interrelations between humans.[58] Humans are thus created as relational beings. They relate to God, to each other and to the rest of creation. They are representatives of God in this world to care for his work as stewards. The *imago dei* should be manifested not only in a few human characteristics, as early Reformed theology argued, but in the totality of human existence. He says: "The whole person, not merely his soul; the true human community, not only the individual; humanity as it is bound up with nature—it is these which are the image of God and his glory."[59] The *imago dei* explains what human beings are and not what they have.[60]

Conclusion

The biblical idea of *imago dei*, as it was argued by Calvin and is currently applied in the Reformed tradition, has concrete implications for Christian anthropology and social ethics. Not only does this concept explain the core value of human dignity, but it is essential to any approach to humaneness and human relationships.

God invested humankind with human dignity, not a dignity equivalent with God, but before God. The richness of this dignity lies in the relationships of humankind—the relation with God, with each other and with

---

[57] J. Moltmann, *God in Creation* (Minneapolis: Fortress, 1997), 1.

[58] J. Moltmann, "The Original Study Paper: The Theological basis of Human Rights and the Liberation of Human Beings," in A.O. Miller, *A Christian Declaration of Human Rights* (Grand Rapids: Eerdmans, 1977), 1.

[59] Moltmann, *God in Creation*, 221.

[60] See also C.J.H. Wright, *Old Testament Ethics for the People of God* (Leicester: Inter-Varsity Press, 2004), 119 and N. Vorster, *Restoring Human Dignity* (Potchefstroom: Potchefstroom Theological Publications, 2007), 75.

creation. Human dignity also enables humans to fulfil their calling to be stewards of creation. Preuss says: "From the beginning, God has given the world to humanity. The world—and that does simply mean fellow human beings—is the object of human moral behaviour and discourse (cf. Ps. 8) and humanity may and should order the world responsibly before this God and in relationship with him."[61]

Although Calvin did not use the term "human dignity" or "human rights" as they are understood in modern constitutionalism, he laid the foundations for the development of such a Reformed ethics of human dignity and human rights with his emphasis on the *dignitas* of human beings due to the *imago dei*. He paved the way for an anthropology that appreciates core moral directives such as compassion, humaneness, life and love and which serves as a corrective to all forms of anthropologies founded in racism, xenophobia, tribalism and sexism. In spite of the modern inclination to accuse Calvin of a pessimistic view of humankind due to his emphasis on total depravity in his soteriology, he laid the foundation of the modern "human face" and immense potential to the social relevance of Reformed ethics today. This can be seen as a reason for the renewed interest in the ideas Reformed ethics can offer regarding the human rights debate and to the development of bio-ethics.

---

[61] H.D. Preuss, *Old Testament Theology* (Louisville: Westminster Press, 1991), vol. 1, 238.

CHAPTER FOURTEEN

CALVIN STUDIES IN NORTH AMERICA

I. John Hesselink

Prior to World War II

Prior to World War II serious, academic Calvin studies in North America were almost non-existent. Only six significant books about Calvin were written by Americans during this period: a biography of Calvin by Williston Walker, the church historian at Yale University (1906);[1] a less important biography of Calvin by Albert Hyma of the University of Michigan;[2] a doctoral dissertation at the Free University in Amsterdam by another Dutch-American, Herman Kuiper, *Calvin on Common Grace*;[3] a collection of essays on Calvin by B.B. Warfield of Princeton Seminary published under the title *Calvin and Calvinism* by Oxford University Press in 1931;[4] a study of Calvin and French humanism the same year by Quirinus Breen, a historian of Christian Reformed background;[5] and, surprisingly, a study of Calvin's ethics by Georgia Harkness the same year (1931).[6] I say surprisingly because she was a Methodist and women Calvin scholars were almost non-existent in either Europe or the United States until the 1970s.

It is not that there weren't many Calvinists during this period, but few, if any, of them were serious Calvin scholars. The so-called Princeton 'divines,' for example, who taught at Princeton Seminary in the late nineteenth century—Archibald Alexander, Charles Hodge, and A.A. Hodge—were staunch Calvinists but not Calvinians. They were often more influenced

---

[1] Williston Walker, *John Calvin, the Organizer of Reformed Protestantism (1509–1564)* (New York: G.P. Putnam's Sons, 1906), reprint (New York: Schocken Books [1969]).

[2] Albert Hyma, *A Life of John Calvin* (Grand Rapids: Eerdmans, 1934). Cf. Hyma's *Christianity and Politics* (New York, 1938).

[3] Herman Kuiper, *Calvin on Common Grace* (Grand Rapids: Smitter Book Co., 1930).

[4] B.B. Warfield, *Calvin and Calvinism* (New York: Oxford University Press, 1931). Warfield taught at Princeton Seminary from 1887 to 1921, so obviously all these essays were published prior to the date of the publication of this book.

[5] Quirinus Breen, *John Calvin: A Study in French Humanism* (Grand Rapids: Eerdmans, 1931), second edition (Hamden: Archon Books, 1968). Cf. Quirinus Breen, *Christianity and Humanism: Studies in the History of Ideas* (Grand Rapids: Eerdmans, 1968).

[6] Georgia Harkness, *John Calvin, the Man and His Ethics* (New York: Holt, 1931).

by 17th century orthodox theologians such as Francis Turretini and later Scottish Common Sense Philosophy than by Calvin.

At best, one could say that there was only incidental interest in Calvin prior to 1940. Again, conservative Presbyterians and Reformed scholars of Dutch background (particularly Christian Reformed) were more interested in Calvinism than the reformer himself. These people, with their Dutch and Presbyterian counterparts, held conferences in the United States sponsored by the "Calvin*istic* Action Committee." These periodic conferences continued until 1957,[7] and were usually held at Calvin College and Seminary in Grand Rapids, Michigan. They were international in scope but the papers that were given were almost always about Calvinism, not Calvin. A breakthrough occurred in 1959 when a symposium of *Calvin* studies was published by the Calvinistic Action Committee, edited by Jacob T. Hoogstra of Calvin College.[8] The contributors include two well-known French Calvin scholars, Pierre Marcel and Jean-Daniel Benoit; four Dutch scholars, A.D.R. Polman, J. Vanden Berg, G.B. Wurth, and G.C. Berkouwer; two South African scholars, H.G. Stoker and J. Chr. Coetzee; three Americans, Wm. Childs Robinson, J.H. Robinson, and C. Gregg Singer; one Englishman, Phillip Hughes; and one Canadian, W. Stanford Reid.

The Breakthrough—The 1950s

Whereas Georgia Harkness could write in 1931 that "Calvin's theology is in eclipse,"[9] all of that turned around radically after World War II. An immediate impetus to Calvin studies, particularly on a popular level, was the republication of all of Calvin's commentaries in the late '40s by the Eerdmans Publishing Company. The old Edinburgh edition of Calvin's commentaries had been out of print for many years and was hard to come by. In the meantime, Leroy Nixon, a Reformed Church in America pastor in New York City, was concerned about making Calvin's sermons available in English. In rapid succession he published a volume of sermons titled *The Deity of Christ* (1950), sermons on the passion and resurrection of Christ; the ascension of Christ; and Pentecost and the return of Christ; *The Mystery of Godliness* (1950), sermons on 1 and 2 Timothy and Titus;

---

[7] The conference papers of the 1957 gathering were published under the title *American Calvinism: A Survey*, ed. Jacob T. Hoogstra (Grand Rapids: Baker, 1957).

[8] Jacob T. Hoogstra, *John Calvin: Contemporary Prophet* (Philadelphia: Presbyterian and Reformed Pub. Co., 1959) and (Grand Rapids: Baker, 1959).

[9] Georgia Harkness, *John Calvin*, vii.

and Sermons from Job (1952).[10] In more recent years a number of other volumes of Calvin's sermons have been translated by Americans.[11]

In the 1950s a few important Calvin studies appeared, the most influential of which was John T. McNeill's *The History and Character of Calvinism*.[12] Although the title refers to "Calvinism," the first half is about the Swiss reformers, with several chapters devoted to Calvin. Here, for the first time in many years a judicious portrait of Calvin emerges. First published in 1954, it is still in print and serves as a useful text for introductory courses on Calvin. The fact that McNeill taught most of his career at the University of Chicago Divinity School and Union Seminary in New York, both distinguished liberal institutions, added a certain 'authority' to his positive presentation of Calvin.

In the 1950s dissertations were being written on Calvin by Americans but few were published. There were four exceptions: Walter Steuerman, *A Critical Study of Calvin's Concept of Faith* (1952); John F. Jansen, *Calvin's Doctrine of the Work of Christ* (1958); Paul Van Buren's Basel dissertation, *Christ in Our Place: The Substitutionary Character of Calvin's Doctrine of Reconciliation* (1957); and most important, Edward Dowey's influential study, *The Knowledge of God in Calvin's Theology*. Originally a dissertation under the supervision of Emil Brunner, it was first published in 1952 and was republished as late as 1994 in a third edition.[13] Dowey didn't publish a major work on Calvin again, turning his energies to studies of Bullinger and other matters, but this one book has had wide-ranging influence.[14]

---

[10] All the while Nixon was writing a book about Calvin's preaching: Leroy Nixon, *John Calvin: Expository Preacher* (Grand Rapids: Eerdmans, 1950).

[11] A sampling: *John Calvin's Sermons on the Ten Commandments* (Grand Rapids: Baker, 1980), and *John Calvin: Sermons on the Book of Micah* (Phillipsburg: P&R Publishing, 2003), both by Benjamin Wirt Farley; *Calvin's Sermons on 2 Samuel*, Chapters 1–13, by Douglas Kelly (Edinburgh: Banner of Truth, 1992); *John Calvin: Sermons on the Acts of the Apostles*, chapters 1–7, by Rob Roy McGregor (Edinburgh: Banner of Truth, 2008); and *Sermons on Genesis*, chapters 1–11; also translated by Rob McGregor (Edinburgh: Banner of Truth 2009).

[12] John T. McNeill, *The History and Character of Calvinism* (New York: Oxford University Press), 1954. McNeill also played a significant role in the publication of "The Library of Christian Classics" (25 volumes) of which he was one of three editors.

[13] Edward A. Dowey, Jr., *The Knowledge of God in Calvin's Theology* (New York: Columbia University Press, 1952), third edition (Grand Rapids: Eerdmans, 1994).

[14] In a blurb for the third edition Heiko Oberman wrote, "This lucid and substantial book will be hailed throughout the world of scholars and students of sixteenth century history."

Ford Lewis Battles, Heiko Oberman, and Brian Gerrish

Another impetus to Calvin studies in the English-speaking world was the new translation of the *Institutes* by Ford Lewis Battles and edited by John T. McNeill in 1960. This was not only far more accurate than the earlier translations of Allen and Beveridge but also provided many invaluable footnotes and references. Battles published a beautiful book on *The Piety of John Calvin: An Anthology Illustrative of the Spirituality of the Reformer,*[15] but many other essays on Calvin by Battles were published together in a posthumous volume, *Interpreting John Calvin*, edited by one of his students, Robert Benedetto.[16]

Battles influenced many students, both at Pittsburgh Theological Seminary and Calvin Theological Seminary, where his career was cut short by his untimely death in 1979. One of his outstanding students was Donald K. McKim whose publications—many related to Calvin—are too numerous to mention.[17] Prior to Battles' death in 1979, however, he was instrumental in organizing the Calvin Studies Society of North America, now probably the largest society devoted to Calvin research in the world.

In the meantime, two distinguished Reformation scholars ended up in the United States and held influential posts, viz., Heiko Oberman,[18] a Dutchman, who began his teaching career at Harvard University and ended it at the University of Arizona, and Brian Gerrish, an Englishman who taught most of his career at the University of Chicago Divinity School. Two early students of Oberman's have had distinguished careers of their own, viz., Jane Dempsey Douglass and E. David Willis, both of whom taught at Princeton Seminary for many years until their retirement.[19]

---

[15] Ford Lewis Battles, *The Piety of John Calvin* (Grand Rapids: Baker Book House, 1978).
[16] Ford Lewis Battles, *Interpreting John Calvin*, edited by Robert Benedetto (Grand Rapids: Baker Books, 1996).
[17] McKim is especially noted for the many books he has edited. Two recent ones: *The Cambridge Companion to John Calvin* (Cambridge: Cambridge University Press, 2004); and *Calvin and the Bible* (Cambridge, Cambridge University Press, 2006).
[18] Oberman's writings covered a wide range of late medieval and Reformation subjects. A slender, but significant, study of Calvin was published in the Netherlands while Oberman was teaching at the University of Arizona, viz., *Initia Calvini: The Matrix of Calvin's Reformation* (Amsterdam: Koninklijke Nederlandse Academie van Wetenschappen, 1991). Two posthumously published works also deal with Calvin: Heiko Oberman, *The Two Reformations: The Journey from the Last Days to the New World*, edited by Donald Weinstein (New Haven: Yale University Press, 2003); and *John Calvin and the Reformation of the Refugees*, edited by Peter A. Dykema (Geneva: Librairie Droz, 2009).
[19] Douglass is best known for her book *Women, Freedom and Calvin* (Philadelphia: Westminster, 1985); Willis for *Calvin's Catholic Christology. The So-Called Extra Calvinisticum in Calvin's Theology* (Leiden: E.J. Brill, 1966).

Brian Gerrish's major Calvin study came out late in his career, *Grace and Gratitude: The Eucharistic Theology of John Calvin;*[20] but earlier he had published many shorter studies of Calvin[21] and inspired a number of his students to write doctoral dissertations on Calvin.

Gerrish has also had his share of outstanding students: one of the first was Jill Raitt, who wrote on Beza, and was one of the early presidents of the Calvin Studies Society.[22] Other students of Gerrish whose dissertations have been published are Gerrit Wilterdink;[23] Randall Zachman (more about him later); Thomas J. Davis, who has specialized in Calvin's eucharistic theology;[24] Dawn De Vries (Gerrish's wife);[25] Dennis Tamburello, another Roman Catholic;[26] and David Puckett, a Southern Baptist.[27]

Robert Kingdon and Historical Studies

The above dissertations were all historical-theological, but while Brian Gerrish was motivating young scholars in this realm, the church historian Robert M. Kingdon was inspiring young scholars to do strictly historical studies, often focusing on Geneva. Among his early students at the University of Iowa were E. William Monter[28] and Raymond Mentzer,[29] now both university professors themselves. After moving to the University of

---

[20] Brian Gerrish, *Grace and Gratitude: The Eucharistic Theology of John Calvin* (Minneapolis: Fortress Press, 1993).

[21] Cf. the collection which contains several essays on Calvin: Brian Gerrish, *The Old Protestantism and the New: Essays on the Reformation Heritge* (Edinburgh: T & T Clark, 1982) and (Chicago: University of Chicago Press, 1982).

[22] It is also noteworthy that Jill Raitt was the first Roman Catholic president of the Society.

[23] Garret Wilterdink, *Tyrant or Father? A Study of Calvin's Doctrine of God*, 2 vols. (Bristol: Wyndham Hall Press, 1985).

[24] Thomas J. Davis, *The Clearest Promises of God: The Development of Calvin's Eucharistic Teaching* (New York: AMS Press, 1995); and *This Is My Body: The Presence of Christ in Reformation Thought* (Grand Rapids: Baker Academic, 2008). Davis also gives credit to professors Susan Schreiner and Martin Marty for assistance in his dissertation.

[25] Dawn De Vries, *Jesus Christ in the Preaching of Calvin and Schleiermacher* (Louisville: Westminster John Knox, 1996).

[26] Dennis Tamburello, *Union with Christ: John Calvin and the Mysticism of St. Bernard* (Louisville: Westminster John Knox, 1994). Tamburello is professor of religious studies at the Roman Catholic Siena College in New York.

[27] David Puckett, *John Calvin's Exegesis of the Old Testament* (Louisville: Westminster John Knox, 1995). Puckett is Professor of Church History at Southeastern Baptist Seminary in Wake Forest, North Carolina.

[28] William Monter, *Studies in Genevan Government 1536–1605* (Geneva: Droz, 1964).

[29] Raymond Mentzer, *Sin and the Calvinists: Morals Control and the Consistory in the Reformed Tradition* (Kirksville: Truman State University, 2002).

Wisconsin, he spent the rest of his career supervising many more dissertations on Calvin and the Reformation.[30] In addition, several of them have
teamed up with Kingdon to produce a critical edition of the *Registers of
the Consistory of Geneva in the Time of Calvin*.[31] Kingdon himself has been
a prolific author. His seminal work is *Geneva and the Coming of the Wars
of Religion in France*.[32] He has subsequently published several books and
countless articles beyond his studies of the Geneva Consistory Registers.[33]

In the field of biblical studies related to Calvin, David Steinmetz,[34] professor of the History of Christianity at Duke University Divinity School,
has played a key role. Two of his former students are now distinguished
professors in their own right, viz., Richard Muller and Susan E. Schreiner.
Schreiner is Associate Professor of Church History and Theology in the
Divinity School at the University of Chicago. She is best known for two
books: *The Theater of His Glory: Nature and the Natural Order in the Thought
of John Calvin*;[35] and *Where Shall Wisdom Be Found? Calvin's Exegesis of Job
from Medieval and Modern Perspectives*.[36]

Calvin College and Seminary Graduates

Richard Muller, Professor of Historical Theology at Calvin Theological
Seminary, is primarily a specialist in seventeenth century orthodoxy,

---

[30] One is Glenn S. Sunshine. His most recent book is *The Reformation for Armchair
Theologians* (Louisville: Westminster John Knox, 2005).

[31] Robert M. Kingdon (ed.), *Registers of the Consistory of Geneva in the Time of Calvin*,
vol. 1 (1542–1544) (Grand Rapids: Eerdmans and the H.H. Meeter Center for Calvin Studies, 2000). Kingdon was assisted by Thomas A. Lambert and Isabella Watt. M. Wallace
McDonald was the translator.

[32] Robert Kingdon, *Geneva and the Coming of the Wars of Religion in France* (Geneva:
Droz, 1956).

[33] Robert Kingdon, *Sex, Marriage and Family in John Calvin's Geneva*, together with
John Witte, Jr. (Grand Rapids: Eerdmans, 2006). Witte, Professor of Law and Ethics and
director of the Center for the Study of Law and Religion at Emory University, is being rec-
ognized as one of the newer Calvin scholars in the United States. Cf. his *God's Joust, God's
Justice, Law and Religion in the Western Tradition* (Grand Rapids: Eerdmans, 2006). There
are frequent references to Calvin and Calvinism in this book. Also John Witte, Jr., *The
Reformation of Rights: Law, Religion, and Human Rights* in *Early Modern Calvinism* (Grand
Rapids: Eerdmans, 2007).

[34] David Steinmetz, *Calvin in Context* (New York: Oxford University Press, 1995).

[35] Susan Schreiner, *The Theater of His Glory: Nature and Natural Order* in *The Thought
of John Calvin* (Durham: The Labyrinth Press, 1991).

[36] Susan Schreiner, *Where Shall Wisdom be Found? Calvin's Exegesis of Job from Medieval and Modern Perspectives* (Chicago: University of Chicago Press, 1994). Recent essays on
Calvin's biblical studies by both Steinmetz and Schreiner are found in *Calvin and the Bible*,
ed. Donald K. McKim (Cambridge: Cambridge University Press, 2006).

his magnum opus being the four-volume *Post-Reformation Reformed Dogmatics*.[37] Even here, however, he deals with Calvin occasionally, and more specifically in *Christ and the Decree: Christology and Predestination in Reformed Theology from Calvin to Perkins*,[38] and above all in an influential study, *The Unaccommodated Calvin: Studies in the Foundation of a Theological Tradition*.[39]

Not only Muller, but earlier members of the Calvin College and Seminary faculty began turning their attention from Calvinism to studies of Calvin himself. A transitional figure is H. Henry Meeter (after whom the Center for Calvin Studies is named), who taught for thirty years in the Bible Department at Calvin College. His book, *The Basic Ideas of Calvinism*[40] was a required text at the college for many of those years. In this text the theology of Calvin himself is also treated. A similar figure in the Department of Religion and Theology at Calvin College was John Bratt who taught there twenty-eight years (1947–1975). He produced no major study of Calvin, but as the editor of a festschrift in his honor noted, he "continually promoted interest in the heritage of John Calvin." In this festschrift, *Exploring the Heritage of John Calvin: Essays in Honor of John Bratt*,[41] all of the contributors wrote essays on Calvin and all were members of the Department of Religion and Theology at the College.[42]

This interest in Calvin's theology at Calvin College and Seminary continues today in the persons of Philip C. Holtrop (emeritus), *The Bolsec*

---

[37] Richard Muller, *Post-Reformation Reformed Dogmatics* (Grand Rapids: Baker Academic, 2003).

[38] Richard Muller, *Christ and the Decree: Christology and Predestination in Reformed Theology from Calvin to Perkins* (Grand Rapids: Baker, 1986, 1988).

[39] Richard Muller, *The Unaccommodated Calvin: Studies in the Foundation of a Theological Tradition* (New York: Oxford University Press, 2000). Cf. Richard Muller, *After Calvin: Studies in the Development of a Tradition* (New York: Oxford University Press, 2003).

[40] H. Henry Meeter, *The Basic Ideas of Calvinism* (Grand Rapids: Baker, 1939), sixth edition revised by Paul A. Marshall (Grand Rapids: Baker, 1990).

[41] David Holwerda (ed.), *Exploring the Heritage of John Calvin: Essays in Honor of John Bratt* (Grand Rapids: Baker, 1976).

[42] Space limitations prevent the listing of the titles of the essays, but the contributors were John H. Primus, Louis A. Vos, David Holwerda, Theodore Minnema, Gordon Spykerman, Clarence J. Vos, Willis P. De Boer, and Leonard Sweetman, Jr. A bibliography of Bratt's writings was contributed by Peter De Klerk, Theological Librarian of Calvin Seminary at that time and the first compiler of The Calvin Bibliography which has appeared each year in the Fall issue of *Calvin Theological Journal*. Cf. Wilhelm, H. Neuser, Herman J. Selderhuis and Willem van't Spijker (eds), *Calvin's Books: Festschrift for Peter DeKlerk* (Heerenveen: Groen, 1997). Of the 22 contributors only three were North American, viz. Joseph Tylenda, Jelle Faber and Brian Armstrong.

Controversy on Predestination from 1551 to 1555;[43] William R. Stevenson, Jr., Professor of Political Science at Calvin College, who wrote *Sovereign Grace: The Place and Significance of Christian Freedom in John Calvin's Thought*;[44] Raymond A. Blacketer, *The School of God: Pedagogy and Rhetoric in Calvin's Interpretation of Deuteronomy*;[45] and Karin Maag, the author of *Seminary or University? The Genevan Academy and Reformed Higher Education 1560–1620*[46] and many essays on Calvin. Perhaps even more importantly, she is currently the Director of the H. Henry Meeter Center for Calvin Studies. Located at Calvin College, the Center has become a focal point for Calvin research. Hundreds of budding Calvin scholars have spent a summer or longer periods at the Center for Calvin Studies and have benefited greatly from its rich resources.

Roman Catholic Authors and Women Authors

Two other developments in Calvin studies in the post-war period are the number of Roman Catholic contributors and the large number of women Calvin scholars. In the former category sympathetic and perceptive studies of Calvin were already written in the early 1970s. Several Catholic theologians showed an interest in Calvin's Eucharistic theology, e.g., John R. Meyer[47] and Joseph Tylenda.[48] Major studies were published by Lucien

---

[43] Philip C. Holtrop, *The Bolsec Controversy on Predestination from 1551 to 1555*, 2 vol. (Lewiston, Canada: Edwin Mellon Press, 1993).

[44] William R. Stevenson, Jr., *The Place and Significance of Freedom in John Calvin's Thought* (New York: Oxford University Press, 1999). His mentor and former teacher at the University of Massachusetts was Glenn Tender, author of *The Political Meaning of Christianity*. Cf. Ralph C. Hancock, *Calvin and the Foundation of Modern Politics* (Ithaca: Cornell University Press, 1989).

[45] Raymond A. Blacketer, *The School of God: Pedagogy and Rhetoric in Calvin's Interpretation of Deuteronomy* (Dordrecht: Springer, 1995).

[46] Karin Maag, *Seminary or University? The Genevan Academy and Reformed Higher Education 1560–1620* (Aldershot, England: Ashgate, 1995). Maag is also the translator of Jean-Francois Gilmont, *John Calvin and the Printed Book* [Sixteenth Century Essays and Studies, 72] (Kirksville: Truman State University Press, 2005).

[47] John R. Meyer, "Calvin's Eucharistic Doctrine: 1536–39," *Journal of Ecumenical Studies* 4/1 (1967), 47–65; and "Mysterium Fidei and the Later Calvin," *Scottish Journal of Theology* 25 (1972), 392ff.

[48] Joseph Tylenda published eight essays on Calvin's doctrine of the Lord's Supper in a variety of journals. I cite only two of them: "Calvin and Christ's Presence in the Supper— True or Real?" *Scottish Journal of Theology* 27 (1974), 65–75; and "The Calvin-Westphal Exchange: The Genesis of Calvin's Treatises against Westphal," *Calvin Theological Journal* 9 (1974), 182–209.

Joseph Richard, O.M.I., *The Spirituality of John Calvin*;[49] Kilian Mcdonnell, O.S.B., *John Calvin, the Church and the Eucharist*,[50] and the French-American, the late George H. Tavard, who taught courses on Calvin most of his career at the Methodist Theological School in Ohio. His last book is *The Starting Point of Calvin's Theology*,[51] a study of Calvin's early publication *Psychopannychia*. Finally, there is the outstanding study by Carlos M.N. Eire, the Yale historian of Cuban background: *War Against Idols: The Reformation of Worship from Erasmus to Calvin*.[52]

The number of women Calvin scholars has grown greatly since the mid-1980s. I am aware of at least thirteen, four of whom have already been mentioned in other contexts, viz., Jane Dempsey Douglass, Susan Schreiner, Dawn De Vries, and Karin Maag. Others are: Suzanne Selinger, *Calvin Against Himself: An Inquiry in Intellectual History*;[53] a veteran Calvin scholar who has published widely, Jeannine E. Olson, *Calvin and Social Welfare: Deacons and the Bourse Francaise*;[54] Mary Potter Engel, *John Calvin's Perspectival Anthropology*;[55] Serene Jones, *Calvin and the Rhetoric of Piety*;[56] Barbara Pitkin, *What Pure Eyes Could See: Calvin's Doctrine of Faith in Its Exegetical Context*;[57] Karen Spierling, *Infant Baptism in Reformed Geneva: The Shaping of a Community*;[58] Bonnie L. Pattison, *Poverty in the Theology of Calvin*;[59] Pamela Ann Moeller, *Calvin's Doxology: Worship in*

---

[49] Lucien Joseph Richard, O.M.I., *The Spirituality of John Calvin* (Atlanta: John Knox, 1974).

[50] Kilian McDonnell, O.S.B., *John Calvin, the Church and the Eucharist* (Princeton: Princeton University Press, 1967).

[51] George H. Tavard, *The Starting Point of Calvin's Theology* (Grand Rapids: Eerdmans, 2000).

[52] Carlos M.N. Eire, *War Against Idols: The Reformation of Worship from Erasmus to Calvin* (Cambridge: Cambridge University Press, 1986).

[53] Suzanne Selinger, *Calvin Against Himself: An Inquiry in Intellectual History* (Hamden: Archon Books, 1984).

[54] Jeannine E. Olson, *Calvin and Social Welfare: Deacons and the Bourse Francaise* (Selingsgrove: Susquehanna University Press, 1989).

[55] Mary Potter Engel, *John Calvin's Perspectival Anthropology* (Atlanta: Scholar's Press, 1988).

[56] Serene Jones, *Calvin and the Rhetoric of Piety* (Louisville: Westminster John Knox, 1995). Cf. Amy Plantinga Pauw and Serene Jones (eds), *Feminist and Womanist Essays on Reformed Dogmatics* (Louisville: Westminster John Knox, 2006).

[57] Barbara Pitkin, *What Pure Eyes Could See: Calvin's Doctrine of Faith in Its Exegetical Context* (New York: Oxford University Press, 1999).

[58] Karen Spierling, *Infant Baptism in Reformed Geneva: The Shaping of a Community* (Burlington: Ashgate, 2005).

[59] Bonnie L. Pattison, *Poverty in the Theology of Calvin* (Eugene: Wipf and Stock, 2006).

the 1559 Institutes with a View to Contemporary Worship Renewal;[60] and Martha Moore-Keish, *Do This in Remembrance of Me.*[61] Special attention must be given to Elsie Anne McKee, for she is one of the best known and most widely published Calvin scholars in the United States. Her position at Princeton Seminary also helps extend her influence. Her doctoral dissertation at the University of Geneva was on *John Calvin on the Diaconal Almsgiving.*[62] She followed that with *Elders and the Plural Ministry: The Role of Exegetical History in Illuminating John Calvin's Theology,*[63] and then edited and translated portions of *John Calvin: Writings on Pastoral Piety.*[64] Her most significant achievement is the first English translation of the 1541 French edition of Calvin's *Institutes.*[65]

Canadian Authors

Thus far I have cited only American, i.e., U.S.A. writers. The Canadians also deserve recognition, but unfortunately there are only a few Canadian Calvin scholars. One might point to the late W. Stanford Reid, the long-time leader of conservative Presbyterians in Canada, but he wrote as much about Calvinism as Calvin himself.[66] There are only three full scale studies of Calvin by Canadian authors as far as I know: *The Nature and Function of Faith in the Theology of John Calvin* by Victor A. Shepherd;[67] the other, also originally a dissertation, *Jesus Christ and Creation in the Theol-*

---

[60] Pamela Ann Moeller, *Calvin's Doxology: Worship in the 1559 Institutes with a View to Contemporary Worship Renewal* (Allison Park: Pickwick Publications, 1997).

[61] Martha Moore-Keish, *Do This in Remembrance of Me* (Grand Rapids: Eerdmans, 2008).

[62] Elsie Ann McKee, *John Calvin on the Diaconal Almsgiving* (Geneva: Droz, 1984).

[63] Elsie Ann McKee, *Elders and Plural Ministry: The Role of Exegetical History in Illuminating John Calvin's Theology* (Geneva: Droz, 1988).

[64] Elsie Ann McKee (ed.), *John Calvin: Writings on Pastoral Piety* (New York: Paulist Press, 2001). This is in the series "The Classics of Western Spirituality." McKee has also published two volumes on Katharina Schütz Zell, a sixteenth century woman reformer.

[65] Elsie Ann McKee (ed.), *Institutes of the Christian Religion: 1541 French Edition* (Grand Rapids: Eerdmans, 2009).

[66] W. Stanford Reid (ed.), *John Calvin: His Influence in the Western World* (Grand Rapids: Zondervan, 1982). Cf. W. Stanford Reid, "Calvin's View of Natural Science," in Edward J. Furcha (ed.), *Papers from the 1986 International Calvin Symposium McGill University* [ARC Supplement, 3] (Montreal: Faculty of Religious Studies, 1987). Some of the Canadian contributors in this volume have also written elsewhere on Calvin and hence should be listed: William Klempa, Joseph C. McLelland, Egil Grislis, and David Demson.

[67] Victor A. Shepherd, *The Nature and Function of Faith in the Theology of John Calvin* (Macon: Mercer University Press, 1983), reprint (Vancouver: Regent College Publishing, 2004).

ogy of John Calvin by Peter Wyatt;[68] and *The Concept of Equity in Calvin's Ethics* by Guenther H. Haas.[69]

A Miscellany

The following books defy classification. Some are seminal studies that continue to be influential: Philip Walker Butin, *Revelation, Redemption and Response: Calvin's Trinitarian Understanding of the Divine-Human Relationship*;[70] W. Fred Graham, *The Constructive Revolutionary: John Calvin and His Socio-Economic Impact*;[71] Christopher Elwood, *The Body Broken: The Calvinist Doctrine of the Eucharist and the Symbolization of Power in Sixteenth Century France*;[72] Stephen Edmondson, *Calvin's Christology*;[73] I. John Hesselink, *Calvin's Concept of the Law*,[74] and *Calvin's First Catechism: A Commentary*;[75] Ward R. Holder, *John Calvin and the Grounding of Interpretation*;[76] John H. Leith, *John Calvin's Doctrine of the Christian Life*;[77]

---

[68] Peter Wyatt, *Jesus Christ and Creation in the Theology of John Calvin* (Allison Park: Pickwick Publications, 1996).

[69] Guenther H. Haas, *The Concept of Equity in Calvin's Ethics* (Waterloo, Ontario: Wilfried Laurier University Press, 1997).

[70] Philip Walker Butin, *Revelation, Redemption and Response: Calvin's Trinitarian Understanding of the Divine-Human Relationship* (New York: Oxford University Press, 1995). Butin was until recently the president of San Francisco Theological Seminary.

[71] W. Fred Graham, *The Constructive Revolutionary: John Calvin and His Socio-Economic Impact* (Richmond: John Knox Press, 1971), reprint ([East Lansing]: Michigan State University Press, 1987). Cf. Edward Dommen and James D. Bratt (eds), *John Calvin Rediscovered: The Impact of His Social and Economic Thought* (Louisville: Westminster John Knox, 2007).

[72] Christopher Elwood, *The Body Broken: The Calvinist Doctrine of the Eucharist and the Symbolization of Power in Sixteenth Century France* (New York: Oxford University Press, 1999). Elwood is Professor of Historical Theology at Louisville Presbyterian Theological Seminary and is also the author of *Calvin for Armchair Theologians* (Louisville: Westminster John Knox, 2002).

[73] Stephen Edmondson, *Calvin's Christology* (Cambridge: Cambridge University Press, 2004). Edmondson is Associate Professor of Church History at Virginia Theological Seminary.

[74] I. John Hesselink, *Calvin's Concept of the Law* (Allison Park: Pickwick Publications, 1992). This is a revision of Hesselink's doctoral dissertation under the supervision of Karl Barth at Basel University.

[75] I. John Hesselink, *Calvin's First Catechism: A Commentary* (Louisville: Westminster John Knox, 1997). Cf. Introduction to *Calvin on Prayer* (Louisville: Westminster John Knox, 2006) and the chapter on "Calvin's Theology" in Donald K. McKim (ed.), *The Cambridge Companion to John Calvin* (Cambridge: Cambridge University Press, 2004).

[76] Ward R. Holder, *John Calvin and the Grounding of Interpretation* (Leiden: Brill, 2006). Holder is Assistant Professor of Theology at St. Anselm's College, Manchester, New Hampshire.

[77] John H. Leith, *John Calvin's Doctrine of the Christian Life* (Louisville: Westminster John Knox, 1989). This was originally Leith's doctoral dissertation at Yale Divinity School. Leith had a distinguished career at Union Theological Seminary in Virginia (1959–89) and

Benjamin Milner, *Calvin's Doctrine of the Church*;[78] John L. Thompson, *Calvin and the Daughters of Sarah*;[79] and Davis A. Young, *John Calvin and the Natural World*.[80] I don't know the legal nationality of (Sueng Hoon) Paul Chung (Korean background) but since he teaches at San Francisco Seminary as an adjunct faculty member, his book should be listed here: *Spirituality and Social Ethics in John Calvin: A Pneumatological Perspective*.[81]

There are also two smaller early studies that should not be omitted: John Murray, *Calvin on Scripture and Divine Sovereignty*;[82] and Benjamin A. Reist, *A Reading of Calvin's* Institutes.[83] Also important are two books that contain papers that were presented during the anniversary year: *John Calvin's Impact on Church and Society 1509–2009*, edited by Martin Ernst Hirzel and Martin Sallmann.[84] This book originated in Switzerland but two of the contributors are Americans (James Bratt and Christopher Elwood). The other is *Calvin for Today*, edited by Joel Beeke.[85] This consists of papers that were given at a conference in Grand Rapids sponsored by the Puritan Reformed Seminary in Grand Rapids. A few years earlier a book of quite a different nature appeared that merits mention: *John Calvin: Suffering—understanding the love of God*, Selections from the writings of John Calvin, compiled and annotated by Joseph A. Hill.[86] Hill is Associate Professor, Emeritus, of Biblical Studies and Greek at Geneva College, Beaver Falls, PA. Again I want to single out a few books that deserve special attention,

---

has published several studies related to Calvin and the Reformed tradition, e.g., John H. Leith, *An Introduction to the Reformed Tradition* (Atlanta: John Knox Press, 1977) and John H. Leith, *The Reformed Imperative* (Philadelphia: Westminster Press, 1988).

[78] Benjamin Milner, *Calvin's Doctrine of the Church* (Leiden: Brill, 1970). At one time Milner taught at St. John's College in Annapolis, Maryland.

[79] John L. Thompson, *Calvin and the Daughters of Sarah* (Geneva: Droz, 1992). Thompson is Professor of History and Theology at Fuller Theological Seminary.

[80] Davis A. Young, *John Calvin and the Natural World* (Lanham: University Press of America, 2007). Young is emeritus Professor of Geology at Calvin College.

[81] (Sueng Hoon) Paul Chung, *Spirituality and Social Ethics in John Calvin: A Pneumato-logical Perspective* (Lanham: University Press of America, 2000). Another scholar of Korean background who teaches in the United States at King College in Bristol is Sung Wook Chung, author of *Admiration and Challenge: Karl Barth's Theological Relationship with John Calvin* (New York: Peter Lang, 2002).

[82] John Murray, *Calvin on Scripture and Divine Sovereignty* (Grand Rapids: Baker, 1960).

[83] Benjamin A. Reist, *A Reading of Calvin's Institutes* (Louisville: Westminster John Knox, 1991).

[84] Martin Ernst Hirzel and Martin Sallmann, *John Calvin's Impact on Church and Society 1509–2009* (Grand Rapids: Eerdmans, 2009).

[85] Joel Beeke (ed.), *Calvin for Today* (Grand Rapids: Reformation Heritage Books, 2009).

[86] Joseph A. Hill (ed.), *John Calvin: Suffering—understanding the love of God* (Webster, New York: Evangelical Press, 2005).

first William J. Bouwsma's *John Calvin: A Sixteenth Century Portrait*.[87] No book on Calvin in the English language has ever evoked the response that this one did. It was reviewed and discussed not only in almost every theological journal in the United States and Great Britain but also in secular magazines and newspapers including *The New York Times* and *The Wall Street Journal*. What was surprising is that Bouwsma, long-time Professor of History at the University of California, Berkeley, was primarily a Renaissance scholar, not a Calvin specialist.

One of the leading 'younger' Calvin scholars in the United States is Randall C. Zachman, an Episcopalian, who is Professor of Reformation Studies at Notre Dame University. His doctoral dissertation written under the supervision of Brian Gerrish at the University of Chicago Divinity School was on *The Assurance of Faith: Conscience in the Theology of Martin Luther and John Calvin*.[88] Subsequently he published many scholarly essays on Calvin in various journals, many of which were collected in the book *John Calvin as Teacher, Pastor, and Theologian: The Shape of His Writings and Thought*.[89] This was followed by his magnum opus, *Image and Word in the Theology of John Calvin*,[90] a huge work which breaks new ground in Calvin studies.

Charles Partee is a veteran Calvin scholar who has crowned his study of Calvin with a monumental *The Theology of John Calvin*.[91] It is the largest one-volume comprehensive theology of Calvin in any language[92] and is bound to elicit considerable response because of its passionate and often polemical nature. A comparable work in terms of size and scope is *A Theological Guide to Calvin's Institutes: Essays and Analysis*, edited by David W.

---

[87] William J. Bouwsma, *John Calvin: A Sixteenth Century Portrait* (New York: Oxford University Press, 1988). Cf. William J. Bouwsma, *The Waning of the Renaissance 1550–1640* (New Haven: Yale University Press, 2000).

[88] Randall C. Zachman, *The Assurance of Faith: Conscience in the Theology of Martin Luther and John Calvin* (Minneapolis: Fortress Press, 1993), reprint (Louisville: Westminster John Knox Press, 2005).

[89] Randall Zachman, *John Calvin as Teacher, Pastor, and Theologian: The Shape of His Writings and Thought* (Grand Rapids: Baker Academic, 2006).

[90] Randall Zachman, *Image and Word in the Theology of John Calvin* (Notre Dame: University of Notre Dame Press, 2007).

[91] Charles Partee, *The Theology of John Calvin* (Louisville: Westminster John Knox, 2008). Cf. his earlier study, Charles Partee, *Calvin and Classical Philosophy* (Leiden: Brill, 1977), reprint (Louisville: Westminster John Knox Press, 2005).

[92] The doctoral dissertation of the Roman Catholic scholar Eva-Maria Faber is even longer and is quite comprehensive, but it has a special focus: *Symphonie von Gott und Mensch: Die responsorische Structur von Vermittlung in der Theologie Johannes Calvins* [The responsorial Structure of Mediation] (Neukirchen-Vluyn: Neukirchener, 1999).

Hall and Peter A. Lillback.[93] Many of the contributors are professors or alumni of Westminster Theological Seminary in Philadelphia. This is a solid contribution and serves as a nice contrast to Partee's approach. Two smaller introductions to Calvin's life and theology (particularly the latter) by Presbyterian theologians also appeared during the quincentennial celebration of Calvin's birth, viz., *Calvin* by George W. Stroup, J.B. Green Professor of Theology at Columbia Theological Seminary in Decatur, Georgia,[94] and *John Calvin: Reformer for the 21st Century* by William Stacy Johnson, Arthur M. Adams Associate Professor of Systematic Theology at Princeton Theological Seminary.[95] Both represent fine Calvin scholarship and are written in a clear style that make them quite accessible to lay people as well as specialists.

Another recent contribution—and a valuable one—is the recent biography of Calvin simply titled *Calvin*[96] by Bruce Gordon, formerly a professor at St. Andrews University in Scotland and now Professor of Reformation History at Yale Divinity School. At least four biographies of Calvin have been published in the United States since 2008[97] but none can compare with this one, not only because of its size but also because of scholarly sophistication. It may not supplant the biography of Calvin by the French historian, Bernard Cottret, but it is superior in style, breadth of scholarship, and theological depth. It is not likely to be superseded for many decades.

I cannot refrain from adding one more title, *Calvin, Participation, and the Gift*[98] by my young colleague at Western Seminary, J. Todd Billings,

---

[93] David W. Hall and Peter A. Lillback, editors, *A Theological Guide to Calvin's Institutes: Essays and Analysis* (Phillipsburg: P&R Publishing, 2008).

[94] George W. Stroup, *Calvin* (Nashville: Abingdon, 2009).

[95] William Stacy Johnson, *John Calvin: Reformer for the 21st Century* (Louisville: Westminster John Knox, 2009).

[96] Bruce Gordon, *Calvin* (New Haven: Yale University Press, 2009).

[97] Two of the four shorter biographies are translations from Dutch scholars: Willem van 't Spijker, emeritus professor of church history at the Theological University of Apeldoorn in the Netherlands, and his successor Herman J. Selderhuis. Willem van 't Spijker, *Calvin: A Brief Guide to His Life and Thought* (Louisville: Westminster John Knox, 2009), and Herman J. Selderhuis, *John Calvin: A Pilgrim's Life* (Downers Grove: IVP Academic, 2009). The other two by Americans, the president of Westminster Seminary in California, W. Robert Godfrey, and Christopher Mehan, a Roman Catholic journalist who works for the Christian Reformed Church. W. Robert Godfrey, *John Calvin, Pilgrim and Pastor* (Wheaton: Crossway Books, 2009) and Christopher Mehan, *Pursued by God: The Amazing Life and Lasting Influence of John Calvin* (Grand Rapids: Faith Alive Christian Resources, 2009).

[98] J. Todd Billings, *Calvin, Participation and the Gift* (Oxford, England: Oxford University Press, 2007). Subsequently, a book on a similar subject—also a revised doctoral dissertation—was published by a young American scholar, the pastor of Immanuel Orthodox

because in 2009 it received the Templeton Award for one of the twelve best recent theological books in the world. This is a revision of his Harvard Divinity School doctoral dissertation.

Comprehensive as this report is, I am sure I have missed some important works. Any omissions are not deliberate. One can get a more complete picture of Calvin studies in North America by checking the Calvin bibliography in each Fall issue of the *Calvin Theological Journal*, now edited by Paul Fields. There are about 180–200 items in each issue, about half of them by Americans.

Calvin studies are obviously alive and well in North America. After the 500th anniversary of Calvin's birth is past there will no doubt be a letup in the number of books on Calvin, but the research will likely be as lively as ever.

Postscript

It is ironical that the person who has done more to promote an interest in Calvin and his theology in the English-speaking world in the last eleven years is not a historian or theologian but a popular novelist. I am referring to Marilynne Robinson who teaches creative writing at the prestigious writers' school at the University of Iowa. It all started with the publication of "Essays on Modern Thought" in *The Death of Adam*, first published in 1998.[99] In three of those essays she defended Calvin against his detractors and certain misunderstandings. In her Pulitzer prize-winning novel *Gilead*[100] the key figure, a Reverend Ames, is fond of Calvin and gets involved in a discussion of predestination. Similar theological discussions take place in the more recent novel, *Home*,[101] which was awarded the Orange Prize in London in June, 2009.

Robinson has read widely in Calvin and has now come to be regarded as a Calvin scholar. As a result, she has been invited to lecture on Calvin to countless church groups including Unitarians, Roman Catholics, and Southern Baptists, and universities and in places as diverse as New York, Washington D.C., Geneva, London, and most recently at the large Calvin

---

Presbyterian Church in West Allegheny. Mark A. Garcia, *Life in Christ: Union with Christ and Twofold Grace in Calvin's Theology* (Eugene: Wipf & Stock, 2008).

[99] Marilynne Robinson, *The Death of Adam: Essays on Modern Thought* (Boston: Houghton Mifflin, 1998), paperback (New York: Picador, 2005).

[100] Marilynne Robinson, *Gilead* (New York: Farrer, Straus, and Giroux, 2004).

[101] Marilynne Robinson, *Home* (New York: Farrer, Straus, and Giroux, 2008).

conference at the University of Toronto in Canada—"Rediscovering Calvin," June 18–20, 2009. She is also now being invited to write introductions to collections of Calvin's writings such as *John Calvin, Steward of God's Covenant: Selected Writings*.[102] Thus, currently the most effective promoter of Calvin and Reformed theology in the English-speaking world is a novelist and essayist.

---

[102] John F. Thornton and Susan B. Vareene (eds), *John Calvin: Steward of God's Covenant: Selected Writings*, preface by Marilynne Robinson (New York: Vintage Books, 2006). Cf. Emilie Griffin (ed.), *John Calvin: Selections from His Writings*, transl. Elsie Ann McKee, foreword by Marilynne Robinson (San Francisco: Harper, 2006).

CHAPTER FIFTEEN

CALVIN'S THEOLOGICAL HERITAGE IN SOUTH AFRICA: ENGAGING AN AMBIVALENT, CONTESTED AND PROMISING LEGACY

Robert Vosloo

In a paper, read at the International Calvin conference in Geneva in May 2009, the South African Reformed theologian John de Gruchy comments:

> Held together by some common threads and family resemblances, Calvinism in South Africa is not a seamless garment but a patchwork quilt roughly woven together, in some places, badly soiled and in need of repair. There are perhaps as many reasons to decry Calvinism's significance in South African history as there is to regard it in some ways formative. But one way or another it cannot be ignored when it comes to the making and unmaking of apartheid both as an ideology and a social reality.[1]

This remark attests to the fact that the legacy of John Calvin in South Africa is in many ways a complex, ambivalent and contested legacy. On the one hand Calvinism became associated with the religious worldview that provided the theological underpinnings for the support of Afrikaner nationalism, and more specifically for the ideology of apartheid,[2] while on the other hand one also finds traces of Calvin in anti-apartheid memory.[3]

---

[1] J.W. de Gruchy, "Calvin(ism) and Apartheid in South Africa in the Twentieth Century: The Making and Unmaking of a Racial Ideology," in I. Backus and P. Benedict (eds), *Calvin and His Influence, 1509–2009* (Oxford University Press, New York, 2011), 306. His contribution was first read as a paper at the International Calvin conference in Geneva in May 2009.

[2] Trevor Huddleston, for instance, writes as follows in his well-known and moving account of his ministry as an Anglican priest in the 1940s and 1950s in the township of Sophiatown, Johannesburg, published under the title *Naught for Your Comfort* (London: Fontana Books, 1957): "The truth is that the Calvinistic doctrines upon which the faith of the Afrikaner is nourished, contained within themselves... exaggerations so distorting and so powerful that is very hard indeed to recognise the Christian faith they are supposed to enshrine. Here in the fantastic notion of the immutability of race, is present in a different form the predestination idea: the concept of an elect people of God, characteristic above all else of John Calvin... Calvinism, with its great insistence on 'election,' is the ideally suitable doctrine for White South Africa. It provides at the same moment a moral justification for White supremacy and an actual day-to-day reason for asserting it" (50).

[3] For a more extensive discussion of this theme, see R.R. Vosloo, "Calvin and Anti-Apartheid Memory in the Dutch Reformed Family of Churches in South Africa" in J. de Niet,

The story of Calvin's reception and influence in South Africa is thus a multifaceted story with several interwoven and conflicting strands.[4] It is— like the story of Reformed life and theology in South Africa in general—a story of many stories.[5] Actually, as Dirkie Smit has observed, it is difficult to speak of Calvinism in South Africa in the singular, given the divided and ambiguous history of the Reformed tradition in South Africa.[6]

In order to engage with the ambivalent and contested nature of Calvin's theological heritage in South Africa today, it is of vital importance not to speak a-historically about Calvin's legacy. In this regard, I will make a few brief historical theological comments on the viewpoints that linked Calvin and Calvinism to what is sometimes called Afrikaner civil religion. This is followed by a discussion of the ways in which Calvin was used by some theologians from the Dutch Reformed family of churches[7] to critique the

---

H. Paul, and B. Wallet (eds), *Sober, Strict, and Scriptural: Collective Memories of John Calvin, 1800–2000* (Leiden: Brill, 2009), 217–244. Sections of this article draw on that essay. Cf. also R.R. Vosloo, "Remembering John Calvin in South Africa today?" *Nederduitse Gereformeerde Teologiese Tydskrif* 51 Supplementum (2010), 423–435.

[4] For a discussion of how Calvin's legacy found form in different ways in the South African context from 1652 onwards through various colonial settler communities (who brought different streams of the Reformed tradition to South Africa), as well as how these communities were shaped by the encounter with indigenous peoples, see De Gruchy, "Calvin(ism) and Apartheid in South Africa." See also Gideon Thom, "Calvinism in South Africa" in W.S. Reid, *John Calvin: His Influence in the Western World* (Grand Rapids: Eerdmans, 1982), 345–363. For another discussion of Calvin's influence in South Africa, see Dolf Britz and Victor d'Assonville, "Calvin in Africa," in H.J. Selderhuis (ed.), *Calvin Handbook* (Grand Rapids, Eerdmans, 2009), 557–563, 505–512.

[5] Cf. D.J. Smit, "Reformed Theology in South Africa: A Story of Many Stories," *Acta Theologica* 12/1 (1992), 88–110, as well as D.J. Smit, "On Adventures and Misfortunes: More Stories about Reformed Theology in South Africa," in G. Harinck and D. van Keulen (eds), *Vicissitudes of Reformed Theology in the Twentieth Century* (Studies in Reformed Theology, vol. 9) (Zoetermeer: Meinema, 2004), 208–235. Compare also D.J. Smit, "What does it mean to live in South Africa and to be Reformed?" *Reformed World* 58/4 (2008), 263–283. These three articles can also be found in D.J. Smit, *Essays on Being Reformed: Collected Essays 3*, ed. Robert R. Vosloo (Stellenbosch: SUN MeDIA, 2009), 201–258.

[6] D.J. Smit, "Morality and Politics—Secular or Sacred? Calvinist Traditions and Resources in Conflict in Recent South African Experiences" (Paper read at conference on "Das Politische Problem religiöser Liberalität in Christentum und Islam Konsultation" [The Political Problem of religious Liberality in Christendom and Islam Consultation], Berlin, 3–5 July 2009), 1. This paper has subsequently been published in Smit, *Essays on Being Reformed*, 513–549. W.A. de Klerk makes a similar point: "To say that the key to the Afrikaners is Calvinism is not enough. As is the case with all apostles, there are as many Calvins as there have been restatements or 'revisions' of the original philosophy." W.A. de Klerk, *The Puritans in Africa: A History of Afrikanerdom* (Harmondsworth: Penguin Books, 1975), 125.

[7] The term "Dutch Reformed family of churches" refers to the Dutch Reformed Church, the Dutch Reformed Mission Church, the Dutch Reformed Church in Africa, and the Reformed Church in Africa. These churches historically had mainly white, "coloured", black and Indian members respectively. In 1994 the Dutch Reformed Mission Church

theological presuppositions associated with Afrikaner neo-Calvinism. Against this historical theological backdrop, the final section of the paper offers a few searching remarks regarding the promise of reclaiming the legacy of Calvin amidst the challenges posed by the current South African context.

The Calvinist Paradigm and Afrikaner Civil Religion

In an influential article "The roots and fruits of Afrikaner civil religion," written in 1983, the well-known South African missiologist David Bosch observes that it is still the dominant view that the religio-political views of the Afrikaner, which reached their maturity in the mid-twentieth century, have their roots in Calvinism. According to this view, which is often referred to as the "Calvinist paradigm," the outlook since the 17th century, and increasingly during subsequent centuries, has been inspired by a strictly Calvinist view of life. Bosch continues:

> This led them to regard themselves as a chosen people, to identify themselves with Israel of old, and to believe that they have been called by God to Christianize and civilize the original inhabitants of the sub-continent. This awareness of being a chosen people blended with the Calvinist doctrine of election and predestination and lead to the belief that they—the Afrikaners—were the elect of God in contradiction to the other races; because this was so, any form of 'gelykstelling' (=equal treatment) of Blacks and Whites would be contrary to the ordinances of God.[8]

The interesting point that Bosch makes with regard to the "Calvinist paradigm" is that it had been advocated not only by scholars critical of Afrikaner nationalism,[9] but also by some Afrikaner scholars, particularly

---

and the largest part of the Dutch Reformed Church in Africa united to form the Uniting Reformed Church in Southern Africa. There are, of course, important theological strands in other Reformed churches in South Africa that reflected on the realities of apartheid South Africa in the light of Calvin's legacy, for instance the serious scholarly work by theologians of the Gereformeerde Kerk associated with the University of Potchefstroom, as well as the work by theologians within the mainly English-speaking Reformed Churches. One can also reflect on the reception of Calvin in the Nederduitsch Hervormde Kerk, another Afrikaans-speaking Reformed church in South Africa.

[8] D.J. Bosch, "The Roots and Fruits of Afrikaner Civil Religion" in J.W. Hofmeyr and W.S. Vorster (eds), *New Faces of Africa: Essays in Honour of Ben (Barend Jacobus) Marais* (Pretoria: University of South Africa, 1984), 14–35, 15.

[9] Cf. T.D. Moodie, *The Rise of Afrikanerdom: Power, Apartheid and the Afrikaner Civil Religion* (Berkeley: University of California Press, 1975) and S. Patterson, *The Last Trek: A Study of the Boer People and the Afrikaner Nation* (London: Routledge, 1957).

since the 1870s, and even more from the 1930s onwards. As Bosch puts it in a later article: "Thus both friend and foe agreed that Calvinism shaped Afrikanerdom; the one, however, wished to prove how *bad* Calvinism was, the other how *good* it was."[10]

Bosch is also mindful of the fact that some scholars have challenged this so-called Calvinist paradigm. He attends especially to the meticulous scholarly critique of André du Toit, from which he quotes: "A critical investigation will show that there is simply no contemporary evidence for the presence among early Afrikaners of a set of popular beliefs that might be recognized as 'primitive Calvinism' nor of any ideology of a chosen people with a national mission: nothing of this kind appears in the contemporary accounts of traveller or other well-placed observers before the 1950s, nor are such views articulated at all by Afrikaners themselves before the last decades of the 19th century."[11] Although Bosch argues that Du Toit probably overstates his case, he nevertheless agrees that it is hard to refute Du Toit's central thesis that the "Calvinist paradigm" cannot be historically substantiated. Furthermore, Bosch remarks that the picture of the heroes of Afrikaner history as devout Calvinists is probably overdrawn: "It is therefore most probable that those scholars are correct who contend that Afrikaners of the 18th and early 19th centuries were, at most,

---

[10] D.J. Bosch, "The Afrikaner and South Africa," *Theology Today* 43/ 2 (1986), 204. For a discussion of the features, failures and future of Calvinism in South Africa, see also D.J. Bosch, "A Calvinist perspective on the future of democracy in South Africa" in K. Nürnberger (ed.), *A Democratic Vision for South Africa* (Pietermaritzburg: Encounter Publications, 1991), 188–195.

[11] Bosch, "The Roots and Fruits of Afrikaner Civil Religion," 16. See also A. du Toit, "No Chosen People: The Myth of the Calvinist Origins of Afrikaner Nationalism and Racial Ideology," *American Historical Review* 88/4 (1983), 920–952. In a later article Du Toit again asserts the fact that very little of the historical construction of the Calvinist paradigm will withstand rigorous critical scrutiny. See A. du Toit, "Puritans in Africa? Afrikaner 'Calvinism' and Kuyperian Neo-Calvinism in Late Nineteenth Century South Africa," *Society for Comparative Study of History* 27 (1985), 209–240. Du Toit concludes his argument: "... (I)n comparative and historical perspective the reputation of authentic Calvinism is quite overblown: it is meager in substance and its historical foundation is shallow. The theory of an authentic Calvinist tradition going back to a primitive Calvinism nurtured in the isolated *trekboer* society of the open frontier, and ultimately derived from the golden age of 'seventeenth century Calvinism' is a historic myth" (234). For a more recent discussion of the link between Calvinism and the idea of the Afrikaner as a chosen people, see Giliomee, H., *The Afrikaners: Biography of a People* (Cape Town: Tafelberg, 2003), 175–179. For a description of "Calvinism" in the Afrikaner school of historiography, see also R.M. Britz, "Die begrip 'Calvinisme' in die Afrikaanse geskiedskrywing. 'n Oorsigtelike tipering" [The Concept 'Calvinism' in Afrikaans Historiography: An Overview], *Skrif en Kerk* 15/2 (1994), 196–218.

Calvinist only in a cultural sense and that very few of them actually lived according to the central tenets of the Calvinist faith."[12]

It is not possible to give a detailed discussion of the influence of Calvin and Calvinism on Afrikaner identity in this paper, but even the cursory remarks above demonstrate that an over-simplified description and uncritical acceptance of the "Calvinist paradigm" is problematic. In order to understand Afrikaner "civil religion"[13] (as it is associated with Afrikaner nationalism), one has to acknowledge a more complex interplay of forces. Bosch identifies three forces in this regard: "The religious roots of Afrikaner nationalism, as it reached maturity in the 1940s and 1950s, are ... to be traced back to the influences of orthodox evangelicalism, Kuyperian Calvinism, and neo-Fichtean romanticism. It is, indeed, a curious blend of all three of these, having gleaned from what best suited the peculiar situation of the Afrikaner."[14]

Much has been written on these three influences on the development of Afrikaner nationalism, as well as on the formation of the identity of the Dutch Reformed Church.[15] Given our focus on the reception of Calvin and his legacy in South Africa, suffice it to say that it is also important to keep in mind that Kuyperian Calvinism (one can also speak of Afrikaner neo-Calvinism in this regard) underwent serious adaptation and distortion in the light of the way its proponents interpreted local needs.

---

[12] Bosch, "The Roots and Fruits of Afrikaner Civil Religion," 18. See also Bosch, "The Afrikaner and South Africa," 206.

[13] For a thorough discussion on the use and usefulness of the notion of "civil religion" in South African discourse, see Dirkie Smit's article "Civil Religion—in South Africa?" in D.J. Smit, *Essays in Public Theology: Collected Essays 1*, ed. Ernst M. Conradie (Stellenbosch: Sun Press, 2007), 101–123. See also F.E. Deist, "Notes on the Context and Hermeneutic of Afrikaner Civil Religion," in J.N.J. Kritzinger and W.A. Saayman (eds), *Mission in Creative Tension: A Dialogue with David Bosch* (Pretoria: SA Missiological Society, 1990), 124–139. Deist later published an extensive study on the exposition of Scripture in the Dutch Reformed Church, with an informative chapter on "Calvinism and Biblical Science." See F.E. Deist, *Ervaring, Rede en Metode in Skrifuitleg: 'n Wetenskapshistoriese ondersoek na die Skrifuitleg in die Ned. Geref. Kerk 1840–1990* [Experience, Reason and Method in Exegesis: A Scientific-historical Study of the Biblical Exegesis of the Dutch Reformed Church 1840–1990] (Pretoria: RGN, 1994), especially 155–260.

[14] Bosch, "The Roots and Fruits of Afrikaner Civil Religion," 32.

[15] See, for instance, Bosch, "The Roots and Fruits of Afrikaner Civil Religion," 25–32; Bosch, "The Afrikaner and South Africa," 208–213; D.S. Bax, *A Different Gospel: A Critique of the Theology Behind Apartheid* (Johannesburg: Presbyterian Church of Southern Africa, 1979), 28–37; A.J. Botha, *Die evolusie van 'n volksteologie* [The Evolution of a Theology of the *Volk*] (Bellville: UWC, 1984), 164–187; J. Kinghorn (ed.), *Die NG Kerk en Apartheid* [The Dutch Reformed Church and Apartheid] (Johannesburg: MacMillan, 1986), 58–69; Willie Jonker, "Kragvelde binne die Kerk" [Forcefields within the Church], *Aambeeld* 26/1 (1998), 11–14.

From the 1930s onwards the South African version of Kuyperian Calvinism grew in strength. For instance, at the Theological Seminary of the Dutch Reformed Church at Stellenbosch a form of confessional neo-Calvinism became more visible. Calvinism became equated with a certain type of confessional orthodoxy.[16] It is a question whether this form of Calvinism was really infused by an in-depth engagement with Calvin, yet Calvin and Calvinism were definitely used as an identity marker and rhetorical device. In addition, this strand of Calvinism rather uncritically embraced the rising Afrikaner nationalism and patriotism.

This strand of Calvinism, to which prominent theologians of the Afrikaans-speaking Reformed Churches contributed, is especially reflected in an influential series called *Koers in die krisis* [Direction in the Crisis], of which the first volume was published in 1935 under the editorship of H.G. Stoker and F.J.M. Potgieter.[17] This series consisted of a wide range of essays, including international contributions, collected by the Federation of Calvinist Student Organizations in South Africa. The aim of *Koers in die krisis* is well mirrored in the last paragraph of the editorial preface of the first volume: "May this work be to the honour of God and the benefit of the *volk*, and may it conquer the heart of our *volk*. And may it unite all the Calvinists in South Africa, whatever their church, province or profession, to common Calvinist action in South Africa!"[18]

Kuyperian Calvinism, or the way it was interpreted in South Africa, thus seemed to be congruent with the rapidly growing nationalism of the 1930s and 1940s. An increasing number of young theologians from the Dutch Reformed Church and the Reformed Church (*Gereformeerde kerk*) studied at the Free University of Amsterdam and a South African version of Kuyperian theology became deeply entrenched. The Kuyperian notion of the separate spheres of life and the principle of the sovereignty of each of these spheres, together with the principle of diversity as something rooted in creation, was adapted to form an apartheid theology based

---

[16] For a discussion of this strand of confessional (neo)Calvinism in the aftermath of the Du Plessis-case, see R.R. Vosloo, "Konfessionele Calvinisme na die Du Plessis-saak" [Confessional Calvinism after the Du Plessis Case], *Nederduitse Gereformeerde Teologiese Tydskrif* 51 Supplementum (2010), 275–288.

[17] See H.G. Stoker and F.J.M. Potgieter (eds), *Koers in die krisis I* [Direction in the Crisis] (Stellenbosch: Pro Ecclesia, 1935). See also H.G. Stoker and J.D. Vorster, *Koers in die krisis II* (Stellenbosch: Pro Ecclesia, 1940) and H.G. Stoker and J.D. Vorster, *Koers in die Krisis III* (Stellenbosch: Pro Ecclesia, 1941).

[18] Stoker and Potgieter, *Koers in die Krisis I*, xii (my translation).

on the principle of the diversity of people (with biblical support from texts like Genesis 11 and Acts 17:26).[19]

Calvin Against Calvin: Perspectives from the Work and Witness of Beyers Naudé and Willie Jonker

The growing dominance in white Afrikaner Reformed churches of a more confessional (or confessionalistic) Calvinism, and the way it was linked to Afrikaner nationalism, was responsible for the fact that an exclusivist "volkskerk" ecclesiology gained a stronger foothold in the Afrikaner churches. However, a number of dissident voices in the 1940s and 1950s, such as Bennie Keet and Ben Marais, were challenging what Jaap Durand described as "the seemingly monolithic theological structure of the Dutch Reformed Church."[20] From the 1960s onwards one further finds how a few theologians and church leaders drew on a different understanding of Calvin. They were motivated by the need to critique the hegemony of the "Calvin" who became associated with Afrikaner nationalism and apartheid discourse. The question regarding the true legacy of Calvin thus itself became a point of struggle. The efforts to develop an alternative reading of Calvin ought therefore to be situated rhetorically within this context. Within such a context the image of a more "ecumenical Calvin" emerges. In order to substantiate this claim, one briefly may recall aspects of the work and witness of Beyers Naudé and Willie Jonker, two prominent figures in church and public life in South Africa who in their different ways drew on Calvin and the Reformed tradition.

Beyers Naudé

In 1969 Beyers Naudé, the famous Afrikaner anti-apartheid activist, wrote an article published in *The Rand Daily Mail* under the heading "What Calvin *really* stood for," in which he asserts: "Calvin did not proclaim or

---

[19] See, for instance, J.C. Adonis, "The Role of Abraham Kuyper in South Africa: A Critical Historical Evaluation" in C. Van der Kooi and J. de Bruijn (eds), *Kuyper Reconsidered: Aspects of his Life and Work* (Amsterdam: VU Uitgeverij, 1999), 259–272, as well as, from a Dutch perspective, G. Harinck, "Abraham Kuyper, South Africa, and Apartheid," *The Princeton Seminary Bulletin* XXIII/2 (2002), 184–187.

[20] J.J.F. Durand, "Afrikaner Piety and Dissent" in C. Villa-Vicencio and J.W. De Gruchy (eds), *Resistance and Hope: South African Essays in Honour of Beyers Naudé* (Cape Town: David Philip / Grand Rapids: Eerdmans, 1985), 39.

support an exclusive ideology based on the domination of any group, culture or race over others...If he were to come alive and be in South Africa today, he would be the first to protest against and combat many of the concepts proclaimed by and posturing as Afrikaner Calvinism."²¹ This remark underlines the fact that it was important for many Reformed Christians to reclaim Calvin as a moral role-model and place themselves in line with the basic tenets of his theology. This served as a strategy to give authority and legitimisation to their own position, as well as to disarm rhetorically and theologically those who in their eyes had distorted the tradition.

Naudé, who came from a very prominent Afrikaner family, brought his understanding of the Reformed tradition into critical conversation with his perception of the reasons for the Afrikaner's nationalistic outlook. In his article "What Calvin *really* stood for," Naudé responded to the fact that Calvin had been a point of focus in a notorious speech in parliament by Albert Hertzog, the son of the former prime minister J.B.M. Hertzog, who soon after this speech became the leader of the *Herstigde Nationale Party*, a political party to the right of the ruling National Party. Hertzog argued that Afrikaner-Calvinism is not reconcilable with liberalism, as expressed by most of the English-speaking community in South Africa. On the other hand, an eminent Calvin scholar, André Hugo, stated during a speech at the University of Cape Town that true Calvinism shows correspondences with what was known in South Africa as "liberalism." In his article Naudé argues that a comparison of these statements reveals conflicting views on Calvinism and that it is no wonder that the average citizen, both Calvinist and non-Calvinist, is confused about what Calvin really said. In order to answer the question as to which of these opposing readings of Calvin is correct, Naudé asserts that the answer is only to be found through a careful and objective study of Calvin's pronouncements, writings and actions. There is no doubt in Naudé's mind that Hertzog's use of Calvin, which drew on the neo-Calvinism of people such as the previous editor of *Die Kerkbode*, Andries Treurnicht (who at that stage was the editor of the conservative newspaper *Hoofstad*, and later became the leader of the Conservative Party, which broke away from the National Party in 1983), cannot be derived from Calvin himself. The main pillar for these argu-

---

²¹ Beyers Naudé, "What Calvin *really* stood for," *The Rand Daily Mail* (29 April 1969), 13. This article was reprinted in Afrikaans in the journal *Pro Veritate*. See Beyers Naudé, "Waaroor het dit eintlik vir Calvyn gegaan?" *Pro Veritate* (15 May 1969), 6–8.

ments against liberalism is the claim that God established the diversity of nations at creation and at Babel, and that this "biblical" principle is propounded by Calvin. According to Naudé, such a use of the principle of diversity to sustain race and national identity, and justify the separation of nations and races, has no grounds in Calvin's writings or in the Reformed Confessions.

Another line of critique that Naudé utilises against the position that uses Calvinism to affirm the ideology of apartheid and to critique English "liberalism" is the affirmation of Calvin's ecumenical concern, not only towards German and Swiss Lutherans, but also towards the *English* Anglicans (Naudé's emphasis). In this regard Naudé quotes at length from Calvin's famous letter of 29 March 1552 to the Archbishop of Canterbury, in which he responded to the invitation to a synod to discuss the possibility of greater unity between the churches of the Reformation. For Naudé, Calvin's ecumenical vision is at the heart of Calvin's thought, thus making Calvinism in essence an ecumenical movement. Naudé even asserts: "If Calvin were to come to life and live in South Africa today, I am convinced that he would be a staunch and active supporter of the Christian Institute of Southern Africa."[22] Here we see the focus on "the ecumenical Calvin" as reaction against the ultra-conservative depiction of Calvin in Afrikaner neo-Calvinism. In this regard one should keep in mind that Naudé's change of view regarding apartheid was deeply influenced by his contact with ecumenical bodies like the World Council of Churches. Naudé's emphasis on the importance of ecumenism was furthermore related to his belief that church unification within the Dutch Reformed family of churches would serve as a powerful prophetic critique against apartheid.

Naudé is moreover interested in the question why there was no protest against the use of Calvinism to justify an unjust racial standpoint, noting the close historical intertwinement of the Dutch Reformed Church with the Afrikaner *volk*: "It is an association so intimately linked and interwoven with all other areas of the life of the Afrikaner that any direct criticism by an Afrikaner on this very sensitive point would immediately be regarded as a betrayal of everything the Afrikaner holds dear, with resulting ostracism and expulsion from the Afrikaner community."[23]

Over against these uses of Calvin in Afrikaner neo-Calvinism, Naudé wants to posit "another Calvin." Therefore Naudé makes a serious plea,

---

[22] Naudé, "What Calvin *really* stood for," 13.
[23] Naudé, "What Calvin *really* stood for," 13.

and in this process he describes himself as "a staunch Calvinist," to the members of the churches to reject the false views of this neo-Calvinism, since it does serious damage to a true understanding of Christianity in general and Calvinism in particular. Naudé concludes: "If only South Africa were to heed the true message of Calvin, how vastly different our whole ecclesiastical and political life would be."[24]

Willie Jonker

The Stellenbosch theologian Willie Jonker is another important theological figure to consider in our reflection on the reception of Calvin in South Africa. Jonker is arguably, together with Johan Heyns, the most important Dutch Reformed systematic theologian in the latter part of the twentieth century in South Africa. He is especially known for his confession of guilt for apartheid on behalf of the Dutch Reformed Church at the Rustenburg church conference in 1990, to which Archbishop Desmond Tutu responded with a word of forgiveness. Jonker wrote his doctoral dissertation under G.C. Berkouwer at the Free University of Amsterdam and after his return to South Africa he worked as a pastor in congregations in Johannesburg and Potchefstroom. The question of the unity of the church was central to his thinking, and he also did important research on church polity during the early 1960s, culminating in the work *Die Sendingbepalinge van die Ned. Gereformeerde Kerk in Transvaal.*[25] In this critique of the 1935 mission policy of the Dutch Reformed Church that played such an important role in the attempt to provide a moral justification for apartheid, Jonker suggested a church denomination across colour lines. Jonker's thinking challenged the deeply rooted association between the Dutch Reformed Church and Afrikaner nationalism. He was soon branded as a "liberal" and experienced the pain of rejection in a very acute manner. After teaching theology at the University of South Africa (UNISA) in Pretoria for a brief period and at Kampen in The Netherlands, Jonker was called to Stellenbosch. His colleague was professor F.J.M. Potgieter, who wrote his doctoral dissertation on Calvin under Valentijn Hepp at the Free University in

---

[24] Naudé, "What Calvin *really* stood for," 13.
[25] W.D. Jonker, *Die Sendingbepalinge van die Ned. Gereformeerde Kerk in Transvaal* [The Mission Ordinances of the Dutch Reformed Church in Transvaal] (Bloemfontein: Sendingboekhandel, 1962).

Amsterdam.[26] There clearly was tension between Jonker's and Potgieter's views on apartheid. In his autobiography *Selfs die kerk kan verander* (Even the Church Can Change) Jonker writes that he could not help but see a fundamental interrelation between Potgieter's Kuyperian Calvinism and his right-wing political sentiments.[27]

Jonker's reading of Calvin, however, moved in another direction to the one offered by Potgieter. In his essay, "Die aktualiteit van die sosiale etiek" (The Relevance of Social Ethics) Jonker argues that Calvin's thought makes room for an approach to social ethics that does not slide into individualism or view the current social structures as an unchangeable and eternal order created by God.[28] Therefore the church is not interested in mere conservative restoration, but has the responsibility to deal with social and political questions in the light of God's Word.[29] For these insights Jonker also draws on André Biéler's work *La pensée économique et sociale de Calvin*. In an important footnote he affirms Biéler's view that Calvinism must be a permanent force for political and societal reformation and transformation. Christians must therefore always be a disturbing presence in society because of their protest against all forms of injustice. This is also the reason why Calvin addressed issues such as poverty and wealth, interest and wages.[30] For Jonker the consequences of the Reformed legacy, in the footsteps of Calvin, are clearly evident for contemporary society:

> As long as we confess that Christ is the Lord and that his rule must be proclaimed over every inch of our earthy reality...we cannot close our eyes to injustice, poverty, oppression and frustration...The way of a pietistic escapism which argues that the church and politics have nothing to do with the burning social and political questions of the day, is not an option for us.[31]

In an address at a conference in Geneva in 2007 on the theme "How to celebrate the legacy of John Calvin?," Dirkie Smit, who was a doctoral student of Jonker, reflects on the excitement they experienced as students at Stellenbosch when they heard Jonker speak on Calvin and read

---

[26] See F.J.M. Potgieter, *Die verhouding tussen teologie en die filosofie by Calvyn* [The Relationship between Theology and Philosophy in Calvin's Thought] (Amsterdam: Noord-Hollandsche Uitgevers Maatschappij, 1939).

[27] W.D. Jonker, *Selfs die kerk kan verander* (Cape Town: Tafelberg, 1998), 126.

[28] W.D. Jonker, "Die aktualiteit van die sosiale etiek" in P.A. Verhoef, D.W. de Villiers, and J.L. De Villiers (eds), *Sol Iustitiae* (Cape Town: NGKU, 1973), 78–107.

[29] See Jonker, "Die aktualiteit van die sosiale etiek," 85.

[30] See Jonker, "Die aktualiteit van die sosiale etiek," 102.

[31] See Jonker, "Die aktualiteit van die sosiale etiek," 96–97 (my translation).

the *Institutes* with him. Smit, who currently is professor in Systematic Theology at Stellenbosch, writes about Jonker:

> He was also known as deeply Reformed, as steeped in Calvin and the Reformed confessions, but also as deeply critical of apartheid, as a dissenter, as disloyal to the *volk*, perhaps even dangerous, as a personal friend of Beyers Naudé, Jaap Durand and others who were known to reject the pervasive ideology, as a public voice arguing for the visible unity of the church, for reconciliation instead of separation, for justice instead of self-preservation and self-privileging.[32]

For Smit and many of his contemporaries, the writings of Jonker that appealed to Calvin and his legacy in order to make a plea for the reformation of the Reformed Churches in South Africa were highly influential. Smit comments on Jonker:

> He was appealing to the tradition against tradition. He was appealing to the community against the community. He was appealing to our deepest identity in order to critique our actual identity. He did that so often, in his lectures and in his sermons. He would often claim in so many words that there was something different in our tradition, even in the Dutch Reformed Church itself, something more than meets the eye, that there have been other people, other voices, and although they may now be completely silenced, temporarily suppressed and forgotten, their presence and their convictions are still there to guide us and to inspire us—like Calvin.[33]

Throughout his career Jonker consistently reflected on the challenges of society from a Reformed perspective, often with reference to Calvin and the emphasis on the important role of Scripture.[34] A reading of Jonker's work reveals especially his debt to Calvin's insights into the ecumenical nature of the church. Jonker can be viewed as an ecumenical theologian

---

[32] See D.J. Smit, "Why Do We Celebrate the Legacy of John Calvin? Views on Calvin's Ethics from a South African Perspective," *Reformed World* 57/4 (2007), 306–307. Jonker also wrote a revealing two-part series in *Die Kerkbode* (14 and 21 August 1974) under the title "Selfliefde en Selfhandhawing" [Self-love and Self-preservation]. These articles, drawing specifically on Calvin, must be understood within the context of the emphasis on "our own" (*die eie*) within Afrikaner nationalism.

[33] Smit, "Why Do We Celebrate the Legacy of John Calvin," 328.

[34] See, for instance, W.D. Jonker, "Heilige Skrif en sosiale etiek by Calvyn" [Holy Scripture and Calvin's Social Ethics], *Bulletin van die Suid-Afrikaanse Vereniging vir die bevording van Christelike Wetenskap* 39 (1973), 31–37 and W.D. Jonker, "Die moderne belydenisbeweging in Suid-Afrika—en Calvyn" [The Modern Confessing Movement in South Africa—and Calvin], *In die Skriflig* 27/4 (1993), 443–461.

with an emphasis on the unity and catholicity of the church as challenge
to an uncritically relationship between church and *volk*.[35]

Black and Reformed: A Painful Paradox

This brief discussion of aspects of Naudé's and Jonker's work and witness with reference to Calvin affirms that there were church leaders and
theologians who challenged the dominant "volkskerk" ecclesiology, often
with an appeal to Calvin's own teaching and to the Reformed confessional
tradition. In so-called black Reformed circles the theological inspiration
for the struggle also came from the tradition of Calvin, Kuyper, Barth and
the Church Struggle in Germany. Smit comments: "This of course had the
result that controversies raged about the conflicting claims to represent
this tradition—a major part of the struggle was the struggle between Calvin
and Calvin, Kuyper and Kuyper, Barth and Barth, not to mention Calvin
against Kuyper and Barth against Kuyper."[36]

Amid the painful reality of apartheid, a central question in black
Reformed circles was whether one can embrace Calvin in the light of the
fact that "Calvinism" has been so closely tied with Afrikaner nationalism. In a doctoral dissertation, completed at the theological seminary at
Kampen in the Netherlands and significantly entitled *A Cry for Life: An
Interpretation of 'Calvinism' and Calvin*, L.R. Lekula Ntoane grappled with
exactly this question. Ntoane refers to the fact that black Reformed Christians, who experienced the demonic and dehumanising effect of apartheid, could not do otherwise than to pose some serious questions:

> Is 'Calvinism' truly and genuinely representative of Calvinian tradition? Are
> the views espoused in it a reflection of the teachings and intentions of its
> initiator? Are the views expressed both in 'Calvinism' and Calvinian tradi-
> tion reconcilable with the message of Jesus Christ? Is it worthwhile for black

---

[35] If "ecumenical" is understood as a vague qualifier abstracted from soteriological concerns, the description of Jonker as an ecumenical theologian is problematic. See, in this
regard P.F. Theron, "Willie Jonker as Gereformeerd-Katolieke teoloog" [Willie Jonker as
Reformed-Catholic Theologian], *Nederduitse Gereformeerde Teologiese Tydskrif* 51 (2010),
179–190. P.F. (Flip) Theron himself is also well-known in South African circles for articu-
lating an ecclesiological vision that challenged church divisions among racial lines. For a
short summary essay that captures well his though in this regard, see P.F. Theron, "Die
kerk as eskatologiese teken van eenheid" [The Church as Eschatological Sign of Unity] in
P. Meiring and H.I. Lederle (eds), *Die eenheid van die kerk* [The Unity of the Church], Cape
Town: Tafelberg (1979), 6–13.

[36] Smit, "Morality and Politics—Secular or Sacred?," 4.

Christians who have adopted and embraced this tradition to remain loyal to it?[37]

Another South African theologian who studied at Kampen is Allan Boesak, who later became moderator of the Dutch Reformed Mission Church and played a prominent role in the church struggle against apartheid, alongside influential figures like Desmond Tutu, Frank Chikane and Beyers Naudé.

What makes Boesak of special concern for the purposes of this paper is the fact that he consciously and continuously referred to Calvin in his rhetoric against the injustices in apartheid South Africa. For instance, in his keynote address at the national conference of the South African Council of Churches (SACC) in July 1979 at Hammanskraal, Boesak quotes at length from Calvin to emphasize that God hears the cry of the oppressed, the cry "How long, O Lord?"[38] At this same conference the SACC adopted a resolution that encouraged acts of civil disobedience against the apartheid laws. The South African Minister of Justice, Alwyn Schlebusch, responded to this resolution by stating that the government was becoming impatient with such statements that threatened the stability of the country. Boesak responded by writing an open letter to Schlebusch, again drawing on Calvin.[39] In this letter Boesak addresses the routine warning by the government that pastors and churches must stay "out of politics" and confine themselves to their "proper task," namely the preaching of the Gospel. For Boesak, the Gospel to be preached is not something meant only for the inner life, for the soul, but for the whole of human existence. The Lordship of Christ applies to all spheres of life, including the social, political and economic spheres. Boesak also wants to make it clear that he makes the plea for civil obedience as a Christian, and more specifically as a Reformed Christian, and that he has done nothing else but to place himself "squarely within the Reformed tradition as that tradition has always understood sacred scripture on these matters."[40] It is Boesak's basic conviction that Christian obedience to the state or any earthly authority is always linked to obedience to God, and therefore the Christian's concern

---

[37] L.R.L. Ntoane, *A Cry for Life: An Interpretation of "Calvinism" and Calvin* (Kampen: Kok, 1983), 124.

[38] A.A. Boesak, *Black and Reformed: Apartheid, Liberation, and the Calvinist Tradition*, ed. Leonard Sweetman (New York, 1984), 23–24.

[39] See Boesak, *Black and Reformed*, 32–41.

[40] Boesak, *Black and Reformed*, 35.

is whether the government accepts responsibility for justice. When justice is lacking, the government comes into conflict with God and then resistance is demanded and warranted. Boesak underlines this idea with a reference to the letter that Calvin wrote to King Francis, published as the prologue to his *Institutes*, from which he quotes: 'For where the glory of God is not made the end of government, it is not a legitimate sovereignty, but a usurpation.'[41]

In addition, Allan Boesak furthermore played a leading role in the founding of the Alliance of Black Reformed Christians in South Africa (ABRECSA). At the first conference of ABRECSA at Hammanskraal in October 1981, Boesak gave an importance address entitled "Black and Reformed: Contradiction or Challenge?"[42] In this address Boesak asks the burning question: "What does it mean to be black and Reformed in South Africa today?"[43] For Boesak the fact that Reformed Christians, and specifically the Dutch Reformed Church, played such an important role in justifying apartheid theologically had the result that the use of the self-designation 'black and Reformed' expresses a painful paradox.

At the heart of Boesak's address is the question of the relation between the Reformed tradition and social justice. In this regard Boesak emphasises, by drawing on Calvin, that the government shows its Christian character not by good religious intentions, but by "the care of the poor, the protection of the weak and the needy, the suppression of the evil, the punishment of oppression, the equable distribution of wealth, power, privileges and responsibilities."[44] For Boesak, Calvin's concern for social justice is, however, not reflected in the policies of those who claim spiritual kinship with him. Hence Boesak wants to use Calvin against the "Calvinists." Boesak continues to argue that South African history might have been different if Reformed Christians had taken Calvin's vision on human solidarity more seriously. Apart form his views on inter-human solidarity, Calvin also plays an important role in the section of Boesak's address where he attends more closely to a Reformed view on government. Boesak accepts Calvin's view that governments are instituted by God for the just and legitimate administration of the world. Therefore the government is not naturally an enemy. This view does not imply for Boesak a blind

---

[41] See Boesak, *Black and Reformed*, 38.
[42] For an edited version of this address, see Boesak, *Black and Reformed*, 83–99.
[43] Boesak, *Black and Reformed*, 84.
[44] Boesak, *Black and Reformed*, 90.

acceptance of government, but offers an important criterion for judging government. Governments must serve in a just and legitimate way. Boesak then notes that in terms of both the modern concept of democracy, and in terms of Calvin's understanding of legitimacy, the South African government is neither just nor legitimate. According to the Reformed tradition— and Boesak quotes Calvin at length in this regard—government is only to be obeyed "*insofar* as its laws and instructions are not in conflict with the word of God."[45] In he light of these remarks, Boesak returns towards the end of his address to the idea of the painful paradox of being black and Reformed in South Africa. He affirms that black Reformed Christians have no reason to be ashamed of their tradition, but warns against the way in which adherents of this tradition have often displayed self-righteousness, arrogance and self-sufficiency in a way that leads to a harmful isolationism. Therefore his conviction that "the Reformed tradition has a future in this country only if black Reformed Christians are willing to take it up, make it truly their own, and let this tradition once again become what it was: a champion of the cause of the poor and the oppressed, clinging to the confession of the lordship of Christ and the supremacy of the word of God."[46]

I draw on this important address because it contains many of the ideas that also resonate throughout Boesak's numerous sermons and speeches during the church struggle against apartheid.[47] Many of these ideas are also reflected in the ABRECSA charter adopted in 1981, especially in the section on the theological basis of the charter.[48] Of special importance

---

[45] Boesak, *Black and Reformed*, 92.

[46] Boesak, *Black and Reformed*, 96.

[47] See, for instance, A.A. Boesak, *Die Vinger van God: Preke oor Geloof en die Politiek* [The Finger of God: Sermons on Faith and Politics] (Johannesburg: Ravan Press, 1979); A.A. Boesak, *Walking on Thorns: Sermons on Christian Obedience* (Geneva: World Council of Churches, 1984); A.A. Boesak, *If this is treason, I am guilty* (Grand Rapids: Eerdmans, 1987), and A.A. Boesak, *Comfort and Protest: The Apocalypse from a South African Perspective* (Philadelphia: Westminster Press, 1987). See also A.A. Boesak, *The Tenderness of Conscience: African Renaissance and the Spirituality of Politics* (Stellenbosch: Sun Press, 2005). The many references to Calvin in this work of Boesak affirm the enduring impact of Calvin on his thought and rhetoric. The title of this work is, of course, taken from Kuyper's remark in his Stone lectures that "Calvinism understood that the world was not saved by ethical philosophizing, but only by the restoration of the tenderness of conscience" (as quoted by Boesak, *Tenderness of Conscience*, 213). See also the many references to Calvin in Boesak's recent book: A.A. Boesak, *Running with Horses: Reflections of an Accidental Politician* (Cape Town: Joho Publishers, 2009).

[48] For the ABRECSA charter, see John W. de Gruchy and Charles Villa-Vicencio (eds), *Apartheid is a Heresy* (Grand Rapids: Eerdmans, 1983), 161–165.

is also the fact that the charter indicates the need for black Reformed Christians to contribute to the ecumenical field and, in this regard, a special opportunity arose with the World Alliance of Reformed Churches' meeting held at Ottawa, Canada in 1982. This meeting indeed became an important marker in the church struggle against apartheid. A document, written by Boesak, was sent from ABRECSA to all the delegates before the meeting. This document, with the title "God Made Us All, But...Racism and the World Alliance of Reformed Churches," is a plea for the World Alliance to play a more active role in the struggle against racism in South Africa. In this document, racism is described as structured sinfulness with the added reference that racism has made it impossible to share in the natural expression of unity within the body of Christ, namely the Lord's Supper. Here Boesak quotes Calvin at length:

> Now since he has only one body, of which he makes us all partakers, it is necessary that all of us be made one body by such participation...We shall benefit very much from the sacrament if this thought is impressed and engraved upon our minds: that none of the brethren can be injured, despised, rejected, abused, or in any kind offended by us, without at the same time disagreeing with Christ; that we cannot love Christ without loving him in the brethren; that we ought to take the same care of our own brethren's bodies as we take care of our own; for they are members of our body; and that, as no part of our body is touched by any feeling of pain which is not spread among all the rest, so we ought not to allow a brother to be affected by any evil, without being touched with compassion for him.[49]

These words gain special significance from the fact that controversy erupted when the delegations of the black Dutch Reformed Churches refused to share Holy Communion with the members of the white Dutch Reformed Church.[50]

The work of ABRECSA and the meeting at Ottawa, and the role of Allan Boesak in particular (who was elected president), prepared further ground for the process, which resulted in the Dutch Reformed Mission Church calling a *status confessionis* with regard to apartheid, leading to the adoption of the Belhar Confession.[51] A reading of the speeches, sermons and

---

[49] Boesak, *Black and Reformed*, 107. Cf. Calvin, *Institutes* IV.7.38.

[50] For a discussion of these events, see J. Christoff Pauw, *Anti-apartheid Theology in the Dutch Reformed Family of Churches: A Depth-hermeneutical analysis* (Amsterdam: Vrije Universiteit, 2007), 187–194.

[51] For the draft confession of the Belhar and the accompanying letter, as well as for some informative essays on the confession, see G.D. Cloete and D.J. Smit, *A Moment of Truth: The Confession of the Dutch Reformed Mission Church* (Grand Rapids: Eerdmans, 1984).

documents surrounding these events shows that, while one must not overestimate the influence of Calvin in this regard, one does find that Calvin
was put to rhetorical and theological use in the attempt to respond to the
realities of apartheid South Africa.

The Promise of Calvin's Legacy for South Africa Today?

Even a brief overview of Calvin's theological reception in twentieth-cen-
tury South Africa reveals the presence of many "Calvins," including the
depiction of Calvin as anti-liberal defender of the values of the *volk*, Calvin as ecumenical figure, and Calvin as advocate for social justice and
civil disobedience. These different portrayals of Calvin ought to be kept
in mind when considering the promise of Calvin's theological heritage
amidst the challenges and opportunities posed by the current South African context.

In late August 2009, a conference was held at the Theological Faculty of
Stellenbosch on the theme of "Calvin's relevance for today?" The confer-
ence program identifies some major opportunities and challenges that the
Reformed tradition faces during the present transformation of the South
African society, including:

i) the opportunity to embody its own unity more visibly through renewal
of its own structures and order, through common worship and confession and through shared life and service, thereby overcoming destructive divisions of the past;

ii) the opportunity to proclaim and practice real reconciliation, thereby
dealing with alienation and pain of yesterday and distance and distrust
of today;

iii) the opportunity to witness publicly, through words and deeds, to God's
compassionate justice, both through its own discipleship and calling on
state, society and public opinion.[52]

Given the divisions, alienation and injustice associated with South Africa's
apartheid past, it is indeed a challenge to embody unity, to proclaim and
practice real reconciliation, and to witness publicly to God's compassionate justice. In response to these challenges, a critical and constructive engagement with Calvin's legacy can provide important theological
resources. I would like briefly to highlight three aspects of Calvin's thought

---

[52] For a discussion of a similar set of challenges, see D.J. Smit, "Calvin in Südafrika:
Lange Zeit zutiefst ambivalent" [Calvin in South Africa: for a Long Time Most Deeply
Ambivalent], *Bulletin SEK-FEPS*, Sonderausgabe "calvin09" (2009), 24–25.

that hold particular promise, namely, Calvin's commitment to the unity of the church, Calvin's affirmation of hospitality towards strangers, and Calvin's economic and social witness.

Calvin's Commitment to the Unity of the Church

In anticipation of the 500 year anniversary of Calvin's birth, a group of scholars met in Geneva in April 2007 to reflect on the question "What is the significance of Calvin's legacy?" The report which followed from the consultation identified eight areas that were considered to be of particular interest for today. The last area that the report discusses deals with Calvin's commitment to the unity of the church, arguing that Calvin lived out his passionate commitment to the unity of the body of Christ within the reality of an already fragmented church. The report concludes:

> Calvin's thinking about the nature of Christian community, his willingness to mediate controversial matters such as the Lord's Supper, and his tireless efforts to build bridges at every level of church life, stand as a contemporary challenge. Calvin challenges churches to understand the causes of continuing separation and, in accordance with scripture, to strive towards visible unity by engaging in concrete ecumenical efforts, all for the sake of the gospel's credibility in the world, and the fidelity of the church's life and mission.[53]

These words are especially relevant to the South African context in light of the long-standing divisions mainly along racial lines within the Dutch Reformed family of churches. In the discussion above I mentioned that Calvin's legacy in South Africa often was associated with a form of Afrikaner

---

[53] "What is the significance of Calvin's legacy? Report on an International Consultation," *Reformed World* 57/4 (2007), 234–235. On Calvin's understanding of the unity of the church, see also Lukas Vischer, *Pia conspiration: Calvin on the Unity of Christ's Church* (Geneva: John Knox Series 12, 2000). Cf. also Eva-Maria Faber's essay "Mutual Connectedness as a Gift and Task: On John Calvin's Understanding of the Church" in M.E. Hirzel and M. Sallmann (eds), *John Calvin's Impact on Church and Society: 1509–2009* (Grand Rapids: Eerdmans, 2009), 122–144. Calvin was also interested in questions related to church order and the actual unity of the church. In South Africa, as elsewhere, the challenge remains to address issues of church unity and church polity in a responsible theological way. See also the influential study by W. Nijenhuis, *Calvinus Oecumenicus. Calvijn en de eenheid der kerk in het licht van zijn briefwisseling* ('s Gravenhage: Martinus Nijhoff, 1959), as well as Douglass, J.D., "Calvin, Calvinism and Ecumenism" in *Reformed World* 55/4 (2005), 295–310. For an engagement with Nijenhuis, Vischer and Douglass, see L.J. Koffeman, "Calvinus Oecumenicus? De O-factor van Calvijn" in R. Reeling Brouwer, B. de Leede, and K. Spronk (eds), *Het calvinistisch ongemak: Calvijn als erflater en provocator van het Nederlandse protestantisme* [The Calvinist Inconvenience: Calvin as Testator and Provocator of Dutch Protestantism] (Kampen: Kok, 2009), 185–200.

neo-Calvinism, which was characterized by a narrow confessionalism and an uncritical allegiance to a *volkskerk* ecclesiology. The question can still be asked today whether such an ecclesiology, albeit in a more subtle form, is still not one of the most important stumbling blocks on the road to church reunification.

In South Africa one furthermore finds a theological strand that challenged the hegemony of the "Calvin" of Afrikaner neo-Calvinism, often drawing on a more ecumenical understanding of Calvin's theology, as is seen in the work and witness of Beyers Naudé and Willie Jonker, but the names of many others can also be mentioned. This strand, which found powerful expression in the Belhar confession with its focus on unity, reconciliation and justice, deserves in my view to be amplified within South African Reformed church life. Churches are faced with the challenge of overcoming destructive divisions of the past in light of the confession that Christ's body is one, thereby giving visible form to this costly unity.

In 2006 a spirit of optimism regarding church reunification reigned, envisioning 2009 as the year in which to realize this goal. A worship service glorifying God for the gift of reunification would have been a wonderful way for the Dutch Reformed family of churches to celebrate the 500 year anniversary of Calvin's birth. Sadly this goal did not materialise, since enthusiasm for church reunification was then at a low point. Therefore the celebration of Calvin's birth was not merely an occasion for joy in light of his rich theological heritage in South Africa, but also a time for mourning our painful divisions and lamenting our formal division. Yet at the same time, Calvin's commitment to the unity of the church encourages us to keep on working toward the goal of reunification and reconciliation within the Dutch Reformed family of churches, inspired and sustained by a biblical and theological vision.

The "Displaced Calvin" as Resource for a Graceful Theology of Hospitality

May 2008 saw a violent outbreak of xenophobic attacks in South Africa. During this time I was working on a paper for our annual meeting of the Theological Society of South Africa, entitled "The Displaced Calvin: 'Refugee reality' as a Lens to Re-examine Calvin's Life, Theology and Legacy."[54] The rampant xenophobic violence that was then very much in the news,

---

[54] Cf. R.R. Vosloo, "The Displaced Calvin: 'Refugee reality' as a Lens to Re-examine Calvin's Life, Theology and Legacy," *Religion and Theology* 16 (2009), 35–52. The conference

as well as the distrust and distance characteristic of past and present social life in South Africa, caused me to look at Calvin in a different way. Given the fact that we are living in a world of growing migration, displacement and xenophobia, we may well discover that Calvin's life and theology, with all its limitations, may provide surprising insights that can aid in the reclaiming of a graceful theology of hospitality.

Such an endeavour is strengthened by the recognition of Calvin's own refugee experiences. Calvin himself was a refugee who ministered to other refugees in places like Strasbourg and Geneva. The impact of the "refugee reality" on Calvin's ministry and theology contributes, in my view, to a more responsible—and exciting—interpretation of Calvin the theologian. It opens to door to rediscover certain neglected themes in his theology, such as exile and hospitality,[55] as well as to re-evaluate some much-discussed doctrines such as election and providence.[56]

In this regard, it remains important, however, to affirm the need for a sensitive historical hermeneutic that is mindful of the continuity and discontinuity between Calvin and our time, between sixteenth-century religious refugees and 21st-century economically and politically displaced persons.[57] Nevertheless, Calvin's engagement with reality was deeply drenched in

---

theme for the meeting of this particular Theological society was "Grace, Space, and Race: Towards a Theology of Place in (South) Africa Today."

[55] See, for instance, the Dutch theologian H.J. Selderhuis' discussion of the "exile motif" in Calvin's 1557 Commentary on the Psalms in his inaugural lecture. H.J. Selderhuis, *Calvijn als asielzoeker* [Calvin as an Asylum Seeker] (Apeldoorn: Theologische Universiteit, 1997), as well as in H.J. Selderhuis, *Calvin's Theology of the Psalms* (Grand Rapids: Baker Academic, 2007).

[56] Heiko Oberman has argued that in Calvin's case the puzzling doctrine of predestination was born out of the experience of exile. "The Calvinist doctrine of predestination is the mighty bulwark of the Christian faithful against the fear that they will be unable to hold out against the pressure of persecution. Election is the Gospel's encouragement to those who have faith, not a message of doom for those who lack it. In particular, it responds to the anguish that Calvin already had felt in the early wave of persecution...Rather than providing grounds for arrogance, predestination offers all true Christians the hope that even under extreme distress they will persevere until the end." H.A. Oberman, *The Two Reformations* (New Haven: Yale University Press, 2003), 114–115. Cf. J.D. Douglass, "Pastor and Teacher of the Refugees: Calvin in the Work of Heiko A. Oberman," in T.A. Brady et al. (eds), *The Work of Heiko A. Oberman: Papers from the Symposium of His Seventieth Birthday* (Leiden: Brill, 2003), 51–65.

[57] Jacques Derrida rightfully reminds us that we ought to distinguish prudently between the categories of the foreigner in general, the immigrant, the exiled, the deported, the stateless or displaced person. See his address to the International Parliament of Writers in 1996 in Strasbourg, published in J. Derrida, *Cosmopolitanism and Forgiveness* (London: Routledge, 2001).

his reading of Scripture, and the Bible's emphasis on the need to show hospitality to "the widows, orphans, and strangers" found many echoes in his sermons, letters, commentaries, the *Institutes* and other theological tracts. In this sense Calvin's life and theology may have continuing significance to sustain a Reformed theology of hospitality towards modern "widows, orphans, and strangers," or in the interpretative language of the report of the 2007 Genevan consultation on Calvin's legacy, "those who are defenceless, displaced, hungry, lonely, silenced, betrayed, powerless, sick, broken in body and spirit, and all those who suffer in our globalizing and polarizing world."[58]

Part of the challenge facing South Africa, and our globalizing world, today has to do with the need to affirm ethnic identity and cultural diversity. Dealing with identity and difference is, however, no easy matter. The way some South African theologians used the legacy of Calvin to proceed from the emphasis on difference and diversity to separateness and exclusion serves as constant reminder not to abstract diversity talk from a deep concern for human dignity, hospitality and justice. In this regard Calvin remains an important conversation partner—also for Reformed churches in South Africa.

Calvin and Social and Economic Justice

The year 2002 saw the celebration of 350 years of Reformed church life in South Africa.[59] During this year, the Stellenbosch economic historian Sampie Terreblanche's book *A History of Inequality in South Africa 1652–2002* was published.[60] In this work, Terreblanche, who is from a Reformed background, traces in a detailed way the exploitation of indigenous people by dominant settler communities from the advent of European colonialism to the end of apartheid in 1994. He furthermore extends his discussion to the "new South Africa," arguing that although the transition to democracy is a very significant political development, a similar socio-economical development has not yet followed. In addition, Terreblanche criticises the

---

[58] "What is the significance of Calvin's legacy?," 234.

[59] For a collection of essays reflecting on this heritage, see P. Coertzen (ed.), *350 Jaar Gereformeerd/ 350 Years Reformed 1652–2002* (Bloemfontein: CLF, 2002).

[60] S. Terreblanche, *A History of Inequality in South Africa 1652–2002* (Pietermaritzburg: University of Natal Press, 2002).

ruling ANC government for abandoning its redistributive ideals, as well as the corporate sector for its ruthless pursuit of its own interests. Even those who may not fully agree with Terreblanche's analysis and proposals will have to admit the stark reality of economic inequality and injustice in South Africa. In such a context Reformed Christians and communities can indeed welcome the renewed interested in the economic and social witness of Calvin,[61] as well as the fact that the World Alliance of Reformed Churches has placed the issue of economic and ecological justice on their agenda. At the general assembly in Debrecen, Hungary in 1997, the WARC called for a *processus confessionis* regarding economic justice and ecological destruction. This process was continued in Accra, Ghana in 2004 with the Accra Declaration's strong, albeit controversial, criticism of the global economic system. This declaration draws on expressions from the Reformed confessional tradition, including the Belhar confession. Not surprisingly, these Reformed and ecumenical concerns on justice with regard to the economy and all of creation have found expression in the South African theological context.[62]

Hopefully the renewed interest in Calvin's social and economic thought will continue to impact Reformed theology and praxis in South Africa, leading to a critical and constructive engagement between Calvin's theology and our context. In appropriating insights from Calvin relevant to our current social and economic life it is important to not extract from

---

[61] See especially the renewed influence of the work of André Biéler in this regard. His book *Calvin's Economic and Social Thought* (Geneva: WCC Publications, 2005) is an important source that provides stimulus for the conversation on Calvin's social and economic witness, not the least through the book's extensive quotations from Calvin's work. See also E. Dommen and J.D. Bratt, *John Calvin Rediscovered* (Louisville: Westminster John Knox, 2007), as well as the thought-provoking statement "The Economic and Social Witness of Calvin for Christian Life Today: Statement of an International Consultation, Geneva, 3–6 November 2004," *Reformed World* 55/1 (2005), 3–7.

[62] Cf. e.g. an interesting collaborative project between the Beyers Naudé Centre for Public Theology at Stellenbosch University and the Evangelischer Entwicklungsdienst (EED), together with the Evangelisch-reformierte Kirche and the Uniting Reformed Church in Southern Africa, called the Joint Gobalisation Project. A book resulting from the consultations of this group has just been published, which includes contributions from different academic disciplines. See A.A. Boesak and L. Hansen (eds), *Globalisation: The Politics of Empire, Justice and the Life of Faith* (Beyers Naudé Centre Series on Public Theology, Volume 40) (Stellenbosch: Sun Press, 2009). Of special interest is Matthias Freudenberg's essay on "Economic and Social Ethics in the Work of John Calvin" (153–172), as well as Dirkie Smit's essay "Theological Assessment and Ecclesiological Implications of the Accra Document 'Covenanting for Justice in the Economy and Earth'—Tentative Comments for Discussion (173–184).

Calvin's thought a social and economic theory abstracted from his theological concerns. Moreover, the value of engaging Calvin as conversation partner in search for social and economic justice in our globalised world extends beyond his contribution to an adequate theological framework, to the way in which his economical and social ideas found embodiment in offices and institutions. Calvin's Christian vision for church and society was a deeply public vision that required practical concretisation.

Within the South African context, as elsewhere, such a public Christian vision of compassionate justice, and the concomitant need for the church, in the words of the Belhar Confession, to "stand where the Lord stands, namely against injustice and with the wronged" and "to witness against all the powerful and privileged who selfishly seek their own interests and control and harm others" is often hampered by a growing movement towards a more consumer-driven privatised spirituality. This form of spirituality is vulnerable to a type of pietistic escapism that robs Christians of the sources for engaging from deep Reformed theological commitments with the burning social, economic and political questions of the day. Such an escapist spirituality is not to be equated with Calvinist piety. The challenge remains for Reformed churches in South Africa today to find a way between, on the one hand a narrow confessionalism, and on the other hand a sentimental, privatised and often anti-theological (if not anti-intellectual) spirituality. In taking on this challenge, Reformed Christian communities in South Africa may well discover that Calvin's life and theology offer unexpectedly rich and as yet untapped resources.

CHAPTER SIXTEEN

CALVIN AND FRANCE: A PARADOXICAL LEGACY

Paul Wells

Anniversaries are plagued by pervasive anachronisms. It seems like Calvin was responsible for a good deal more in the modern world than he could have imagined in his wildest dreams. Whether it be individualism, the growth of liberal economics, civil liberties, the separation of Church and State, Calvin seems to have had some hand in it, or so it is claimed.

However, Yves Krumenacker, the latest French biographer, states rather bluntly that "Calvin wasn't concerned to make a new epoch, other than that of the kingdom of God. His principal concern was that all of life, beginning with his own, be subject to the will of God."[1] If, continues Krumenacker, Calvin's work opened a number of perspectives, he would have been horrified by modern secular society. The paradox is that he may well have aided and abetted developments that he himself would not have viewed with enthusiasm.[2]

On the one hand, Calvin's body of thought has to be weighed in the balance; for this he is responsible. On the other hand, there is the legacy in terms of how his ideas were appropriated or what their effects were. The danger is to amalgamate the two. In so far as Calvin and his beloved *patrie* are concerned the two must be distinguished, and in several ways.

Bearing this caveat in mind a number of issues enter into discussion concerning the work of Calvin and his legacy in French history, society and culture. Firstly, there are enigmas concerning the religious influence of Calvin that are felt acutely in secular France. Secondly, his opposition to traditional Catholicism helped engender a culture of criticism and a spirit of negativity toward religious belief that rumbles on right up to the present. Thirdly, Protestantism, as a minority, later became an ally with forces that essentially were not Christian. This identity born of necessity distanced it from classical Calvinism in alliances with Enlightenment free-thinking. This too remains a feature of French Protestantism until

---

[1] Yves Krumenacker, *Calvin: Au-delà des légendes* (Paris: Bayard, 2009), 518–519.
[2] Krumenacker, *Calvin*, 520–525, 545.

the present day. Finally, as a result of these processes, Calvin's thought became virtually unknown not only within French Protestantism, but in society as a whole.

We will present each of these strands without proposing to give more than some hypothetical ideas about the development of the Calvin legacy in France. To set the scene we will begin by speaking about Calvin's vision of the ills of civilization.

Humanity through a Glass Darkly

Albrecht Dürer's woodcut the "Four Horsemen of the Apocalypse" (1498) portrays the trauma of conquest, war, famine, and death. Such were the fears of Calvin's time.[3] Human tyranny is relentless and Calvin knew it. Living in comfort it is easy for us to forget that elsewhere people are suffering from poverty, political or religious oppression and injustices that engender misery. But Calvin will never let us forget this.

A profound consciousness of the reality of human nature is present on almost every page of the *Institutes*, positively in statements about human iniquity and negatively in the systematic destruction of the illusions of merit. And yet by way of contrast, the creation is a theatre of great beauty richly endowed for humans.[4] André Biéler states that "Laughter, pleasure, work, personal success, social prosperity and all that makes for the good life, is assumed with good conscience and confidence by Calvin."[5] But like Rudyard Kipling, Calvin could have said that where every prospect pleases only man is vile.

Calvin is frequently presented as a great pessimist. True, he shared few of the expectations for human nature of his humanist contemporaries, but his view of the plight of humanity was more than an expression of his personality or even the influence of Augustine. It came from a sustained reading of Scripture and its message: because man is what he is only God's grace can provide any lasting consolation.

Because of this the author of the *Institutes* became one of the untouchables of modern culture. Calvin will not allow us to hide behind the masks of illusions of goodness or progress. If the Reformation was, as has been

---

[3] Cf. Rev. 6:1–2.

[4] Cf. Susan Schreiner, *The Theater of His Glory. Nature and Natural Order in the Thought of John Calvin* (Durham, NC: Labyrinth Press, 1991).

[5] A. Biéler, *Calvin's Economic and Social Thought* (Geneva: WCC Publications, 2006), quoted by Rémi Teissier du Cros, *Jean Calvin, de la réforme à la revolution* (Paris, L'Harmattan, 1999), 141.

claimed, the victory of Augustine's doctrine of grace over his doctrine of the church,[6] was not Calvin's doctrine of sin a triumph over a certain ideal of freedom as well?[7] This perhaps explains why he has enemies across the board, from humanist free-thinkers to present day evangelicals. In France some of Calvin's greatest opponents have come, and still do, from the camp that is sociologically known as "Calvinist".[8] French Protestants have a profound distrust of Calvin that runs to André Gide's gibe "J'ai cette figure en horreur".[9]

Myths and the legends about the abominable Calvin abound in the popular imagination. One has the impression that even professional historians free themselves from such caricatures only with great effort, if at all. Bernard Reymond's recent essay on what to do with the "big bad Calvin" is a case in point.[10] The fact of the matter is that for many sentimentalists who love humanity, Calvin's vision of man seems to be demeaning for human nature. Such a theme is hardly endearing to a nation that vaunts having brought light and freedom to the nations and sees its history as exemplary for the liberation of the oppressed.

We propose to leave aside these caricatures and consider the influence of Calvin not only in the French context but also in a specific sense in relation to the paradoxes that arise within his own thought.[11]

Calvin: A Paradoxical Personality?

A "positive promising shift in Calvin historiography is...away from the dogmatically motivated study of Calvin's theology and from the related assumption that the primary purpose of an exposition of Calvin's doctrine is to provide a significant point of departure for contemporary theologizing."[12]

---

[6] Benjamin B. Warfield, *Calvin and Augustine* (Philadelphia, P&R.: 1980), 322.

[7] Reinhold Niebuhr says this is where the Reformation lost out to humanism, *The Nature and Destiny of Man*, II (London: Nisbet, 1943), 191–220.

[8] Abraham Kuyper, *Lectures on Calvinism* (Grand Rapids: Eerdmans, 1961), 12ff.

[9] Franck Lestringant, " 'J'ai cette figure en horreur': Gide et Calvin ['I abhor this figure': Gide and Calvin]," in *Bulletin de la Société de l'histoire du protestantisme français* 155 (2009), 305–320.

[10] Bernard Reymond, *Le protestantisme et Calvin: Que faire d'un aïeul si encombrant? [What to do with a cumbersome ancestor?]* (Geneva: Labor et Fides, 2008).

[11] Cf. Irena Backus, *Life Writing in Reformation Europe* (Reading: Ashgate Publishing, 2008), 125–186.

[12] Richard Muller, *The Unaccommodated Calvin* (Oxford, Oxford University Press, 2000), viii.

This shift not only allows a re-evaluation of the relation between Calvin and Reformed scholasticism but also a balanced evaluation of Calvin's influence. If we are honest we cannot simply praise or blame Calvin, but see that his complex personality gave rise to a variegated legacy.[13]

Calvin often showed great humanity, compassion and friendship. His commentaries on the Good Samaritan are exemplary in this respect: the greatest stranger is our neighbour, humanity itself implies we belong to a family, a sentiment we are to entertain without respect of persons, be they friends or enemies, worthy or not. God demands that we show to all men the love we ought to bear for him according to this principle: we must love whosoever, if we love God.[14]

Such sentiments seem incompatible with Calvin's temperament. He had a notorious short fuse with regard to those who did not see things his way. Was this not his Achilles heel? How is love to all men because they are humans compatible with the Servetus incident or with his harsh treatment of his enemies? Calvin seems to prove the impracticality of faith for those who think "God is not great", as say the modern anti-theists.

Calvin's intransigence hangs heavy over history and the Reformed tradition. Many of the people we honour for their theology were rather thin in their humanity. Too often the lines are drawn between orthodoxy and compromise. The image of the rigid Calvin survives more readily in the modern mind than Calvin's many words of compassion and goodness that are easily forgotten.

The paradox is that a compassionate Calvin seemed to be struggling to shed the skin of the intolerant Calvin. Apologists whitewash Calvin as a child of his time. Servetus was, after all, his only burnt offering. However, we are not satisfied; the legacy of the intolerant Calvin has marked history more than the humanity of Calvin.[15] Even the witness of Theodore Beza in his life of Calvin, which is joy and light next to the tabloid Bolsec,[16] raises doubts about Calvin's temper and his relational difficulties. Calvin's legacy points to the danger of occupying moral high ground and the practical

---

[13] Cf. Andrew Pettegree, "The Spread of Calvin's Thought" in Donald K. McKim (ed.), *The Cambridge Companion to John Calvin* (Cambridge: Cambridge University Press, 2004), 207–224.

[14] Calvin, *Institutes*, II.8.46, 55.

[15] If there were not a difficulty would books and articles have been written on the subject by the likes of Richard Stauffer and Olivier Millet? No-one writes on the humanity of Luther.

[16] Herman Selderhuis, "L'image de Calvin: chez Bolsec, Calvin et les autres," *Bulletin de la Société de l'Histoire du Protestantisme Français* 155 (2009), 281–288.

difficulty of living with opposition. For many of our contemporaries the nature of religious belief itself is the root of such insoluble difficulties.

The root of the problem seems to have been in the tension between Calvin's desire for ultimate orderliness, "things being in their right place" and the impossibility of resolving certain tensions in the human situation.[17] The linkage between Word and Spirit, both of which occupy a central place in his theology, is neither necessary nor automatic. Calvin was convinced he was the arbiter of truth and yet he could not make his view prevail or avoid schism. His desire for doctrinal purity could not, in and of itself, procure unity on these terms within Christianity.[18] The enigma is that Calvin's attitude seemed to break the key in the lock instead of opening the door.

Perhaps this paradox served to reinforce the modern myth that religious convictions must necessarily lead to intolerance and inquisition, something frequently taken for granted in our global situation today. In contrast to Protestant cultures, in France it favoured the development of anti-religious attitudes. It contributed to the perception that religion itself is not the solution but a profound problem for the good of man. At the turn of the 20th century, Auguste Sabatier,[19] the apologist of liberal Protestantism, contrasted the old religions of authority with the religion of the Spirit. He saw both Catholicism and the religion of the Reformation as doomed expressions of authoritarianism.

A Contribution to a Culture of Criticism?

Toward the end of his life Calvin tended to encourage greater flexibility and adaptation in ecclesiastical matters, but with the advent of the St Bartholomew massacre (1572) and the wars of religion, his followers in France favoured the earlier polemical writings not the later more conciliatory Calvin. In the face of persecution this is understandable, but it seems that Calvin later lost control of his troops. Beza was more of an influence as time drew on.

---

[17] Cf. Paul Helm on tensions of Word and Spirit, *Calvin. A Guide for the Perplexed* (Edinburgh: T & T Clark, 2008), 124–126.

[18] The remarks of R. Ward Holder, "Calvin's Heritage", in McKim, *Cambridge Companion to John Calvin*, 254–256.

[19] Auguste Sabatier, *Les religions d'autorité et la religion de l'Esprit* [*The authoritarian religions and the religion of the Spirit*] (Paris: Fischbacher, 1903).

Francis I (1517–1547), to whom Calvin dedicated his Epistle to the King in the *Institutes*, left his mark on the situation. He subdued the Church of France and co-ordinated it completely with the absolutist system, which could not be made secure while the Church was free. In France everything centred in the king and what was not pleasing to him would not long be heard.[20] The dominant policy can be summed up: one king, one law, one faith. The unity of kingdom, faith and Church was maintained by force and terror. France had no parliament and there had been no meeting of the Estates general since 1506.[21] Under Francis I no protestant congregation was established. These began to appear like mushrooms overnight after 1555.

The wars of religion left a profound mark on France and ended with the uneasy truce of the Edict of Nantes in 1598.[22] Pope Clement VIII is reputed to have commented: "liberty of conscience granted to all is the worst thing in the world." This situation which granted Protestants limited freedom, but satisfied neither side, lasted until the revocation of the edict under Louis XIV in 1685. An estimated 400 000 Huguenots subsequently left France, in their ranks some of the ablest minds and finest spirits of the nation.

There is little doubt that there is a marked difference between what Calvin wrote and strands of his thought that led to other developments. He was fundamentally conservative but there exists in his thought an unresolved paradox between the necessity to be subject to authority and those passages, such as the final chapter in the *Institutes*, in which he appears to open the door to resistance and revolt. His followers soon took advantage of this ambiguity and justified resistance to absolutism. In France there arose a line of opposition spokesmen who advocated the use of force. The hope that the Edict of Nantes would be applied lead Protestants to affirm royal supremacy, even under persecution, but when absolutism became rigid theories of resistance soon surfaced. A line can

---

[20] Norbert Rouland, *L'Etat français et le pluralisme* [The French State and pluralism] (Paris: Odile Jacob, 1995), *passim*; John T. McNeill, *The History and Character of Calvinism* (Oxford: Oxford University Press, 1954), 328.

[21] Calvin evoked the three Estates of the kingdom as a defense for the people against tyrannical rulers. A hope of redress was continually expressed with reference to the Estates, although they had played little part since 1506 and in 1561 did nothing for Protestants.

[22] The wars began with the massacre of Protestants in a church service at Wassy in 1562 and continued until the Edict of Nantes in 1598.

be traced from François Hotman[23] and the 'monarchomaques' to Pierre Jurieu,[24] Jacques Basnage, Jean Claude and Pierre Bayle who all advocated active opposition in the name of liberty of conscience.[25] Outside of France this current developed with the likes of John Knox, Samuel Rutherford, Johannes Althusius and John Milton who considered regicide a viable solution for tyranny.[26]

The tragedy of the Huguenots was the tragedy of France and indirectly of Europe. The triumph of their enemies was that of absolute intolerant power. By the time he died in 1715 Louis XIV thought he had dealt with the Protestant problem.

How can Calvin's influence be assessed in the light of these developments? It is too easy to say that Calvin is the champion of liberty of conscience and a major factor in the development of democracy. In his situation at Geneva, Calvin faced great uncertainties but above all a wall of almost monolithic opposition in the power of the crown and the power of Rome. It is not surprising that the note of his trumpet was uncertain, something between obedient non-resistance and possible opposition to tyranny. Theoretically Calvin was an enemy of tyranny in all its forms—the devil, sin, error, anarchy and the abuse of absolute power by civil or ecclesiastical authority. He could reconcile theoretically the contradiction of resistance and obedience as complementary expressions of Christian freedom of conscience before the Lord. One can submit internally to hostile power in obedience to God, but one can also justify, to a certain extent, external resistance against injustice for conscience's sake and out of concern for *le pauvre peuple.*

---

[23] François Hotman, a close friend of Calvin who escaped with his life from the St Bartholomew massacre, wrote *Franco-Gallia* (1573) a manual of resistance that interpreted French history in the light of popular sovereignty and representation. François Hotman, *La Gaule française* (Paris: Fayard, 1991).

[24] Jean Claude wrote *Complaints of the Protestants* (1686). Pierre Jurieu (1637–1713) penned *The sighs of enslaved France aspiring for liberty* (1689–90) stating that the French king had taken the place of the State and removed the people's rights. Jurieu noted that the Estates elected the king and calls for a meeting of the Estates to depose Louis XIV—a revival of the ideas of Hotman, Duplessis-Mornay and Langet. However, these authors were not republicans and not 'democratic' in the modern sense.

[25] Cf. Natacha Salliot, "Philippe Duplessis-Mornay lecteur de Calvin: d'une Institution à l'autre," *Bulletin de la Société de l'Histoire du Protestantisme Français* 155 (2009), 209–220 and Hubert Bost, "Calvin au prisme du Dictionnaire de Bayle," *Bulletin de la Société de l'Histoire du Protestantisme Français* 155 (2009), 245–265.

[26] Paul Wells, "La théorie politique 'réformationelle' et le pacte social," *La Revue réformée* 58 (2007/5), 41–66.

It can be argued that both attitudes are liberating as the exercise of the individual conscience lies at the heart of both and that together they contribute to the rise of modern freedom.[27] However the paradox inherent in his thought on freedom and resistance does lead to a variegated history. As resistance developed later, the plea for freedom of conscience and tolerance gave the impression that religion was always a divisive factor. A culture of rejection and criticism was one of the outcomes. The French mentality, if one can speak of such, is characterised as much by defensive and critical attitudes as it is by supposed Cartesian rationalism.

The French always appear to think that someone is trying to get the better of them and that good intentions ultimately hide a desire to manipulate or some attendant evil. Trench society is characterised by confrontation and opposition, a far cry from the polder attitudes of colder climes. The civil war generated by religious opposition deeply marked the culture and made revolution one viable outcome.

Calvin and the Development of Non-Calvinistic Protestantism

In his recent essay on the legacy of Calvin, Bernard Reymond argues that the influence of Calvin was much less than is often thought.[28] In spite of Reymond's exaggerations it cannot be denied that Calvin never occupied a position of unique influence in the development of Calvinism, and even less in France than elsewhere. Also, as Carl Truman suggests, the language of identity and difference is less suggestive in describing the relation of Calvin and later Protestantism than that of continuity and discontinuity.[29]

This is particularly true of French Protestantism that bears only passing relation to Calvin's theology. The relation is hardly one of continuity but more of disaffiliation. During the age of the Enlightenment and following the failure of the Camisard rebellion at the beginning of the 18th century,

---

[27] Mario Turchetti, "Contribution de Calvin et du calvinisme à la naissance de la démocratie moderne" [Contributions of Calvin and of Calvinism at the birth of the modern democracy], in Martin Ernst Hirzel and Martin Sallman (eds), *Calvin et le calvinisme. Cinq siècles d'influences sur l'Eglise et la société* [Calvin and calvisnism. Five centuries of influence upon Church and the society] (Geneva: Labor et Fides, 2008), 290–326. Turchetti proposes (324) that from this double freedom of conscience comes, across the centuries, the spirit at the heart of an a-religious attitude to law and in France, *laïcité*. The argument is hardly convincing.

[28] Reymond, *Le protestantisme et Calvin*, 52–77.

[29] Carl Truman, "Calvin and Calvinism" in McKim, *Cambridge Companion to John Calvin*, 225–244.

the Reformed churches in France were weakened by reduction in numbers. Persecution, emigration, lack of leadership and controversies arising from duress left only a husk of Reformed Protestantism. In this fragile condition, the French churches were profoundly affected by rationalism and the current philosophy, but not by the new evangelical awakenings taking place in the Anglo-Saxon world and elsewhere. They were confronted by the aggressive secularism of the Enlightenment that assumed the supremacy of the State over the Church and its right to coerce subjects in ecclesiastical matters.

In this context, Protestantism in France found an ally in the free-thinking that developed exponentially throughout the century. The typical attitude toward this was not negative but selective. Protestant thinking was increasingly characterised by the motifs of tolerance, individual freedom and attitudes that were tributary of the developing deism and the *Encyclopedia*. Protestants entertained the idea that new light can be expected to break out and hoped for this in terms of social progress and liberty. Calvin was effectively obscured by the Enlightenment. Yves Krumenacker speaks about the dissolution of Calvinism and notes that in Protestant sermons toward the end of the 18th century the divinity of Christ is almost totally absent. Protestants seem to have maintained the Geneva liturgy while shunning the Geneva preaching.[30] When Rabaut St Etienne spoke on behalf of Protestants before the National Assembly in 1798 his request was typical: "It is not toleration that I claim but liberty."

The absence of the direct influence of Calvin in France after the start of the 17th century is often forgotten. It can be documented by reference to editions of the *Institutes*. B.B. Warfield stated that "During Calvin's lifetime the publication a new edition of the "Institutes" in French was an almost annual affair...however, after his death, its publication stopped abruptly." Here are some salient facts assembled in his article "On the literary history of the 'Institutes' ":[31]

1. only a single edition was published in the 17th century (1609);
2. a French pastor at Bremen, Charles Icard, published a new edition in 1713;

---

[30] Krumenacker, *Calvin*, 564.
[31] Benjamin B. Warfield, "On the Literary History of the 'Institutes' ", in B.B. Warfield, *The Works of Benjamin B. Warfield*, ed. E.D. Warfield, W.P. Armstrong, C.W. Hodge (Grand Rapids: Baker, 1981/2), reprint from (New York: Oxford University Press, 1927–1932), vol. 5, 373–428, particularly 394ff.

3. this edition was reprinted at Geneva in 1818;
4. apart from the Brunswick edition by Baum, Cunitz and Reuss (1865) one edition appeared in Paris (Charles Meyrueis) in 1859;
5. subsequently an adaptation in modernised French of the 1560 *Institutes* was published in 1955 by Jean Cadier and Pierre Marcel.[32]

Surprisingly, perhaps, this means that there were only four editions of the *Institutes* in 350 years. The contrast with the numerous editions in English or other languages, to say nothing of the practice of making abridgments, is striking. As Warfield summarised: "the appearance remains strong that Calvin's theology has found fewer eager readers among his compatriots—whether in France or Geneva—in the nineteenth century than it did in the sixteenth century".[33] The fact that there were between these dates only two editions with short print runs (and that would probably have had low availability in France for obvious reasons), shows how minimal the direct influence of Calvin on Protestant history in fact was. To make virtual connections between the thinking of Calvin and later Protestantism, including a filiation with the French revolution does not stand this test.

We can sum up that in France, a combination of persecution and free-thinking gave birth to a new, non-Calvinistic Protestantism, one that identified with the Reformation and Calvin not ideologically but nominally, and had more affiliation with Enlightenment trends than with the Calvinistic tradition.

Only in this way did an emasculated and persecuted Protestantism, a Protestantism different from Calvin's, contribute to the development of an anti-authoritarian culture as it arose in revolutionary times. In this way later Protestants saw themselves as actors, although they only had a minor part, in the movement of progress in France and the modern world.

The continuity of Reformation and Revolution is more a popular fiction than a historical reality. Calvin himself could well have been an anti-revolutionary.

---

[32] The new edition published in 2009 translated by Marie de Védrines and Paul Wells is the first translation in modern French (Cléon d'Andran, Aix-en-Provence/Ed. Excelsis, Ed. Kerygma, 1514 pp.).
[33] Warfield, "Literary History", 396.

Conclusion

Over the years, Calvin's thought became virtually unknown not only in Protestantism but in French society as a whole. The fifth centenary is providing an opportunity to know Calvin, perhaps for the first time, with critical distance a necessary ingredient.

Our impression after reviewing some features of French Protestant history leads us to believe that simple models for interpreting these complex developments are to be avoided. To present Calvin as the father of modern liberties, as the defender of freedom of conscience and the advocate of tolerance, of the ideal of democracy, is a gross oversimplification. Calvin lived in an age of authoritarianism, tyranny and confusion. From his perspective the best defense against these was the authority of the Word of God, the justice flowing from justification and the assurance of the future Kingdom. To make Calvin and his Camisard inheritors forerunners of the French revolution, deemed to be either a catastrophe for the natural order or an explosion of freedom and the expression of the sovereignty of the people, depends on the existence of a number of non-existent missing links. The same might perhaps be said about the ongoing debate concerning Calvin and capitalism.

In a more modest way we have tried to show that paradoxes in Calvin's thought in three areas are not without influence. They play a part because the thought of Calvin is either derided or abandoned. Because of this, French history and culture developed with their own particular character, different from developments in Protestant societies.[34] The largely negative image of Calvin in the French culture zone, including Protestantism, has fashioned a historical legacy that takes positively what Calvin may have considered negatively. So in relation to modernity Calvin's influence is a paradoxical one:

1. Calvin's view of human sinfulness has often been interpreted in such a way as to show that God must be against man, and therefore man must be free of God to fulfil his destiny on earth;
2. His own character and polemics made Calvin something of a scarecrow. Religion, it is assumed, must always lead to violence and division;

---

[34] There has been much debate about Protestant and Catholic societies since the publication of Napoléon Roussel, *Les nations Catholiques et les nations Protestantes* (Paris: Meyrueis, 1854). Cf. P. Besnard, *Protestantisme et capitalisme. La controverse post-wébérienne* [The controversy post-Weber] (Paris: A. Colin, 1970).

3. The constitution of a Protestant party in France, its opposition to cen-
   tralised power and its later alliance with Enlightenment freethinking
   contributed to a culture of criticism and fear of authority in any form.
   Such sentiments are profoundly characteristic of the French mind-set.
4. The ignorance of Calvin in France has meant that Protestantism has
   been linked with factors that have little to do with the Gospel itself or
   with the Reformation for that matter—tolerance, free-thinking, liberty
   and the primacy of the individual conscience.

Taken together these factors make up the ingredients of a typically French
dream, the republican myth of salvation. Liberty, equality and fraternity,
human life without God, without religion or transcendence and in a spirit
of criticism of authority makes the way of progress a perpetual conflict
against injustice and evil. Together these go to make up *laïcité* which is
essentially contrary to Calvin's ideal that God is sovereign over all of creation and human activity and that the goal of Christian living is union
with Christ.

INDEX OF NAMES

INDEX OF SUBJECTS